"Yes, this is a theological interpretation
more. Leithart boldly argues that God
whose triune love determines what we s.   ....plicity to
mean. While scrupulously Protestant in attention to the biblical text,
Creator builds creatively on the metaphysical insights of theologians as
varied as Milbank, Bulgakov, and Jensen. Leithart's scintillating composition makes for joyful music, echoing the triune song that sings creation
into being."

Hans Boersma, Saint Benedict Servants of Christ Professor in Ascetical
Theology at Nashotah House Theological Seminary

"Few prolific theologians are always worth reading, but Peter Leithart is
the rare exception. Here he explores and praises the triune Creator in
critical dialogue with the recent turn to Aquinas in some Reformed and
Catholic circles. His construal of Aquinas's perspective is itself worth
the price of the book and will stimulate a rich debate!"

Matthew Levering, James N. Jr. and Mary D. Perry Chair of Theology at
Mundelein Seminary

"This deeply learned and wide-ranging study boils down to a simple
conviction: God can be known and he can be named. Peter Leithart's
voice is fresh and refreshing. Though thoroughly orthodox, he is hard
to label. His extraordinary learning is all tethered to the defense of the
historic wisdom of the church. This book is a must-read for any
thoughtful Christian."

William Edgar, professor emeritus of apologetics, Westminster Theological
Seminary, and author of *A Supreme Love*

"'Let there be' an advance in the doctrine of God debates! Leithart moves
the conversation forward through his learned exposition of Greek metaphysics, critical analysis of perceived tensions in Thomas Aquinas's
thought, exhilarating theological exegesis of the opening lines of
Scripture, and proposals for how classical theism could be more thoroughly evangelized. He invites us to revisit (or revise) popular con-
struals of simplicity through the doctrine of the Creator. It is that God,
and that God only, whom we know and with whom we have to deal.
Benefit from this exercise of 'scriptural purification'—Leithart's iconoclastic effort to demolish conceptual idols that run from the language of
God's revelation in the Bible."

James R. Wood, assistant professor of ministry at Redeemer University

"*Creator* is theological exegesis at its finest. Leithart brings forth from the oldest of biblical wineskins startling fresh insights, enabling him to critique classical and process theism alike with his alternative 'metaphysics of Genesis.' Creation here becomes the site for a new battle for the Bible and for the doctrine of God. To read Genesis 1 with Leithart is an exhilarating, even intoxicating experience."

Kevin J. Vanhoozer, research professor of systematic theology at Trinity Evangelical Divinity School

"In *Creator*, Peter Leithart guides the reader through a profound reflection on the foundational creation account of the Scriptures, Genesis 1. Framed by an exploration of the Greek philosophical tradition and the church's relation to it, Leithart calls the church to take our stand 'in the beginning,' at the place where 'God created,' and from there to receive the Word of the triune God. Through his lively prose, Leithart challenges the church to ground our theological reflection in the doctrine of creation, which means to adopt a heart of childlike trust in the Word of the Creator."

Joel Lawrence, executive director of the Center for Pastor Theologians

CREATOR

A THEOLOGICAL
INTERPRETATION
OF GENESIS 1

PETER J.
LEITHART

Academic

An imprint of InterVarsity Press
Downers Grove, Illinois

InterVarsity Press
P.O. Box 1400 | Downers Grove, IL 60515-1426
ivpress.com | email@ivpress.com

InterVarsity Press® is the publishing division of InterVarsity Christian Fellowship/USA®. For more information, visit intervarsity.org.

All Scripture quotations, unless otherwise indicated, are taken from the New American Standard Bible®, copyright 1960, 1962, 1963, 1968, 1971, 1972, 1973, 1975, 1977, 1995 by The Lockman Foundation. Used by permission.

The publisher cannot verify the accuracy or functionality of website URLs used in this book beyond the date of publication.

Cover design: David Fassett
Interior design: Jeanna Wiggins
Cover Image Credits: © Emilija Manevska / Getty Images, Jan Brueghel the Elder and Peter Paul Rubens, The Garden of Eden with the Fall of Man. Mauritshuis, The Hague / Geheugen van Nederland / Wikimedia Commons, Stuartia Malacodendron Image from Stirpes Novae aut Minus Cognitae (1784) by Pierre-Joseph Redouté and Charles Louis L'Héritier de Brutelle. Original from Biodiversity Heritage Library / Raw Pixel

ISBN 978-1-5140-0216-2 (print) | ISBN 978-1-5140-0217-9 (digital)

Printed in the United States of America ∞

Library of Congress Cataloging-in-Publication Data
Names: Leithart, Peter J., author.
Title: Creator : a theological interpretation of Genesis 1 / Peter J.
   Leithart.
Description: Downers Grove, IL : IVP Academic, [2023] | Includes
   bibliographical references and indexes.
Identifiers: LCCN 2023017102 (print) | LCCN 2023017103 (ebook) | ISBN
   9781514002162 (print) | ISBN 9781514002179 (digital)
Subjects: LCSH: Bible. Genesis, I–Criticism, interpretation, etc. |
   Creation–Biblical teaching.
Classification: LCC BS651 .L353 2023 (print) | LCC BS651 (ebook) | DDC
   231.7/65–dc23/eng/20230621
LC record available at https://lccn.loc.gov/2023017102
LC ebook record available at https://lccn.loc.gov/2023017103

30   29   28   27   26   25   24   23 | 12   11   10   9   8   7   6   5   4   3   2   1

TO THE READER:

"I have a mind to fill this [book]
with profitable wonders. . . .

I will fill it with those Truths

you love without knowing them;

and with those things which,
if it be possible,

shall shew my Love to you,

in communicating most enriching
Truths to Truth,

in exalting her beauties
in such a soul."

THOMAS TRAHERNE,
Centuries of Meditation 1.1

CONTENTS

Preface   ix

Acknowledgments   xiii

1   Apophaticism, Accommodation, Anthropomorphism   1

2   Logos, Mythos, Creation   28

3   Simplicity, Partially Baptized   67

4   Creator   116

5   Triune Creator   165

6   Metaphysics of Genesis   210

7   God Speaking and God Seeing   255

Conclusion   303

Bibliography   305

Name Index   325

Subject Index   329

Scripture Index   337

PREFACE

Creator was conceived in a rare fit of self-assessment. I have neither the desire, patience, nor skill to write a systematic theology, but several years ago, musing over my published books, I realized I had inadvertently covered nearly every locus of systematic theology. A prolegomenon of sorts: *Against Christianity*. On hermeneutics: *Deep Exegesis*. On God: *Traces of the Trinity* and sections of *Deep Comedy*. On covenant: Commentaries on all the "First and Seconds" of the Old Testament. On Christology: A monograph on Athanasius, a student's guide to the Gospels, and commentaries on Matthew and 1 John. On soteriology: *Delivered from the Elements of the World*. On ecclesiology and related topics: Nearly everything, specifically *The End of Protestantism*, *Blessed Are the Hungry*, three books on baptism, and the Theopolis Fundamentals series, published in omnibus form as *On Earth as in Heaven*. On Ethics: *Gratitude* and *The Ten Commandments*. On political theology: *Defending Constantine* and *Between Babel and Beast*. On Eschatology: *Deep Comedy*, *God of Hope*, and a two-volume commentary on Revelation.

The big lacuna was the doctrine of creation, including anthropology. It was a surprising discovery. I talk and write about creation all the time. I learned from Jim Jordan to trace every biblical theme and theological question back to Genesis 1–3. I criticize other theologians for their faulty views of creation. I have tossed around the insult "Gnostic" with abandon, though not, I think, unjustly. Critics of "pure nature" and the nature/supernature dualism—Henri de Lubac, Alexander Schmemann, and John Milbank especially—haunt everything I write.

Once I noticed the gap, I determined it was time to come clean and make explicit what I had been assuming about creation all along. I initially planned to write a medium-sized book on God, creation, and man. I intended to address controverted questions about the days of creation, the age of the earth, the whole tangled knot of creation-evolution, but only in passing. I hold "fundamentalist" views on all those questions, but I worry that theologians and biblical scholars expend so much energy on disputed points that we miss the theological grandeur of the biblical account of creation. I am interested in how long the days of creation are, but I am, for the purposes of this project, far more interested in what Genesis 1 tells us (if anything) about God's relation to time. I believe God created light on the first day, but I am far more interested in meditating on the speaking God and exploring the ontological priority of light. Animal species did not emerge over millions of years but were, I believe, created on days five and six of the creation week; yet I am more interested in exploring what Scripture means when it calls them "living souls." To put it simply: I intended to write a book of theology, not apologetics.

A few months into my research, I worked through Matthew Levering's *Reconceiving the Doctrine of Creation*, which devotes several chapters to theology proper. I realized that working on creation gave me an opportunity to work on trinitarian theology in more depth (another long-standing obsession on which I have written comparatively little) and to decide once and for all (for now) what I think of "classical theism" (a phrase I avoid as much as possible in this book). After reading Levering, my sights simultaneously narrowed and expanded: Narrowed with respect to this book, which focuses on the doctrine of God the Creator;

expanded, because this book got pretty big and also because I intend to write two further books on creation, one a "revisionary metaphysics" of created reality and the other a study of biblical anthropology. Ultimately, Lord willing, a trilogy: *Creator, Creation, Man*.

ACKNOWLEDGMENTS

I owe debts to many people. First on the list are those friends who have diligently, doggedly attended my Sunday School class devoted to "An Excruciatingly Detailed Exposition of Genesis 1," which has now produced an excess of excruciation by moving on to Genesis 2. I'm grateful to Pastor Rich Lusk and the elders of Trinity Presbyterian Church for giving me a venue to millimeter my way through the text.

I gave several lectures on "classical theism" at the 2019 Pastors Conference at Church of the Redeemer in Monroe, Louisiana, and I am thankful to our host, Pastor Steve Wilkins, and for discussions there with my Theopolis colleagues Alastair Robert and Jeff Meyers. During 2021–2022, I taught a Theopolis Regional Course on creation at Exodus Church, Wichita; All Saints Presbyterian Church, Fort Worth; Christ Covenant Church, Chicago; Trinity Presbyterian Church, Birmingham, Alabama; and Christ Church, Cary, North Carolina. I am grateful to the pastors of those churches—Kyle Lammott, Jeff Niell and Steve Jeffery, Jon Herr, Rich Lusk, and Duane Garner—for hosting our courses and hosting me. Thanks too to the Theopolis staff, especially Emma Leithart, for managing logistics. I presented some of the material in chapter five at the New Saint Andrews College Grad Forum in the fall of 2021; thanks to Timothy Edwards for the opportunity, and to Pastor Doug Wilson, Tim Harmon, and others for their questions and challenges.

David Sedley was kind enough to answer an out-of-the-blue email question about Aristotle, and Jonathan McIntosh gave feedback on an inchoate initial version of the argument of chapter four.

I am grateful for my long friendships and collaborations with the Biblical Horizons group, including Jim Jordan, Jeff Meyers, Rich Bledsoe, and others. Jim taught and wrote about Genesis with unprecedented insight, and I could not have written *Creator* without making his thoughts my own. Long ago, Jeff excited my interest in trinitarian theology with a series of lectures at a Biblical Horizons conference.

Thanks, finally, to Dan Reid of InterVarsity Press, who first accepted my proposal, and to David McNutt, who took up the project after Dan retired, gave me the green light when I changed the scope of the book midstream, and demonstrated preternatural patience when I missed my deadline by a year and a half.

Creator is dedicated to my wife, Noel Jordan Leithart. Her contributions to this and all my other writings are incalculable. They are all her books as much as mine. Through four decades and counting, she has taken up my slack in a thousand ways, attending to life's practicalities and leaving me free to putter away at my books and peck away at my keyboard. She has *never* been overawed, not with me or anyone else, but she has been fiercely, relentlessly supportive, my loudest cheerleader and best friend. Because the Lord has blessed us beyond measure, we have been immeasurably fruitful. In every way, the fruitfulness is *ours*, neither mine nor hers alone. Together, always and in everything, together.

I love you.

You are my Queen.

Easter 2023
Beth-Elim
Gardendale, Alabama

1

APOPHATICISM, ACCOMMODATION, ANTHROPOMORPHISM

Creator is largely a theological commentary on portions of Genesis 1:1–2:3, an attempt to articulate a fundamental theology explicitly and rigorously controlled by the Bible's first chapter.

I would prefer to jump right in. You may do so by skipping to chapter two. Alas, I cannot. I must, reluctantly, begin before I begin, with a brief defense of my assumptions about the task of theology, which, for me, means assumptions about Scripture and how it is to be read. My reluctance rises from several sources. As Jeffrey Stout famously put it, methodological discussions are like a speaker's throat-clearing before he begins to speak.[1] One needs a clear throat, to be sure, but too much academic speech is swallowed up in throat-clearing, question clarifying, framing. It is easy to forget that frames exist not for themselves but for the sake of the painting; we clear our throats so our throats are clear to *say* stuff. Fortunately for you, this chapter is comparatively brief. I could not explain or defend all my assumptions without writing a complete

---

[1] Jeffrey Stout, *Ethics After Babel: The Languages of Morals and Their Discontents* (Princeton, NJ: Princeton University Press, 2001), 163.

prolegomenon, and I cannot in good conscience subject readers to more "ahems" than is strictly necessary.

I am also reluctant because method too often pre-determines the outcome of an investigation. As Jean-Luc Marion observes, *meta-hodos* implies we begin "at the end of the path . . . onto which [we] have just barely set forth." Method allows us to "run ahead of the phenomenon, by *fore*-seeing it, *pre*-dicting it, and *pro*-ducing it."[2] Method immanentizes the eschaton and attempts to survey the territory to be explored from an impossible position outside, or on the far side of, the territory. Method bewitches us into thinking it guides us from the beginning toward a reliable end, but in fact method is discernible only in retrospect. We can only know the *meta-hodos* from the end of the *hodos*. Discovery occurs when we are confronted by an other, often a new acquaintance. Method saves time by netting and taming the other as soon as we meet him, without the fuss of listening to what he has to say, without considering whether or not he knows a better path toward our destination.[3] This is bad form in general, fatal when the Other is the Creator.

Every way of proceeding is shaped by substantive convictions about the subject matter that is yet to be studied. Sometimes, the convictions arrive from outside the subject at hand. Even the "clean" methods of the physical sciences are never purely methodological,[4] since they rest on metaphysical premises about

---

[2]Jean-Luc Marion, *Being Given: Toward a Phenomenology of Givenness* (Stanford, CA: Stanford University Press, 2002), 9-10.

[3]Summing up Gadamer's objections to "method," Anthony Thiselton writes: "Interpreters conditioned by their own embeddedness in specific times, cultures, and theological or secular traditions need to *listen*, rather than seeking to 'master' the Other by netting it within their own prior system of concepts and categories. This premature assimilation of the Other into one's own prior grooves of habituated thought constitutes the 'control' and advance commandeering that Gadamer calls 'Method.'" In Roger Lundin et al., *The Promise of Hermeneutics* (Grand Rapids, MI: Eerdmans, 1999), 134.

[4]Stephen Shapin, *Never Pure: Historical Studies of Science as if It Was Produced by People with Bodies, Situated in Time, Space, Culture and Society, and Struggling for Credibility and Authority* (Baltimore: Johns Hopkins University Press, 2010).

causation, the law-like regularities of created phenomena, the irrelevance of supernatural factors—none of which have been or can be proven by the method they are used to support.[5]

There is no way round the knotted aporia at the origin of all human exploration: We must know what we are looking for before we begin, yet we cannot. We cannot immanentize the eschaton, and yet we *must* if we are going to move toward the end at all. Every human investigation requires contact with the already before we grope toward the not yet.

This aporia is perhaps most evident in theology. "He who is not with Me is against Me," Jesus says, and we must know the Jesus we befriend in order to come to know him (Mt 12:30; Lk 11:23). Theology is for disciples. For theologians, the only *meta-hodos* that truly meets the requirement is the *hodos* who is also *telos*, who is also Truth and Life.

We must know God in order to know God more deeply. As Karl Barth insists, it will not do to begin by positing a generic divine being in order to work our way up to the true God. Christian theology seeks to know, praise, and proclaim the one living God, the Father who begets the eternal Son by his eternal Spirit, the God who is a communion of three equal divine persons. Any theology that seeks to know God while prescinding from incarnation and Pentecost is founded on idolatry, no matter that the living triune God is clumsily squeezed into the idolatrous frame. This gets very much to the problem I investigate and seek to correct in this book, for the heart of my critical argument is that Christian theology has been tainted by a failure to integrate creation fully into its doctrine of God. To put it provocatively, much Christian theology has unwittingly posited a nonexistent idol and attributed creation to that idol, rather than to the living God who is Father, Word, and Spirit.

---

[5]Rupert Sheldrake, *The Science Delusion* (London: Coronet, 2012).

One aspect of this aporia is directly pertinent to *Creator*: This book is an extended exercise in theological interpretation of the creation account, but any understanding of the truth value of Scripture depends on a prior understanding of creation. Our understanding of the function and force of the words of Genesis 1 depends on our understanding of the teaching and content of Genesis 1. This is an aporia indeed, for we cannot begin to grasp how we are to construe the words of Genesis without having already construed the words of Genesis 1 in some particular fashion. Without trying to relieve the tangled tension that meets us at the outset, I believe some pathways are more consistent with the content of Genesis 1 than others. I focus the discussion by posing this question: Are the words of Scripture adequate to convey the truth God intends to reveal? This, of course, is a species of a more general question about creation: Is *creation* capable of conveying the truth God intends to reveal?

The Christian tradition has answered yes, but the yes has quivered and wobbled. Below I seek to steady a few wobbles and worries—worries about babbling theologians, about the babbling God, about the words with which we babble.

BABBLING THEOLOGIANS

For many theologians, T. S. Eliot's words about words, about their strain, slippage, and imprecision, apply most especially to words about God.[6] Though revelation authorizes us to use the language of creation to speak of God, it must, it is said, be "hedged about with the cautionary reminder that the sense in which some words are used cannot be the primary and familiar one."[7] These qualifications on our language about God are

---

[6] "Burnt Norton," *Four Quartets*.
[7] Rowan Williams, *Understanding and Misunderstanding "Negative Theology"* (Milwaukee, WI: Marquette University Press, 2021), 14.

rooted in the metaphysical conviction that God is so transcendent that our words are, at best, distant pointers to the one who is beyond speech and thought. Nothing we can say positively can capture "what it is 'like' to be God" because finite minds have no "adequate perspective on unlimited actuality as such."[8]

The majority tradition of the church has oscillated between positive and negative theology, modulated between cataphatic and apophatic registers, often treating the apophatic as a moment in what is primarily a cataphatic quest.[9] In one of his theological *Orations*, Gregory of Nazianzus insists that negative theology is not a stopping point for theology: "He who is eagerly pursuing the nature of the Self-existent will not stop at saying what He is *not*, but must go on beyond what He is not, and say what He *is*; inasmuch as it is easier to take in some single point than to go on disowning point after point in endless detail, in order, both by the elimination of negatives and the assertion of positives to arrive at a comprehension of this subject."[10]

Gregory follows with an analogy:

A man who states what God is *not* without going on to say what He *is*, acts much in the same way as one would who when asked how many twice five make, should answer, not two, nor three, nor four, nor five, nor twenty, nor thirty, nor in short any number below ten, nor any multiple of ten, but would not answer ten nor settle the mind of his questioner upon the firm ground of the answer. For it is much easier, and more concise to show what a thing is not from what it is, than to demonstrate what it is

---

[8]Williams, *Understanding and Misunderstanding*, 17.

[9]In fact, every negation implies some positive knowledge. See Charles Hartshorne, *The Divine Relativity: A Social Conception of God* (New Haven, CT: Yale University Press, 1967), 34-36.

[10]*Oration* 28.9. Translation by Charles Gordon Browne and James Edward Swallow in Philip Schaff and Henry Wace, eds., *Nicene and Post-Nicene Fathers, Second Series*, vol. 7 (Buffalo, NY: Christian Literature, 1894).

by stripping it of what it is not. And this surely is evident to every one.[11]

Here, apophasis is the fruit of cataphasis, not the opposite.

Pseudo-Dionysius is a key figure here. He recognizes the interplay of apophatic and cataphatic discourses, and insists we name God only by names authorized by Scripture. In principle, everything in creation can name God since God is the cause of each thing. Dionysius encourages the multiplication of the names of God. Cataphatic theology does not say too little; it says more than it can possibly know, and, for that reason, should speak to excess.[12] Excess saves us from the prim and frugal idolatry of using a few favored names for God, which can seduce us into thinking we have snagged God on a concept.

At the same time, multiplication of names creates a crisis for naming as such. At its height, when applied to God, language is destined to collapse into paradox. God is light, Dionysius says, following Scripture. But God is also darkness. Employing both names does not yet arrive at the pinnacle of learned ignorance. We attain that peak when we both affirm and deny all cataphatic descriptions, and then proceed to negate the contradiction between them. God is light *and* God is not light, but the paradox that

---

[11]*Oration* 28.9. Of recent efforts to characterize Thomas Aquinas as a thoroughgoing apophaticist, Victor Preller's is among the most rigorous. Preller claims that Thomas formulates an "apophatic rule" according to which "in this life God is radically *unintelligible*." Preller, *Divine Science and the Science of God: A Reformulation of Thomas Aquinas* (Princeton, NJ: Princeton University Press, 1967), 28. For a rejoinder, see Kevin Hector, "Apophaticism in Thomas Aquinas: A Re-Formulation and Recommendation," *Scottish Journal of Theology* 60, no. 4 (2007): 377-93. Hector regards Thomas's apophaticism as a "strategy" that opens up into positive claims about God.

[12]Summarizing Pseudo-Dionysius and Thomas Aquinas, Denys Turner writes, "God is beyond our comprehension not because we cannot say anything about God, but because we are compelled to say too much, more than we can know how to mean. In short, for the pseudo-Denys and for Thomas following him, the 'apophatic' consists in the superfluity of the 'cataphatic,' the darkness of God consists in the excess of light." Turner, "Tradition and Faith," *International Journal of Systematic Theology* 6, no. 1 (2004): 34.

surpasses mere contradiction is the confession of God as bright darkness, dark brilliance, a celestial darkness visible. This ultimate paradox violates the normal semantic rules and represents, according to Denys Turner, "the collapse of our affirmation and denials into disorder, which can only be expressed . . . in bits of collapsed, disordered language, like the babble of a Jeremiah."[13]

The way of Dionysius is, without doubt, dizzying, delicious, yet Turner's final comment gives pause. It marks one of the potholes along the apophatic way. It is not clear which portions of Jeremiah Turner considers "babbling." Even if some passages of the prophet merit that label, surely babbling does not characterize the whole. Is Jeremiah "babbling" when he warns of impending disaster, when he rebukes Judah's kings, when he instructs the exiles to settle down to seek the peace of Babylon, when he encourages the residents of Jerusalem to surrender to Nebuchadnezzar? Most of Jeremiah is perfectly lucid, and even when he speaks of Yahweh, he does not "babble." Dionysian apophaticism threatens to nullify the possibility of sense in the biblical text, not only when it speaks about God but when it speaks about anything. "God said" does not mean God spoke, because God utterly transcends what we think of as "speech." "God made" does not refer to a specific activity of God. "Day" does not mean a period of time. All these words mean something ineffably beyond words.[14] We know them only in their erasure.[15]

---

[13]Denys Turner, *The Darkness of God: Negativity in Christian Mysticism* (Cambridge: Cambridge University Press, 1998), 22.

[14]As Jonathan Tran notes, this is a theological version of the philosophical dilemma that posits that some reality is "necessarily on the far side of human language and thought," which we "cannot quite reach because we are stuck in, and so blocked by, language." "Linguistic Theology: Completing Postliberalism's Linguistic Turn," *Modern Theology* 33, no. 1 (2016): 47-68.

[15]I evoke the deconstructive formula as a reminder of the faddish apophaticism of postmodern theory. See Daniel Bulzan, "Apophaticism, Postmodernism and Language: Two Similar Cases of Theological Imbalance," *Scottish Journal of Theology* 50, no. 3 (1997): 261-87.

This pothole is the product of more basic instabilities in apophatic theology. There is, for starters, a risk of misplaced mystery. Language, it seems, more or less transparently grasps creation and discloses finite realities. Language as such is univocal; only language about God is problematic. On these premises, if Scripture says, "Jeremiah said," it means, straightforwardly, "Jeremiah said," but if Scripture says, "God said," it must be hedged with caution signs. But the world itself is full of mystery, for in its depth creation is nothing but the created effulgence of the glory of the Creator.[16] Our capacity to name and shape the world through words at all is a continuous miracle, a daily aftershock of the Creator's first magical *fiat lux*.[17] Mystery does not suddenly confront us when we begin to speak about God. Mystery confronts us at every turn, in every encounter with anything at all, because every encounter is an encounter with the Creator in his creation. God is not a creature, yet if we must "babble" about God, then all speech is reduced to babbling. But then if babbling is all we do, perhaps we should conclude that, for creatures, babbling simply is the form that rational speech takes. We babble, but compared to *what*?

There is also a risk of a false transcendence, which leads immediately to a false immanence. Apophaticism can be formulated in a way that posits a zero-sum game between the transcendence and immanence: To the degree God is transcendent, to that degree he is not immanent. The more transcendent he is, the less he is thinkable, speakable, and knowable by creatures. In reality, true transcendence is not in opposition to immanence; on the contrary, they are mutually determinative. *Because* God is transcendent, unbounded by temporal and spatial limits, he is

---

[16]Hartshorne, *Divine Relativity*, 40-41.
[17]I hope to address the theology of language in more depth in a future volume on anthropology.

immanent, present, and active in every space and time. His immanence in every space and time implies, in turn, his transcendence of spatial and temporal limits. By the same token, the oddness of our talk about God, a marker of God's transcendence, is not in opposition or tension to the ordinariness of our talk about God. God-talk is at once the oddest of human talk *and* the most ordinary. It is the most ordinary *because* it is the oddest.[18]

God is not hidden away at the inaccessible peak of an ontic hierarchy of being. He is the transcendent source of being; he is Creator. Because God is triune, further, there is a perfect convertibility between God and his manifestation as Word: "his hiddenness—his transcendence—is always already manifestation."[19] False transcendence is the transcendence of the non-Creator, a God who may or may not create, a God who may or may not be related to creatures.[20] As I will argue at length in chapter four, no such non-Creator exists, for the living God *has* created. On trinitarian and creationist premises, every disclosure of God discloses the God who shows himself. Appeals to transcendence that render us mute implicitly deny God's transcendence is the transcendence

---

[18]John Frame, "God and Biblical Language: Transcendence and Immanence," in John W. Montgomery, ed., *God's Inerrant Word* (Minneapolis: Bethany House Fellowship, 1974). Frame speaks of transcendence and immanence as "perspectivally related." Jeremy Begbie observes that some accounts of God's transcendence make it appear that "language is something by its very nature that God would long to escape," on the assumption that "something so finite and susceptible to corruption could have no integral role in God's purposes." *Redeeming Transcendence in the Arts: Bearing Witness to the Triune God* (Grand Rapids, MI: Eerdmans, 2018), 111.

[19]David Bentley Hart, *The Hidden and the Manifest: Essays in Theology and Metaphysics* (Grand Rapids, MI: Eerdmans, 2017), 147. It seems to me that Hart's strongly apophatic approach in *Experience of God: Being, Consciousness, Bliss* (New Haven, CT: Yale University Press, 2016), 142, comes close to precisely the false transcendence he rejects in Plotinus.

[20]This is the key point in Franz Rosenzweig's refutation of Maimonides. Scripture is not concerned with God or man in isolation from one another, but with the event of their meeting in time. Anthropomorphism expresses a theology of the Creator. See Rosenzweig, *Kleinere Schriften* (Berlin: Schocken, 1937), 521. I rely on the summary found in Leora Batnitzky, *Idolatry and Representation: The Philosophy of Franz Rosenzweig Reconsidered* (Princeton, NJ: Princeton University Press, 2000), 21-23.

of the Trinity, the Father who manifests himself in the Word who, by the Spirit, is the manifestation of the Father. Apophatic appeals that negate the propriety of biblical language implicitly deny that God's transcendence is the transcendence of the Creator, who is, *for us*, always already related to creation. False transcendence offers a grammar for theology that claims to contextualize the Bible, but in so doing often obliterates the Bible. False transcendence does not merely nullify this or that statement of Scripture, but erodes the very possibility of Scripture: For how can a God beyond manifestation manifest himself in the fixed and determinate words of a text?

We can cut through the fog more simply: we in fact *do* speak of God. We may speak of God badly, but the church has recognized such a thing as proper speech. If we do speak well of God, we must be capable of doing so. We use language—often quite ordinary, albeit modified, language—to speak of God. As Jonathan Tran points out, the fact that we fill in the concept "God" with terms like transcendence, eternity, simplicity, unity, triunity, reveals the *abundance* of language, not its poverty. Of course, we cannot encompass or fully comprehend God. We cannot subject him to our conceptual control. He is a living God, a God capable of surprise. But then we cannot encompass or comprehend *anything* in its fullness, for *nothing* is under our control—most especially nothing that is alive. Whatever we say about our God-talk, we must insist God's purpose is "not to render us dumb."[21] God transcends language not because our words are nonsensical, or because they say nothing determinate about God. God created language; he has spoken, and his speech is recorded in Scripture; he can ensure that his speech communicates exactly what he wants it to communicate. He transcends language because there is

---

[21]Begbie, *Redeeming Transcendence in the Arts*, 112.

always *more* to say of him, *always forever* more to say, even after he has spoken the "last word" of final judgment.

Apophatic cautions are sometimes brought forward as a reminder that our knowledge of God arises not in scientific scrutiny but in personal encounter. We cannot claim to know God when we know creed, confession, or even the contents of Scripture, but only when we know *him*. It is a salutary reminder. Yet, once again, it does not imply that our knowing of other things is otherwise. Despite its marketing to the contrary, scientific knowledge is not impersonal and objectivized but arises from deep communion with reality.[22] Importantly, a personal encounter does not exclude, but *requires*, determinate knowledge. The ways I know my wife and children exceed words, but I would never have achieved that knowledge without words. Even when the Word becomes flesh to dwell among us, he talks and talks and talks. And even after the resurrection, he spends a fair proportion of his time leading Bible studies with his disciples (Lk 24).[23] We commune with God in, with, under, and through his talk to us and our backtalk.

BABBLING GOD

Let us grant, as the church has done, that we can make positive claims about God. The question then is, Is Scripture up to the task? Is it adequate to reveal God? The church has answered yes, but with worries and a wobble.

Commenting on John 3:22-29, Augustine quotes Psalm 35:1, which describes God as light and fountain. Augustine wonders, How can he be both? He replies with this lovely passage:

---

[22]See, for instance, Evelyn Fox Keller's *A Feeling for the Organism* (Times Books, 1984), on the genetic research of Barbara McClintock. More generally, Michael Polanyi, *Personal Knowledge: Towards a Post-Critical Philosophy* (Chicago: University of Chicago Press, 2015; first published in 1958); Esther Meek, *Loving to Know: Covenant Epistemology* (Eugene, OR: Cascade, 2011).

[23]Thanks to my pastor, Rich Lusk, for this way of putting the point.

On earth a fountain is one thing, light another. When you are thirsty you look for a fountain, and in order to get to the fountain you look for light; and if it is not daytime, you light a lamp in order to get to the fountain. Now that fountain itself is the light; for the thirsty it is a fountain, for the blind it is light. Let the eyes be opened to see the light, may the mouth of the heart be opened so as to drink from the fountain; what you drink, that is, what you see, what you hear. God becomes everything for you, because he is for you the fullness of the things that you love. If you are thinking of visible things, bread is not God, water is not God, this light is not God, a garment is not God, a house is not God. In fact, these things are visible and distinct from one another; bread is not water, and a garment is not a house; and these things are not God, for they are visible. For you God is everything; if you are hungry, he is bread for you; if you are thirsty he is water for you; if you are in the dark he is light for you, because he abides imperishable; if you are naked he is the garment of immortality for you when this perishable thing shall put on imperishability and this mortal thing shall put on immortality (I Cor 15:54). . . . What have lamb and lion got in common? Each name is applied to Christ: Look, there is the Lamb of God (Jn 1:29). How about "lion"? Look, the Lion from the tribe of Judah has conquered (Rv 5:5).[24]

Augustine then sums up: "Everything can be said about God, and nothing that is said is worthy of God. Nothing is more extensive than this poverty of speech. You look for a suitable name, you cannot find one; you look for something to say in any way at all, and you find everything."[25] Augustine runs on and on about the glories of God, gives him name upon name upon name, and then pulls out the rug: "Of course, this is all inadequate. All that I have

---

[24]Augustine, *Homilies on the Gospel of John, 1–40*, trans. Edmund Hill (New York: New City, 2009), 13.5.
[25]Augustine, *Homily on the Gospel of John* 13.5.

said is unworthy of God." Why should it be unworthy? Inadequate *to what purpose?*

It is a common theological tick.[26] Herman Bavinck, who quotes the passage, does the same. Because God reveals himself, we have "the right to name him on the basis of his self-revelation." We can use human words because God does, and "manifests himself in human forms." Scripture is not anthropomorphic here and there, but "anthropomorphic through and through," culminating in God's "self-humanization" in the incarnation. *All* biblical descriptions of God "are derived from earthly and human relations." He has a soul and spirit; a face, eyes, eyelids, ears, nose, mouth, arms, legs, and, unlike idols, his organs are in working order; he rejoices, grieves, expresses anger and delight, hates and loves; he searches, knows, intends, forgets and remembers, speaks, calls, commands, sees, smells, hears, walks, meets, visits, writes, heals, kills and makes alive, washes and anoints and clothes; he is bridegroom, father, judge, king, warrior, architect, gardener, shepherd, physician; he has all the accoutrements of a king—throne, footstool, rod, scepter, sword, bow and arrow, shield, chariot. Scripture even describes him by reference to nonhuman creatures: he is lion, eagle, lamb, hen, sun, morning star, spring, food and drink, rock and refuge, stronghold, shadow, road, and temple.[27]

Then the tick: These names "present a peculiar intellectual difficulty." Why? The knowledge these names offer is not "fully

---

[26]And an ancient tick. See Mark Sheridan, *Language for God in Patristic Tradition: Wrestling with Biblical Anthropomorphism* (Downers Grove, IL: IVP Academic, 2015), who explores, among other things, Origen's criteria for identifying passages where the literal sense is "unworthy of God."

[27]Bavinck, *Reformed Dogmatics*, vol. 2: *God and Creation*, trans. John Vriend, ed. John Bolt (Grand Rapids, MI: Baker, 2004), 95-101. Bavinck is in the mainstream of Christian theology here. As we shall see, Thomas argues that all creatures bear some resemblance to the Creator. Bavinck quotes Bonaventure: Because God is Creator of all, "we must transfer to the divine that which pertains to the creature." Since every creature glorifies God, so "every name that is ascribed to creatures might glorify him" (102-3).

adequate to the subject." There is no exhaustive "fit" between the names and the God to whom the names refer. How can God be both nameless and the bearer of infinite names?[28] Bavinck resolves the difficulty with an appeal to accommodation: "We have the right to use anthropomorphic language because God himself came down to the level of his creatures and revealed his name in and through his creatures."[29]

The obvious thing to say is what Thomas Aquinas says: Every created thing resembles God in some specific fashion simply because God created it that way. Its resemblance is its essence. In naming God from creation, we are naming him by the created resemblances he made, resemblances he presumably made just so we might speak of him. Conversely, God possesses every perfection of creation as Creator, in the way of eminence. God is *not* a rock—not because he bears no resemblance to a rock, but because his rockiness is so infinitely realized that no created rock or collection of rocks can fully express his eternal rockiness. He is not an idol, because he does not have malfunctioning eyes, ears, nose, hands, and feet (Ps 115:1-8). God has no physical hands as idols do, but he has infinite manuality. He has no physical eyes, but he has the eternal original power of which our capacity for sight is a shadow and symbol. The biblical logic is: He who created the eye, does he not see? He who created the ear, does he not hear? He who created the tongue, can he not speak? The one who created arms and hands acts with a mighty hand and an outstretched arm (Ps 94:9). The heavenly Father is the father by whom every earthly fatherhood (*patria*) is named (Eph 3:14-15). And then we can also say: The one who created passionate creatures, does he not love, have compassion, show wrath toward sin?

---

[28]Dionysius, *Divine Names* 596C-D, in *Pseudo-Dionysius: The Complete Works*, trans. Colm Luibheid (Mahwah, NJ: Paulist, 1987).
[29]Bavinck, *God and Creation*, 104.

If we can say this, why the wobble? Why the pseudohumble confession of inadequacy?

Anthropomorphism is not projection from finite to infinite. In the order of knowing, it seems so. In the order of being, it is the opposite: It is authorized from top down. Scripture uses anthropomorphic and cosmomorphic language of God because God created man in his image and the cosmos as a manifestation of his glory. It is not accommodation. The Bible uses anthropopathic language of God because our human capacity for emotion is a reflex of God's emotional life. We can speak of God using the categories of creation because he created them to be used in our speaking of and to him.[30]

Bavinck says all this. So, why the tick? Having created a world that comprehensively speaks of God, why would God prohibit us to use the language he made? How could it possibly be inadequate or inappropriate?[31] Why is it unworthy of God when we use created things as God intended them to be used? Where does the instinct to explain away the "crudeness" of Scripture come from?

The Bible is embarrassing. Even many who believe Scripture is inspired by God find much in it that is "unworthy of God." Who

---

[30]Brian Howell, *In the Eyes of God: A Contextual Approach to Biblical Anthropomorphic Metaphors* (Eugene, OR: Pickwick, 2013), 57, makes a related point about theological language: "There is a spectrum of meaning within any given divine predicate that is neither located exclusively within the human, nor the divine realms. Rather, this semantic field ranges from the 'natural' to the 'supernatural,' with both God and humans potentially capable, with some concessions, of action involving elements of both ends of the spectrum. . . . The fact that these denotations can be transferred to the divine and human subjects demonstrates that the nature of the action is derived as much from its context as its actor."

[31]Science's hostility to anthropomorphism is one source of our deep alienation from creation and from ourselves. Teleology and purpose, it is said, are human projections onto nature. If so, it is hard to see how human beings can be natural and also persons who act with ends and purposes. Our relation to nature thus becomes purely instrumental. See the compact, brilliant argument of Robert Spaemann, *Essays in Anthropology: Variations on a Theme* (Eugene, OR: Cascade, 2010), 9-12.

can believe a book that describes God in such blatantly anthropo-morphic terms? Who can believe early humans lived for centuries? Who can believe the world was created in six normal days? Accommodation is a method, or a trick, to relieve the shame of devoting a lifetime of study to a children's picture book. It is a way of justifying the thoroughly anthropomorphic, pictographic Bible to its cultured despisers. Accommodation is the theologian's wink that tells everyone he knows just how childish the Bible is. He knows, as Calvin does, it is as if God stoops to babble to us as a mother to her infant, since we are incapable of grasping whatever adult speech about God would be.[32]

Despite this suggestion, Calvin of course takes the specific words and sentences of the Bible with the utmost seriousness. Others, not so much. If the Bible is baby talk, then grownups are apt to search for more dignified ways to talk. Maimonides and his many heirs provide a pious rationale for exterminating the Bible's accommodated anthropomorphism. He turns the iconoclastic impulse of Judaism against Judaism's own text. Religious language must be purged of conceptual idols as much as worship has been purged of material idols. "God is our rock" forms an idolatrous image in the brain, which must be ground to powder like the golden calf. Unsurprisingly, pure, grown-up language about God turns out to be metaphysical language. Eventually the impulse turns against "God" as such, since the adults in the room eventually realize *any* determinate statement about God is an illegitimate attempt to fix and limit him.[33]

John Polkinghorne puts accommodation to a similar use when he writes that the "human writings [of Scripture] bear witness to timeless truths, but they do so in the thought forms and from

---

[32]John Calvin, *Institutes of the Christian Religion* 1.13.1.

[33]Moshe Halbertal and Avishai Margalit, *Idolatry*, trans. Naomi Goldblum (Cambridge, MA: Harvard University Press, 1994), 2-3.

the cultural milieu of their writers." As a result, "we find atti-
tudes expressed in the Bible that today we neither can nor should
agree with."[34] Accommodation allows Polkinghorne to uphold a
version of Scriptural authority, while overtly denying the truth
value of what Scripture actually asserts. More fundamentally, his
version of accommodation assumes the writers of Scripture
intend to communicate timeless truths, *rather than* an account of
history. In this form, accommodation does not *lead to* liberalism;
it *is* liberalism.[35]

Even when accommodation is used within an orthodox context,
it is a source of many confusions and is ultimately theologically
insupportable. A first confusion: It is often assumed that abstract
theological language eludes accommodation in a way that concrete, poetic language does not.[36] If accommodation is right,
though, it applies to *all* human speech about God; it is dumbed all

---

[34]John Polkinghorne, *Science and the Trinity: The Christian Encounter with Reality* (New Haven, CT: Yale University Press, 2004), 45-46.

[35]As George Lindbeck points out, liberalism treats doctrinal claims as symbols of reli-
gious experience. Lindbeck, *The Nature of Doctrine: Religion and Theology in a Postliberal Age*, 25th anniv. ed. (Louisville: Westminster John Knox, 2009), 17-18. Markus Barth saw Bultmann's demythologizing as an example of accommodation gone to seed; quoted in Hans Urs von Balthasar, *The Glory of the Lord: A Theological Aesthetics*, vol. 1: *Seeing the Form* (San Francisco: Ignatius, 1983), 316. See also the role of accommodation in Kenton Sparks, *Sacred Word, Broken Word: Biblical Authority and the Dark Sayings of Scripture* (Grand Rapids, MI: Eerdmans, 2012), 52-55. Spinoza is a key figure here, the thinker in whom opposition to anthropomorphism, cultivation of "higher criticism," and promotion of liberal theology converge with liberal political theory.

[36]This is explicit in Pseudo-Dionysius. He distinguishes "conceptual" from "percep-
tual" names, which correspond both to the distinction between the things that im-
mediately flow out erotically from the Creator and the things that are flow further down, and to the distinction between unity and multiplicity. Given God's nature, the simplest and most abstract names are the most fitting. Naming God begins with "the first things," which are the most abstract and conceptual names, and then moves down toward the more concrete names. "My argument traveled downward," he writes, "from the most exalted to the humblest categories, taking in on this downward path an ever-increasing number of ideas which multiples with every stage of the descent" (*Divine Names* 712A). The movement is from the "most exalted" to the "humblest" of God's names (*Mystical Theology* 1033C). Those at the top of the hierarchy are "similar similarities," while those lower down are "dissimilar similari-
ties." All created things name God, Dionysius insists, yet some names are more

the way down. To say "God is a rock" is no *more* accommodated than saying "God is a Spirit, infinite, eternal, and unchangeable in his being, wisdom, power, holiness, justice, goodness, and truth." "God is simple, eternal, impassible, immutable, *actus purus*" is no less accommodated than "God is my sun and shield." The abstract metaphysical terminology feels more impressive, but, strictly speaking, it is just as childish.

The difference between "Yahweh is my shepherd" and "God is *esse ipsum*" is not the difference between accommodated and non-accommodated. Rather, the first is more obviously metaphorical than the latter. Which leads to a second confusion: Metaphor and accommodation are *not* the same thing, though they are frequently conflated. The recourse to accommodation devalues the figurative language of Scripture in favor of a truth stripped of ornamentation and poetry. Scriptural language is implicitly cast as primitive, and this exerts pressure on theologians to transcend Scripture in search of a more sophisticated, more culturally acceptable, idiom, which often involves learning to speak with a Greek accent.

The attempt to transcend metaphor does not work, in any case. Another confusion: Even abstract language rests on metaphor that has concrete, physical roots.[37] "God is simple" stands in contrast to multiparted composites, but still evokes a homogeneous physical entity or substance—perhaps especially a fluid. "In him we live" seems more ontologically substantive than "he sits on the circle of the heavens," but the former is also a spatial metaphor, which portrays God as a container of our lives, movements, and existence. The prepositions "of him, through him, and to him"

---

divine than others. God is more Being than He is Rock. For more, see Denys Turner, *The Darkness of God*, chap. 2.

[37] See George Lakoff and Mark Johnson, *Metaphors We Live By* (Chicago: University of Chicago Press, 2003); Lakoff and Johnson, *Philosophy in the Flesh: The Embodied Mind and its Challenge to Western Thought* (New York: Basic Books, 1999).

describe physical relations—of origin, instrumentality, and destination. When we attempt to ascend out of the this-worldly idioms of Scripture, we do not ascend into a higher reality. We remain within the creation, using created things to describe the Creator. There is no alternative for creatures. Happily, we need no alternative to speak God's words after him and back to him.

Even in its best forms, accommodation is theologically insupportable.[38] It suggests God must adjust to circumstances outside his control. Yahweh faces an ancient cultural context full of poetic myths and primitive beliefs, and he has to adjust his mode of communication to make himself heard. He brings Israel from Egypt into a world of suzerainty treaties, so he adopts and adapts the form in his rule over Israel. But where did these treaties come from? Yahweh is Lord of history, who orchestrates and arranges the world as he pleases. He is never faced with a world that is not of his own making, and so does not need to adjust to it. Rather, he arranges the world to be just the sort of world he wishes to speak into. If the suzerainty treaty form—if that is what the Sinai covenant is—is lying around for Yahweh to pick up, it is because he put it there.

Accommodation suggests God does not take full responsibility for his own speech. Why does God allow the biblical writers to attribute passions and actions to God that are manifestly "inappropriate" to deity? Why does his covenant with Israel take the form it does? Why does Genesis 1 recount the origins of the world as it does? God has to speak this way because he has to make himself understood to the primitive minds of ancient hearers. "Don't blame *me*," God might say. "*Of course*, I know Genesis 1 does not describe how it actually happened. *Of course*, I too am a

---

[38]The next few paragraphs summarize Vern Poythress, *Interpreting Eden: A Guide to Faithfully Reading and Understanding Genesis 1-3* (Wheaton, IL: Crossway, 2019), 323-40.

theistic evolutionist. But this was all I could expect these ignorant ancient peoples to understand. Babbling to infants; it's all babbling to infants." If we cannot imagine a blame-shifting God, we should not imagine a God who fails to say what he wants to say because of outside pressures.

In the eternal life of the triune God, God responds to God. In the creation, God responds to God-as-God evaluates the words and works he speaks and does in the world (see chap. 7). Scripture is included within God's address to God, embedded within the covenant God makes with his people, which he enables his people to keep. Yahweh commissions Moses to write the covenant documents and deposit them in the ark of the covenant. The covenant is two sided, as God the covenant Lord and Father binds himself to his people, and the covenant document is likewise two-sided. Scripture is God's word to himself as well as to Israel. In committing himself to Israel, the covenant God commits himself to himself, to be God-for-Israel. As Vern Poythress points out, Scripture's intratrinitarian location comes to unique expression in Jesus' prayer in John 17. There, as in all Scripture, "God addresses us, but he also addresses himself as the second party." When we receive Scripture, "the Holy Spirit stands with us, indwelling us" as the hearer of the Word of the Father. The Son speaks and the Spirit hears, but the receptive Spirit is the Spirit who indwells us to enable our reception. In our hearing the Word of the Son, the Spirit also hears. Scripture's language is not accommodated language suitable to children. It is the way God talks to God about God.[39]

To close the circle: Accommodation often betrays a faulty theology of creation. By some definitions, accommodation is the claim that God speaks in a form suited to our capacity as hearers.

---

[39]Vern Poythress, *The Mystery of the Trinity: A Trinitarian Approach to the Attributes of God* (Phillipsburg, NJ: P&R, 2020), 645.

God speaks in human language because he speaks to humans. He refers to created things to reveal his character, because he speaks to creatures surrounded by created things. If that is what accommodation means, it is true and important. It is also just another way of talking of creation as such. God creates by Word; creation is his speech to us. By virtue of creation, we are surrounded by the inescapable speech of God (Rom 1:18-20). That is accommodation enough.

Typically, though, accommodation is a *second* condescension, over and above creation itself. This is the Augustinian tick we noticed above. Scripture speaks with creation in all kinds of ways, Bavinck says, but then adds, "Of course, this is because God stooped down from his proper height." Why do we need this second stoop? Was the condescension of creation itself not adequate?

Behind these ticks and tricks is the unacknowledged assumption that creation as such is not capable of conveying God's self-revelation. In the view of many theologians, the concrete stuff of the world—light, rocks, stars, the sun, shields and bucklers—is not an adequate vehicle for informing us truly about God. In order to know God as he really is, we need him to descend. Or, we need to ascend from "God is a rock" and "our God is a consuming fire" to "God is immutable" or "God is morally perfect."[40] Once again, the move does not work. Whether the words are Hebrew or Hellenistic, some medium separates the Creator's voice from the creature's ear, producing inescapable static and distortion. This second accommodation betrays a desire to bypass history, bodies, words, Scripture in pursuit of a contact with God that does not have to deal with the crudities of creation. There is

---

[40]Again, this is explicit in Dionysius: "The sheer crassness of the signs is a goad so that even the materially inclined cannot accept that it could be permitted or true that the celestial and divine sights could be conveyed by such shameful things" (*Celestial Hierarchy* 141B-C).

a gnostic impulse here: Something stands in God's way—recalcitrant matter, evanescent time, chaos—and makes it impossible for God to speak clearly. This second condescension suggests creation is not *entirely* good, not entirely God speaking "to the creature through the creature."[41]

I leave it to Robert Jenson, on whom I will rely periodically throughout this book, to put my point with blunt clarity: "The Bible's language about God is drastically personal: he changes his mind and reacts to external events, he makes threats and repents of them, he makes promises and tricks us by how he fulfills them. If we understand this language as fundamentally inappropriate, as 'anthropomorphic,' we do not know the biblical God."[42] And that means we simply do not know God at all because the biblical God is the only available option.

Put it positively: Creation is a suitable vehicle for speaking of God because creation is itself an image of the glory of God. It is the created effulgence of the uncreated glory of the Trinity.[43] When Scripture says, "God is a sun" or "God is a rock," it is not imposing a theological meaning on atheological material reality. The innermost being of all things is its revelation of the glory of the Creator. Of course, Scripture speaks of God by speaking of the creation. What other language does he need? What other language do we need? What other language could there possibly be?

IN ALL THE SCRIPTURES

Ahem . . . ahem . . . ahem. I am almost finished, about ready to begin speaking. My throat is so clear that I may break out in song.

---

[41]The phrase is Hamann's from *Aesthetica in nuce* in *Hamann: Writings on Philosophy and Language*, ed. Kenneth Haynes (Cambridge: Cambridge University Press, 2007), 75.

[42]Robert Jenson, *Systematic Theology*, vol. 1: *The Triune God* (Oxford: Oxford University Press, 1997), 222.

[43]David Bentley Hart, *The Beauty of the Infinite: The Aesthetics of Christian Truth* (Grand Rapids, MI: Eerdmans, 2004), 240.

Before I do, let me make a few more commitments explicit. First, let me state a fundamentalist presupposition that has been implicit throughout this chapter. I believe God speaks in the normal sense of the word *speak*. He appeared in Eden to utter audible words to Adam, then to Adam and Eve. He confronted Cain, instructed Noah, called Abram and promised him land and seed, consoled Hagar in the wilderness, thundered from Sinai, spoke to Solomon in a dream, came as Word of Yahweh to prophets. After speaking in many portions and in many ways, he spoke in the last days through his Son (Heb 1:1-3).

Scripture is God's Word in written form. It contains *nothing* unworthy of its divine Author. What Scripture teaches, God teaches. It is our final rule for all theology and Christian practice. Through Scripture, the Spirit tests, judges, and corrects every creed and theological claim, and the Bible also has the theological, and therefore the philosophical, resources we need to formulate a positive theology and biblical metaphysics.[44] Scripture does not need to be "translated" into metaphysical terms to provide the "grammar" of divinity. Of late, "classical theism," with its emphasis on metaphysical perfections such as simplicity, immutability, eternity, and impassibility, has been put forward as that grammar. I propose the Bible and the creed ("I believe in God the Father Almighty, Creator of heaven and earth") as a more suitable and stable grammar, to which all other conceptualities must be drastically subordinated.

Second, *Creator* is a theological reading of Genesis 1, but Genesis 1 does not stand alone. There is heuristic value in isolating a single chapter and asking what it can tell us on its own. We should make

---

[44]Every important philosopher in the Western tradition intrudes on theology, though sometimes without much attention to or understanding of the texts and resources of theology. See chap. 2 below for a discussion of some of the theological dimensions of Hellenic philosophy.

our initial approach to understanding the meaning of the phrase
"image of God" (Gen 1:26-27), for instance, by asking what kind
of God has been introduced in the first twenty-five verses of the
chapter. In its immediate context, we learn that man is the image
of a God who creates, speaks, makes, has a Spirit, and so on. That
is where we should begin our theological anthropology, but it is
not where we end our theological anthropology. Genesis 1 is only
the first chapter of a very long book, and, besides, many passages
of Scripture refer to and illuminate the creation account. Though
I offer a close reading of the Hebrew text of Genesis 1, my theological interpretation will range across the canon.

There are two justifications for pursuing a *sensus plenior*. First,
later writers of Scripture not only allude to earlier sections of
Scripture but comment on those earlier Scriptures. John employs
terminology from Genesis 1 to make his own theological claims.
With "in the beginning" and his references to the Word, "coming
into being," light and darkness, and his enumeration of a sequence of days, John signals that his account of the life of Jesus
marks a new genesis for the world. Redemption is new creation,
as the God who spoke the worlds into being speaks again, as the
God who spoke creation unveils himself in his Word, now taber-
nacled among us in our flesh.

Yet John 1 is not simply a new covenant rewriting of Genesis 1.
It is also a *commentary* on the original account.[45] We can infer
from Genesis 1 that the Word was "in the beginning with God,"
that "all things came into being" by the Word, and that the Word
is the source of both light and life. We might even be able to infer
that the Word of creation "enlightens every man." What is revealed in the incarnation is the divinity of the Word, the fact that
the Word who is in the beginning, by whom God made all things,

---

[45]Peder Borgen, "Logos Was the True Light: Contributions to the Interpretation of the
Prologue of John," *Novum Testamentum* 14, no. 2 (1972): 115-30.

who is light and life, *is* God and God-toward-God (*pros ton theon*, Jn 1:1). What is revealed in the incarnation is also the *personhood* of the Word, the fact that he is not only a divine utterance but a divine *he*, who bears the glory of his Father as the only begotten of the Father. This is not merely, I suggest, a new covenant insertion into John's riff on Genesis. John interprets Genesis 1 in the light of the gospel, justifying a fresh reading of the creation account. Though not explicit, this is the logic of Augustine's trinitarian reading of Genesis 1,[46] and it will be the logic behind my trinitarian reading as well. We do not know the Trinity from the opening chapter of the Bible, but in the light of the remainder of the Bible, we find the hints of Trinity inescapable.

We reach the same conclusion through a different route. Jesus said the substance of Scripture is the suffering and glory of the Christ (Lk 24). Every page of Scripture speaks of Jesus the Christ. And if all Scripture is about Jesus, then it is also about the Father of the incarnate Son and the Spirit by whose anointing Jesus is the Christ. Just as we search for Jesus on every page of Scripture, so we expect to find the other divine persons on every page. Even without the direct commentary of John 1 and other passages, a christological—that is, a true—reading of the creation account would necessarily yield a *trinitarian* reading.

Finally, and briefly: I say *plenior*; I actually mean *plenissimus*. I am after the fullest sense I can discover. I will squeeze everything I can out of textual features large and small. Thus I will suggest a radical reorientation of theology proper by emphasizing the theological, as well as textual, primacy of Genesis 1:1 (chap. 4), draw theological conclusions from the literary texture and the divine plurals of Genesis 1 (chap. 5), indulge in an extended numerological speculation to lay foundations for a "metaphysics of

---

[46]Especially in *Literal Meaning of Genesis.*

Genesis" (chap. 6), and meditate on the echoes and re-echoes across the creation days to formulate an understanding of the Creator's relationship to created time (chap. 7). My sources are eclectic, and I will frequently, tastelessly, mix theological genres and styles, shifting from tedious exegesis to flights of mystical speculation with little warning and no hesitation. It may appear that I believe I can find a fully developed trinitarian theology in Genesis 1. I do not. But I do believe the Bible is a single book and that we can only plumb the depths of its first chapter if we see it through the prism of every other chapter. And I believe the church's creedal and theological tradition provides further resources to illumine the creation account.

Call it maximalism if you like. Call it a "kitchen sink" hermeneutic because I do not intend to leave out that crucial piece of kitchen gadgetry. For this reason, I do not offer a completed system with tidy, totalized, smoothed edges. The coherence I aim for is biblical, and I pick up whatever is at hand to illumine and fill out a scriptural metaphysics. *Creator* is more suggestive than systematic; it is a form of bricolage, though the bits and pieces form a whole, something akin to Irenaeus's mosaic portrait of a beautiful prince.

I am prepared to have much of *Creator* dismissed as childish mythology. I relish the dismissal, for being childish puts me in the best theological company. All theologians *should* be, and the best theologians *are*, companions of the divine Child who calls us to follow him as little children. That is not a call to naiveté or innocence. It is a call to play at the edges of viper's dens, heedless to our safety.[47] The methodological principle that has most consistently guided me over the decades is encapsulated in a little poem by G. K. Chesterton:

---

[47]I learned this many years ago from Pastor Toby Sumpter.

Stand fast! And keep your childishness.
Read all the pendant's creeds and strictures,
But don't believe in anything
That can't be told in colored pictures.[48]

---

[48]G. K. Chesterton, "Lines Written in a Picture Book," *G. K. Chesterton Collected Works*, vol. 10: *Collected Poetry, Part I* (San Francisco: Ignatius, 1994), 304.

2

LOGOS, MYTHOS, CREATION

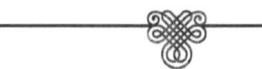

Some readers will have heard haunting echoes of the dreaded, discredited "Hellenization thesis" reverberating in the background of chapter one. My criticism of translating biblical into philosophical idiom and my criticisms of accommodation seem perilously close to the claim that the early church was corrupted by her subjection to the abstractions of Hellenistic philosophy. This historical thesis is often allied with a theological program of *de*-Hellenization, an effort to purge Greek thought from theology and to replace it with Hebraic thought forms.

I do believe Christian theology has been adversely affected by Greek thought forms, and this entire book is an exercise in scriptural purification. Yet *Creator* is not grounded on the Hellenization thesis. The shape of my argument is more of the pox-on-every-house variety.

On the one hand, the anti-Hellenization-thesis position sometimes fails to recognize the thoroughly religious character of the Greek philosophical heritage. Ancient metaphysics was not an academic discipline but a way of life that included a way with the gods or, in some cases, with "God."[1] The fundamental categories

---

[1]Pierre Hadot, *What Is Ancient Philosophy?*, trans. Michael Chase (Cambridge, MA: Belknap, 2004).

of Greek philosophy and science were transformations of mythic tropes and patterns, and the religious dimensions were never set aside. The clash between the church and Greek philosophy was a clash between rival theologies.

Yet, on the other hand, the clash did *not* end in Christianity's thoroughgoing subjection to metaphysics, nor an apostasy from the gospel or biblical teaching. The story of early Christian theology is much rather the story of a complex series of battles, triumphs, and truces between Greek and biblical conceptualities. The result was, in general, a deep transformation of Hellenic thought by the Bible, especially by the doctrine of creation *ex nihilo* and the dogmas of the Trinity and, especially, the incarnation.[2] These doctrinal claims stretched prior Greek conceptualities all out of recognizable shape, in order to put them to use in speaking of, praying to, and worshiping the God and Father of Jesus Christ. We can see it happening already in the New Testament, which uses the Greek language and, to some degree, Greek intellectual categories to proclaim and elaborate a gospel for both Jews and Gentiles. The result, in Robert Jenson's words, is neither the triumph nor the renunciation of metaphysics but its revision and transformation.[3] By and large, the church *won* the battle.

Yet, finally, I do not believe the gospel *entirely* vanquished her enemies. Theologians have taught distorted, unbiblical notions about God, sometimes under the influence of one or another form of Greek metaphysics. Modern theology has, in turn, taught

---

[2]See Johannes Zachhuber, *The Rise of Christian Theology and the End of Ancient Metaphysics: Patristic Philosophy from the Cappadocian Fathers to John of Damascus* (Oxford: Oxford University Press, 2020), who argues that the Christian revolution in metaphysics occurred not in the trinitarian debates of the fourth century but in the christological debates of the fifth and sixth centuries.

[3]Robert Jenson, *Theology as Revisionary Metaphysics: Essays on God and Creation* (Eugene, OR: Cascade, 2014); Klaus Hemmerle, *Theses Towards a Trinitarian Ontology* (Brooklyn, NY: Angelico, 2020), 14, 19-20.

distorted, unbiblical notions about God under the influence of Kant, Heidegger, or Derrida. Identifying and purging those false teachings is one of the perpetual tasks of theology. Theology will remain, among other things, revisionary metaphysics until kingdom come.

This chapter and the next expand on the last two paragraphs. In this chapter, I show the continuity between Greek religion and Greek philosophy, *mythos* and *logos*, poetry and philosophy, between, in Marcus Terentius Varro's terms, fabulous and natural theology.[4] I attempt to escape the risks of offering a potted history by focusing primarily on a single text, Plato's *Timaeus*. In the next chapter, I examine the Christianization of Greek metaphysics, once again avoiding potted-history-ness by examining Thomas Aquinas's modifications of divine simplicity in some depth. From the beginning, I have selected evidence to highlight the fact that biblical teaching about creation is a, perhaps *the*, crucial site of conflict between the rival theologies.

QUEST FOR THE *ARCHĒ*

What is the source of everything that is? Where does it all come from?

In the beginning, Greek poets, especially Hesiod and Homer, answered by composing myths that told of Gaia and Chasm and Eros, a succession of gods, and a series of dynastic conflicts between fathers and sons that culminated in the triumph of Zeus and the Olympians.[5] The divine beings of these myths are supersized human beings, with supersized passions and (literally)

---

[4] Augustine, *City of God* 6.
[5] The basic plot line is borrowed from Mesopotamian and ancient Near Eastern myths, with Zeus standing in for Marduk or Bel. See Walter Burkert, *The Orientalizing Revolution: Near Eastern Influence on Greek Culture in the Early Archaic Age* (Cambridge, MA: Harvard University Press, 1998); M. L. West, *The East Face of Helicon: West Asiatic Elements in Greek Poetry and Myth* (Oxford: Clarendon, 1999).

titanic battles, their primary difference from humans being their immortality, which is to say, their immunity to the devastations of time and death.

According to the standard account, Greek philosophy originates with the Presocratics, who are said to have embarked on a novel form of human inquiry.[6] Between Homer and Plato, *mythos* shifted in meaning, as *logos* occupied a larger role in Greek talk about talk. Though, at one level, *logos* encompasses both *epos* and *mythos*, Plato attaches values to *logos* that generate a set of oppositions between *logos* and *mythos*. *Logos* is verifiable speech;[7] *mythos* is unverifiable discourse because it refers to persons and events of ancient times or because it refers to a world of gods and demons beyond the sensible world. Myths are the province of diviners, initiators, and poets, whose *logoi* cannot be proven; the philosopher, by contrast, subjects all discourse to the interrogation of reason, and thus can escape the prison-cave of opinion and arrive

---

[6]The Presocratic achievement is novel, yet these writers are indebted to the poets. For a general overview of the connections, see *The Presocratic Philosophers: A Critical History with a Selection of Texts*, ed. G. S. Kirk and J. E. Raven (Cambridge: Cambridge University Press, 1957), 8-72. On Parmenides in particular, see Maja E. Pellikaan-Engel, *Hesiod and Parmenides: A New View on their Cosmogonies and on Parmenides' Proem* (Amsterdam: Hakkert, 1978); Edwin F. Dolin Jr., "Parmenides and Hesiod," *Harvard Studies in Classical Philology* 66 (1962): 93-98; Eric A. Havelock, "Parmenides and Odysseus," *Harvard Studies in Classical Philology* 63 (1958): 133-43; Mark D. Northrup, "Hesiodic Personifications in Parmenides A 37," *Transactions of the American Philosophical Association* 110 (1980): 223-32. Manuel Knoll, *Antike griechische Philosophie* (Berlin: De Gruyter, 2017), 15-35, details mythical elements in Thales and concludes that the philosophical aspects of Hesiod force us to relocate the beginning of philosophy to Hesiod rather than Thales. Knoll draws on Olof Gigon, *Der Ursprung Der griechischen Philosophie: Von Hesiod bis Parmenides* (Basil/Stuttgart, 1968). See also the brief discussion in Jean-Pierre Vernant, *Myth and Society in Ancient Greece*, trans. Janet Lloyd (New York: Zone Books, 1990), 215-18; and the philosophically rich interpretation of Hesiod found in Marcel Detienne and Jean-Pierre Vernant, *The Cuisine of Sacrifice Among the Greeks* (Chicago: University of Chicago Press, 1986), esp. chap. 2.

[7]As early as Heraclitus, *logos* refers not only to a form of discourse but to the inner rationality of things that philosophical discourse reveals: *logos/logoi* disclose *Logos*. See Gregory Vlastos, *Plato's Universe* (Las Vegas: Parmenides, 2005; first published in 1975), 8; Eva Brann, *The Logos of Heraclitus* (Philadelphia: Paul Dry Books, 2011).

at truth. *Logos* progresses by argument; *mythos*, like history, is nonargumentative. *Philosophia* has the dialectical tools to verify or falsify statements.[8]

The earliest philosophers deploy the resources of *logos* in a quest for the *archē*, the source, principle, or cause of all things.[9] Beginning from the belief that the world is a *kosmos*, an ordered and unified system intelligible to the mind, they ask: What explains cosmic unity and order? Whatever it is, it must have a causal relationship with the cosmos. The quest for an *archē* is a quest for an origin, whether something resembling a creator or a metaphysical principle in which things cohere.[10]

In the nature of the case, the quest for an *archē* introduces a distinction between sense and intellect. We can discern cosmic order, but the explanation of the order lies beyond the world of sense. The sun rises and sets with great regularity, but the sun itself cannot explain why the sun rises and sets with great regularity. The *archē* is the "nonevident" explanation for the sensible phenomena of experience. To find this *archē*, one must be able to

---

[8]Luc Brisson, *How the Philosophers Saved Myths: Allegorical Interpretation and Classical Mythology*, trans. Catherine Tihanyi (Chicago: University of Chicago Press, 2004), 5-26. See also Brisson, *Plato the Myth Maker*, trans. Gerard Naddaf (Chicago: University of Chicago Press, 1998).

[9]Aristotle's survey of earlier metaphysics is a summary of theories of the *archē*. Aristotle himself is still on the quest: Theoretical as opposed to technical wisdom is "scientific knowledge of certain sorts of starting points (*archai*) and causes (*aitiai*)" (*Metaphysics* 981ª28). Henri Frankfort overstates the contrast of *mythos* and *logos*, but, importantly, identifies the Ionian revolution in a shift in the meaning of *archē*. In contrast to their predecessors, philosophers "did not describe an ancestral divinity or progenitor. They did not even look for an 'origin' in the sense of an initial condition which was superseded by subsequent states of being. The Ionians asked for an immanent and *lasting* ground of existence. Arche means 'origin,' not as 'beginning' but as 'sustaining principle' or 'first cause.'" *The Intellectual Adventure of Ancient Man: An Essay on Speculative Thought in the Ancient Near East* (Chicago: University of Chicago Press, 1946), 376.

[10]Paul surely has Genesis 1:1 in mind when he writes of Jesus as *hē archē* (Col 1:18), but has he also read his Aristotle? Is he saying to the Colossians something similar to what he says at Mars Hill: "The *arche* you search for in ignorance, I announce to you"?

ascend from phenomena to source, from effect to cause. If there is an unbridgeable chasm between appearance and reality, the search for an *archē* fails. In that case, the *kosmos* then has no explanation, and we are forever confined to the phenomena. We may be tempted toward skepticism: Perhaps what we perceive as order is not order at all; perhaps we are deluded. Yet the order of the world seems undeniable, and philosophers embark on their quest in hope that there is a discoverable, articulable *logos* at the end.[11]

Physical explanations (if such they were) are bound to fail. If water is (as Thales said) the principle of reality, cosmic order is explained by something *within* the cosmos.[12] But if the *archē* is among sensible phenomena, then *it* needs to be explained, and we face an infinite regression of *archai*.

Greek philosophers begin from the observation that the sensible world has two features, plurality and mobility, a process of coming to be and passing away. The sensible world is full of distinct things (trees and mailboxes, finches and Fabergé eggs), and these things are in constant motion (trees grow, mailboxes open and close, finches fly, Fabergé eggs tragically break).

---

[11]I am aware I am skimming over differences among philosophers and philosophies. Bear with me; I will get more specific in a moment. For the time being, I am relying on Gerson, *God and Greek Philosophy* (London: Routledge, 1994), 5-14, though I disagree with Gerson insofar as he minimizes the religious impulses behind philosophy. The quest for an extrasensory explanation of sensible phenomena is not confined to ancient thought. Modern science likewise posits occult forces like gravity to "save the appearances" that have no *apparent* explanation.

[12]There is much dispute about what Thales meant. The full statement, as recorded by Aristotle (*Metaphysics* 983ᵇ6), is: "The earth floats on water, which is in some way the source of all things" (Kirk and Raven, *The Presocratic Philosophers*, citation 86). If he means that water is the *source* of earth, he remains quite close to mythical conceptions, in which "the deep" or a liquid chaos is often the first principle. Whatever he means, Thales does not exclude divinity. After identifying water as the *archē tēs physeos*, he adds "all things are full of *daimonon*" (Kirk and Raven, *Presocratic Philosophers*, citation 91), and he also claims that a divine power (*dynamin theian*) penetrates and moves the "elemental moisture" (Kirk and Raven, *Presocratic Philosophers*, citation 95).

Reflection on these features of the sensible world generates, by way of negation, a rough sketch of the *archē*. Within the swirl of plural and changing phenomena, we discern elements of unity and fixity. The world of things sometimes verges toward the "confusion of a welter,"[13] yet somehow it all holds together. How? There must, it seems, be a source prior to the multiplicity, a *one* that embraces and holds together the many. Ergo: The *archē* must be One.

Despite their teeming multiplicity, things do have one sameness: their very existence. And that suggests the existence of a source of their miraculous common existence. Despite their mobility and mutability, further, things are continuous with themselves. Trees grow yet remain trees; when a Fabergé egg (tragically) breaks, the pieces are identifiably pieces of a Fabergé egg. A thread of immobility runs through the turning world; there is sameness in the midst of difference, and it must come from something other than the world. Ergo: The *archē* must be self-same, immobile.

Coming to be and passing away are forms of becoming. Sensible things come to be when they are generated by some other sensible thing—children from parents, mailboxes from the postal service, Fabergé eggs—*real* ones—from a Russian craftsman. But an *archē* is not the product of becoming of any kind; it is underived, because a derived *archē* would itself have an *archē*: a daft idea.[14] Ergo: A genuine *archē* must be purely originary, an ungenerated starting point.

---

[13] William Desmond, *Being and the Between* (New York: SUNY Press, 1995), 232.
[14] As Plato writes, "The beginning (*arche*) is ungenerated. For everything that is generated must be generated from a beginning, but the beginning is not generated from anything; for if the beginning were generated from anything, it would not be generated from a beginning. And since it is ungenerated, it must be also indestructible." *Phaedrus* 245D, trans. Harold N. Fowler (Cambridge, MA: Harvard University Press, 1925).

The "attributes" of the *archē* are teased out from observation determined by the *archē*'s function as a cornerstone, lynchpin, or capstone of the cosmos. To serve as *archē*, the *archē* must be one rather than many; unchanging, atemporal, and immobile rather than temporal and mutable; simple and smooth rather than jagged and cobbled together; an origin that is in no way originated. In effect if not in intent, the attributes of the *archē* are decided by negation of the sensible world: Whatever the world *is*, the *archē* is *not*, and vice versa. I believe in one *archē*, unchangeable and ingenerate—so goes the creed. Though the reasoning is philosophical, it is not accidental that the outcome coheres with myth: The *archē* of *logos* possesses the same immunity to the ravages of time and change as the gods of *mythos*. Had Homer and Hesiod encountered the philosophical *archē*, they would have recognized the scent of divinity about it.[15]

As I mentioned above, this entire line of reasoning depends on our ability to construct or discover a bridge to span the gap between the world of experience and the unknown *archē*. But the

---

[15]Even philosophers who offer rigorously immanent *archē*-ology remain theologians. Heraclitus, it seems, aspired to be a consistent physicist whose cosmological *archē* is not a "once" but a "what," a principle of origination and growth internal to the cosmos. There is no beginning: "This world order (*kosmos*) did none of gods or men make, but it always was and is and shall be" (Kirk and Raven, *Presocratic Philosophers*, citation 220). Consistent with this premise, Heraclitus denies the divinity of the heavenly bodies, stating the modern-sounding theory that the lights in the sky come from bowls "in which the bright exhalations are collected and form flames" (Kirk and Raven, *Presocratic Philosophers*, citation 227). Yet Heraclitus's world is not bereft of divinity. In a mysterious passage, he describes God as "day night, winter summer, war peace, satiety hunger; he undergoes alteration in the way fire, when it is mixed with spices, is named according to the scent of each of them" (Kirk and Raven, *Presocratic Philosophers*, citation 207). Even this consummate philosopher of *physis*, who aspires to purge Hesiod's cosmogony of its "naive" theology and metaphysics, remains a theological philosopher of the *archē*. My summary depends on David Sedley, *Creationism and Its Critics in Antiquity* (Berkeley: University of California Press, 2007), 8. See also A. P. D. Mourelatos, "Heraclitus, Parmenides, and the Naive Metaphysics of Things," in *Exegesis and Argument: Studies in Greek Philosophy Presented to Gregory Vlastos*, ed. E. N. Lee et al., Phronesis Supplement 1 (New York: Humanities, 1973).

philosophical pursuit of the *archē* reaches an early impasse, a
burned-out bridge, in the poem of Parmenides.[16] He is unrelent-
ing in his insistence that the *archē* is one, underived, immobile,
and immutable. Parmenides seems to achieve the ultimate apotheosis of *logos*, elevating the logical principle of noncontradiction
to a fundamental ontological claim. Logically and metaphysically,
A either *is* or *is not*, with no middle ground. *To be* is simply *to be*.
Being is *not*, as Aristotle will later insist, said in many ways. Being
is absolutely homogeneous, unmixed with nonbeing, smooth and
pure, without gaps that would negate its continuity with itself,
with nothing outside. In fact, the formula "nothing outside" is
nonsensical since, strictly, "there is no 'outside.'"[17] Everything
that exists is simply a facet of the one thing that exists, and the
one thing that exists is divinity.[18]

According to Parmenides, the *archē* cannot be different merely
from sensible reality. It has to be "absolutely different from
anything."[19] It has to be utterly different in the *manner* of its
existence. It cannot *possess* being. It must *be* Being. Yet Being-
itself cannot manifest itself in the sensible world. If you could find
traces of Being-itself in the world of sense, then Being-itself would
not be completely other to the world of sense. But if there is no
connection with the *kosmos*, how is the *archē* an *archē* of the
kosmos? Parmenides places contradictory demands on the *archē*:
To be Being, Being must be absolutely different from beings and
from the realm of beings as such; it is ontological, transcendent

---

[16]Once again, we note the continuity between religion and philosophy. Parmenides
composes a philosophical poem, rather than an argument. He receives *sophia* and
thus becomes a *philo-sophos*, by ascent to a goddess.

[17]Desmond, *Being and the Between*, 232.

[18]Cornford, *From Religion to Philosophy*, 216, notes that, despite Parmenides's obvious
distance from Olympianism, his concept of Being is indebted to mythic theology:
"the attributes of unity, perfect continuity, and divinity (now construed in the
Olympian sense of deathless immutability) exclude and negate plurality, and the
changing movement of life."

[19]Gerson, *God and Greek Philosophy*, 26.

to the ontic. But an *archē* can be an *archē*—the explanatory principle of the sensible world—only if it is *not* absolutely different,
only if the sensible world has some discernible connection to the
archē.[20] As a result of this contradiction, Parmenides concludes
that Being is known only in the way of pure reason, purged of any
appeal to sense or nature. Goodbye, natural theology![21] Goodbye
science, while we are at it: Even if we discover Being, it can teach
us nothing about the origin or order of the *kosmos*. No wonder
Parmenides has to take a mystical chariot into the realm of the
goddess to discover wisdom. He is not going to run into lady
wisdom on the street corner.

Parmenides is at war with himself, and this internal strife can
only lead to an incoherence that becomes evident when we consider how Parmenides deals with the problem of not-being. Not-
being seems inherent to the changing world of phenomena; multiplicity can exist only if we can say "X *is not* Y," "the cat *is not* the
mat on which it sits." For Parmenides, though, it is an insult to
Being even to speak of "nothing." Giving the nonexistent a name
treats it as if it were something. Strictly, we must be silent about
nothing. And we cannot explain our silence because that too would
insult the absoluteness of Being. Univocity (Being is Being is Being),
which markets itself as the apotheosis of *logos*, is in the end the
"death of logos" that reduces philosophy to a "metaphysical silence

---

[20]Gerson (*God and Greek Philosophy*, 26) suggests we imagine that fire is the *archē*:
A distinction between fire and its being follows because "fire exists" or "fire is
real" gives us two pieces of information: what exists and that it exists. If this is
so, the nature of fire does not explain its own being nor can being explain fire,
unless it is separated from fire, in which case fire does not exist, counter to the
initial hypothesis. . . . A true *arche* must be perfectly undivided. Once, however,
the *arche* is identified with being itself and it is discovered that being is neither
multiple nor changing, showing how it explains anything about the multiple and
changing appearances seems an impossible task. For nothing about the plural
and changeable world as such seems to have anything to do with what being is.

[21]Parmenides, on Lloyd Gerson's reading, is not "an eccentric natural theologian" but
"a metaphysician or philosopher of being who rejects natural theology altogether"
(*God and Greek Philosophy*, 28).

that logically should not even explain itself."[22] And Parmenides himself cannot avoid saying "not," thereby contaminating the pure homogeneity of Being. He is "reduced to commanding us not to think the 'not,'" but he subverts his command in the speaking of it, since it is a "no-saying" and "is itself a form of the 'not.'"[23]

As the Stranger in Plato's *Sophist* notes, Parmenidean Being has drastic epistemological and ethical consequences. A disciple of Parmenides, the Stranger finds he must commit philosophical parricide because Parmenides makes it impossible to distinguish truth from error. If "it is" is the truth of all, then all that *is* is true, including even falsehoods and phantasms. A hallucination of a Fabergé egg, or a counterfeit, *is* as much as a real egg. Truth and falsehood are indeterminate because both share in Being. A perfect univocal monism paradoxically leads to a radical equivocal relativism; the apotheosis of *logos* destroys the entire point of *logos*, which is to discern between truth and falsehood.[24]

The quest for an *archē* thus leaves Hellenic philosophy with a fundamental dilemma between existence and unity: Is there any unity in the flux of a Heraclitean cosmos? On the other hand, do identifiable beings exist if, as Parmenides announces, all is one?[25]

---

[22]Desmond, *Being and the Between*, 232.

[23]Desmond, *Being and the Between*, 234. Desmond presents a version of Plato's argument in his *Parmenides*, on which, see Elizabeth Anscombe, "A New Theory of Forms," *The Monist* 50, no. 3 (1966): 408-9; also Cornford, *Plato and Parmenides* (London: Kegan, Paul, Trench, Trubner, 1939); Samuel Scolnicov, *Plato's Parmenides* (Berkeley: University of California Press, 2003); Robert Roecklein, *Plato versus Parmenides: The Debate over Coming-into-Being in Greek Philosophy* (Lanham, MD: Lexington Books, 2011), 121-58.

[24]To claim that one is caught up in false belief or has expressed falsehood in words, the Stranger says, one must "assume that what is not is; only on that assumption will a false thing said or believed turn out to be something that is." But this is precisely what Parmenides excludes, with his exclusion of the thought "that the things that are not are." *Sophist* 273a in *Plato: Thaetetus and Sophist*, ed. Christopher Rowe (Cambridge; Cambridge University Press, 2015). See Eva Brann, *The Music of the Republic: Essays on Socrates' Conversations and Plato's Writings* (Philadelphia: Paul Dry Books, 2011), 278-303.

[25]Anton C. Pegis, "The Dilemma of Being and Unity," in *Essays in Thomism*, ed. Robert Brennan (Eugene, OR: Wipf & Stock, 2014 [1942]), 152.

Plato aims to surmount the Parmenidean impasse. To see how he does so, we can briefly examine Plato's rejoinder to another Presocratic, Anaxagoras. Anaxagoras posits a creative *nous* (mind) that organizes matter. Before mind gets to work, the world's ingredients are homogeneous. The original stew does not include shoes and ships and sealing wax, cabbages and kings, or even the four elements. It is an undifferentiated mixture of the properties that constitute stoicheic pairs of opposites.[26] *Nous* forms a vortex that separates out wet, dry, hot, and cold from the something-nothing that is both all these properties and none. As each quality spins out, it combines with other properties in its proper place. Cold and dry are thrown together as heavy earth; hot and dry combine as light fire. This separation is always only partial. No sheerly wet wetness nor purely hot heat exists; nor is anything made of a single element. Though the portions of binary qualities change, "in everything there is a portion of everything."[27]

Anaxagoras evades the Parmenidean impasse by introducing a saving duality between the noetic *archē* and everything else. *Nous* escapes mixture. It alone is pure; mind "is all alone by itself."[28] It has to be pure because if it were mixed with anything it would be mixed with all. Mixed things change but, unmixed, mind is immutable. Mixed things have physical properties, but, though *nous* is a very fine kind of stuff, it is not physical. Immutability, immobility, and immunity to mixture are *nous*'s defining qualities.[29] Once again we catch a whiff of archaic divinity.

---

[26]See G. E. R. Lloyd, *Polarity and Analogy: Two Types of Argumentation in Early Greek Thought* (Indianapolis: Hackett, 1992).

[27]Kirk and Raven, *Presocratic Philosophers*, citation 509.

[28]Kirk and Raven, *Presocratic Philosophers*, citation 503.

[29]This paragraph is indebted to Sedley, *Creationism and Its Critics*, 8-25. Anaxagoras believes in a form of "intelligent design," but *nous* is not a "Creator" in the Christian sense. The cosmos neither becomes nor perishes. *Nous* sets things spinning. Or, *nous* is a farmer that sows the seeds of development within the cosmos. It is *not* the kind of entity that brings things into being.

Socrates was initially enthusiastic about Anaxagoras. The notion of mind as "the disposer and cause of all" he found delightful and admirable. If mind produces the cosmos, it can dispose all things for good, placing each thing where it belongs, forming a cosmos of justice and beauty. *Nous* searches for the state of being, doing, or suffering that is best for each thing. Anaxagoras seems to offer what Parmenides does not, a conscious, purposeful world maker. Alas. When he read Anaxagoras, Socrates was disappointed. He "could not imagine that when [Anaxagoras] spoke of mind as the disposer of [things], he would give any other account of their being as they are except that this was best." The more Socrates learned of Anaxagoras, the more disappointed he became. Instead of attributing the order of things to intelligence, he introduces other causes—"air, and ether, and water, and other eccentricities." It is as if Anaxagoras begins by saying mind is the cause of Socrates's actions, then changes direction and explains Socrates's specific actions by reference to his body parts: "I sit here because my body is made up of bones and muscles" and "I am able to bend my limbs, and this is why I am sitting here in a curved posture." By introducing thousands of causes, Anaxagoras forgets mind, "the true cause."[30]

For Socrates and Plato, a proper cosmogony and metaphysics has to include a good *archē* who deliberately forms the best of all possible worlds. In Anaxagoras, *nous* ultimately functions as a quasi-naturalistic, scientific cause. Plato and Socrates oppose the naturalizing theories of the *physiologoi*, insisting that the order of things can only be accounted for by something outside that order. In the *Timaeus*, Plato introduces the right kind of *archē*, the demiurge. The demiurge is *not* a mere symbol of a naturalistic principle of coming to be or growth. He is "father" to the world he

---

[30]*Phaedo* 98C, in *Euthyphro, Apology, Crito, Phaedo*, trans. Benjamin Jowett (Amherst, NY: Prometheus, 1988). For analysis, see Sedley, *Creationism and Its Critics*, 86-89.

orders, a being who "rejoices" over creation, which is made in the image of the eternal gods.[31] For the first time, a *philosopher* speaks of a cosmic artificer who is more Zeus than *nous*.[32] Plato's goal is an overt *r*emythologization of cosmogony.[33]

PLATO AND MYTHOS

This is perhaps a surprising claim, given Plato's overt hostility to poets, poetry, and *mythos*, a hostility built into his fundamental metaphysical assumptions.[34] A visible representation of a thing is less than its eidetic reality. Time is a moving image of eternity and a chair a shadow of the ideal chair, of lesser ontological weight for being copies. As representations of the sensible world, poetic myths are doubly false, shadows of shadows. Poets lie. Homer and

---

[31]Plato, *Timaeus* 37C-D.

[32]Francis Cornford, *Plato's Cosmology: The Timaeus of Plato* (Indianapolis: Hackett, 1997 [1937]), 34.

[33]Walter Burkert sums up the transition this way: "Heraclitus . . . seems to develop a 'biomorphic' model into a 'phytomorphic' model, the principle of growing according to inner laws, as plants do. . . . And yet hardly any of Heraclitus' successors can do without the concept of creator. Parmenides introduces a female *daimon* who 'governs everything,' and creates divine powers such as Eros; Anaxagoras gives a similar function to *Nous*, 'Mind,' the leading power for all differentiation; Empedocles has 'Love' constructing organs and organisms in her workshop; it was only Democritus who, criticizing Anaxagoras, tried to exclude 'mind' from the shaping of macrocosm and microcosm. The reaction came with Plato and Aristotle: Plato's *Timaeus* finally established the term 'creator,' *demiourgos*." "Logic of Cosmogony," in *From Myth to Reason? Studies in the Development of Greek Thought*, ed. R. G. A. Buxton (Oxford: Clarendon, 2002), 95-96. See also Vlastos, *Plato's Universe*, 25, who argues that Plato offers a "theological cosmogony" in response to the Presocratics.

[34]Plato's argument against poetry is in *Republic* 10 (595a-606c). There are, of course, multiple complexities in interpreting Plato's works. He never appears in his own dialogues or speaks in his own person; Socrates is typically his mouthpiece of wisdom, but it is not altogether clear whether Plato endorses everything Socrates says; the various dialogues do not agree fully with one another. Thus, one must be cautious about attributing a view stated in a Platonic dialogue to Plato, and about assuming there is a single metaphysical vision running through all the dialogues. I use a deliberate simplification: "Plato" is a stand-in for "the teaching of the Platonic dialogues" and I assume, as most interpreters have, that there is sufficient coherence among the dialogues for us to speak meaningfully of a "Platonic" position on this and that. Eric Perl, *Thinking Being*, 19-22, suggests the dialogues form a "woven tapestry," coherent enough to justify locutions like "Plato says X."

Hesiod are the fathers of lies, though, Plato recognizes, some lies
are noble.

Socrates insists he is not a "myth-teller,"[35] since he does not
construct imitations of things that never were nor will be. When
he constructs a myth or formulates an image, it is an image of
what *is*. To arrive at appropriate images, Socrates first engages in
an interior argument, which leads to true opinions written into
his soul "as by an inner scribe."[36] To make these images, a philosopher must be able to see likeness and unlikeness, to discern
the truth and also the difference between truth and copy. Socrates
and Plato freely revise myths and literary works for their own
purposes, adjusting them to the cause of truth.

Plato's hostility to Homer and Hesiod has a more specific
source: Their poems are not merely lies but *bad* lies, morally evil
because they depict reprehensible violence and sexual predation,
blasphemous because they attribute these immoral actions to the
gods. The greatest of lies, Plato says, are the lies about Ouranos,
who swallowed his children, and Kronos, who retaliated against
his father by castrating him. Even if these stories are true, they
ought not be told to the young but should be buried in silence.[37] In
the passage of the *Republic* where Socrates condemns the lies of
the poets, he explicitly names Hesiod and alludes to *Theogony*.
The passage forms a *locus classicus* in the combat between *mythos*
and *logos*, poetry and philosophy.[38] Plato specifically condemns

---

[35] *Republic* 61B5.

[36] Brann, *Music of the Republic*, 154. Brann quotes *Philebus* 38E. This entire paragraph
depends on Brann's exposition of Socratic images.

[37] Plato, *Republic* 377-78.

[38] Aristotle is, if anything, even more emphatic. He dismisses "Hesiod and all the theologians" who "made the starting-points (*archai*) to be gods and what is born of gods"
who feed on nectar and ambrosia. There is no need for a serious investigation of
"mythical subtleties" but the philosopher should instead "cross-question those who
use the language of demonstration to learn from them why in the world from the
same things come . . . beings that are eternal and . . . beings that pass away" (*Metaphysics* 1000ª9-18). Yet Aristotle too is a theologian.

poetic *theology*, which opens up the path toward a distinctly philo-sophical conception of divinity.[39]

What may appear to be a clean break with poetic *mythos*, however, is *not*. The boundaries between Greek myth and Plato's philosophy are fuzzy and permeable.[40] Plato does not leave Homer behind. The first word of the *Republic* is *katebēn*, "I went down," an echo of Homer's account of Odysseus's descent to Hades: *katebēn domon Aidos eisō*, "I went down into the house of Hades."[41] The scene is critical to Homer's epic. To achieve his *nostos*, his "homecoming" to Ithaca, Odysseus has to pass through death. For his part, Socrates is headed to the Piraeus, the seaport of Athens, to observe a festival for a newly founded religion and to pray to the chthonic goddess, probably Bendis. Several myths of the

---

[39]See Francis Cornford, *Principium Sapientiae: A Study of the Origins of Greek Philosophical Thought*, ed. W. K. Guthrie (New York: Harper, 1965), 146-55.

[40]The general argument has been frequently made. See Francis Cornford, *From Religion to Philosophy: A Study in the Origins of Western Speculation* (Minneola, NY: Dover, 2004; first published in 1957); Cornford, *Principium Sapientiae*; McEvilley, *The Shape of Ancient Thought: Comparative Studies in Greek and Indian Thought* (New York: Allworth, 2002); from an eccentric Girardian angle, Guiseppe Fornari, *Dionysus, Christ, and the Death of God*, vol. 1: *The Great Mediations of the Classical World* (East Lansing: Michigan State University Press, 2021); Raymond Barfield, *The Ancient Quarrel Between Philosophy and Poetry* (Cambridge: Cambridge University Press, 2011), 10-31. See also the older, exhaustive treatment in J. A. Stewart, *The Myths of Plato* (London: Macmillan, 1905). For an overview of the scholarship on *mythos* and *logos*, see Glenn Most, "From Logos to Mythos," in Buxton, *From Myth to Reason?*, 25-50. I focus on Plato and Hesiod, first, to give the argument a degree of texture that would be lacking in a more general argument, and, second, to zero in on the *Timaeus*, the pagan creation account that has the most direct, broadest, and most lasting influence on Christian theology. But the argument can be broadened, since many ancient philosophers were able to draw back the veil of myth to discover wisdom. In the third century BC, for instance, Berossus offered allegorical interpretations of Babylonian myths, and others interpreted the Egyptian myth of Atum as an allegory of the emergence of the many from the primordial one. On pre-Hellenic philosophy, see Frankfort, *Intellectual Adventure of Ancient Man*; more recently, Marc van de Mieroop, *Philosophy Before the Greeks: The Pursuit of Truth in Ancient Babylonia* (Princeton, NJ: Princeton University Press, 2016). On the philosophical content of the Bible, see Yoram Hazony, *The Philosophy of Hebrew Scripture* (Cambridge: Cambridge University Press, 2012); Dru Johnson, *Biblical Philosophy* (Cambridge: Cambridge University Press, 2021).

[41]*Odyssey* 23.252.

Republic mimic this opening line, as they describe descent into and ascent from underground territories, most famously in the allegory of the cave, which Socrates explicitly compares to Hades. From Socrates's first words, we steel ourselves for a harrowing but necessary descent to the realm of the dead.

The *Republic* also ends with a cluster of Homeric allusions. Socrates says the reincarnational Myth of Er does not come from "Alkinous," a reference to the Phaeacian king who hosts Odyssey. Er's journey resembles that of Odysseus, and Er even sees the soul of Odysseus, standing alone as the one soul who learned the lessons of his life.[42] Similarly, when Socrates introduces the climactic allegory of the cave, he "quotes from that part of the *Odyssey* in which Odysseus, having descended into the underworld, is told by the shade of Achilles that he would rather be a serf to a poor man than ruler over all the dead." The effect is "to link the situation of human beings in a political community with that of the shades in Hades, and the situation of the philosopher, whose quest for wisdom enables him to transcend the cavelike horizons of a political community, with that of Odysseus, a visitor to Hades."[43] Allusion is not, of course, endorsement, and Plato is always busy revising myth. Plato worries that Homer's Hades provokes fear and reworks the *katabasis* of Odysseus to foster courage in the face of death.

Plato's Homeric frame is not window dressing. The *Republic* offers a "new, specifically *philosophic* odyssey," an updated, intellectually

---

[42]Jacob Howland, *The Republic: The Odyssey of Philosophy* (Toronto: Twayne, 1993), 49. For a complementary analysis of the *Republic*, see Brann, *Music of the Republic*, 108-245. Brann finds more Herakles than Odysseus. Like the former, Socrates engages in a battle and multifaceted labor of argument. He teaches his audience letters (as Herakles did), founds a city, is delivered from drowning, uses his rhetorical music to release a Theseus who is confined to Hades, confronts a Cerberus (118-22).

[43]Howland, *Republic*, 49. See also Andrea Capra, "Plato's Hesiod and the Will of Zeus: Philosophical Rhapsody in the *Timaeus* and the *Critias*," in *Plato and Hesiod*, ed. G. R. Boys-Stones and J. K. Haubold (Oxford: Oxford University Press, 2010), 201-2.

sophisticated *nostos* that brings the exiled soul to its true home. Plato's first aim is to convince the soul it is indeed exiled, not an easy task, since our "prephilosophical contexts have . . . shaped our desires and beliefs, have impressed on us judgments of the goals and paths of life." Philosophy disturbs our contentments in order to show that our most cherished *nomoi* are inimical to full human life.[44] Once he has detached citizens from their illusions, Socrates can lead them out of the cave toward the light. The *Republic* is a philosophical harrowing of Hades.

Is the rescue successful? Can it be? The Homeric precedent leaves us pessimistic: Odysseus does *not* bring his men home, nor does he remain in Scheria, the golden city of the Phaeacians. The *Republic* has a similar mood. It begins with a detailed sketch of the ideal regime, but that is not the climax of the dialogue. As Odysseus leaves the "height" of Scheria to return to Ithaca, so Socrates shifts "from the nature of the best regime to the problem of individual salvation." His "tour of regimes and souls makes it clear that the community cannot be saved along with the individual."[45] In the light of its mythic model, the *Republic* is revealed not as a utopian political treatise but as a call to transcend politics for the philosophical life. It is haunted by the tragic sense that the political community as such, like Odysseus's band of friends, is beyond hope. Few shall be saved.

If the *Republic* is *mythos* transmuted into *logos*, the same is more self-evidently true of the *Timaeus*.[46] Despite his rejection of

---

[44]Howland, *Republic*, 49.

[45]Howland, *Republic*, 53.

[46]The *Timaeus* is the best-known of the Greek cosmogonies and has an enormous role in the Western philosophical tradition, known to Plotinus, Augustine, Dionysius, Boethius in late antiquity. Throughout the Middle Ages, it was the only complete Platonic work available in Latin and offered as the primary evidence for the Christian claim that Plato read Moses. It is a major source of some of the most enchanting and persistent ideas of Western civilization—the music of the spheres, the theory of humors, the notion that the sphere is the perfect geometric shape, the four elements, the significance of the human body. Along with Genesis, it presented the

Hesiodic theology, Plato draws on, echoes, and mimics Hesiod throughout his own account of origins.[47] At one level the similarities are obvious. Both the *Theogony* and the *Timaeus* are accounts of how the world began.[48] Both Hesiod and Plato think the world is formed from an original something. In the *Theogony*, the initial state includes three entities: Chasm, Gaia, and Eros.[49] Though *chasm* refers to an empty space or gap (perhaps the gap opened by the separation of heaven and earth), it is early linked etymologically with *cheisthai*, "to flow," and comes to refer to flux or chaos. For Hesiod, chasm forms the "fluid substrate" of all things and is the source of change and hence of evil.[50] As such, it anticipates the "receptacle" in Plato's cosmogony, which also functions as substrate that the demiurge tames into cosmic order.

---

universe as good because it is the product of conscious divine design. See R. B. Rutherford, *The Art of Plato: Ten Essays in Platonic Interpretation* (Cambridge, MA: Harvard University Press, 1995), 285-96.

The *Timaeus* is divided into two large sections. Initially, Timaeus describes the works of reason, carried out by the demiurge. The demiurge forms the body and soul of the cosmos, makes the celestial gods, generates the Olympian gods, and carefully shapes the human body and soul. Midway through, Timaeus changes tack and introduces a new set of characters. The Receptacle, the Chasm (or chaos), the Primary Bodies formed from combinations of triangles, Motion, and the Senses. For more complete analyses of the dialogue, see Cornford's classic, *Plato's Cosmology*; Sedley, *Creationism and Its Critics*, 95-132; Gabriela Roxana Carone, "Creation in the *Timaeus*: The Middle Way," *Apeiron* 37 (2004): 211-26; Vlastos, *Plato's Universe*; Sarah Broadie, *Nature and Divinity in Plato's Timaeus* (Cambridge: Cambridge University Press, 2011). See also Louis Markos, *From Plato to Christ: How Platonic Thought Shaped the Christian Faith* (Downers Grove, IL: IVP Academic, 2021), 95-117.

[47]Though he wrote in the eighth century BC, Hesiod still looms large in the literary culture of classical Athens. The *Theogony* was best-known of the Greek creation myths. See E. E. Pender, "Chaos Corrected: Hesiod in Plato's Creation Myth," in Boys-Stones and Haubold, *Plato and Hesiod*, 218. David Sedley says Hesiod is "close to the center of Plato's cultural universe" (Sedley, "Hesiod's *Theogony* and Plato's *Timaeus*," in Boys-Stones and Haubold, *Plato and Hesiod*, 247). Sedley details how the *Theogony* set the agenda for philosophical musings on origins in *Creationism and Its Critics*, 2-4. On Hesiod's debt to Near Eastern mythology, see Walter Burkert, *The Orientalizing Revolution*, and M. L. West, *The East Face of Helicon*.

[48]The very fact that Plato wrote a dialogue on the origin of the world is notable. Parmenides did not, believing as he did that it was "impossible for anything to come into existence" (quoted in McEvilley, *Shape of Ancient Thought*, 54).

[49]My discussion here follows Sedley, "Hesiod's *Theogony* and Plato's *Timaeus*," 246-58.

[50]Sedley, "Hesiod's *Theogony* and Plato's *Timaeus*," 253.

Both Hesiod and Plato link the chasm/receptacle with time, change, instability, and evil, over against beings that more or less effectively impose stability and good. Timaeus claims the cosmos is not eternal but "has come into existence" (*gegonen*).[51] Yet a visible "all" already exists (*pan hoson en horaton*) when the demiurge begins. The demiurge's labor is to bring order out of disorder (*eis taxin . . . ek tēs atasias*) since the former state is superior to the latter.

Beyond these broad parallels, there are many similarities of detail. The polarity of demiurge and receptacle is gendered, like the various male-female polarities of Hesiod's *Theogony*. The male represents the principle of stability and order, while the feminine, a womb fertile with novel beings, is a principle of change and disorder. The demiurge's efforts to persuade chaos have erotic overtones, as he sweet-talks the turbulent female entities to conform to the models he seeks to copy. Behind Plato's "assemblage of created deities" is "Hesiod's model of the world as a divine family," though Plato's divine household is far less dysfunctional than Hesiod's.[52] In Hesiod's *Works and Days*, women are proximate sources of evil. Pandora, Zeus's ambiguous gift to Epimetheus, releases evils in the world because of her insatiable curiosity. Plato's misogyny is metaphysical. The male soul is the pinnacle of *psyche*. Yet, because the good demiurge seeks to make the world as full a copy of the original Form as possible, he populates the world with lesser souls. The first degenerate soul is the feminine, followed by the souls of other living creatures.

The most obvious textual link between Hesiod and Plato is Timaeus's quick summary of the creation of the gods that takes place at a critical juncture in the dialogue. Timaeus describes the demiurge's formation of four classes of creatures that correspond

---

[51]Plato, *Timaeus* 28B.
[52]Sedley, "Hesiod's *Theogony* and Plato's *Timaeus*," 237.

to the four *stoicheia* (elements): Land animals with earth, fish with water, birds with air, and stars with fire. Of these deities, Timaeus can formulate a plausible opinion, but with respect to other gods, he relies on tradition handed down from those who are themselves children of the gods. (Surely they know their own ancestors!) In quick summary, he reproduces Hesiod's lineage of the gods: "Let the generation of these gods be stated by us, following their account, in this wise: Of Ge and Uranus were born the children Oceanus and Tethys; and of these, Phorkys, Cronos, Rhea, and all that go with them; and of Cronos and Rhea were born Zeus and Herod and all those who are, as we know, called their brethren; and of these again, other descendants."[53]

The demiurge enlists these deities to assist with the creation of man. After this speech, Timaeus moves into a new phase of the discourse, where the demiurge disappears from view and other eternal powers and factors take center stage.[54] The demiurge's creation of the gods and of man, a passage full of overt borrowings from Hesiod, forms the climax of the first section of Plato's discourse.[55]

Timaeus's implicit recourse to etymology to explain the term *demiurge* is another nod to Hesiod. In his speech to the freshly

---

[53]Plato, *Timaeus* 40E-41A, trans. R. G. Bury (Cambridge, MA: Harvard University Press, 1929); cf. *Theogony* lines 132-38, 453-58. On this passage, see Pender, "Chaos Corrected," 223-26. To be sure, even here Plato diverges from Hesiod. There is no being corresponding to the demiurge in Hesiod. When the *Theogony* opens, three principles or figures already exist—Chasm, Gaia, and Eros. In an act of ecstatic parthenogenesis, Gaia produces Ouranos, with whom she then copulates, in the power of Eros, to form other beings. For Timaeus, all of these beings are directly born of the demiurge, whom he calls "the one who generated them all."

[54]Note the explicit transition from *logos* to *anagke* in *Timaeus* 47E-48A.

[55]More generally, Friedrich Solmsen finds a continuity between Hesiod's "mythical genealogy" and Plato's "dialectical genealogy," both of which "aim . . . at setting up intellectually satisfactory relationships between kindred entities." Both, in short, "construct pedigrees (*gene*) based on material and substantial rather than on accidental similarities." "Hesiodic Motifs in Plato," in *Hesiode et son influence*, ed. Kurt von Fritz et al. (Geneve: Vandoeuvres, 1960), 180.

created gods, the demiurge identifies himself as *demiourgos* and *pater*, adding all these works (*ergon*) came to be *di' emou*, "through me." The close textual proximity of *demiourgos* with *ergon* and the prepositional phrase *di' emou* hints that the demiurge is identifying himself as the One-Through-Whom the cosmos is.[56] Earlier, Timaeus reflects on the etymological appropriateness of the words Ouranos and *kosmos*,[57] and Plato's interest in etymologies is evident throughout his work, most notably in the *Cratylus*. In etymologizing divine names, Plato is probably inspired by the *Theogony*, which assigns the Muses names to match their artistic roles and which links the name Aphrodite with her origin from the foam that bubbled from the sea where Kronos threw the genitals of Ouranos ("Aphrodite" is "Foam-Born" [*aphrogenea*]).[58] Plato's etymology of demiurge is inspired by Hesiod's *Works and Days* (9-10), where he links the name Zeus to the preposition *dia*. Plato defends this specific etymology in the *Cratylus*, noting that the king of the pantheon is the one through whom all things live (*di' hon zēn*).[59] For both Hesiod and Plato, the high god is the *archē*, the source of the cosmos. Yet Plato diverges: While Hesiod sings of Zeus's rise to power and his achievement of divine *dikē*, Plato's demiurge is a Zeus-like father and creator from the beginning. He is Zeus *undramatized*, Zeus *without his story*.[60]

---

[56]Plato, *Timaeus* 41A. On this passage, see Mario Rigali, "Hesiod in the *Timaeus*: The Demiurge Addresses the Gods," in Boys-Stones and Haubold, *Plato and Hesiod*, 261.

[57]Plato, *Timaeus* 28B. See Rigali, "Hesiod in the *Timaeus*," 262.

[58]Rigali, "Hesiod in the *Timaeus*," 263.

[59]Plato, *Cratylus* 396a. See Rigali, "Hesiod in the *Timaeus*," 265-67.

[60]See Cornford, *Principium Sapientiae*, 153: "Looking back over the 'quarrel' between philosophers and poets, we see that it turned chiefly on the rationalist's objections to the anthropomorphism of the myths." Ignoring "the mythical adventures of humanized gods," the philosopher speaks of a god who is "at first the immortal and imperishable power of motions and consciousness animating the whole body of the world." This deity is not a person, nor an object of worship, but the single *archē* that determines the *physis* of things. This, Cornford argues, reverts to a pre-mythical stage of religious thought, of "superhuman power diffused throughout Nature." Solmsen offers a specific example of the turn from anthropomorphism, time, and

The *Theogony* leaves other faint traces on the *Timaeus*. The latter begins with the promise of a triadic feast of discourse that will trace the history of creation from its origins (Timaeus's discourse) through the wars and death of the heroes (the subject of the *Critias*) to the contemporary world (the subject of a discourse by Hermocrates). In the event, Plato composed only half of the sequence, the *Timaeus* and the unfinished *Critias*. Yet the planned trilogy resembles the triadic scheme of Hesiod's *Theogony* and *Works and Days*.[61] Timaeus seems to suggest four principles—the Forms, the demiurge, the cosmos, and the receptacle or space within which the Form's copies take shape, yet he never speaks of the demiurge and the receptacle in the same context. Even when Timaeus introduces new powers and "characters," a Hesiodic gravitational pull keeps bringing him back to a triad.[62]

Finally, the elemental structure of Plato's cosmos seems to be indebted to mythological domains. Ancient myth distributes different cosmic realms to different gods. Zeus, like Marduk/Bel, is the sky god, equipped with the thunderbolt; Poseidon is the god of water; Hades the god of the underworld. In philosophical cosmogonies, these regions are translated into depersonalized *stoicheia*, each of which combine two properties of the double binary of cold/hot and wet/dry. Zeus the sky god becomes hot-dry fire,

---

story. In *Republic* 3, Plato explicitly employs Hesiod's myth of the four ages, each of which links a particular stage of human life with a metal. Plato picks up the qualitative distinctions among men of different types but ignores the temporal sequence. Some people in every age, including Plato's own, are golden (Solmsen, "Hesiodic Motifs," 182). Further, Plato tarnishes the luster of Hesiod's age of Kronos, by emphasizing the absence of political order. What matters for human life is not easy abundance of material goods, but peace, justice, happiness, which are dependent on shame (192).

[61]Capra, "Plato's Hesiod," 204.
[62]Pender, "Chaos Corrected," 237: "Perhaps . . . Plato, with the *Theogony* as his archetypal model, wants to utilize the triad as a successful narrative and explanatory motif, while recognizing that any single triadic group would simply prove insufficient to the needs of his own complex discourse."

Poseidon the cold-wet water, Hades the cold-dry air or hot-wet earth.[63] The elements are depersonalized and denarratized, but they occupy the same territories and play much the same role as the mythic gods.[64]

I draw this modest preliminary conclusion: The *Republic* is a philosophical *Odyssey*; the *Timaeus* is a philosophical *Theogony*.

PLATO BEYOND PARMENIDES

It must be conceded: The *Timaeus* is a *philosophical Theogony*, a transmutation of *mythos* into *logos*. But why does Plato retain mythic elements at all? Why not posit an eternal cosmos, or follow Anaxagoras's lead by attributing order to depersonalized *nous*? Why the demiurge? Why the gods?

Plato's form is partly determined by the subject matter. Timaeus explicitly presents his account of origins not as a logically airtight argument but as an *eidos mythos*, a plausible story. It cannot be otherwise. The cosmos itself is a copy, and any effort to describe its origin has a truth status appropriate to the thing it describes. The world exists as the realm of sense rather than in

---

[63]Cornford, *From Religion to Philosophy*, 17-18, 60-65. Plato gives a quasi-mathematical account of the elements. Corporeal things must be visible and tangible, and thus must be composed of fire (for visibility) and earth (for solidity). Two cannot be joined without a third to mediate their union, and since the world is three-dimensional it requires two mediators: Water and air are thus placed between fire and earth, with proportionate relations ("air being to water as fire to air, and water being to earth as air to water") (*Timaeus* 32B-C).

[64]Anton Pegis writes that the *Timaeus* is marked by the dilemma of being and unity that marks all Greek philosophy. It offers "intelligibility minus unity; intelligence minus autonomy." It portrays "a continual war against interior forces of division, plurality and even disintegration" and treats being as a force that "stems the barbarism of eternal matter by a transcendence which is a confession that the barbarians are continually threatening the gates of reality as well as those of the Roman empire." It is, on the one hand, a "necessitarian world," yet, on the other hand, a "dismembered world," a world "lacking in individual beings as its intelligibility, sealed in determinateness, [and] lacking in unity." If there is order here at all, it is an order achieved at the price of sacrificing reality (Pegis, "Dilemma of Being and Unity," 170). This summary brings the *Timaeus* close to mythic cosmology, in which Zeus must continuously battle back the forces of chaos.

the realm of intelligible things, and so humans can only arrive at opinions (*doxai*) or beliefs (*pistoi*) about it, never rational truth.[65]

But the subject matter does not fully account for the shape of Plato's cosmogony. He includes the gods because he *believes* in the gods.[66] Further, he introduces mythic elements in order to parry Parmenides. He does this at two levels, one metaphysical having to do with his theory of Forms, the other metaphys-mythical, which has to do with the mediation of the demiurge. Without the demiurge, Plato's quest for the *archē* or *archai* runs aground.[67]

---

[65]Alternatively: Elsa Grasso, "Myth, Image and Likeness in Plato's *Timaeus*" in *Plato and Myth: Studies on the Use and Status of Platonic Myths*, ed. Catherine Collobert, Pierre Desiree, and Francisco J. Gonzalez (Leiden: Brill, 2012), argues that the dialogue is *eikos mythos* not because it deals with the sensible world but because it offers the most rational account of divine genesis (351). See also Luc Brisson, who writes that a "reasonable myth" is one "describing the work of reason (that of the demiurge) involved in world-making, which is therefore practical, not theoretical" ("Why Is the *Timaeus* Called *Eikôs Mythos* and *Eikôs Logos*?" in Collobert, et al., *Plato and Myth*, 391).

[66]Gerd Van Riel claims historians of philosophy have misread Plato because they conflate Plato's theology with Aristotle's. For the latter, theology and metaphysics merge in the unmoved mover who is both the highest metaphysical reality and "god." According to Aristotle, "god is pure act, pure form, self-thinking thought . . . and the final cause of the universe," the "cornerstone of metaphysics." Many have read Plato's various statements about God, the Good, and the gods through this Aristotelian lens, but that, Van Riel argues, is anachronistic. Plato's gods (note the plural) are "a multitude of divine souls, each of whom has the specific task of looking after (part of) the sensible world." To be sure, Plato often writes of *theos*, "god," but he uses the singular interchangeably with the plural *theoi*. "God" does not refer to a single transcendent deity; rather, Plato uses the singular as an abstract term: "'god' as a singular noun does not refer to one sole god, but rather describes all of the gods in their essential features." Plato wants to purify archaic, mythical, poetic images of the gods, in order to stress the goodness of the gods and in order to speak rightly of the gods. That is why he expels the poets with their degrading stories about the gods from his republic. But he is still a polytheist, more archaic than often believed. See Van Riel, *Plato's Gods*, Ashgate Studies in the History of Philosophical Theology (London: Routledge, 2013), 3, 38. Adam Drozdek argues, by contrast, that Plato is a monotheist and the gods are analogous to angels in Christian cosmology. *Greek Philosophers as Theologians: The Divine Arche* (London: Routledge, 2007), 163-64.

[67]Thus Cornford claims Plato ends up "Olympianizing" the Forms: "Plato, in his final attempt to formulate a cosmology, falls back on the mythical horn of the dilemma, which Parmenides has the courage to avoid. He is forced to attribute to his deified Intellect and impossible impulse of desire," the demiurge. Thus "the mythical form of this whole cosmology is not a poetical dress" and Plato could have stated it as *logos* if he could. Immutable logos provides "a scheme of classification" but it cannot

I begin with Plato's metaphysical rejoinder to Parmenides. For Parmenides, *to on*, "Being," is outside time and space, whole, continuous, unmoved, without beginning or end. Being has divine attributes, and perhaps Parmenides considered Being to be god. Clearly, Being is not like the traditional gods of mythology, except in its immunity to change, time, and death. It is "divinity in pure form, the essence of divinity abstracted from the world of the gods of mythology."[68] Parmenides has often been read as a pantheist who claims Being is the only existing thing and that sensible things are illusory. When he writes the *Timaeus*, Plato retains a Parmenidean ontology for the intelligible world. The Forms are perfect but have no agency or autonomy. They are determinedly self-identical.

This is evident, for instance, in Plato's account of time. Time, Timaeus claims, is a moving image of eternity, organized by heaven into units of days, nights, months, years, which form the *mere chronou*, "parts of time." The tensed terminology of temporal existence does not apply to eternal being. Time is the form of becoming and motion, and motion does not exist for *to on*, which is entirely *akinetos*.[69] Timaeus's linkage between motion and time, on the one hand, and immobility and eternity, on the other, is rooted in a more basic duality, between "Same" and "Other." Sameness is perfection; thus, the cosmos is a sphere, since that is the most self-similar of all shapes.[70] Being perfect, *to on* is indivisibly the same. To form the changeable cosmic soul that moves

---

produce anything: "To account for the existence of anything whatever, we have to ascribed to it the unworthy and lower faculty of desire, and give this desire an unworthy and lower object" (*From Religion to Philosophy*, 260-61). Cornford does not believe Plato intends the demiurge to be taken literally. However necessary the mythic flavoring is, the demiurge is a "mythic symbol" of divine reason, not an object of worship (*Plato's Cosmology*, 38).

[68] Adam Drozdek, *Greek Philosophers as Theologians*, 50.

[69] Plato, *Timaeus* 37D-38A.

[70] Plato, *Timaeus* 33B: *panton teleotaton homoitaton te auto heauto*.

in the pageant of time, the demiurge must mix the sameness of Being with the divisibleness and difference of bodily becoming—that is to say, to form a compound of Same and Other midway between them. It is a challenging recipe: Same and Other are, Timaeus wryly says, "naturally difficult to mix," and the demiurge needs the aid of Being to accomplish the task. Once compounded, he distributes the mixtures in different portions to various regions of the cosmos.[71]

On Plato's premises, this is perfectly sound. If *to on* is not purely the same, it can become Other and cease to be Being. If *to on* is accompanied by a second, a co-eternal Other, then the ultimate thing must be a third something that unites the two. "That which embraces all intelligible living creatures," Timaeus argues, "could never be second, with another beside it." If it were, there would need to be "yet another living creature, which would embrace them both, and of which they two would each be a part." In that case, the cosmos would not be modeled on the one or the other, but on the third that encompasses the two.[72]

We find a similar account of the Form of the Living Thing in *Timaeus* 51E-52A: "There is, first, the unchanging Form, ungenerated and indestructible, which neither receives anything else into itself from elsewhere nor itself enters into anything else anywhere, invisible and otherwise imperceptible; that, in fact, which thinking has for its object."[73] Two different things cannot "come to be in the other in such a way that the two should become at once one and the same thing and two." Beauty is its self-same self only because it does not enter into anything else, whether in earth or heaven, but remains "always in and by itself."[74] To

---

[71]Plato, *Timaeus* 34B-35B.
[72]Plato, *Timaeus* 31A.
[73]This is Cornford's translation, *Plato's Cosmology*, 192.
[74]Plato, *Symposium* 211A.

remain independent, the Form must not receive anything from elsewhere. Being cannot remain continuous, eternal, immobile if it receives another into itself, or if it enters into another.

At the same time, Plato is already moving from Parmenides, insofar as he believes the sameness of *to on* is capable of being mixed, and indeed, *must* be mixed, with otherness. This maneuver is crucial to Plato's effort to lend ontological ballast to the sensible world, to carve out space to say, "It is," of temporal things. Instead of treating time and change as illusion, he views them as shadows and images. Plato refuses the binary choice of Parmenides—A *is* or *is not*—and so affirms a qualified form of "being" exists in the multiple, changing world of the many.[75] He looks for a path through the Parmenidean impasse.

A *KOINONIA* OF FORMS

In the *Timaeus*, Plato does not develop the full metaphysical apparatus to support this qualified notion of Form. He does in the *Sophist*.[76] At the outset of that dialogue, Theaetetus and a visitor to Athens (the Stranger) are trying to understand what a sophist is. Is the sophist a hunter preying on rich young men, a salesman of virtue and eloquence, a professional wrestler in the *agōn* of words? Does the sophist possess the gift of separating and distinguishing, which purifies the soul of his hearer? The Stranger and Theaetetus finally fasten on the sophist as a maker of spoken images, but this too requires a distinction, for there are *poietes* of likeness and makers of apparitions.

From there, the *Sophist* opens into a metaphysical analysis of images that pinpoints the failure of Parmenides. An image is like the thing it images, but it is *not* that thing. *Not* being the original is the very essence of the image. Here, then, is a form of being

---

[75]Desmond, *Being and the Between*, 235.
[76]Here I follow Brann, *Music of the Republic*, 278-303.

whose very essence is *not*-being. An apparition makes the point even more sharply, for a false image is not only *not*-original, but it is also *not-like* the original, not in a truthful way. An apparition is a double negation of the being that serves as its model, yet, paradoxically, this double negation is just what the apparition *is*. Images and apparitions can exist, and be identified as images and apparitions, only if Nonbeing is.

As I have noted briefly above, this puts the Stranger, a disciple of Parmenides, on a collision course with his master, whose key axiom is that Being *is*, with the corollary that Nonbeing is *not*. How can he get past Parmenides? After all, it seems commonsensical to say "Being *is*" and "Nonbeing *isn't*." To justify the existence of Nonbeing, and so to affirm the is-ness of images and apparitions, the Stranger redefines Nonbeing as "Other." That eventually leads to a reconsideration of the Forms. Along with Being (*to on*), the Forms include Rest and Motion. These last two oppose one another and so cannot partake of one another. Yet both *are*, and therefore both share in Being. Lurking behind this analysis are, once again, the greatest of kinds, Same and Other, but the Stranger realizes these cannot be simple opposites. Same and Other also partake of Being: Every form is self-same and thus participates in the Same, yet each Form is also other to the others, and thus each partakes in the Other. Even Being itself partakes of the Other, since it is self-same as itself only by being *other than* Rest, Motion, Same, and Other.[77] The Forms, thus, are interwoven with one another to form a *koinonia*, a communion of kinds.[78] The *Sophist* makes explicit the antinomy between unity and being that runs through Greek metaphysics. The Stranger

---

[77]Brann, *Music of the Republic*, 289.

[78]As Elizabeth Anscombe points out, Plato already appealed to the *koinonia* of Forms in the *Republic* 476C, though there the question was about participation in a Form *by* others, which makes the Form appear multiple. In the *Sophist*, Plato is raising the prospect of Forms participating *in* others ("New Theory of Forms," 406).

steers between Parmenides and Heraclitus by insisting that Being must be diverse if it is to be intelligible. In the process, Being loses its unity. The world of the *Sophist* has only the "unity of an ordered whole which maintains within itself the distinct articulation of its members."[79]

All Forms partake of Other since each is other to the others. Surprisingly, *otherness* becomes the Form that binds the kinds into an interwoven communion. As each participates in Other, it is both distinguished from and related to every other, through the common share in the Other. The power of the Other is "at the heart of all this community, participation, and interweaving," since the Other is the "power by which a being is what it is only by being other than *and therefore related to* everything else."[80] This ontological communion of kinds makes images possible since the image both *is* and *is other than* the original.[81] It makes it possible for us to distinguish images from originals and illusion from reality.

The communion of forms in the *Sophist* resolves tensions in the cosmogony of the *Timaeus*. Time, as noted above, is a "moving image" of eternity. The dazzle of the image is apt to seduce us into ignoring its conceptual gaps. Plato appeals to the Forms as a way of stabilizing thought and language about the world of Becoming, and, more deeply, to provide an ontological anchor for an intelligible cosmos. The Forms provide a set of *archai*, with the Form of the Good sometimes suiting up to play the role of master *archē*.

---

[79]Pegis, "Dilemma of Being and Unity," 157. Pegis continues the story: Plotinus will attempt to save unity from the infection of plurality, but, because he shares Plato's antinomy, he can do so only by elevating the One above intelligibility. The only unity that can be established is "a barren unity whose eminence over being is also an isolation from the intelligibility of being" (158).

[80]Brann, *Music of the Republic*, 289.

[81]This supports Adrian Pabst's claim that Plato presents a "relational" ontology. See *Metaphysics: The Creation of Hierarchy* (Grand Rapids, MI: Eerdmans, 2012), 2-3, though he arrives at the conclusion by a different route.

Yet Plato never clearly explains how the world of Becoming is related to the world of forms.[82]

How does time mimic eternity? To answer this, we need first to specify the time Timaeus has in mind. It is not the experienced time of the soul, or the human time of birth, growth, and death, or the social and political time of war and peace, of plenty and penury. Instead, he speaks of cosmic time, the regular motion of the sun, moon, and stars, which mark out the units of time. As Eva Brann puts it, "the similarity-feature that links the heavenly clock to its heavenly paradigm is the steadiness of its circular celestial motion."[83] In its stately majesty, celestial motion resembles the perfect immobility of eternity.

But from the perspective of the *Sophist*, time is an image of eternity because it is not simply *opposite* to the eternal world of forms. There is instead an analogy between the communion of Forms in the Form of the Other and the motions and flows of temporal existence. "It is" is *not* the only word, even in the intelligible realm of the Forms, because even among the Forms there is both "It is" and "It is other." Since the Forms form a communion of one with other, they can serve as the original of which flowing time—each moment other to every other—is the copy.[84]

---

[82]Brann, *Music of the Republic*, 275. The chapter title is "Time in the *Timaeus*." *Methexis* or "participation" is the typical answer to the question, but see below on the problems surrounding *methexis*.

[83]Brann, *Music of the Republic*, 277. Brann cites Aristotle's argument in *Physics* 264[b]9 that circular motion is "the most stable, continuous, and regular motion there is."

[84]"There is a quite wondrous anticipation of Trinitarian ontology here, for the God who eternally *is* is not pure self-sameness; there is in God both *this* and *that*, *one* and *other*. Indeed, there is in God a "not," for the Father is *not* the Son, nor the Son the Spirit, nor the Spirit the Father. In the triune God is a "relative" and "relational" non-being. For trinitarian ontology, nonbeing is not simply the opposite of being, but the "motor of [being's] internal movement." Piero Coda, *From the Trinity: The Coming of God in Revelation and Theology* (Washington, DC: Catholic University of America Press, 2020), 494-95. From this, Coda draws the further inference that the existence and life of the Trinity is not continuous possession but continuous dispossession and *kenosis*. The Father possesses himself as the source of divine love *only* in that he dispossesses himself in his self-gift to the Son. Each person is himself "only

At this point, Parmenides is *very* dead. The Stranger's parricide is highly successful. Plato's alternative metaphysics lends ontological weight to the sensible world, without lending *ultimate* ontological weight. Coming to be and passing away are not illusions. Saying *this* and *that* is not a lie. It is possible, epistemologically and ethically, to distinguish truth from illusion. If the *archē* is a *koinonia* of Forms, the multiple, moving ontic realm can be a genuine image of the ontological. The metaphysics of the *Sophist* buttresses a "creationist" understanding of origins, yet it does not *produce* it. Being the original of the moving, multiple world is not the same as being the *origin*. To cross the bridge from Forms to formed, Plato needs an active, intelligent mediator. He needs a craftsman who looks a lot like a character from a myth.

THE DEMIURGE AND THE FORMS

In part, the demiurge is a solution to problems raised by the theory of Forms and the related concept of *methexis*, "participation." It is a vexed concept. Aristotle dismisses it with the sharp comment that Plato never explains what it means.[85] Plato himself understands the difficulties. The title character in the *Parmenides* asks whether the participant shares all or only part of the Form. Neither answer is coherent: If it shares the whole Form, it seems it will *be* Form, but it cannot share a part because Forms are not the kinds of things that have parts. One solution is to deaden the Forms, reducing them from soul-like living things to concepts, but in the process, *methexis* is transmuted from an ontological reality into a logical and linguistic principle. Plato cannot abide this reduction: "Zeus!" cries the Stranger of the

---

insofar as they are not (in themselves, independently of others), but gives themselves totally and thus receive themselves in turn" (495, alluding to A. Brunner and von Balthasar).

[85] Aristotle, *Metaphysics* 987^{b}10-14. See Pabst, *Metaphysics*, 16.

Sophist, "Are we in any case going to be so easily persuaded that change and life and soul and wisdom are truly absent from what completely is, and that it does not live, or think, but sits there in august holiness, devoid of intelligence, fixed and unchanged." Theaetetus agrees: "That would be a quite shocking account of things for us to accept."[86]

Unless the Forms are alive, mobile, and wise, they cannot serve as *causes* of the cosmos. On the other hand, if the Forms *are* alive and mobile, can they do their duty as fixed anchors of the sensible world? Plato's solution is to insert the demiurge in the between space, with a foot in both worlds. He has access enough to the *koinonia* of living Forms to use them as models, but he can also have contact, without undue contamination, with the cosmos he constructs.[87] The Forms and the demiurge *must* work in tandem. The Forms provide the patterns and the ontological stability for a world of change and flux, but the Forms come to expression in sensible things only through the mediation of the demiurge.[88]

We see this collaboration at various points in the *Timaeus*. At the outset of his monologue, Timaeus distinguishes the world of being from the world of becoming. *To on* is described in strong Parmenidean terms, as that which always is, while *to gignomenon* is always becoming and never reaches the rest of *to on*.[89] Becoming results from some cause (*aitios*); the cause of the whole is the demiurge. To ensure that the world of time and motion is

---

[86]Plato, *Sophist* 248E. See the discussion of the problems of *methexis* in Cornford, *From Religion to Philosophy*, 255-56.

[87]The contact is not intimate. The demiurge does not, like YHWH *'elohim*, form man from dust and breathe into his nose. He delegates the dirty work to the lesser gods.

[88]Plato introduces the demiurge "to provide the permanent intellectual activity . . . for Forms to do their work" (Gerson, *God and Greek Philosophy*, 69).

[89]Plato, *Timaeus* 28A. The foundation of the duality appears to be epistemological rather than ontological. *To on* is what came be known by reasoning, while *to gignomenon* is what is known by *alogike* sensation. Without much by way of argument, Timaeus bakes these associations into his scheme: being : becoming :: truth/reason : belief :: model : copy.

as good as possible, the demiurge keeps "his gaze fixed on that which is uniform, using a model (*paradeigma*) of this kind."[90] Thus the cosmos is a copy (*eikon*) not of the demiurge himself but of the eternal paradigms to which the demiurge gazes. Specifically, the cosmos is made after the pattern of the intelligible living thing that contains within itself all intelligible living things, the most beautiful of all intelligible things.[91] Specific features of the sensible world must be as they are because they are imitations of the model. Because the intelligible living creature is one, so also the cosmos is a unity that contains all visible, sensible living things.[92] Because the cosmos copies the divine archetype, it too must be divine, generated by the demiurge to be a "blessed god."[93]

Other mythical entities prove necessary as well. The demiurge is between, but he is still too close to the world of Being to become completely entangled in becoming. So, the demiurge forms the "divine" cosmos, the divine lights of heaven, and summons the various gods of Hesiod—Gaia and Ouranos, Okeanus and Tethys, Kronos, Rhea, Zeus, and Hera. Timaeus does not venture a full account of the origin of these "other divinities" (*allon daimonon*) but relies instead on the testimony of those who descended from the gods, since they are aware "no doubt, [of] their own forefathers."[94] In the demiurge's speech to the gods, he claims paternity and indicates that they are dependent on his continuing

---

[90]Plato, *Timaeus* 28B. On the meaning of *paradeigma*, see William J. Prior, "The Concept of *paradeigma* in Plato's Theory of Forms," *Apeiron* 17 (1983): 33-42.

[91]The Greek phrase is *noeta zoa panta ekeino en heato perilabon exei*. While Plato sometimes implies an identity between the demiurge and the form of the living thing, they cannot be completely identical, since "the demiurge is *nous* and the Forms are *noeta*" (Gerson, *God and Greek Philosophy*, 69).

[92]Plato, *Timaeus* 30C-D.

[93]Plato, *Timaeus* 34B (*eudiamona theon auton egennesato*).

[94]Plato, *Timaeus* 40E. This passage has often been interpreted as ironic, but Cornford persuasively argues that there is no reason to doubt Plato's sincerity (*Plato's Cosmology*, 138-39).

favor. Since they were generated, they can dissolve; yet they will *not* dissolve on account of the goodwill of the demiurge, "a bond greater and more sovereign than the bonds wherewith, at your birth, you were bound together."[95] He delegates to the gods the task of generating mortal beings, since he is incapable of generating any beings without making them "equal unto gods." The ungenerated demiurge can make only divine beings, but the generated divine beings have the capacity, by imitating the generative power of the demiurge, to fashion generated mortals.[96]

The ontological status of the demiurge has been debated since antiquity: Does Plato believe he has named an actual being responsible for the form of the universe? Plato's account does not leave room for much of anything else.[97] The *eide* provide the ontological stability for the cosmos. The communion of Forms is Plato's *archē*, the principle of order and unity. Because an *eidos* is purely what it is, "simply itself and nothing beyond itself," it provides an anchor for the unity within the multiplicity of finite beings.[98] Yet, precisely because each *eidos* is self-same, it cannot itself produce its copy. They cannot serve as origin, because an origin must have the power to originate beyond itself, and so the power to extend itself into another. Nor can the *koinonia* of forms

---

[95]Plato, *Timaeus* 41A-B.

[96]Plato, *Timaeus* 41C. Behind this is the assumption that like makes like, a logical or metaphysical principle to which the demiurge is subject.

[97]Nor, for that matter, does the text. Sedley argues that Timaeus argues for an *archē* that is an actual beginning of the cosmos, not merely a causal principle (*Creationism and Its Critics*, 98-107); also Broadie, *Nature and Divinity*, 5, who claims that both the temporal beginning and the separate demiurge are essential to Plato's argument and warns that chiseling off or smoothing out bits of the *Timaeus* endangers the whole system. See also Broadie, "Theological Sidelights from Plato's *Timaeus*," *Proceedings of the Aristotelian Society* 82 (2008): 1-17. Gregory Vlastos, "Creation in the *Timaeus*: Is it a Fiction?" in *Studies in Greek Philosophy, Volume II: Socrates, Plato and their Tradition*, ed. Daniel W. Graham (Princeton, NJ: Princeton University Press, 1995), 265-79, answers the question of his title with "Probably not." For a contrary view, see Gabriela Roxane Carone, "Creation in the *Timaeus*: The Middle Way," *Apeiron* 37, no. 3 (2004): 211-26.

[98]Desmond, *Being and the Between*, 235.

reproduce itself. The Forms need a mediator to replicate them in the sensible world. Plato, in effect, divides the two functions of the *archē*: Understood as "principle of order," the *archē* is the *koinonia* of forms; understood as "cause of order," the *archē* is the demiurge. He does not, and cannot, unite the two functions into a single *archē*.

And that means Plato cannot do without myth. The mythic form of the *Timaeus* is not simply a persistence of primitive modes of thought, nor simply accommodation, nor even, as Timaeus admits, the proper form of speech for a probable account of origins. The mythic demiurge is a *metaphysical* necessity. Plato needs the kind of "creator" he posits to make sense of the origin of the world.[99]

CONCLUSION

Christian thinkers have long seen parallels between Plato's cosmogony and the creation account of Genesis. We can understand why. Above all, the demiurge is *good*. Plato's deletion of stories of Zeus's violence and sexual shenanigans is a crucial theological innovation.[100] The framer of worlds is elevated above the combats of the gods, not to mention the combats of men. He is a father, a careful craftsman who designs things as well as they can possibly be. His care in making the world is a reflection of his own character, for "He was good, and in him that is good no envy arises ever concerning anything."[101] Because he is free from envy, he

---

[99]The Socrates of Xenophon expresses a similar "anti-scientific creationist" or religious cosmogony. See Sedley, *Creationism and Its Critics*, 78-86.

[100]As Gregory Vlastos points out, the demiurge is not, like the Olympians, a strategist or schemer but possesses the reason of a mathematician, engineer, and, above all, an artist (*Plato's Universe*, 26).

[101]Plato, *Timaeus* 29E. For the Greeks, it is hardly a given that a deity will be without envy. Rather the opposite: "The envy of the gods is one of the deepest convictions in Greek theology" (Vlastos, *Plato's Universe*, 27). Can you say "Euripides"? A god beyond envy opens up new possibilities for piety; such a god can be *imitated* without ethical danger (Vlastos, *Plato's Universe*, 28).

desires everything to be "so far as possible, like unto himself."[102] Plato's account is recognizable to readers of Genesis precisely because he resorts to myth. With his speaking and making and doing, *'elohim* more closely resembles the demiurge than he does a Form.

Yet under the surface, there are major differences between Genesis and the *Timaeus*. There is nothing in Genesis comparable to the geometric scheme of Timaeus, nor any obvious suggestion of *stoicheia* from which sensible things are constructed.[103] In Plato, the world never comes to full reality, but exists only as shadow-play—*good* shadow-play, as good as it can possibly be, yet finally mere shadow-play. Nothing is at stake for the demiurge or the Forms; they have no skin in the game and cannot assume skin to enter the game. *'Elohim* makes *things*, complex systems, rather than components of systems. As a result, Genesis does not open up the gap between appearance and reality that structures much Platonic discourse. For Genesis 1, what you see is what there *is*: light, water, sky, earth, trees and grasses, sun, moon, stars, birds, fish, lions and tigers and oxen and snakes. Those are creatures of God, whether directly spoken from his mouth or mediated through some created reality. Unlike the demiurge, *'elohim* does not disdain to create any of these things. The ungenerated Creator is capable of generating *non*divine beings; the eternal God makes times and things that move and change in time.

The demiurge is not the sole cause of the universe. He is not the unbounded creator of possibility but subject to necessities outside himself and outside his control. He creates a spherical cosmos, in

---

[102]Plato, *Timaeus* 29E-30A.

[103]There is a possible parallel in the sequence of the first half of the creation week: Fire is perhaps implied by the reference to the Spirit in Genesis 1:2. Light (perhaps) pertains to air, the structuring of creation is largely a hydraulic operation (days two and three), and plants, land animals, and man are generated from earth. Thus: fire, air, water, and earth.

which every place on the surface is equidistant from the center, making the sphere "the most perfect and most self-similar" shape, because the "similar is infinitely fairer than the dissimilar."[104] The demiurge does not determine that similar is fairer than dissimilar; he inherits the aesthetical principle.

In the second section of the dialogue, indeed, the demiurge disappears and Timaeus offers an account of origins that depends not on a reasoning designer but on the operations of necessity.[105] New forces are introduced alongside necessity—the wandering cause, the receptacle, space, and something like preexisting matter, and these confront a being now called *theos* as a chaos that needs to be ordered.[106] This god organizes the inchoate proto-elemental material into triangles, then combines triangles to form the solid atoms that constitute the basic particles of the four elements. The god proceeds by distinguishing and purifying, disentangling elements from one another and giving each a purity of atomic shape that determines its physical and sensible properties. Not only does the god confront an existing material, but he is again beholden to standards of goodness and beauty from outside—for example, the geometric rules that determine the organization of atoms by triangles.[107]

---

[104]Plato, *Timaeus* 33B (*monisas murio kallion homoion anomiou*).

[105]Plato, *Timaeus* 48A.

[106]Cornford writes, "It is the familiar experience of every craftsman that his material limits the scope of his design and may hinder it from reaching a perfection he can imagine but never achieve" (*Plato's Cosmology*, 165). "Hinder" may be too strong (see Sedley, *Creationism and Its Critics*, 116), but Cornford is right to argue that the demiurge confronts *anagke* and has to adjust and adhere to its demands. Plato is misunderstood when his demiurge is conflated with the omnipotent God of the Bible, which has no place in Greek thought (*Plato's Cosmology*, 163, 165).

[107]Plato, *Timaeus* 53C: "It is absolutely necessary (*pasa anagke*) that depth should be bounded by a plane surface; and the rectilinear plane is composed of triangles." Despite superficial resemblances to modern *mathesis*, William Desmond is right to call attention to the different role that geometry plays in Plato, as opposed to, say, Newton or Kepler: "The eikonic making of the world is not motivated by *geometry*: the demiurge is motivated to create out of a desire to make the world the *most beautiful and good possible*." In Pascalian terms, "This is a matter of *finesse* and not geometry.

Most fundamentally, in the *Timaeus*, as in all of Plato, divinity exists on both sides of what Christians mark out as the Creator-creature boundary. Platonism offers "an analysis of being in which there is no such distinction between God and creatures," because "divinity" spreads out to include both "creator" and the living thing that is the cosmos: "It is . . . inevitable that what is divine in Platonism should have some of the attributes which, in a Christian world, belong to creatures," and vice versa. In the *Timaeus* as in all Plato's writings, the dividing line is between the immutable divine and the changeable cosmos, or between intelligibility and matter, *not* between Creator and creation.[108]

Despite genuine convergences and resemblances between the *Timaeus* and Genesis, they present *rival* accounts of the origin of the universe and, in doing so, present rival accounts of the Originator. Plato's resort to myth is not a residue but a metaphysical necessity, and that means his metaphysics of the Creator and creation is bound up with a revised mythical theology. Platonism is fundamentally ill-equipped to "explain the nature of God and of creatures by means of a metaphysics of being in which there is, strictly speaking, neither the one nor the other."[109] Greek myths were a target for the earliest Christian apologists, and if Christians renounce the myth, we must also be ready to oppose the metaphysics. Creation is the site of a fundamental, inevitable clash between the Bible and Greek metaphysics.

In Plato's demiurgic making *geometry serves finesse*. And finesse concerns the discernment of what is most good and beautiful, and the ultimate 'yes' to these." For the demiurge, who creates without envy and so forms for the good of the thing made, "the *aesthetics of being*, rather than the geometrics . . . are more ultimately motivating, more moving." *Art, Origins, Otherness: Between Philosophy and Art* (New York: SUNY Press, 2003), 220.

[108]Pegis, "Dilemma of Being and Unity," 173.

[109]Pegis, "Dilemma of Being and Unity," 173.

3

SIMPLICITY, PARTIALLY
BAPTIZED

Greek metaphysics and Christian theology have been entangled
since the beginning of the church's history. It need not have been
so.[1] Had God chosen a wandering Andean, the intellectual
terrain plowed by Plato, Aristotle, and their followers would not
have been the church's first promised land. In fact, he chose a
wandering Aramean and sent his Son into a world of Greek
speakers and Greek thinkers. Contingent though it is, the entan-
glement of Hellenism and Christian faith is a historical fact.

Evaluation of that fact has been and remains hotly contested.
For all the heat, the church's response has been remarkably consistent. On the assumption that the "all" that belongs to us
(1 Cor 3:21-23) includes Plato, Aristotle, and Plotinus, Christian
thinkers have sifted through the dust of pagan Greece for treasures and resources to clarify, adorn, and expound the gospel. Yet,
the church has *never* regarded pagan thinkers as benign sources
of pure truth. Plunder from Egypt must be purified in fire,[2] and
the hair and nails of the beautiful captive woman must, as the law

---

[1] Robert Jenson, *Systematic Theology*, vol. 1: *The Triune God* (Oxford: Oxford University
Press, 1997), 207.
[2] Augustine, *On Christian Teaching* 2.40-42.

requires, be cut and pared before she is received into Israel (Deut 21:10-13).[3] As the exposition of the Creator's word, sacred doctrine bears his authority to clarify philosophical obscurity, elaborate partial truth, pass judgment on other truth claims, and correct metaphysical error.[4] The theologian who uses philosophy should not mix water and wine but imitate Jesus by turning the one into the other.[5] Many theologians would agree with the conclusion of chapter one: Plato may get closer to the truth than others, but he does not *tell* the truth about creation or the Creator.

Theology has been consistently honored as reigning queen of the sciences, whom philosophy, along with all natural and social science, serves as a handmaid. If theology is not the master discourse, placing and correcting other discourses, it will inevitably be displaced by another master discourse, for as John Milbank says, "the necessity of an ultimate organizing logic . . . cannot be wished away."[6] Robert Jenson's phrase "revisionary metaphysics" is, to my knowledge, relatively new.[7] The concept is as old as the church, inherent in the practice of Christian theology, evident

---

[3]"Whatever we find said well and reasonably among our enemies, or we read anything said among them wisely and knowingly, we must cleanse it also from the knowledge which is among them, remove and cut off all that is dead and worthless—namely all the hairs of the head and the nails of the woman taken from the spoils of the enemy—and so at last make her your wife when she has nothing of the things which are called dead through infidelity. She has nothing in her head, nothing in her hands, lest she bring something unclean or dead either in her thoughts or in her deeds. For the women of our enemies have nothing pure because there is no wisdom among them with which something unclean was not mixed." *Origen: Homilies on Leviticus 1–16*, trans. Gary Wayne Barkley (Washington, DC: Catholic University of America Press, 1990), 7.6.7. For the persistence of this image, see Henri de Lubac, *Mediaeval Exegesis: The Four Senses of Scripture* (Grand Rapids, MI: Eerdmans, 1998), 1:211-24.

[4]Thomas Aquinas, *Summa theologiae* 1.1.5 (hereafter cited parenthetically in the text as *ST*). See John Milbank and Catherine Pickstock, *Truth in Aquinas* (London: Routledge, 2001).

[5]Aquinas, *In Boeth. De Trin.*, 2.4.ad 5, quoted in Simon Oliver, *Philosophy, God, and Motion* (London: Routledge, 2013), 87.

[6]Milbank, *Theology and Social Theory: Beyond Secular Reason* (Oxford: Blackwell, 1990), 1.

[7]Robert Jenson, *Theology as Revisionary Metaphysics: Essays on God and Creation* (Eugene, OR: Cascade, 2014).

already in Paul's preaching and letters. It is not the *whole* task of theology, since the Bible, as I will seek to demonstrate, generates fresh theological and philosophical insight never dreamed of by pagan philosophy. We can, we should, start with the Bible to formulate theologies of everything. I will attempt this in the second half of this book. Still, attention to and revision of inherited concepts are inescapable tasks.[8] As Barth said, the theologian is a quality-control officer called to test the proclamation of the church by assessing its conformity to Scripture.[9]

Some of the transformations are obvious. Despite frequent use of Aristotelian categories, concepts, and argumentative strategies, no theologian has mistaken Aristotle's unmoved mover, the final cause of an eternal universe, for the triune Creator. Neoplatonic turns of argument recur regularly among various theologians, but everyone knows the difference between the Trinity and the Plotinian triad of One, Mind (*nous*), and Soul (*psychē*). No Christian thinker has ever attempted to formulate a metaphysics without guidance from Scripture—not Augustine, nor Anselm, Aquinas, Bonaventure, Barth, Bulgakov, and on through the alphabet.

Examples at this level of generality, however, do not capture the depth of the revisionary work of Christian thought. It is not as if Aristotle's notions of substance, accident, matter, form, categories, and so on remained intact and were simply put to new uses. Christian theology did not simply adopt Plotinian claims about the simplicity of the One. Though they shared the Neoplatonic instinct to oppose simplicity to composition, they could not deny the convertibility of unity and intelligibility in the Christian

---

[8]As the church penetrates Africa and Asia, her thinkers and teachers will have to engage in the same labor with regard to traditional African and Asian thought and cultural forms.

[9]Karl Barth, *Church Dogmatics* 1/1: *Doctrine of the Word of God*, trans. Geoffrey Bromiley (London: T&T Clark, 2004), 250.

God. In the process of putting inherited concepts to new uses, Christian thinkers, wittingly or not, transformed those concepts down to gritty details. In Augustine, Christ took Platonism captive; in Aquinas, Jesus made Aristotle and Neoplatonism his bondservant; in Cornelius Van Til, he enlisted—wonder of wonders!—Idealism to preach the gospel. In all these cases, Christ demanded, and secured, repentance, for neither Plato nor Aristotle nor Kant could come into the kingdom unbaptized. First they must die, then rise a new creation.

Examples of the biblicization of metaphysics are countless.[10] Rather than offering a potted history that skims across the

---

[10]For instance: In articulating post- and pro-Nicene trinitarian theology, Gregory of Nyssa formulated an unprecedented concept of "person." The triune persons, he argued, are not merely collections of properties or causal relations, but distinct and unique persons because of the joyful *koinonia* they share. See Lucien Turescu, *Gregory of Nyssa and the Concept of Divine Persons* (Oxford: Oxford University Press, 2005); Khaled Anatolios, "Personhood, Communion, and Trinity in Some Patristic Texts," in *The Holy Trinity in the Life of the Church* (Grand Rapids, MI: Baker, 2014), 147-64; Joseph Ratzinger, "Concerning the Notion of Person in Theology," *Communio* 17, no. 3 (1990): 439-54. Augustine alters the Aristotelian category of "relation" when applying it to the simple triune God (*On the Trinity* 5.5-7). On Augustine's exposure to Aristotle's *Categories*, see *Confessions* 4.16. For a technical exposition of Augustine's modification of Aristotle, see Paul Thom, *Logic of the Trinity: Augustine to Ockham* (New York: Fordham University Press, 2012), 19-51. More fundamentally, Augustine elevates "relation" to the divine sphere, as a fundamental ontological category, something that Aristotle would have firmly rejected. On this, see Giulio Maspero, "Life as Relation: Classical Metaphysics and Trinitarian Ontology," *Theological Research* 2 (2014): 31-52. The christological debates of the sixth century spark a "turn to the individual" that can be characterized, with slight exaggeration, as an "ontological revolution." See Johannes Zachhuber, *Theology and the End of Ancient Metaphysics: Patristic Philosophy from the Cappadocian Fathers to John of Damascus* (Oxford: Oxford University Press, 2020). Thomas Aquinas modifies Aristotelian concepts of relation and act/potency in order to explicate a metaphysics of creation. See Mark Gerald Henninger, "Aquinas on the Ontological Status of Relations," *Journal of the History of Philosophy* 24, no. 4 (1987): 491-515; more generally, Henninger, *Relations: Medieval Theories 1250–1325* (Oxford: Clarendon, 1989). Far from introducing an alien metaphysics into a Scripture setting, Thomas is, in the main, transforming metaphysics in the light of revelation, and, in particular, modulating classical metaphysics into a metaphysics of creation. See David B. Burrell, *Freedom and Creation in Three Traditions* (Notre Dame: Notre Dame University Press, 1993), 33: "Aquinas' alterations of the metaphysics he received from both Aristotle and Avicenna are all in the direction of securing a characterization of creature and creatures . . . it is the exigencies of revelation that transformed the metaphysics Aquinas received into one

surface of two millennia, I focus on the idea of divine simplicity, first as it appears in Aristotle and Plotinus and then as it is modified by Thomas Aquinas. By examining this specific question in some detail, I demonstrate the Christian transformation of simplicity. At the same time, I probe the *limits* of that transformation—limits that will become especially critical in chapter four.

While I focus on simplicity, I recognize simplicity cannot be isolated from other things theologians say and do not say about God. Thus in this chapter and the next, I implicitly address other attributed perfections—God's immutability, impassibility, immobility, eternity. Simplicity is arguably foundational to this complex of attributes. Because he is simple, God is not a complex of potency and act; being *actus purus*, he cannot change. Insofar as movement is a species of change, or change a species of movement, a God without parts must also be an *immobile* God. Thomas Aquinas makes these links (or leaps) explicit in the *Summa Contra Gentiles*,[11] where his argument from motion rests on assumptions about God's lack of potency and provides the initial basis for his claim that God is eternal (*SCG* 1.15): "For whatever begins or ceases to be suffers this through movement or change. Now it has been shown that God is altogether

---

properly his own." See also the oft-cited statement of Josef Pieper: The "fundamental idea" of Thomas's philosophy "by which almost all the basic concepts of his vision of the world are determined" is "the idea of creation, or, more precisely, the notion that nothing exists which is not *creatura*, except the Creator Himself; and in addition, that this createdness determines entirely and all-pervasively the inner structure of the creature." *The Silence of St. Thomas Aquinas*, trans. John Murray and Daniel O'Connor (South Bend, IN: St. Augustine's Press, 1957), 47. To explain the meaning of "nothing" in *creatio ex nihilo*, Anselm alters the Aristotelian notion of accidental change and imagines an "absolute privation," to which creation answers as gift (*Monologion* 7-10). See Kenneth Schmitz, *The Gift: Creation* (Milwaukee, WI: Marquette University Press, 1982).

[11] I use the translation of Laurence Shapcote in *Saint Thomas Aquinas, Summa contra Gentiles, Books I-II*, Works of St. Thomas Aquinas 11 (Green Bay, WI: Aquinas Institute, 2018). References are cited parenthetically as *SCG*.

unchangeable. Therefore, he is eternal, having neither beginning nor end." Because eternal, God suffers no succession, neither the coming to nonbeing of the past nor the not-yet-being of the future. Immutability, impassibility, eternity are tightly knotted, and simplicity keeps the knot tied.[12] If, as I argue, simplicity is imperfectly evangelized, that defect will reverberate throughout our theology.

WHOSE SIMPLICITY?

Plato's late theory about the *koinonia* of Forms has played almost no role in Christian theology.[13] Instead, most theologians adapted principles and arguments from Aristotle or the "Neoplatonic" syntheses of Plato and Aristotle that came to highest expression in Porphyry, Plotinus, Iamblichus, and Proclus.[14] These pagans appear to provide a grammar of monotheism compatible with Christian faith, and simplicity is a basic rule of that grammar.

The unmoved mover unveiled at the conclusion of Aristotle's argument from motion fits the standard profile of a proper *archē*, set from the time of the Presocratics. God is eternal, immovable, and "separate from perceptible things." The mover is "without magnitude . . . without parts and indivisible." Since it causes the motions of an eternal cosmos, it must itself be eternal. It does not have a finite magnitude, and there is no such thing, Aristotle

---

[12]Isaak Augustus Dorner harshly but justly observes that many theologians argue in circles: "God is immutable because simple and simple because immutable," and these conclusions "contain no grounds for the one or for the other." *Divine Immutability: A Critical Reconsideration*, trans. Robert R. Williams and Claude Welch (Minneapolis: Fortress, 1994), 136.

[13]For an exception, see Ryan Haecker, "Splitting the Difference: Contradiction and the Trinity in Plato's 'Sophist,'" *Macrina Magazine*, January 15, 2022, available at https://macrinamagazine.com/issue-9-contradiction/guest/2022/01/15/splitting -the-difference-contradiction-and-the-trinity-in-platos-sophist.

[14]On Aristotle, see David Bradshaw, *Aristotle East and West: Metaphysics and the Division of Christendom* (Cambridge: Cambridge University Press, 2007). On Plotinus, see Panagiotis Pavlos, "Christian Insights into Plotinus' Metaphysics and his Concept of Aptitude (*elitedeiotes*)," *Akropolis* 1 (2017): 5-32, and the literature cited there.

believes, as an infinite magnitude. It is, finally, "impassive and inalterable."[15] Unlike the Being of Parmenides, Aristotle's god is alive and happy, indeed, supremely happy, for it is eternally and uninterruptedly engaged in active understanding, the activity "that is to the highest degree best . . . of what is to the highest degree best." It is pure intellect occupied with the best possible object, itself.[16]

Aristotle's mover is too much a composite for Plotinus, who insists that, in order to be *absolutely* One, the *archē* must be beyond intellect and being:

> There must be something simple prior to all things and different from all things after it, being by itself, not mixed with the things that come from it, all the while being able to be present to other things, having what those other things have in a different manner, being truly one, and not having its existence different from its being one. . . . For if it is not simple, beyond all combination and composition and not truly one, it would not be a principle.[17]

---

[15] Aristotle, *Metaphysics* 1073ᵃ1-13. The related argument in *Physics* ends the same conclusion: "The immovable mover . . . seeing that it remains simple, selfsame, and in the same, will move things with a movement that is one and simple" (*Physics* 260ᵃ13-18). Below, I examine the differences between these two presentations of the argument. I am using the translations of C. D. C. Reeve, *Aristotle: Metaphysics* (Indianapolis: Hackett, 2016); and *Aristotle: Physics* (Indianapolis: Hackett, 2018). Note: The mover needs these "attributes" to maintain his place as the capstone of a pyramid of beings, but the mover needs these attributes only if he is included within the cosmos and is not a truly transcendent source of all things. If he transcends the world as creative source, there seems no reason why a "highest being" cannot be infinitely mobile, rather than immobile.

[16] Aristotle, *Metaphysics* 1072ᵇ13-29.

[17] *Enneads* 5.4.1, in *Plotinus: The Enneads*, ed. and trans. Lloyd P. Gerson (Cambridge: Cambridge University Press, 2019). Note the proximity to pre-Socratic conceptions of the *archē*. Paul Gavrilyuk explains the logic: "Non-simple things are composed, and composed things ontologically depend on their parts in the sense that if a part is removed, the thing is no longer what it used to be. Things that are composed of parts . . . can be explained by describing those parts, which in this case become epistemologically prior to the compound. Parts make and explain the compound. That which is first in the order of being and explanation cannot be preceded by something else, such as the parts of which it is composed. Therefore, that which is first cannot be compound, but only simple in the strongest sense of

This One cannot be Aristotle's transcendent mover, characterized by Intellect (*nous*), because mind is multiple, a composite of "it is" and "it thinks." Thought inevitably involves a split between the subject-thinking and the object-thought. Even a mind thinking itself, as Aristotle's god does, implicitly bisects itself.[18] Everything but the One is both itself and another; the One alone "merely is itself, and truly itself."[19]

Plotinus proposes a second hypostasis, *nous* or Intellect, as a "repository of the intelligible paradigms of the material world, of the Platonic forms," but *nous* cannot be the highest principle because multiple Forms would render it multiple.[20] Unlike Aristotle, Plotinus mounts no explicit cosmological argument for the primacy of the One. He frequently asserts that oneness is prior to

---

the word" ("Plotinus on Divine Simplicity," *Modern Theology* 35, no. 3 [2019]: 5). The epistemological point is not obviously true. I have many parts, but I cannot be explained by dissecting me into the physical, temporal, or metaphysical parts that make the compound that is me. Ontologically, it is not clear that parts are prior to wholes, or that the causation is in one direction, from parts to wholes. Let us say I am made up of two parts—body and soul. Let us say too, for the sake of argument, that I am an Aristotelian-leaning metaphysician. My body is matter, but that matter does not explain anything at all without the soul that informs it; unformed matter is neither explicable nor an explanation. Matter individualizes, but only insofar as it is in-formed by form. The material part of me is only analyzable because of the prior unity of form and matter; it is my body only if it is composite. So you cannot explain the whole that is me by describing the physical part of me. Nor can you explain my soul apart from the life the soul lives in my physical body. I could grant that wholes are composed of their parts; but we must equally say that parts are the parts they are because of the whole of which they are part. The relation of parts and whole seems more "perichoretic" or "perspectival" than monodirectional. For a discussion of the primacy of wholes, see Jonathan Schaffer, "Monism: The Priority of the Whole," *Philosophical Review* 119, no. 1 (2010): 31-76.

[18]Plotinus, *Enneads* 5.6.2: "If that which is first thinks, something will exist in it, and therefore it will not be first, but second, and not one, but many, and thereby all the things that it thinks. For even if it thinks of itself, it will be many."

[19]Plotinus, *Enneads* 6.8.21.

[20]Gavrilyuk, "Plotinus on Divine Simplicity," 5. Plotinus's One has what Paul Gavrilyuk calls "industrial strength" simplicity; with a nod to Anselm, he describes it as "that which nothing simpler can be conceived." Plotinus cites the Parmenides of Plato's dialogue as a source (*Enneads* 2.9.3; 5.1.8).

multiplicity,[21] often adverting, as proof, that the numeral 1 proceeds all other numbers.[22] Like the numeral 1, the One is first in a
series, the cause of the existence of all composites, producing the
unity that is identical to each existent's existence.

In its utter simplicity, the One is beyond predication. We
cannot speak without speaking of "something," but the One is *not*
a something.[23] Strictly, it is false to call it "One" or to say "it
exists." To say the latter is to distinguish *that* it is from *what* it is,
and so to insult its purity. This does not mean Plotinus can say
nothing of the One, or that he contradicts himself whenever he
speaks of it.[24] We can speak truly of the One so long as we do not
imply composition. The stark simplicity of the One does not exclude certain narrowly construed forms of complexity, most importantly, causal relations to composite things. In fact, the One
possesses everything possessed by compounded beings, though
not complexly.[25] Plotinus speaks of the One's power, infinity, om-
nipresence, and goodness. "Good" is, in fact, the most frequent
of Plotinus's designations for the One, suggesting that Plato's
"Form of the Good" is an inspiration.[26] Though the One is beyond

---

[21]E.g., Plotinus, *Enneads* 3.8.9.

[22]*Enneads* 5.3.12. Plotinus's is a tragic metaphysics, since it assumes that any surplus
from the origin is a diminution, less perfect from the origin. Origin is always superior to destination, *archē* nobler than *telos*, "whence" always more valuable than
"whither" (*Enneads* 3.8.8). Trinitarian theology upends the "basic science" of an-
tique metaphysics by insisting on a Second Person who is equal to the First in power
and glory; and then also insisting on a Third. See my *Deep Comedy: Trinity, Tragedy,
and Hope in Western Literature* (Moscow, ID: Canon, 2006).

[23]Plotinus, *Enneads* 5.3.13.

[24]Here I follow the generous reading of Plotinian theology found in Lloyd Gerson,
Plotinus (London: Routledge, 1994), 2-35.

[25]Plotinus, *Enneads* 5.3.15.

[26]Though he acknowledges Plato's influence, Gerson argues that Plotinus's One is not
identical to the Form of the Good: Plato never says the Form of the Good causes the
demiurge or the divine mind; it is solely the cause of the existence and intelligibility
of the *Forms*. Plato never attributes personal qualities to the Form of the Good, even
analogously, and Plato does not hesitate to describe the Form of the Good as an Idea,
even though it is beyond *ousia*. For Plotinus, a One that is beyond *ousia* must, by definition, also be beyond *nous* (*Plotinus*, 15).

nous, it is not without intelligence; how else could it generate Intellect? It is beyond *nous* only insofar as *nous* is plural, because plurality is a blemish. For Plotinus, the One is in some sense alive, though, once again, without composition, movement, or change.[27] Plotinus uses personal language to describe the One, though, once again, always under cover of negation.[28]

Nor is the One entirely beyond our knowledge. Plotinus denies the One can be an object of discursive reasoning (*dianoia*), but it can be known through *hypernoesis*, an absorption or union into the One. Our approach to the One is not through dialectic but through ascent, "the refuge of a solitary in the solitary."[29] Since we are multiple, composite beings, striving toward union with the One means undoing our specific forms of existence. We strive for union by simplifying ourselves, shedding the encumbrances of the body and the weighty multiplicities of sensible reality.[30] There is an intoxicating sacrificial magnificence to Plotinian piety: To save our life, we must lose it.[31]

Exquisite as this picture may be, it suffers from internal tensions if not outright contradictions. The One is known only by an "ecstasy that carries the soul outside of itself," but in speaking or writing of the One, Plotinus does not and cannot express that ecstasy. As philosopher, Plotinus is *outside* the One, and his philosophy is necessarily "a fall or degeneration," perhaps "evil."[32]

---

[27]Caleb Cohoe argues, by contrast, that the One is entirely incapable of self-knowledge because it involves the same composite of "knower" and "known" involved in any knowledge. "Why the One Cannot Have Parts," *Philosophical Quarterly* 67 (2017): 768.

[28]The One is "father" and unbounded love (Plotinus, *Enneads* 6.7.32; 6.8.15).

[29]Plotinus, *Enneads* 6.9.11. Or, as it is sometimes rendered, "the flight of the alone to the Alone."

[30]As David Bentley Hart has pointed out, Plotinus ontologizes the tragic ethos of Greek religion. "Christ and Nothing," *First Things*, October 2003.

[31]See Pierre Hadot, *Plotinus, or, The Simplicity of Vision* (Chicago: University of Chicago Press, 1998).

[32]William Desmond, *Being and the Between* (Albany: SUNY Press, 1995), 234.

Plotinus inescapably speaks from the middle realm, suspended between "being" and "nonbeing," removed from the One. To approach the origin, we must abandon discursive thought, which means that philosophy comes to an end just at the moment it attains its end. Plotinus is fully aware that his speaking of the univocal One is equivocal, as his constant qualifications "inoculate the reader, and perhaps himself, from the infection of this necessary equivocity."[33]

The emphatic monism of the One, intended to overcome the persistent dualisms and multiplicities found in Plato, generates a drastic form of dualism between the utterly unique One and the cosmos of compounded things. In William Desmond's parable, the One is an "inscrutable King" locked away in his magic fortress. His subjects wonder what the King is up to, and over time they may even forget he exists. His "inner self-security . . . makes the people outside less secure, for this inscrutability suggests something ambiguous." When terrible things happen outside the castle, the people speculate that it emanates from the King himself. Instead of providing stability, the univocity of the King's isolation generates the terror of uncertainty and equivocity outside.[34]

---

[33]Desmond, *Being and the Between*, 234.

[34]Desmond, *God and the Between*, 60. In a different idiom, Desmond explains: "This univocal securing of the One as beyond all equivocity becomes mired in its own equivocity. In so securing the One, we are made the more insecure about the One. If its relation to the between is one of oppositional dualism, no affirmative meaning can be given, first to the origination of the finite between, second to the promise of our porosity to the divine, third to our traversing the between as the ontological intermedium wherein our self-transcending contributes to its own destiny, and finally in relation to the good of that between and that self-transcending. From an incomprehensible origin, we find ourselves inhabitants of a middle, involuntary exiles waking to taste the bitterness of ontological disorientation in a foreign land that can never be home." Along similar lines, John Milbank remarks that for Plotinus, "Being participates in unity and yet participation appears threatened by the absolute gulf fixed between pure unity [the One], and a unity only thinkable in relation to difference" (*Theology and Social Theory*, 427).

Ultimately, the origin cannot be simply One. A purely unified origin is difficult to distinguish from "inert self-sameness." Self-sameness *cannot* be an *archē*, since an origin must have the capacity to originate something *beyond* itself. An origin that is sheerly one diffuses into equivocity. Only "an originative One that is more than one" can be the cause of the world's existence.[35] To speak of the One, we need an articulate One, a One who has *logos* and is *logos*, a One whose *logos* articulates an intelligible world.

No competent Christian theologian would take Plotinian simplicity onboard without modification. None *has* done so. Plotinus is, at best, ambiguous about the One's capacity for self-knowledge,[36] but no Christian has had the slightest doubt that the Lord knows his own mind through the Spirit who searches the depths of the living God. Augustine retains yet modifies Plotinus by merging the One with Plotinus's second principle, *nous*, placing patterns akin to Plato's ideas in the mind of the One God— thereby rendering him, by Plotinus's lights, multiple rather than simple. Trinitarian theology "further weakened" the Plotinian version of simplicity.[37] Though trinitarians continue to say God is simple,[38] they modify it into something Plotinus would not recognize as simplicity. If the unmoved mover fails Plotinus's exacting standard of simplicity, the God who is Father, Son, and Spirit surely fails too.[39]

---

[35]Desmond, *Being and the Between*, 236.

[36]Plotinus, *Enneads* 5.6.2; 6.9.6.

[37]Gavrilyuk, "Plotinus on Divine Simplicity," 10. See Thomas Wassmer, "The Trinitarian Theology of Augustine and His Debt to Plotinus," *Harvard Theological Review* 53, no. 4 (1960): 261-68.

[38]See Lewis Ayres, *Nicaea and Its Legacy: An Approach to Fourth-Century Trinitarian Theology* (Oxford: Oxford University Press, 2007), 280-88.

[39]As Gavrilyuk points out, divine simplicity creates tensions with the Christian conviction that God acts outside himself: "Divine simplicity requires an obliteration of the distinction between potency and act in God, with the result that God is conceived as *actus purus* (pure act)." If "God is immutably active in a way that surpasses the

The biblical conviction that the world was *created* poses a major challenge to Plotinian simplicity.[40] To explain how the One is the cause of everything that is, Plotinus enlists the Aristotelian concept of *energeia*, "energy" or "activity." For Aristotle, the *energeia* of the unmoved mover is essential to the mover's role in the cosmic order. The mover's *energeia* is eternal self-contemplation; its action is never activity "in another," for if it were directed outward, it could not serve as the immobile, independent cosmic flywheel: "to have an actuality outside of itself would mean that it had a potency in relation to that actuality and hence that it is imperfect in some respect."[41]

Though he borrows *energeia* from Aristotle, Plotinus modifies the concept rather drastically by distinguishing two ways of construing the relation of energy to substance. "There is activity," he writes, "which is activity of the substance [*energeia tēs ousias*] and there is activity which arises from the substance of such things [*energeia ek tēs ousias*]." The former is the "actuality that each thing is" and the latter, which "had to follow of necessity," is "different from it." Fire is double, first the heat that fills out the substance of fire, and then also the heat radiating from it. As a fire actualizes "its native substantiality by remaining fire," it also reaches out to spread heat outside itself.[42] The distinction is somewhat analogous to the classic theological distinction between the *opera ad intra* (works of God within his own triune life)

---

potency-act dichotomy in created things," we are left with the question of "how to reconcile the divine action *ad extra* of any kind with a stipulation that God is simple" ("Plotinus on Divine Simplicity," 10). Gavrilyuk thinks simplicity is essential to Christian theology, but he ends with a variation of Ovid's lament: "*O divina simplici-ties, 'nec sine te nec tecum vivere possum'*"—O simplicity, I cannot live without you, but I can't live with you either!

[40]In the following paragraphs, I follow the careful analysis of Lloyd Gerson, "Plotinus' Metaphysics: Emanation or Creation?" *Review of Metaphysics* 46, no. 3 (1993): 559-74.

[41]Gerson, "Plotinus's Metaphysics," 567.

[42]Plotinus, *Enneads* 5.4.2.

and the *opera ad extra* (works of God outside his triune life, in creation), which has a created reflex in the Thomistic distinction between a creature's "act of existing," which makes a thing what it is, and the thing's outwardly directed acts and doings.

Plotinus comes to this revision of Aristotle by reasoning through his fundamental premises. For Aristotle, Intellect (*nous*) is primary. As we have seen, Plotinus rejects that claim because *nous* is necessarily complex rather than simple. In rejecting the primacy of *nous*, Plotinus also rejects the primacy of *ousia*, "being," because "being" is simply what presents itself to Intellect to be known.[43] As a result, "the *arche* of all is going to be beyond *ousia* and so beyond limit."[44] And if the One is beyond *ousia*, it must also be beyond the *energeia* that is identical with *ousia*. Yet the One cannot be *without energeia*, because a lack of energy would be an imperfection. Nor can activity be *added* to the One, because then the One would no longer be One. The One must thus *be* activity: "If . . . activity is more perfect than is substantiality, and the first thing of all is most perfect, activity would be primary."[45]

What kind of *energeia* is identical to the One? It cannot be the energy *of ousia*, since the One is beyond *ousia*. Thus, its *energeia* of the One must be *energeia ek tēs ousias*, a productive energy that gives existence to *nous* and all the essences contained in *nous*. The One *necessarily* produces a multiplicity of things, though it is not under any internal or external compulsion. Though the One does not possess *ousia*, it does *produce* it through the mediation of *nous*, which is the "*archē* of essence." The One is the source of existence;

---

[43]Eric Perl claims the Parmenidean principle that "the same is for thinking and for being" is the foundational assumption of ancient metaphysics. *Thinking Being: Introduction to Metaphysics in the Classical Tradition* (Leiden: Brill, 2014), 4.

[44]Gerson, "Plotinus's Metaphysics," 568.

[45]Plotinus, *Enneads* 6.8.20. In his *Plotinus*, Gerson sums up Plotinus's theology of the One with the admittedly anachronistic Thomist concept that the One's essence is identical to its existence.

Intellect the source of essence, the particular forms of existence among composite things.[46]

All this enables Plotinus to compare the productive perfection of the One with the generative perfection of all other substances, as he does in this lovely passage:

> All beings, so long as they persist, necessarily, due to the power present in them produce from their own substantiality a real, though dependent, existent around themselves directed to their exterior, a sort of image of the archetypes from which it was generated. Fire produces the heat that comes from it, and snow does not only hold its coldness inside itself. Perfumes especially witness to this, for so long as they exist, something flows from them around them, the existence of which a bystander enjoys. Further, all things, as soon as they are perfected, generate. That which is always perfect always generates something everlasting, and it generates something inferior to itself.[47]

From the energy of its substance, every perfected thing releases an *energeia* from itself; everything gives from itself to every other thing. Nothing holds itself to itself; nothing withholds itself from others. Being most perfect, the One is most productive, most giving. Of all perfumes, the One is the most aromatic.

This is not simply an "emanationist" viewpoint,[48] but neither is it biblical creationism. Plotinus's simple One is incapable of

---

[46]Gerson, "Plotinus's Metaphysics," 571-72.

[47]Plotinus, *Enneads* 5.1.6.

[48]In an "emanationist" account, creation is an extension of the Creator. Think of a thick liquid slowly spreading across a surface. The liquid is the One, the spread is the world it produces; someday, perhaps, the liquid will be sucked back together, the *exitus* completed in a *reditus*. Emanation tends toward pantheism, the belief that creation is divine. Emanation in this sense is a denial of the Creator-creature distinction, of the freedom of God, and of the *otherness* of creation. It is not clear Plotinus actually believed this. Gerson observes that Plotinus's theory is regarded as emanationist partly because he uses the metaphor of "flow" to describe how complex things emerge from the simple One: "Since it is perfect, due to its neither seeking anything, nor having anything, nor needing anything, [the One] in a way overflows and its superabundance has made something else" (*Enneads* 5.2.1). The image proves nothing. Thomas

creating as God does in Genesis 1. It will be illuminating to specify the divergences, by briefly comparing Plotinus to Thomas Aquinas's account of creation.[49]

Plotinus and Thomas Aquinas differ in their understanding of the preexistence of Forms. Plotinus says the One contains all forms "in such a way that they were not distinct."[50] But, as Gerson observes, a vague Form is not a Form at all, and the Forms within the One do not exist in any determinate way: "The Good is enthroned . . . not so that it has a foundation, but so that it may found the Form of the primary Forms, while remaining formless itself."[51] Plotinus *must* say this. If the Forms were distinct *within* the One, the One would no longer be One. If the One itself had a determinate "shape," it too would be multiple—itself and its form—and it would not be capable of producing all things.

For Thomas, by contrast, all things are in God "eminently," in their most *perfect* form. All perfections "pre-exist in God according to a more eminent mode" (*ST* 1.4.2).[52] God is the

---

Aquinas, who *does* believe in creation *ex nihilo*, *also* uses the image of creation "flowing" from God: Creation is "the issuing (*emanationem*) of the whole being from the universal cause, which is God; it is the springing forth (*emanationem*) that we designated by the term 'creation.'" *Summa theologiae*, vol. 8: *Creation, Variety and Evil*, trans. Thomas Gilby (Cambridge; Cambridge University Press, 2006), 1.45.1. Plotinus is not a pantheist. He does say the One is everywhere. If it were everywhere without being nowhere, it would be identical with all that exists. But it is also nowhere, and therefore genuine multiplicity exists (*Enneads* 3.9.4). Etienne Gilson denies Plotinus is a monist; he would be, if the One were Being, but it is beyond Being. *Being and Some Philosophers*, 2nd ed. (Toronto: Pontifical Institute of Medieval Studies, 1952), 24. Wolfhart Pannenberg denies that Plotinus's theory is emanationist because the One retains a degree of freedom. Emanationism comes into Neoplatonism with Proclus. *Systematic Theology*, trans. Geoffrey W. Bromily (London: T&T Clark, 2004), 2:18.

[49]I follow Gerson, "Plotinus's Metaphysics" in the following comparison. One might make a similar point by comparing Thomas's flexible account of simplicity with the starkly Plotinian theology of Avicenna, who concludes, based on simplicity, that creation is absolutely necessary. See Rahim Acar, *Talking about God and Talking about Creation: Avicenna's and Thomas Aquinas's Positions* (Leiden: Brill, 2005), 119-26.

[50]Plotinus, *Enneads* 5.3.15.

[51]Plotinus, *Enneads* 6.7.17.

[52]Translation by Timothy McDermott in *St. Thomas Aquinas, Summa theologiae*, vol. 2: *Existence and Nature of God* (Cambridge: Cambridge University Press 2006).

archetype of all created things. "Rock" exists more eminently in God than in created rocks; God is not impersonal but supereminently personal. To be sure, Thomas insists, all things are eminently in God without violation of his simplicity. Still, by including everything in God by way of eminence, Thomas softens the austerity of Plotinian simplicity. To put it otherwise: for Thomas, God is the source not only of the existence of all things but of their *ousia*. In effect, like Augustine, he merges the first two Plotinian hypostases, *to hen* and *nous*, which means that Thomistic simplicity is "less simple" than its Plotinian variety. Plotinus would surely view Thomas's theology of creation as a ruinous compromise of the Oneness of the One.

Plotinus does not think the *virtuality* of the Forms in the One is equivalent to the *eminence* of the Forms in the One, and as a result he "cannot just infer that the One is eminently whatever its effects are in an inferior way," because that would, once again, compromise simplicity. Thomas believes being is "an actualization of essence" and that God is himself being. As a result, he can pursue a *via eminentiae*, while Plotinus can do no more than deduce "the attributes of the perfectly simple" from his simplicity and from the One's role as first cause.[53] As we have already noted, this opens a chasm between the One and everything else. Thomas does not need to bridge the chasm because, on his creationist metaphysics, it does not exist in the first place.

Thomas does not attribute existence and essence to distinct hypostases and would regard Plotinus's division of the two as a compromise of God's omnipotence. For Plotinus, both the One and Intellect are *archai*, the first of existence and the second of substance. For Thomas, *ousia/nous* cannot be a separate *archē*, for that would suggest a limit on the power of God. As Gerson says, "Plotinus is less

---

53Gerson, *Plotinus*, 27.

concerned with preserving omnipotence than he is with preserving the unqualified simplicity of the first *arche*." God's creative omnipotence shapes Thomas's understanding of possibility. Though Plotinus and Thomas "agree that the *arche* of all cannot do what is logically impossible, Plotinus would say that the structure of logical possibility is grounded in the second *arche*, Intellect, whereas Aquinas will want to say that logical possibility and impossibility are ultimately to be accounted for by the first principle, God."[54] For Plotinus, the One's power is circumscribed by its simplicity. In Thomas, simplicity must bow before the Creator's omnipotence.

Thomas would not recognize Plotinus's or Avicenna's account of origins as a creation at all.[55] Thomas diverges from Plotinian simplicity, and wherever he does, he does so because of his belief in the biblical teaching concerning creation. Genesis 1, in short, forces a revisionist understanding of simplicity, what we must call, from Plotinus's perspective, a complexifying of simplicity. Thomas baptizes simplicity. But he does not complete the task, and so leaves us with a monstrosity, partially baptized metaphysical hybrids—Nephilim.

BAPTIZED IN THE TRIUNE NAME

"God is simple" is a near-universal Christian confession about God. It is *not* the case that every theologian means the same thing when he or she says it.[56] It is highly misleading to present a rigorous

---

[54]Gerson, *Plotinus*, 27.

[55]Anton Pegis writes, "A God who must produce a universe is for St. Thomas Aquinas not a creator. A God who must do what He does and cannot choose to do this or that without violating His goodness is again not a creator. A divine goodness which in order to be good must produce necessarily is not the goodness of a God who is the creator of the universe. A divine goodness which is a necessitated goodness and which therefore is radically incompatible with liberty and self-sufficiency is not the goodness of the Christian God." *Saint Thomas and the Greeks* (Milwaukee, WI: Marquette University Press, 1939), 70.

[56]See, briefly, Christopher Stead, *Philosophy in Christian Antiquity* (Cambridge: Cambridge University Press, 1994), 130-35. Andrew Radde-Gallwitz observes that the

Augustinian or Thomistic doctrine of simplicity and then treat it as the *sine qua non* of the Christian doctrine of God. Arguments of that sort are useful for theological bullying, less so for theological insight. Thomas's treatment of simplicity may be the most coherent account. It may not be. It is certainly not the account given by *every* orthodox theologian. Today's apologists typically defend the strong, Thomistic version of simplicity, and that will be the account I examine below.[57]

To capture Thomas's transformation of simplicity and its limitations, I start at the far end of his treatise on God, where Thomas discusses the triune persons and their relations (*ST* 1.27-43).

---

notion that simplicity entails "that every term one attributes to God names God's essence or substance, and that, metaphysically, God's essence and God's properties are in fact identical" is "precisely the thesis that Basil and Gregory faced in the version articulated by Eunomius of Cyzicus, their principal doctrinal opponent." Though the Cappadocians affirm divine simplicity, "they rightly perceive that the identity interpretation of it, in the version they encounter in Eunomius' theology, conflicts with the inherent complexity of the knowledge of God, and if any theory does this, so much the worse for the theory." *Basil of Caesarea, Gregory of Nyssa, and the Transformation of Divine Simplicity* (Oxford: Oxford University Press, 2009), 114. For surveys of the history of divine simplicity, see Muller, *Post-Reformation Reformed Dogmatics*, vol. 4: *The Triunity of God* (Grand Rapids, MI: Baker Academic, 2003); Jordan P. Barrett, *Divine Simplicity: A Biblical and Trinitarian Account* (Minneapolis: Fortress, 2017), 35-132; Jonathan Marc Platter, "Divine Simplicity and the Triune Identity: A Critical Dialogue with the Theological Metaphysics of Robert W. Jenson" (PhD dissertation, University of Cambridge, 2020), 28-66.

[57]See, for instance, James E. Dolezal, *All That Is in God: Evangelical Theology and the Challenge of Classical Christian Theism* (Grand Rapids, MI: Reformation Heritage, 2017); and *God Without Parts: Divine Simplicity and the Metaphysics of God's Absoluteness* (Eugene, OR: Pickwick, 2011); Steven J. Duby, *Divine Simplicity: A Dogmatic Account* (London: T&T Clark, 2016); and *God in Himself: Scripture, Metaphysics, and the Task of Christian Theology* (Downers Grove, IL: IVP Academic, 2019); Matthew Levering, *Engaging the Doctrine of Creation: Cosmos, Creatures, and the Wise and Good Creator* (Grand Rapids, MI: Baker Academic, 2017), 73-107. David Bentley Hart offers what might be construed as a radicalization of Thomist simplicity in *The Experience of God: Being, Consciousness, Bliss* (New Haven, CT: Yale University Press, 2013), 134-42; and *You Are Gods: On Nature and Supernature* (Notre Dame, IN: University of Notre Dame Press, 2022), 115-22. For an impassioned rejoinder, see Paul Hinlicky, *Divine Simplicity: Christ the Crisis of Metaphysics* (Grand Rapids, MI: Baker, 2016); *Divine Complexity: The Rise of Creedal Christianity* (Minneapolis: Fortress, 2011). From the perspective of analytic theology, see R. T. Mullins, "Simply Impossible: A Case against Divine Simplicity," *Journal of Reformed Theology* 7 (2013): 181-203.

Thomas is well aware his earlier discussion of simplicity could be used against the dogma of the Trinity. He even puts some of his own phrasing in the mouth of the objector. If, the interlocutor says, God is utterly, absolutely simple (*summa simplicitas*), with no diversity (*in Deo non est aliqua diversitas*) or compositeness at all, how can he exist in three distinct persons? How can there be processions in God if "in God, nothing can be moved or be outside" (*in divinis, nihil est mobile neque extraneum*). There is no place for divine processions in an immobile, simple God (*processio in Deo locum non habet*) (*ST* 1.27.1).[58] D. Stephen Long notes how Thomas turns these objections against the objectors, using simplicity to demonstrate how a God can be triune yet *one* God. Simplicity is, Thomas writes, not a subversion of Trinity but a necessary support. Yet Long is also aware that Thomas modifies certain (mis)understandings of simplicity and even rejects certain inferences that might be drawn from a bare affirmation of simplicity.[59] Let us examine Thomas's responses to these objections.

The first point is so obvious we might miss its significance: Thomas insists, as he must, that there *are* processions in God. The *sed contra* statements for articles one and two of question twenty-seven (*Prima Pars*) are quotations from Scripture. Are there processions in God? Yes, because Jesus said "I came forth from God" (Jn 8:42; *ego ex Deo processi*). Is there a procession that can be called "generation"? Yes, because the psalmist says of the Son, "Today I have begotten thee" (Ps 2:7; *ego hodie genui te*). Whatever metaphysical objections might arise against processions and a generation in simple God, Scripture and the gospel speak otherwise. Thomas has already insisted on divine simplicity. As a

---

[58] I am using the translation of Ceslaus Velecky, *Summa theologiae,* vol. 6: *The Trinity* (Blackfriars, 1965).

[59] D. Stephen Long, *The Perfectly Simple Triune God: Aquinas and His Legacy* (Minneapolis: Fortress, 2016), 42-55.

teacher of sacred doctrine, he knows it must harmonize with biblical and creedal teaching about the Son and Spirit.

Within a Christian setting, this is standard-issue theology. No orthodox theologian has said "simplicity" without also saying "Trinity." But it is an epochal, radical departure from anything Aristotle or Plotinus would have recognized as the simplicity of the first principle. Simplicity is no longer purely simple. No intelligible word proceeds from Aristotle's mover, who, with utter uncomplicated simplicity, *is* nothing but "thought thinking itself," his thinking of thinking. For Plotinus, this kind of internal generation is precisely what simplicity *excludes*. Thomas inherits and solidifies the Christian tradition of evangelizing metaphysics, modifying the philosophical inheritance under the pressure of the gospel and biblical teaching. When he affirms simplicity, he makes sure he affirms the simplicity of the biblical God.

Introducing processions into the divine being entails other modifications. To say there are processions is to say that there is something analogous to "movement" within the Godhead, a "whither" and a "whence."[60] Thomas typically avoids calling procession a "movement" since he has already denied mobility in God (see below).[61] He avoids it by distinguishing the divine processions from processions that involve "going forth to something outside" (*ad aliquid extra*). In divine processions, what proceeds remains within the agent, as an "inward procession" (*ad intra*).[62]

---

[60]Robert Jenson's terminology in *Systematic Theology*, 1:338-39.

[61]On the other hand, see *SCG* 1.13; 4.19; *ST* 1.19.1 (*intelligere et velle dicitur motus*); Oliver, *Philosophy, God, and Motion*, 110, 114-17; Wayne Hankey, *God in Himself: Aquinas' Doctrine of God as Expounded in the Summa theologiae* (Oxford: Oxford University Press, 2004), 96-114.

[62]Surely trinitarian theology demands a more paradoxical formulation. Does the Son remain in the Father who generates him? Yes, because the Son is in the Father and the Father in the Son. Is the begotten Son *other than* the Father? Thomas himself will say so. Divine procession thus transcends, scrambles, or cuts across any simple *ad intra/ad extra* distinction.

The best analogies, Thomas thinks, are spiritual and intellectual. Bodily processions involve "movement in space" or action that produces an external effect. Processions in God are not like that. Yet there is, he admits, a distant resemblance between the processions in God and the procession of an idea within a finite intellect: "Whenever anyone understands because of his very act of understanding, something comes forth within him, which is the concept of the known thing proceeding from his awareness of it." This "word of the heart" (*verbum cordis*) is exteriorized in the word spoken (*verbo vocis*). The procession of the Word should not be understood on the analogy of heat passing from fire to a thing heated. Rather it is similar to an "issuing in the mind" (*secundum emanationem intelligibilem*), or an intelligible word that remains in the mind of the thinker.[63]

Thomas intends to "norm" his trinitarian theology by drawing on earlier conclusions about unity and simplicity.[64] But in the process Thomas weakens one of the key uses of simplicity—that is, as a boundary marker between Being and beings, between the ontological and the ontic, between Creator and creature. Beings, said Aristotle and Plotinus, are composite, but the unmoved mover or the One is simple. Distinguishing one versus multiple, immovable versus mobile, ungenerated versus generated: That is how we distinguish the *archē* from everything else. Thomas echoes their conclusion: All created things are composites, but

---

[63]*ST* 1.27.1. John Milbank has rightly made much of Thomas's linguistic analogy, as an episode in the longer story of how the linguistic turn in philosophy is indebted to a linguistic turn in theology. Working within trinitarian categories, Thomas follows Augustine in the view that even within the human mind, ideas take the quasi-linguistic form of "interior words." *Word Made Strange: Theology, Language, Culture* (Oxford: Blackwell, 1997), 92-93.

[64]Long, *Perfectly Simple Triune God*, 50. Long argues that in Thomas's theology, the qualification is reciprocal: The discussion of the divine essence qualifies and regulates trinitarian theology, and trinitarian theology qualifies the treatment of divine essence. I argue below that the qualifying is asymmetrical. Thomas misses the opportunity to introduce trinitarian qualifications from the outset.

God is absolutely simple. Yet, for Thomas, the simple God exists as and by virtue of processions that are the originals of the complex processions of the human mind. Instead of drawing a veil between created structures and divine life, the simplicity of the *triune* God becomes a source, model, and pattern for created existence.[65] The Trinity is not the apotheosis of the *via negative* but falls under the rubric of the *via eminentiae*.[66]

Thomas's discussion of divine generation follows a similar pattern (*ST* 1.27.2). "Generation" has two possible meanings. If it means "coming into being and decaying" or a "change from not existing to existing," it obviously cannot apply to God. But *proprie* it refers to the origination of a living being, and this has several entailments. Living things are born from a living principle that is conjoined to it. The thing born shares a likeness with its origin. Properly speaking, there is generation when a thing born proceeds "with specifically the same nature, as when man comes from man, horse from horse." Generation of organisms is generation of a likeness with a similar nature, and created generation always involves an actualization of potency. In the God who is *actus purus*, there is no such actualization, but the other features of generation *do* apply. As with created things, the generation of the Word in God is an action; it arises from a conjoined source; the generated bears a specific resemblance to the generator; the Word is the same nature as the Father, since in God "to be and to understand are identical" (*in Deo idem est intelligere et esse*). To this

---

[65]For the argument that Thomas makes intentionally inexplicable assertions ("theological dead ends") about the Trinity, see Karen Kilby, "Aquinas, the Trinity and the Limits of Understanding," *International Journal of Systematic Theology* 7, no. 4 (2005): 414-27. Specifically, Kilby thinks the analogy with speech functions precisely to reshape our language so that, applied to God, it is no longer a "carrier of *any* insight into God" (420). As I read him, Thomas is far less sternly apophatic. He thinks he can say true things about the life of God.

[66]Elaborating this point has been *the* key shift in trinitarian theology over the past century. Its presence in Thomas shows he is an early contributor to what today goes under the heading of "trinitarian ontology."

point, Thomas is obviously qualifying the generation of the Second Person in a way that makes it compatible with simplicity, and, in turn, using simplicity to keep the triune persons from drifting off into a loosely affiliated triumvirate.

Yet, to state the obvious again, Aristotle and Plotinus find generation of any sort utterly incompatible with the simplicity of the *archē*. More subtly, in his explanation of divine generation, Thomas introduces yet another drastic alteration of simplicity. The third objection (*ST* 1.27.3) employs Thomas's earlier conclusions in opposition to the notion of divine processions. Generated things receive being (*accipit esse*) from the one who generates. The *esse* of anything generated is *receptum*, and nothing whose existence is received subsists in itself (*per se subsistens*). Thomas has previously proven that God's being *does* subsist in itself. Nothing that receives *esse* can be God, which implies, the objection claims, that if Thomas is wholly consistent, nothing *generated* can be God.

Thomas's reply, revealingly, shifts from the question of receptive being per se to the question whether every received *esse* is accepted in a different subject (*in aliquo subjecto*) or into other material (*in aliqua materia*). If receptive being in God were of this sort, the Word generated would be a different subject and nature from the Father. In God, *esse* is received by one who is consubstantial, *homoousios* with the giver of *esse*. Once this qualification is in place, Thomas accepts the presence of receptivity within God:

> What is begotten in God accepts existence from the begetter, yet
> not so that this existence is received into material or a subject; for
> this conflicts with God's self-grounded existence; we speak
> of "existence accepted" (*esse acceptum*) because he who comes
> forth has divine existence from another (*ab alio habet esse divinum*),
> not because he has existence other than divine existence. For
> both the Word which comes forth spiritually and its source are

contained in the perfection of the divine existence itself. (*ST* 1.27.3, reply to obj. 3)

This simply ignores the force of the objection. Based on the premise of simplicity, Thomas has argued that God subsists *per se* not *ab alio*. Now he introduces, *within* God, a generated Word whose exists *ab alio*, whose *esse* is *received*. Baldly put: The objection states, "Generation implies received being, and this violates your earlier claims about divine simplicity." Thomas's answer is, in effect: "Not when I modify the definition of simplicity to cover the case."

It is a *necessary* adjustment. Thomas's concept of simplicity would not be Christian without it. If he refused to admit receptiveness into God, he would no longer be talking about the God of the gospel. But Thomas does not indicate, perhaps does not realize, how revolutionary it is. In the opening discussion of God, he has lined up receptivity with passivity, dependence, and potency, none of which can be present in God. Aristotle and Plotinus could not countenance receptive *esse* in the *archē*; for them, receptivity, with its associations of passivity and dependence, is a certain indication that we are dealing with something *other than* the first principle. Aristotle and Plotinus would hold the line, upholding their "metaphysical snobbery toward relativity, dependence, or passivity, toward responsiveness and sensitivity."[67] Thomas, thank God, blinks.

Again, this adjustment means the Trinity is not a sheer mystery of revelation but an eminent original of which created being is a resemblance. The whole substance of the creature is, he says, *accepta a Deo*; then he says the Word is *esse acceptum . . . ab alio*. The act of creation reveals the inner life of the Trinity; the generation of the Son is the eternal and necessary root of the Father's free

---

[67]Charles Hartshorne, *The Divine Relativity: A Social Conception of God* (New Haven, CT: Yale University Press, 1967), 50.

act of creating, and the Son's reception of being is the uncreated model of the receptive existence of creatures. The Father is unaltered by creating a world other than himself through his Word, because his eternal life is nothing but generating the Word and breathing the Spirit, nothing but donating himself *ad alios*.

To anticipate: Thomas's initial description of simplicity does *not* anticipate this maneuver. There is a gap between Thomas's initial declaration that God is immobile and his later argument, accurately summarized by Stephen Long, that the "received being of the Word is a divine perfection. . . . God is in God's self gift and reception of being, and reception is a perfection, not a potential that is actualized. This 'movement' constitutes God's perfection."[68] There is a gap between denying receptiveness in God and his conclusion that the Son's divine being is *esse receptum*. We will be left to ask: Why did Thomas not introduce this "movement" and this receptivity when he first started talking of simplicity?

One final illustration of Thomas's transformation of simplicity occurs in his discussion of triune persons. In question thirty, Thomas asks whether there is a plurality of divine persons. Citing Athanasius, he insists there are *plures personae*. According to the third objection, plurality implies number, and, Boethius says, there is no number in God. In reply, Thomas argues that God's unity and simplicity exclude all plurality absolutely speaking (*omnis pluralitas absolute dictorum*), but simplicity and unity do not rule out a plurality of *relations*, since relations are predicated of or to another (*de aliquo ut ad alterum*). Relations do not imply any composition in God, particularly since the relations of the Trinity are subsistent relations.

Once again, Thomas uses simplicity to "norm" trinitarian claims, but only after the trinitarian claims have burst the norm

---

[68]Long, *The Perfectly Simple Triune God*, 49.

from within. For Plotinus, to repeat, plurality of *every* kind is rigorously purged from the unified *archē*. Where Plotinus holds out for purity, Thomas is a theologian of impurity. Thomas rightly insists on plurality within the Godhead, couching it so as not to violate his earlier conclusions. Still, it looks like a fudge, as if Thomas said, plurality of relations does not violate simplicity, so long as I am permitted to redefine simplicity in a way that accommodates plurality of relations.[69]

Here I must go back to the beginning of Thomas's initial discussion of divine essence and prove what I have asserted: Thomas does not initially define simplicity in a way that accommodates procession, receptivity, and plurality of relations. To support my assertion, I need first to retrace the *viae* that open Thomas's treatise.

THE SIMPLENESS OF THE ONE GOD

According to David Burrell, the focus of Thomas's discussion of *simplicitas* (which Burrell translates as "simpleness") is less metaphysical than linguistic.[70] Given what we know about God, the opening sections of the *Summa* aim to establish protocols of appropriate speech about God and to "rule out from him everything inappropriate, such as compositeness, change, and the like" (*ST* 1.1.3). Thomas's treatment of simplicity and compositeness, Burrell observes, is rooted in a centuries-long investigation of language, which assumed an isomorphism between the structure of language and the structure of reality. Our composite

---

[69]Once *relatio* is introduced into trinitarian theology, the concept opens up a large space for forms of "multiplicity" in the simple God. Thomas, for instance, denies that multiple divine ideas entail diversity within God because what God knows in knowing finite things is his own participated *relationes* with those things (*ST* 1.15.2). Plotinus would not have been impressed. According to Long, "Simplicity allows theologians to posit real distinctions in God without losing God's unity or dividing God into three parts" (*Perfectly Simple Triune God*, 23).

[70]David B. Burrell, *Exercises in Religious Understanding* (Notre Dame, IN: University of Notre Dame Press, 1974), 80-140. See also his *Aquinas: God and Action*, 3rd ed. (Eugene, OR: Wipf & Stock, 2016), 13-46.

syntax—subject + a predicate that extends beyond the subject—
points to the composite character of the created world. Subject-
predicate is a linguistic sign of ontological composition, whether
of matter or form, individual and species, genus and difference,
or substance and accident.[71]

Since God is not composite, "no well-formed sentence can
express his way of being."[72] In ordinary speech about creatures,
we say "to be X is to be Y": To be man is to be rational, to be yellow
is to be colored, to be Socrates is to be an Athenian. Nothing can
fill in the Y when we speak of God. Divine predication must take
the form "to be God is to be"—full stop. "We cannot predicate
anything of God, because *the form* itself conveys a composition
that would falsify the statement."[73] Thus simplicity functions as
a metalinguistic rule about "how God may *not* be described."[74]
The only "attributes" that may legitimately be added in the Y-slot
are attributes equivalent to "to be." God is perfect, good, and
eternal because perfection, good, and eternity are nothing but
explications of *esse*.

Burrell's is an intriguing reading of Aquinas.[75] For Burrell's
Thomas, simplicity is much more a premise than a conclusion,
and it functions not as a "doctrine" but as a formal and negative
rule about theological language. Regarding immutability, Burrell
makes a similar point: "None of [Thomas's] arguments are designed to show that change is inimical to God, but rather that

---

[71]Burrell, *Exercises*, 93.

[72]Burrell, *Exercises*, 82.

[73]Burrell, *Exercises*, 96-97.

[74]Burrell, *Exercises*, 92. See also Victor Preller, *Divine Science and the Science of God* (Princeton, NJ: Princeton University Press, 1967), who argues Thomas's "proofs" are designed to show what we *cannot* say about God.

[75]And it runs against the grain of recent treatments of simplicity, which take it as a positive statement about God's being rather than as sheer apophatic caution. Steven Duby for instance, runs through various biblical texts and truths—God's aseity, the fact that he is Creator—and argues that these "entail" simplicity (*Divine Simplicity*, 91-177).

what we must affirm (and deny) of him removes God from any possibility of being in process. We simply have no way to speak of him changing, hence he must be beyond change."[76] Saying God is immutable is not to say he is static or inert. He is pure *act*. What immutability denies is "that mode of motion and change proper to things which exist in potency" (*ST* 1.9.1).[77]

Yet this restrained understanding of simplicity does not escape the question: Where do the standards of "appropriate" talk about God *come* from? Thomas's grammar of Godhead assumes a divine metaphysics; where does he find it? Not in Scripture, it seems, which is full of ordinary "composite" statements about God that cannot, in any obvious way, be reduced to "to be God is to be": To be God is to be God of Abraham, Isaac, and Jacob; to be God is to be God of Exodus; to be God is to be Creator of heaven and earth; to be God is to be the Father who raised Jesus from the dead in the power of the Spirit. Burrell concedes Thomas's motivation may have "stemmed from deep-seated 'hellenic' prejudices against change,"[78] but he thinks this misses the point. Perhaps it misses the point Thomas is making, but the problem stands. To put it starkly: If Thomas's strictures on theological language put most of the Bible under erasure, something has gone wrong.[79]

Negation is not the end of the story for Thomas, however. Having mercilessly curtailed our speech about God, he offers a doctrine of creation that opens up ordinary language as appropriately analogical speech about God.[80] As Creator, God is cause

---

[76]Burrell, *Exercises*, 117.

[77]For citations from questions 2-11 of the *Summa*, I rely on the translation of Timothy McDermott in *Summa theologiae*, vol. 2: *Existence and Nature of God* (Cambridge: Cambridge University Press, 2006).

[78]Burrell, *Exercises*, 117.

[79]I am tempted to say, Burrell is where Thomas would have ended up if he had not cared so much about the Bible.

[80]See Robert W. Jenson, *The Knowledge of Things Hoped For: The Sense of Theological Discourse* (Eugene, OR: Wipf & Stock, 1969), 75-89. Burrell takes Thomas's discussion of resemblance in a rigorously apophatic sense. When he says things

of being, the exemplar cause of all created things, the efficient and final cause of the universe. As noted above, Thomas believes all perfections "pre-exist in God according to a more eminent mode" (*ST* 1.4.2). For Thomas, "every cause causes effects similar to itself in that respect in which it is a cause" (*ST* 1.4.3). This resemblance will necessarily be imperfect since the effects do not "fully utilize the causal power" of the cause (*ST* 1.13.5). Since God is entirely outside every class, the effects will have a "remote resemblance" to him by virtue of participation (*ST* 1.4.3). Remote or not, the traces are literally everywhere. All creatures are imitations of God, most basically in that they are beings, "since he is the primary and universal principle of all being" (*ST* 1.4.3). Every being is, simply as a being, *good*, and one, and so the perfections of the one Creator who is Being are evident in the beings he causes. To speak of created things as good is to name the "created character which causally imitates God's goodness." While they "fall short of his form," still they "do attain some similarity to it" (*ST* 1.13.2). Creation is the basis for analogical predication, a use of human language "that is somehow meaningful on both sides of the division between God and creatures."[81]

Further, Thomas's apophaticism is well-nigh universal. He is modest not only about our ability to know God but about our ability to know *anything*. He sometimes writes as if reason can

---

resemble God insofar as they possess existence, he is aware his claim is "improper if not nonsensical." What then is Thomas doing? Burrell claims his language is "not philosophical but rather poetic." God's *esse* is not the blueprint for a building but rather more like the difference between blueprint and building. This opens up "action" as the key metaphor for *esse*. Essence is analogous to a theatrical role, *esse* is the playing-out of the role (*Exercises*, 102-3). I take Thomas to be making a straightforward claim about creation as an image of the Creator. For a less stringent analysis, see W. Norris Clarke, *Explorations in Metaphysics: Being God Person* (Notre Dame, IN: Notre Dame University Press, 1994), 123-49.

[81]Jenson, *Knowledge of Things Hoped For*, 83, 85.

comprehend finite essences, and so know their truth in its en-
tirety (SCG 1.3), but these are exceptions to a pervasive reserve
about the potency of human knowledge, reason, and arguments.
In his exposition of the Apostles' Creed, he observes that "our
manner of knowing is so weak that no philosopher could perfectly investigate the nature of even one little fly," adding a reference to "a certain philosopher [who] spent thirty years in solitude in order to know the nature of the bee."[82] Arguments are
weak (SCG 1.8), yet they are still useful for the exercise of the
mind, so long as they do not puff us up. Thomas justifies God's
arrangement of a world whose depths reason cannot plumb. If
reason could dispel all mysteries, God would not be widely known.
Reasoning about God is difficult and requires training. Since it
takes a long time to arrive at truth through a process of reasoning,
only those with sufficient leisure can come to a rational knowledge
of God. Because God does not wish to be known only to an elite of
leisured philosophical snobs, he gives the Scriptures to humble
reason and to cover the earth with the knowledge of God as the
waters cover the sea.

Sensible things retain a trace of likeness to God, in that effects
resemble causes as actions reveal the nature of the acting agent.
Since God is cause and causes exceed their effects, we cannot
know *what* God is from an exploration of his effects. But we are
capable of knowing *that* God is, and also know *some* truths about
him, deducible from the knowledge that God is first principle.[83]

Thomas's "demonstrations" (ST 1.2.3) are therefore not merely
demonstrations of the bare existence of some being whom we call
God. Because God is known in his effects, arguments assume and
can draw out positive claims about God. This is why Thomas can

---

[82]"Prologue," available at https://isidore.co/aquinas/Creed.htm.
[83]SCG 1.8: *cognoscat de Deo quia est, et alia huiusmodi quae oportet attribui primo principio.*

appeal to the five *viae* in later arguments, particularly in his discussion of simplicity. God cannot be a body because bodies change, and "God has been shown above to be the unchanging first cause of change" (*ST* 1.3.1, reply 1, citing 1.2.3). God has no potentiality because "we have seen" God is the first existent one, and as such must be fully actualized (*ST* 1.3.1, reply 2, again citing 1.2.3). God is not externally caused because, as already said (*dicimus*), God is the first efficient cause (*ST* 1.3.4, first demonstration, citing 1.2.3). The notion that God is composed of substance and accident has been ruled out by the denial of potency in God (*ST* 1.3.6, citing 1.3.1). Thomas assumes simplicity before he examines it explicitly; it is already embedded in the *viae*. To grasp Thomas's case for divine simplicity, therefore, we need to examine these demonstrations. I will focus on the "first way," the argument from change or motion.

One preliminary point must be made. In Thomas's extended treatment in the *Summa Contra Gentiles* (1.13), the argument from motion is overtly presented as an exposition of Aristotle's argument. Thomas is aware, for instance, that the argument assumes Aristotle's stipulated definition of motion. Toward the end of the discussion, he admits that Plato and Aristotle use "motion" differently. For Aristotle, motion applies only to things that are in potency—that is, to divisible, bodily things. Motion is the "reduction" or the *educere* of potency to act. Plato, by contrast, uses motion in a broader sense to refer to any *operatio*. For Plato, even understanding or thinking is a species of motion. Thomas asks if this affects the conclusion of the argument from motion: Is the first mover self-moved (as Plato would say) or is he *immobile* (as Aristotle would say)? Thomas does not think it matters: *nihil differ*, whether we go with Plato or Aristotle.[84]

---

[84]Thomas eventually exploits the different understandings of motion to suggest a relation of analogy between the (Platonic) *operationes* within the Trinity and the (Aristotelian) potency-to-act motions of creation. See Oliver, *Philosophy, God, and Motion*,

This is important to keep in mind as we assess Thomas's argument. Many have charged that Thomas makes God inert, static, inactive. But his denial of God's mobility assumes a specific, Aristotelian definition of motion: It is "reduction of potency to act." On this definition, there is no contradiction in saying God is immobile while at the same time insisting he is pure activity, action, infinite and unbounded actualization. On this definition, there is no contradiction in saying, on the one hand, God does not move and, on the other, coming close to saying God is an event.

I do not believe Thomas's theology portrays a static God.[85] My complaint against Thomas is more focused and, perhaps, more subtle. The question is whether Thomas's initial account of simplicity is compatible with the modifications he later makes under pressure of the Christian creed. Does he build trinitarian modifications into his understanding of simplicity, or does he initially assume a *non-* (or *anti-*) trinitarian account of simplicity? I will argue the latter and will further argue that this leaves Thomas's theology with a degree of incoherence that becomes evident in his and later treatments of God as Creator (see chap. 4). In the following pages, I adjust the focus slightly, moving from simplicity to immobility. As I have already indicated, for Thomas, these imply one another. Though my discussion is about mobility, it is still an argument about simplicity.

108: "Motion is not that which separates creation from its creator, but is the very means of their analogical relation." It is precisely our capacity to be actualized that enables us to reach our *telos* in God.

[85] Fergus Kerr makes a strong case for a dynamic understanding of Thomas's fundamental theology. Should we not, in charity if for no other reason, assume that Thomas Aquinas, doctor of the church, poet and theologian, wished to speak of a *living* God? See "God in the *Summa theologiae*: Entity or Event," in *Philosophy of Religion for a New Century: Essays in Honor of Eugene Thomas Long*, ed. Jeremiah Hackett and Jerald Wallulis (Dordrecht: Springer, 2004), 63-79. See also the lucid treatment of Thomas and the "God of the philosophers" in Frederick Bauerschmidt, *Thomas Aquinas: Faith, Reason, and Following Christ* (Oxford: Oxford University Press, 2013), 101-7; and W. Norris Clarke's exploration of the relational concept of substance in Thomas in *Explorations in Metaphysics*, 211-28.

The short form of Thomas's argument from motion is found in the *Summa theologiae* 1.2.3, the "first proof" of the existence of God. It goes like this: Some things are in motion. Everything that is in motion is put into motion by another. Things move only if they are in potency in relation to the things that move them. Movement, as we have seen, is actualization of this potency, "nothing else than" the reduction (*educere*) of potency to act. A thing in potency toward movement can move only if it is moved by something that is already actualized. A reduction to act can only be caused by something *in actu*. Only what is actually hot can make something else hot.[86] Fire—not an unstruck match—lights the grill.

Now, a thing cannot be both in potency and in act in the same respect at the same time. Something that is actually hot cannot be potentially hot, but only potentially cold (or, presumably, potentially *hotter*, until it reaches maximal hotness). Since moving and being moved are forms of actuality and potency, a thing cannot be both moving and moved in the same respect at once. Nothing, then, can move itself. Things that seem to move themselves—a scurrying squirrel, a dancing man—are actually being moved by part of themselves—the squirrel by its legs, the man by his limbs and ultimately by his soul most musical.

Given this relation of mover and moved, the regress of motion cannot go on to infinity. Without a first mover, there would be no motion at all. All would be left in potency toward motion, none in act. Subsequent movers move because they are put into motion by a first mover. And this first mover is, Thomas says, "whatever everybody understands by God" (*hoc omnes intelligunt Deum*).[87]

---

[86]The limits of medieval science are evident here. Electricity is not hot in itself, yet it makes my kettle boil. It creates heat as it runs through a conductor, which is not hot either. Heat is generated from two not hot things.

[87]Long rightly points out the difference between this statement and Thomas's later "ta-da" moment, "This is God."

Thomas does not simply replicate Aristotle. In this initial argument, Thomas does not describe the first mover as "unmoved." The term is introduced later, but not here. The absence leaves open the question whether the mover might be in motion in some sense, so long as he is not moved by another. Thomas also departs from Aristotle in refusing to restrict the causal power of the first mover to final causation. In the second argument, indeed, he will argue that the one everyone calls God is the supreme efficient cause (*causam efficientem primam*).[88]

This is critical, and once again illustrates Thomas's revision of Aristotle in the light of Scripture and Christian doctrine. Aristotle presents arguments for the existence of an unmoved mover, identified as "god," in two places: In *Physics, Book Theta*, and in *Metaphysics, Book Lambda*. In the former, he argues that motion is eternal. How is this possible? His argument is the model for Thomas's own argument: An infinite regress of moved-and-moving things is impossible. There must be something that does not move accidentally but necessarily. This cannot be a self-moved mover. Nothing moved is identical with what moves it; nothing that moves can be identical to what it moves. A self-mover is still being moved, and thus is not fully actualized. Thus, to fulfill its cosmic vocation, "a first mover must be immovable."[89]

But what *kind* of cause is the unmoved mover? The argument of the *Physics* ends with an *archē* that functions as an *efficient* cause.[90] *Book Eta* of the *Physics* initiates the search for an efficient cause, which is completed by the argument of *Theta*. Aristotle's treatise *On Coming-to-Be and Passing-Away* alludes to the argument

---

[88]Besides this, Thomas means something different by "being." For him, it is the act of *esse*; for Aristotle, form or essence is the source of being. See Joseph Owens, "The Conclusion of the Prima Via," in John R. Catan, *St. Thomas Aquinas on the Existence of God: The Collected Papers of Joseph Owens* (Albany, NY: SUNY Press, 1980), 142-68.
[89]Aristotle, *Physics* 8.6.258b4-5.
[90]Gerson, *God and Greek Philosophy*, 119.

of book *Theta* in a passage that explicitly identifies the unmoved mover as an efficient cause.[91] Most importantly, "the argument leading up to the unmoved mover is a chain of reasoning in the line of efficient causality, that is, as the moved mover is the efficient cause of the variety of earthly changes, so, presumably, the unmoved mover is the efficient cause of the everlasting circulation locomotion of the moved mover." In short, "nothing in the argument is . . . in need of final causal explanation."[92] To put it crudely, the unmoved mover of the *Physics* causes everlasting motion by pushing along the first moving thing, which becomes the secondary cause of all other motion. The unmoved mover causes in a way analogous to the way a carpenter or hammer causes the driving of a nail, or, to use Aristotle's preferred analogy, the way a sculptor sculpts a bronze statue. Exactly how an *unmoved* mover can serve as an efficient cause is never made clear. It is difficult to see what can fill the explanatory gap, other than magic.

When Aristotle gets to *Metaphysics Lambda*, though, this argument will no longer do. He presents a version of the same argument from motion to an unmoved mover, this time in the perspective of Being rather than *physis*. In this version of the argument, the efficient causation is provided not by the unmoved mover but by fifty-five "inseparable souls of the spheres, the *archai* of their motion and the motion of the 'planets' contained within them."[93] These are not unmoved in an unqualified sense,

---

[91] "Now there are two meanings of 'cause,' one being that which, as we say, results in the beginning of motion, and the other: the material cause. It is the latter kind with which we have to deal here; for with cause in the former sense we have dealt in our discussion of Motion, when we said that there is something which remains immovable through all time and something which is always in motion." *Aristotle, On Sophistical Refutations; On Coming-to-be and Passing-away*, trans. E. S. Forster (Cambridge, MA: Harvard University Press, 1955), 1.3.318.

[92] Gerson, *God and Greek Philosophy*, 119.

[93] Gerson, *God and Greek Philosophy*, 132.

since they are moved by the higher principle that is the unmoved mover. Meanwhile, the latter has become a final rather than an efficient cause. It *must* be so. An efficient cause is, by definition, actualized in another: Rodin is actualized as sculptor only if he produces *The Thinker*. But the unmoved mover of the *Metaphysics* is supposed to be utterly independent of everything, wholly and eternally actualized in itself. There is a mismatch between the first efficient cause of the *Physics* and the absolute first-final cause of the *Metaphysics*.[94]

This leaves Aristotle strung out across various dilemmas. The argument from motion only works if one can ascend from the efficiently caused motion of moving things to an efficient cause, the unmoved mover. There is no bridge from a series of motions to an unmoved mover who is a *final* cause. Yet Aristotle wants to employ the argument of the *Physics* to reach a metaphysical mover. As Gerson says, "The god of the *Physics* cannot satisfy metaphysics and the god of the *Metaphysics* cannot be reached by coherent reasoning within metaphysics."[95] There is "an incoherence between Aristotle's metaphysics and his mode of demonstrating god's existence."[96]

For this reason, Aristotle is unable to fulfill his aspiration to unite physics and metaphysics, to unite all sciences as theology.[97] Though the unmoved mover of the *Metaphysics* is fully actualized substance, it cannot fulfill the function of a purely actual entity. By Aristotle's definition, "The nature of being itself and as such . . . must be that which is derivatively expressed in absolutely every instance of being, every sensible substance, every attribute of a

---

[94]Gerson, *God and Greek Philosophy*, 136.
[95]Gerson, *God and Greek Philosophy*, 134.
[96]Gerson, *God and Greek Philosophy*, 140.
[97]On the definition and aspirations of Aristotle's metaphysics, see Shane Duarte, "Aristotle's Theology and Its Relation to the Science of Being qua Being," *Apeiron* 40, no. 3 (2007): 267-318.

sensible substance, and so on,"[98] for, as Aristotle says, "being is said in many ways."[99] But how can a separated Form be expressed in every being if that Form possesses merely final causality? As Gerson puts it, "If god is only a final cause, it is once again difficult to see how being is derived to everything else in the way required by the *Metaphysics*, that is, in a way such that the science of god will be the science of being of everything else."[100] Nothing else is illuminated by Aristotle's conclusion that "god is the final cause of the motion of the first-moved mover."[101]

As a final cause, the mover is an object of desire, specifically the desire of the first heaven, which transforms the final causality of the mover into efficient causality and then moves all other celestial spheres and eventually puts the sublunary world into motion. Without the unmoved mover, the first heaven would stop its rotation, which would stop the lower spheres, which would stop everything. Absent the mover, "there is a silent, motionless world," nothing but "stillness in the universe."[102] Moved by desire for the mover, everything marches in a stately, circular dance.[103] It is a beautiful picture, especially when Christianized by Aquinas, for whom God is the mover desired by all, the One toward whom all moves, source and end, beginning of creation's journey and creation's restful Sabbath, when God is all in all.

---

[98]Gerson, *God and Greek Philosophy*, 134.

[99]Aristotle, *Metaphysics* 1003^{b}5-6.

[100]Gerson, *God and Greek Philosophy*, 138-39.

[101]Gerson, *God and Greek Philosophy*, 140.

[102]Adam Drozdek, *Greek Philosophers as Theologians: The Divine Arche* (London: Routledge, 2007), 174.

[103]The unmoved mover is a cold fish, hardly sexy enough to awaken a desire strong enough to move the cosmos. Francis Cornford says that Aristotle resorts to mythology to make the mover lovable: "It is only by calling it 'God,' and persuading ourselves that it is alive, and active, and blessed—all of which is manifestly mythical—that we can induce the faintest feeling of attraction towards it." *From Religion to Philosophy: A Study in the Origins of Western Speculation* (Mineola, NY: Dover, 2004; first published in 1957), 261. On the role of myth in Aristotle's thought, see Martin D. Yaffe, "Myth and 'Science' in Aristotle's Theology," *Man and World* 12 (1979): 70-88.

In Aristotle, the "mechanism" runs aground; or, more accurately, the stately parade circles round and round without end, never reaching the joy of rest. Adam Drozdek explains:

> Why should the FH [First Heaven] desire the UM [Unmoved Mover]? What is so desirable in the UM that is a powerful enough reason for the FH to be active, to be in motion, to strive for it? To be like the UM. In what sense? To reach the state of contemplation? If so, why should the FH not do just that, namely contemplate? The FH, being a union of *nous* and aether and as such capable only of actualizing its potentiality, cannot reach the state of contemplation which involves no change. However, maybe the second-best state for the FH would be to think discursively, to reason, to limit its activity to the intellectual sphere. . . . Why then exercise any action on the rest of the world by being an efficient cause? What good does it do the FH? It only distracts it from what is truly desirable, namely from becoming more like the UM which is its telos. If the UM is merely uninterested in the affairs of this world, the FH seemingly would do best by detaching itself from the rest of the world and devoting itself to the intellectual activity whose object is the perfect being, the UM.[104]

If the first heaven were to become *like* the mover, the first heaven would itself become an unmoved heaven, and all below would grind to a halt. The more perfect the first heaven becomes, the more contemplative and indifferent it is, the less useful it is to the world and the less it fulfills its reason for being.[105]

The first heaven will never/can never gain the notice of the mover, much less be united with it. This is not a particular problem for Aristotle, who does not believe the world came into being, and does not have any eschatology. He is content to leave the world going on and on, the first heaven pining away for the

---

[104]Drozdek, *Greek Philosophers as Theologians*, 174.
[105]Drozdek, *Greek Philosophers as Theologians*, 175.

unmoved mover from eternity to eternity, like a country song on scratched vinyl. The first heaven's desire to reach its *telos must* be frustrated, lest the universe become a lifeless, immobile shell of itself. Love makes the world go round, but the only love that does the trick is courtly love—tragic, unrequited love.

Thomas believes love is the deep heart of things, but to make this coherent he must decisively break with Aristotle. Thomas insists God is the *efficient* cause of the world; that is to say, the active Creator of all things. Thus, he can explain how God, who is *ipsum esse*, can be expressed in every existing thing. He can also use the argument from motion to arrive at a metaphysical unmoved mover. Because Thomas's unmoved mover is the efficient cause of created existence, everything that is bears some resemblance to God. The Cause is knowable and known in his effects. In shifting from final to efficient causality, Thomas breaks the tragic frame of Aristotelian metaphysics, and does so because he believes Genesis 1:1: "In the beginning God created the heavens and the earth."

UNBAPTIZED SIMPLICITY

At various points, however, the argument from motion depends on metaphysical assumptions that are incompatible with the trinitarian metaphysics of questions twenty-seven and twenty-eight of the *Summa*'s *Prima Pars*.[106] Thomas, for instance, explicitly denies the possibility of *esse receptum* within God. In the extended treatment of the argument from motion in the *Summa*

---

[106]Kevin Hector harmonizes the theology proper of the *Summa* by arguing that the "God" arrived at through the *viae* is a "placeholder" for the as-yet-unknown cause of the world. Eventually, the placeholder is filled in by positive claims about God. "Apophaticism in Thomas Aquinas: A Reformulation and Recommendation," *Scottish Journal of Theology* 60, no. 4 (2007): 377-93. Perhaps that is Thomas's intent, but in fact he tailors the placeholder in ways that make it ill-suited to the place-filler.

Contra Gentiles, Thomas argues that, absolutely speaking (*simpliciter*), act precedes potency. Individually and in time, I am potentially musical before actually musical, but I would not be potentially musical, I would not be at all, were it not for my actual parents. Push the logic back to the beginning, and we discover the first cause must be actual, fully so, without admixture of potency. Possible things can possibly *not* exist. Since God necessarily exists, he cannot have possible existence. There is, Thomas insists, no potency in his substance (*nihil . . . potentia in sua substantia*).[107]

An absence of potency implies an absence of derivation and passivity. Only a fully actualized being can act as a whole. A being in potency in any respect will act by virtue of some actualized part of itself. But the first agent acts of himself, rather than by virtue of participation in another. Actuality and action form a natural pair, and so too potency and passivity: it is "natural for [a thing] to be passive insofar as it is in potency" (*natum est pati inquantum est potentia*). Since God is "altogether impassible and immovable" (*omnino impassibilis ac immutabilis*), there can be "neither potency nor passivity in him" (*nihil . . . de potentia, sciliet passive*).

Thomas mounts a similar argument later in the *Summa Contra Gentiles*, in the midst of a discussion of the identity of essence and existence in God (1.22). If they are distinct, one must be cause of the other: Existence must be dependent on essence or essence on existence or perhaps both dependent on something else. None of these can be true of God, since necessary existence is by definition *independent* existence: "if it depends on something else, it no longer exists necessarily" (*si ab alio dependet, iam non est necesse esse*).

---

[107]Is there an opening here for potency in *some* respect? Perhaps God is not in potency in his substance, but can be in potency in *relation*? Thomas will rule this out, and on the basis of simplicity. God is his essence; essence and existence are identical. If he is not in potency *in sua substantia*, he cannot be in potency in any other respect either.

But this is Arian metaphysics. Eunomius, not Athanasius or the Cappadocians, equated derived *esse* with secondary *esse*. As Thomas knows, the Son *is* "from another" (*ab alio*), and therefore his necessary existence as eternal Son is derived from and dependent on the Father's act of begetting. We speak rightly of the Son only with passive locutions: He *is* begotten of the Father; as Word, he is spoken. "Patiency" is a feature of triune being and existence. Thomas knows there is derivation within the Trinity but in his opening arguments does not acknowledge that reality. No doubt he would evade the objection by objecting to my terminology. What happens between the Son and the Father is not "dependence" or "passivity," though we must call it that, due to the limitations of human language. Grant the point for the sake of argument, yet my criticism stands: There is that in God (*esse acceptum ab alio*) of which created dependence and passivity are resemblances. This is just what Thomas denies when elaborating the argument from motion.

God's immobility presents a similar problem. As noted above, Thomas's initial argument from motion in the *Summa theologiae* does not end with the declaration that God is *immobile*, but merely with the conclusion that God, as the first mover, cannot be moved by another. Soon enough, that conclusion has modulated into the claim that God is the "unmoving first mover" (*primem movens immobile, ST* 1.3.1),[108] and the related, though distinct, claim that God, being immobile, is *immutabile*. There is a conceptual leap here. The equation of immutability with immobility only seems obvious if we start from the assumption that change is a species of movement, or vice versa, and only if we define movement as the "reduction of potency to act." Certain kinds of immutability—Steph Curry's fixed

---

[108]Jeffery D. Johnson rightly notes the gap between the demonstration of *ST* 1.2 and the claims of *ST* 1.3 in *The Failure of Natural Theology: A Critical Appraisal of the Philosophical Theology of Thomas Aquinas* (Conway, AR: Free Grace, 2021), 116-18.

determination to get the ball in the basket—require supple mobility rather than the opposite. And, finally, Thomas's language is infelicitous: It is too easy to forget Aristotle's stipulated definition of motion and conclude God is a great block of motionless being.

Thomas's argument ignores his later confession that there are processions within God. The trinitarian argument assumes a kind of "movement" in God that the argument from motion denies. To be sure, Thomas would deny, given his definition of motion, that what happens in God is rightly described as "motion." Concede the point once again, and yet on trinitarian grounds we must say: There is that in God (processions) of which created movement and change is the resemblance. As Thomas formulates it, the first *via* has an apophatic destination: From created motion, we are led to an inconceivably immobile mover. In more thoroughly trinitarian terms, the argument from motion might be recalibrated to move along the *via eminentiae*: The partial and intermittent motions of created things point to the infinitely mobile triune God. Indeed, precisely the partial and intermittent acts and movements of creatures constitute their likeness to the Father who generates the Son and breathes forth the Spirit. In the terms set earlier, "mobile" is used here in a Platonic rather than an Aristotelian sense. Thomas to the contrary, the choice between Plato and Aristotle *does* matter. The Aristotelian definition of motion, combined with the conviction that God is *actus purus*, closes off the possibility of discerning supereminent motion in God.

A final illustration, from *Summa Contra Gentiles* 1.13: Aristotle recognizes that the fact that a first mover is unmoved does not necessarily mean he is *absolutely* immovable. Perhaps the first mover is moved by himself. This is initially plausible since "what is of itself is always prior to what is of another" (*quod est per se, semper est prius eo quod es per aliud*). One can imagine, when speaking of motion, that "what is moved first is moved by itself and not by another" (*primum motum . . . est per seipsum moveri, non ab alio*). Aristotle, and Thomas, reject this possibility. It is absurd, Thomas thinks, to suggest that a thing can move itself, for that would mean it is both active and passive in the same respect at the same time, as if a teacher could be taught while teaching.[109]

Here the issue is not one of movement per se, but the priority of mover over the one moved. On Thomas's definition of motion, it is perfectly sensible. Movement is a reduction of potency to act, and before a mover can move another from potency to act it must have actualized its own potency to move. The carpenter only actualizes the hammer's potential to hammer a nail if the carpenter is first actualized as a carpenter, with hands and an arm capable of wielding a hammer. But this apparent common-sensical conclusion is scrambled when we introduce trinitarian considerations. For the Father is not Father prior to begetting the Son. Rather, the Father's begetting and the Son's being-begotten are eternally simultaneous, while absolutely distinct. The Son's being-begotten by another does not come after anything that is in the Father per se, for there is no Father per se except as the One who begets the Son. Thomas will deny the procession is a motion. Grant the point. Yet, if a trinitarian ontology is assumed, we may say: There is that in God of which the simultaneity of cause and effect is a resemblance.

These tensions between Thomas's initial and later doctrine of God raise questions about the plausibility of Thomas's initial arguments. If there is "passivity" and "dependence" and receptiveness in God, then arguments that depend on denial of passivity in God no longer work, or at least they do not work in the same way. We

---

[109]It is an odd argument, coming as it does from a teacher. Surely everyone who has taught is aware that being-taught is part of the process of teaching. We do, after all, hear ourselves speak, and what we speak may never have entered or minds or mouths before a moment of inspiration.

can no longer reason from the universal fact of motion to an unmoving capstone. Nor can we reason from the fact of created motion to the claim that the first mover must be wholly "unmoved" by another, for the Son is "moved" by the Father.

In fact, we need the trinitarian framework to make the argument compelling in the first place. If God is *simpliciter* immobile, how can he create a world in motion? If God lacks potency, where does the potency and patiency of creation *come* from?[110] Thomas says these are qualities of matter, but matter too comes from God, as an effect of the first cause that resembles the first cause. One might say God simply transcends the ontic binary of actuality and potency in his infinite ontological actuality.[111] But this is not Thomas's position, since it would render much of his discussion otiose. Within the Thomistic frame, does there not have to be *some* resemblance between created potency and the divine essence, as there is between every effect and its cause? If we reverse the argument from motion, Parmenides's ontology seems equally, if not more, plausible: Precisely because the first principle is unchanging, so *all* that comes from the *archē* must be unchanging. Why can an immobile cause not be the source of a universe whose apparent mobility is a demonic delusion? Conversely, the fact of a mobile universe leads just as plausibly to an ineffably *mobile* first cause as to an ineffably *immobile* one. Is Thomas falling prey to an instinct to formulate divine metaphysics by simple negation of created metaphysics? If so, is that not an implicit denial of creation?

Thomas's arguments for immobility and simplicity depend on and reinforce a partially baptized metaphysics. Absolute simplicity in the sense Thomas initially presents it follows from his

---

[110]Dorner warns that denial of plurality and process in God produces an "acosmism" that treats these features of the world as illusions (*Divine Immutability*, 95-96).

[111]As David Bentley Hart does in "Providence and Causality: Divine Innocence," in *The Providence of God*, ed. Francesca Aran Murphy and Philip G. Ziegler (London: T&T Clark, 2009), 34-56.

arguments only on the basis of a nontrinitarian ontology. Thomas later uses his unevangelized concept of simplicity to norm his trinitarian doctrine, but at the same time, he modifies simplicity in a way that leaves it unrecognizable to its classical proponents. There would be no need for this modification if Thomas began from an evangelized metaphysics, a trinitarian ontology that, from the outset, names God from the gospel. He norms his trinitarian theology by assumptions and arguments that are not themselves normed by trinitarian theology. Against D. Stephen Long, Thomas's discussion of divine essence and his discussion of Trinity are not mutually qualifying. Indeed, at certain points, priority is given to the nontrinitarian paradigm.

Unlike his later followers, Thomas does *not* write a treatise *de Deo uno*, followed by a treatise *de Deo trino*.[112] He does not begin with a philosophical concept of God, and then try to hang it on a theological concept of God like a suit of borrowed clothes. That is to say, none of this is his *intent*. Yet the Thomists who split the treatise on God were not delusional. They recognized what I have tried to expose here; namely, that Thomas begins with unevangelized ontological categories, only to modify them later. Even without the *uno* and *trino* headings, even though Thomas's entire project is *sacra doctrina* guided by Scripture, yet there is a substantive difference between his discussion of divine essence and his trinitarian theology.[113]

More seriously, Thomas's approach raises questions about the coherence of reason and revelation. Natural reason leads to an

---

[112]Karl Rahner famously charged that Thomas introduced this fateful bifurcation into the doctrine of God in *The Trinity* (Herder & Herder, 1997).

[113]Paul Hinlicky reaches a similar conclusion: Thomas works out his understanding of simplicity protologically, as part of a meditation on God as first cause, but reserves the knowledge of this God to the eschaton. That leaves Thomas oscillating between univocity and equivocity that is not dispelled by calling it "analogy" (*Divine Simplicity*, 36-49).

immobile, simple God, without internal "motions," reception, or relations; by disclosing the Trinity, revelation trumps reason.[114] There are two theologies in the *Summa*, a theology of nature and reason and a trinitarian theology of the gospel, and they are not entirely compatible. To exaggerate crudely for the sake of emphasis: Thomas introduces two *Gods*, and they are rivals. Thomas abominated the theory of double truth, yet the two-story Thomists, who split Thomas into natural/reason versus supernatural/revelation, were not imagining things.

To return to our starting point: Why does Thomas do this? I submit that his theological instincts are inadequately evangelized, and so his doctrine of God is only partially baptized. The first of his two Gods is, like the *archai* of ancient Greece, defined by contrast with the time-full multiplicity of creation; the second, the living God, is known in the gospel of Jesus, sent by the Father in the power of the Spirit.

CONCLUSION

What would it look like to *begin* from an ontology fully baptized in the triune name? It would look something like von Balthasar. He agrees with Thomas: In God, existence and essence are identical. He agrees this marks a basic *dissimilarity* between God and creation, for in all creatures there is a real distinction between *what* something is and the fact *that* it is. Yet von Balthasar adds that even the essence/existence *difference* within creatures, this "polarity that traverses creaturely 'unity,'" bears traces of the life of God. In the Trinity, the "divine hypostases are one with the divine essence and yet distinct in relation to one another." There

---

[114]*On the Power of God* 9.5: "We should say that the plurality of Persons in the Godhead concerns matters subject to faith, and natural reason can neither investigate nor sufficiently understand it." *The Power of God by Thomas Aquinas*, trans. Richard J. Regan (Oxford: Oxford University Press, 2012).

is thus an "original distance" in God that is the source of created polarities of substance/accident, form/matter, essence/existence within creatures. Assume divine simplicity. Still: If all effects resemble the cause, a Creator in whom *no* distance or difference existed could not create composite beings.[115]

The triune persons have an "incommunicable otherness" from one another. They live by giving *and* receiving, making happen *and* letting happen. *Both* sides of each relation are positive; both are divine perfections. In the Trinity, there is divine, eternal reception and *passio*. Passivity is not simply a negation of God's activity; *esse receptum* is a dimension of the purely active life of God. Created receptivity images divine receptivity, the latter being a dimension or facet of the infinite act by which God is God. Thomas presents a God who is active, energetic, eventful, infinitely youthful. But his language, and his unbaptized metaphysics, get in the way. For von Balthasar, God is "beyond all becoming," yet his being is not rigid and static. He is "*energeia*, ever-actual event." And the eventfulness of God, his liveliness, is the foundation of "the possibility of all creaturely becoming." God does not become; but there is that in God of which becoming is an image. There is a source in God's own life for the created distinction between potency and actuality, between action and contemplation, between male and female. There is even in God an archetype of "good death," insofar as each person gives himself in "unconditional self-surrender" for the others.[116] Thomas's partially trinitarian ontology is also a partially creationist ontology, insofar as he sometimes identifies features of created being that bear *no* resemblance to the life of the Creator.

A trinitarian argument from motion might go like this: All is in motion, and that points to a first mover. But this first mover is not

---

[115]Hans Urs von Balthasar, *Theo-Logic: Theological Logical Theory*, vol. 2: *The Truth of God*, trans. Adrian J. Walker (San Francisco: Ignatius, 2004), 83.
[116]Hans Urs von Balthasar, *Theo-Logic*, 2:83.

only the source of motion but the model and pattern of motion, for in him the Father begets and the Son is begotten and the Spirit proceeds from both. The argument from motion points to a first mover, but a first mover eternally, infinitely in "motion," moved with inconceivable motion that infinitely exceeds the movements of creation, yet moved and moving. That is to say, we might conclude the demonstration from motion not with "this is what *everybody* understands by God" but with "this is what *we Christians* understand by God." It would provide a *via* leading us not to deity but to the destination we long and need to go toward, toward Trinity.

4

CREATOR

Let me take stock of where we are. In chapter two, I examined Plato's *Timaeus* in order to demonstrate that it presents a theology of creation and the Creator that clashes with the biblical portrait. Christian theology cannot adopt Platonic metaphysics, or Hellenic metaphysics in general, without alteration, and, as I argued in chapter three, it has not. Because Thomas believes the biblical account of creation, he modifies the Plotinian (Avicennan) account of divine simplicity. Yet he fails to carry through his revisionary metaphysics consistently. His doctrine of God is partially but not fully baptized; it does not die and rise bearing the triune name. This chapter continues a critique of Thomas's understanding of divine simplicity, but now focused on its implications for his doctrine of creation. I will show that creation is a battleground between partially baptized theology and the Bible. At the end of the chapter, I offer a radical proposal to resettle the doctrine of the Creator on firmer ground.

Here is Thomas's dilemma: Suppose a strong notion of simplicity, according to which God is identical to his attributes. Suppose God, as simple, is absolutely immutable. If all of God's attributes are identical to each other and to his *esse*, then God-as-Creator is identical to God-as-God. But can God be Creator *without* creation? If God-as-Creator is identical to God-as-God, perhaps creation is eternal. On the other hand, if creation is not eternal, it seems that God "becomes" Creator, assuming some new relation *ad extra*. If God is simple, he "must" create; or, if God is simple, he *cannot* create, because creation would put in him a "new" relation. Perhaps the name "Creator" does not name God at all but is only a description of a relation that befalls creatures. In short, is the doctrine of creation compatible with the belief that God is absolutely simple and unchangeable?[1]

We can press the question: Could a simple God create *in the way Genesis 1 says God created*? Can a God who is a single sheer act of being perform the variety of actions that Genesis 1 records? Can a simple God speak "light" on day one, "firmament" on day two, and "dry land" on day three? Can a God who is *actus purus* create, speak, hover, make, place, bless, invite, consult? It might be said that these various actions attributed to God are refractions of God's single act of being, the appearances of God's simple *esse* within the order of creation. But if those recorded acts do not correspond in a strong sense to anything God does and says, then Genesis 1 says almost nothing about God but only about God as he *appears*. Indeed, Scripture as a whole seems to be largely placed under similar erasure, for it consistently speaks of God saying and doing *different* things

---

[1]Thomas notes the problem: "Whatever receives something anew must be changed, either essentially or accidentally. Now certain relations are said of God anew (for instance, that he is Lord or governor of a thing which begins anew to exist). Therefore, if a relation were predicated of God as really existing in him, it would follow that something accrues to God anew, and consequently that he is changed either essentially or accidentally: the contrary of which was proved in the first book." *Summa contra Gentiles*, Works of St. Thomas Aquinas (Green Bay, WI: Aquinas Institute, 2018), 2.12. Steven Duby goes so far as to claim that simplicity is "entailed" by creation *ex nihilo*. See *Divine Simplicity: A Dogmatic Account* (London: T&T Clark, 2016), 168. Some contemporary theologians take the opposite view, that the Christian doctrine of simplicity requires creation. See David Bentley Hart, *The Experience of God: Being, Consciousness, Bliss* (New Haven, CT: Yale University Press, 2013), 134-42.

at different times, of God in various states and conditions. Besides, how do we *know* the Scriptural account of God's sayings and doings is an accommodation or a refraction? What independent access do we have to a God-beyond-Scripture who does not say and do as the God of the Bible does? Some philosophical theologians may claim to find pathways to the unrefracted light. For Protestants like me, there is no such path. If Scripture falsifies God, we are of all men most miserable.

No ancient writer poses a challenge to the Christian doctrine of creation more forcefully than Proclus the Successor, a fifth-century philosopher, who challenges the idea of a temporal creation on the basis of a Neoplatonic view of simplicity.[2] In his treatise on the eternity of the world, he poses two alternatives: Either a creator is always creating, in which case he will be an actual creator, or he is merely a *potential* creator until he begins to create. If the former—if the creator is always actualized as creator—then the creation must "likewise always be actually undergoing creation." He cites Aristotle's principle: "When . . . a cause is actual, that which is caused will likewise be actual."[3] On the other hand, if the creation is *not* always actualized, then the creator will not always be actualized as creator until he begins to create.

Suppose God is a potential creator. Proclus argues that this alternative raises a problem that eventually leads back to the eternity of the world. Once again citing Aristotle, Proclus argues that potential things are actualized only by something actual, as cold water becomes hot through the agency of something already hot. A potential creator, then, must be actualized as creator by

---

[2]*Philoponus: Against Proclus on the Eternity of the World 1-5*, trans. Michael Share, Ancient Commentators on Aristotle (London: Bloomsbury, 2004). See R. T. Mullins, *The End of the Timeless God* (Oxford: Oxford University Press, 2016), 108-15.
[3]Philoponus, *Against Proclus* 1.42.6-8.

some other entity that is already actualized. If this is the case, the *actual* creator is the higher being or power who actualizes the first creator; if the higher creator is always actualized, then the secondary creator must also be always actualized, and the creation must be eternal. We can keep retreating, but there must always be an actualized creator to catalyze the potential creators lower down the ladder. We are left either with an infinite regress of potential creators, or an actual creator. If the former, the world would not be at all; if the latter, the world, as an effect of the creator, must be as eternal as the cause. Since the world exists, it must be eternal.

The Christian philosopher Philoponus dismisses Proclus's argument as "sophistical."[4] Proclus mangles Aristotle, who teaches not one but two types of potency and two kinds of actuality. The first type of potentiality is "based on fitness."[5] A child has a natural aptitude to learn grammar because he is a rational animal who is "receptive to acquiring from others the theorems of grammar at the right time."[6] There is also a form of potency based on *capacity*. This is the potency of a grammarian who is not actively practicing grammar, for he still possesses the capacity to grammatize when he is eating, sleeping, or daydreaming about his next round of golf.

"Second potency" is identical to "first actuality." The grammarian is an actualized grammarian, even when he is on the driving range and not actively practicing his skills as a grammarian. Aristotle also posits a "second actuality," which involves the active use of some skill or capacity. The grammarian at his craft is actualized with second actuality.

---

[4]Philoponus, *Against Proclus* 1.45.6.
[5]Philoponus, *Against Proclus* 1.46.12.
[6]Philoponus, *Against Proclus* 1.46.9-10.

Once this distinction is made, Philoponus can sort through the Aristotelian axioms. "When a cause is actual, that which is caused will likewise be actual"[7] applies only to *second* actuality. When a grammarian is practicing grammar, the grammatical perfor- mance will be actualized. But the principle does *not* apply to first actuality. It is possible, Philoponus says, "for a builder to have the capacity to build but not be building and for someone who has the capacity to teach not to be teaching."[8] In these cases, the effect of the actualized builder or teacher is not realized.

Through this distinction, Philoponus is able to assert that God is eternally an actualized Creator (because he always possesses the capacity to create) without implying that the creation is eternal (because God's eternal actuality as Creator is an eternal "first actuality"). Philoponus can also argue that God needs no outside cause or catalyst to spur him to create. Being actualized by first actuality, he can choose to be actualized in second actu- ality, and so be a second-actualized Creator, by his own volition.

It is not clear that Philoponus has really addressed Proclus's argument. A teacher who is actualized as teacher by first actu- ality has, presumably, *taught*. Does a builder who knows how to build but has never *actually* built anything qualify as a builder? Perhaps so, but only in an attenuated sense. So too, a Creator who is actualized as Creator only by first actuality, but has never produced creatures, does not fully qualify as an actualized Creator.

Further, to parry Proclus's argument, Philoponus has to alter the idea of simplicity. As a Christian, Philoponus believes God made the world. It is not eternal. To head off the conclusion that creation is eternal, Philoponus introduces a form of potentiality in God. To be sure, this potentiality is also a "first actuality," but it is nonetheless a form of potency. An advocate of strict

---

[7]Philoponus, *Against Proclus* 1.47.22.
[8]Philoponus, *Against Proclus* 1.48.2-4.

simplicity does not, it seems, have this option available. If God is *actus purus*, there is no potency of any kind in him. Besides, Philoponus is forced to introduce change into the Creator: "Someone who is already in possession of the theorems of grammar, and who is said to be a potential grammarian, does not, when he changes from this [kind of] potentiality to what is known as second actuality . . . change through the agency of another . . . but changes from being inactive to being active by himself, without any intermediary."[9] This arrests Proclus's infinite regression of actualized agents, but at the cost of admitting change or movement from potency to act. Strict simplicity rules out change of any kind. To make his response work, Philoponus has to loosen the linkage of simplicity and immutability. Finally, Philoponus locates God's second actualization as Creator in God's will. This too violates a strict understanding of simplicity in that it frees God's will from his nature or being. We will catch Thomas making a similar move below.

Divine simplicity is vulnerable to Proclus's argument. If the Creator is fully actualized in every respect, without any form of potency, and if the Creator is incapable of change, then it seems the world must be eternal and the Creator must create. Thomas, as we have seen, defines movement as the reduction of potency to act, but if no such movement can take place in God, then God must always be not only *capable* of creating but *actually* creating. And if actually creating, it would seem he must actually be producing the effect of creation.[10] Thomas, we will see, has some ways around this impasse. But the dilemma has driven some

---

[9]Philoponus, *Against Proclus* 1.49.2-5.
[10]See R. T. Mullins, "Divine Perfection and Creation," *Heythrop Journal* 57 (2016): 122-34. One of the most potent recent statements of this critique comes from David Bradshaw in *Aristotle East and West: Metaphysics and the Division of Christendom* (Cambridge: Cambridge University Press, 2007), 244-60, which focuses on Thomas Aquinas.

recent theologians, like T. F. Torrance, to state outright that creation involves a change in God, from non-Creator to Creator, from nonrelated to related.[11]

I have refuted nothing, rejected nothing. I have posed challenges, and challenges are not refutations. But the challenge is deep, and exposes "dilemmas" or aporias at the beginning of our consideration of God. Theologians have, of course, noticed the problem and proposed solutions. I will examine two in detail: Thomas Aquinas's and Sergius Bulgakov's. Neither entirely convinces.

ETERNAL CREATION?

Aquinas deals with the necessity of creation in two related connections—in discussions of the eternity of the world and in treatments of the freedom of God's will. Under the first heading, he asks about the *eternity* of the world but touches on the necessity of the world; under the second, he directly asks whether the world, eternal or temporal, is *necessary*. In my view, Thomas's efforts to reconcile absolute simplicity and free creation fail, and on the way to failing, Thomas makes some fateful theological decisions.

Aristotle teaches the cosmos is eternal, and the dispersion of Aristotle's works in the thirteenth century put the question on the agenda of Arab philosophers and Christian theologians. Some Christian thinkers responded by offering philosophical arguments for a temporal beginning to creation, others by giving theological defenses of Aristotle.[12] Thomas takes a

---

[11]T. F. Torrance, *The Christian Doctrine of God* (London: T&T Clark, 1996), 237: "God was always father, but not always Creator."

[12]Siger of Brabant is the best-known representative of the second group. He argued that, because God is fully actualized, he cannot be a potential Creator but must be Creator of creatures from all eternity. Siger's position raised crucial methodological questions, since he went on to confess a temporal creation as a matter of faith. Faith

mediating position.[13] While he takes it as a given of faith that the "world has not existed from eternity but had a beginning of its duration,"[14] he does not think it heretical to say, "God is able to bring it about that something created by him should always have existed."[15]

Thomas finds nothing *philosophically* incoherent about an eternal creation. Causes must be "before" effects, but this "before" need not be temporal. In fact, causes and effects are temporally simultaneous; the smack of the cue ball occurs in the same instant as the movement of the eight ball. Since God acts through will, he does not have to precede his effects in duration.[16] Creation comes "after" nothing, but this "after" need not be temporal either.[17] To John of Damascus and Hugh of St. Victor, who deny eternal creation by arguing that nothing can be co-eternal with God, Thomas responds with a citation from Boethius, who distinguishes between the (hypothetical) endless duration of creation and the "whole presence of the endless life" that characterizes God's eternity.[18] Even if the world is everlasting, it is not eternal as God is eternal.

On the other hand, Thomas finds nothing philosophically incoherent in the Catholic claim that the world has a temporal beginning. If God willed to create an eternal world, he could have

---

may be philosophical nonsense, yet it must be believed. Thomas, of course, was a resolute opponent of anything that hinted of a theory of double truth. See Frederick Bauerschmidt, *Thomas Aquinas: Faith, Reason, and Following Christ* (Oxford: Oxford University Press, 2013), 108.

[13] Thomas addresses this question repeatedly in *Summa Contra Gentiles* 2.32-37; *de potentia Dei* q. 3; *Summa theologiae* 1.46.2.

[14] Thomas Aquinas, *On the Eternity of the World (De Aeternitate Mundi): St. Thomas Aquinas, Siger of Brabant, St. Bonaventure*, 2nd ed., trans. Cyril Vollert, Lottie H. Kendzierski, and Paul M. Byrne (Milwaukee, WI: Marquette University Press, 1983), 1.

[15] Aquinas, *On the Eternity of the World*, 3.

[16] Aquinas, *On the Eternity of the World*, 5.

[17] Aquinas, *On the Eternity of the World*, 7.

[18] Aquinas, *On the Eternity of the World*, 10.

done so, without contradiction.[19] In reality, he did not, and a temporal beginning is fitting. God's end is his own goodness, and this end is eternally actualized, eternally achieved. Creation adds nothing. Yet the good is self-diffusive. God would diffuse his goodness to an eternal creation, yet the excess (*excessus*) of divine goodness is more apparent "by the fact that creatures have not been always," since that manifests that "all else beside him has him as the author of its being" (*SCG* 2.35). It is more strikingly good for God to diffuse his goodness to creatures that were, a moment before, airy nothings, than to diffuse his goodness to creatures that have accompanied him everlastingly. Philosophically, the debate is a draw. Revelation tips the balance toward a temporal beginning.

To come to this mediating position, Aquinas detaches the concept "creation" from the idea of a temporal beginning. God did not, but *might have*, created an eternal world, without beginning. It would still be a "creation" since it would depend on God for its existence:

> A creature does not have existence except from another; regarded as left simply to itself, it is nothing; prior to its existence, therefore, nothingness is its natural lot. Nor, just because nothing does not precede being in duration, does a thing have to be nothing and being at the same time. For our position is not that, if the creature

---

[19]Thomas consistently locates the cause of creation in God's will. In the *Summa theologiae* 1.46, he answers arguments against eternal creation. If you posit a cause, the objection goes, you posit its effect. When a cause does not have its effect, the cause is partial and needs a further cause to achieve its effect successfully. Since God is the sufficient, final, exemplar, and efficient cause of the world, and since he is eternal, so too the world. *Sed contra*: only God has been from eternity. Since God's will is the cause of things, their necessity does not lie in their being but in the will of God. The necessity of an effect depends on the necessity of its cause. There is no necessity for God to will any but himself, and so "there is no necessity for God to will and everlasting world." Instead, "the world exists just so long as God wills it to." *Summa Theologiae*, vol. 8: *Creation, Variety and Evil*, trans. Thomas Gilby (Cambridge: Cambridge University Press, 2006), 1.46.1.

has always existed, it was nothing at the same time. We maintain that its nature is such that it would be nothing if it were left to itself. We maintain that its nature is such that it would be nothing if it were left to itself.[20]

To be a creature, it is not necessary to originate in time. A creature is something that is wholly dependent on another for its existence, a something that would be nothing at all if left to itself. God would still be Creator even if he were the source of an everlasting creation, even if there were no "in the beginning." To be Creator is to be the Giver who calls not-beings into being. Creation is a *relation*, not a temporal act or a change.[21]

---

[20] Aquinas, *On the Eternity of the World*, 7. Does this adequately distinguish creatures? *Videtur non*: The Son is "from" the Father (as we have seen, the Son is *ab alio* and *esse receptum*). Without the Father's begetting, both Son and the Father would be nothing. Unbegotten by the Father, the Son would not be; if he did not beget the Son, the Father would not be Father, and so would not be. "It would be nothing if left to itself" applies to the triune persons as much as to creation. Once we work through the trinitarian logic, we discover that a temporal beginning is a *necessary* feature of the concept of "creation," if "creation" is to be distinguished from the triune Creator. Regarding the contrast between creation as "timeless relation" and creation as beginning, see Jenson, *Systematic Theology*, vol. 2: *The Works of God* (Oxford: Oxford University Press, 1999), 10-12.

[21] On creation as relation, see Bauerschmidt, *Thomas Aquinas*, 114-19. Bauerschmidt sees this separation of "creation" from "temporal beginning" as a purification (112), but it is odd that a concept can be purified by a theory (eternal creation) that is in fact false. Creation as *relatio* is set against creation as change or action. But to define "creation" as a *relatio*, Thomas must assume creation is instantaneous. In fact, he does not believe this to be the case, or at least he does not believe this is a necessary interpretation of the creation account. He produces his own Heptameron (*ST* 1.67-73) and disagrees with Augustine's conclusion that "there was not just one day." *Summa theologiae*, vol. 10: *Cosmogony*, trans. William Wallace (Cambridge: Cambridge University Press, 2006), 1.74.2. His disagreement is not strong, as he gives reasons in support of both Augustine's theory and his own. Yet the actions of the six days do not enter into his basic understanding what "creation" means. If his definition of creation were thoroughly Heptameranic, he would recognize change is part of the work of creation. For instance, on day three, *'elohim* commands the earth to bring forth vegetation, and it answers in obedience (Gen 1:11-12); on day five he summons the seas to teem with fish (Gen 1:20-22); and on day six he summons cattle, beasts, and creeping things from the earth (Gen 1:24-25). By Thomas's definition, these acts count as "change," since they involve the formation of particular things, not universal existence, and since they involve an actualization of the potency of earth and sea. Yet, in Genesis, these actions are under the general heading of "creation," for on day seven *'elohim* rests from all he "created and made"

Thomas is aware of theologians who appeal to God's eternity and simplicity to prove creation is eternal. By the axiom of simplicity, they claim, God cannot be in potency to create and then, at some logically or temporally distinct "moment," actively create. On Thomas's own premises, potency is reduced to act only by something higher and prior to the agent. Since there is none higher than God, since he is simple and utterly without potency, his act of creating must always be actualized. And if the act is eternally actualized, the effect must be eternally produced (SCG 2.32). Further, a sufficient cause must produce its effect. If the effect does not follow, there must be some defect in the cause. God is eternally the sufficient cause of creatures; otherwise, he would not be *in actu* but only *in potentia*. Since there is no defect in the divine cause, and no hindrance that would prevent God from creating, he must eternally produce his effects (SCG 2.32).

Thomas's responses to these lines of argument are revealing. To be sure, since God is simple, his understanding and willing "must be his act of making" (*suum intelligere et velle sit suum facere*) (SCG 2.35). But we must consider the character of intellect. It determines both the condition of a thing *and* its appropriate time, as "art determines not only that this thing is to be such and such, but that it is to be at this particular time" (SCG 2.35). God's single intellectual-voluntary act "was from eternity" yet "his effect was not from eternity, but from the time when he appointed from eternity" (SCG 2.35). God eternally wills to produce creatures "when the will has appointed the effect" (*quando voluntas effectum esse disponit*) (SCG 2.35). An eternal action need not have an eternal effect. God eternally wills to produce creatures at some suitable *now*.

(Gen 2:1). Thomas to the contrary, in Genesis, creation *does* involve what he calls "change." More on this in later chapters.

This is an almost adequate answer,[22] but Thomas elaborates by distinguishing natural and voluntary causation. An action of nature is determined by nature. If a *natural* cause exists, so must the effect. But the will is not determined by nature or existence but by intention: It "acts not according to the mode of its being, but according to the mode of its purpose" (*non secundum sui esse, sed secundum modem sui propositi*) (*SCG* 2.35). A temporal creation makes it manifest that "his power is not constrained to produce these effects as nature is to natural effects." Rather, his power to produce creation is a voluntary one, and in creating a temporal world, he demonstrates that "he is a voluntary and intelligent agent" (*quod est voluntate agens et intelligens*) (*SCG* 2.35). A temporal creation is suitable because it testifies God's freedom from natural determination. It witnesses to the sovereignty of God's *will*.

Thomas's distinction of nature and will is sensible to some degree. God does not create with the same involuntary inevitability as a pear tree that produces pears. He is not Plotinus's One who merely overflows into multiplicity. His divine nature does not compel him in any way. He *wills* to create. Yet two problems arise, and they are devastating. First, Thomas violates his own premises about divine simplicity. Thomas has insisted God is his *esse*, which is identical to his will, intellect, and action. Yet it is somehow possible for God to act "not according to his being" (*non secundum sui esse*) but according to the intention of his will (*voluntas*).[23] The force of the argument, the force of Thomas's

---

[22]Not entirely adequate because it abstracts "creation" from the biblical account of creation. Suppose God eternally wills to bring the world into existence on a spring afternoon in what will eventually be recognized as 4004 BC. If God created the world as Genesis 1 describes, then on that spring afternoon, determined from eternity, he *spoke* "Let there be light." This may not reflect a new will, but it *is* a new *operum ad extra*. On his premises, if he does not acknowledge the novelty of the action, Thomas is still unable to escape the conclusion that the world is eternal.

[23]Antonio Rosmini runs into a similar contradiction. In creating, the divine mind, he says, "takes from itself (one absolute object) all the types it wishes, not by different acts but by one, most simple act. These types, relative to the divine mind, are the

own convictions about simplicity, push him toward the conclusion that creation is eternal. Based on revelation, he believes
creation has a temporal beginning. So he fudges simplicity at the
last minute to squeeze Genesis 1 into a divine metaphysics constructed *without* Genesis 1. He adjusts an ontology of noncreation
to accommodate a biblical creation. Instead of carrying through
on the logic of his premises, he—happily—blinks.

Then, more seriously, there is the nature of the fudge. To
defend the biblical truth that creation has a temporal beginning,
Thomas detaches the will of God from the being of God. Divine
will floats free, and God now has two modes of acting, one "according to the mode of his being" and another "according to the
mode of his purpose."[24] Loosening the identity of *esse* and will
opens a window for voluntarism.[25] Though Thomas is no voluntarist, his arguments against an eternal creation undermine the
credibility of his claim to be the poster boy of intellectualism. And
the note of voluntarism is fatal: The history and order of creation

---

finalization of its one act. Outside the divine mind, they are real entia, each with a
relative existence to itself." *Theosophy*, vol. 3: *Trine Being (Contd.)* (Durham, NC: Rosmini House, 2011), 163, par. 1309. But how can a simple divine mind *not* wish whatever it wishes?

[24]Thomas's use of "*modum*" may signal his awareness of the problem. He does not
distinguish action "according to *esse*" from action "according to *voluntas*," but distinguishes action in different "modes." Yet the result is the same. System-saving
distinctions are always tenuous and implausible. Trotting out "mode" to protect the
system does *not* protect the system.

[25]Elsewhere, Thomas draws an analogy between the effect of a natural cause and the
effect of a voluntary cause. An effect from the first follows according to the mode of
its form, so "an effect of a cause that acts through will follows from it according to
a form that is preconceived and defined." God is the sufficient cause of the world
from all eternity, yet "this does not demand our postulating that the world made by
him is any other than as it is in the predetermination of his will." He willed it to have
"existence after non-existence," and that eternal will has been realized, with no
additional willing or action needed to catalyze the emanation of the actual creation
(*ST* 1.46.1). Thomas appears to be both a direct and indirect source for voluntarism:
Direct, in that he detaches *voluntas* from *esse* at crucial points; indirectly, insofar as
his predominant intellectualism sparked a voluntarist reaction. On the direct link,
see Wolfhart Pannenberg, *Systematic Theology*, trans. Geoffrey Bromiley (London:
T&T Clark, 2004), 2:148-49.

seem arbitrary, rather than rooted in and reflecting the being of the triune God. As will floats free of *esse*, so economy drifts away from theology, nature from supernature, created existence from union with God.[26]

FREE WILL?

The other relevant thread of argument arises in Thomas's discussion of God's willing in *Summa theologiae* 1.19.2-3.[27] Here the question is not the eternity of the world but its *necessity*. It is again a question of theology proper: Given God's simple *esse*, is creation inevitable?

The first article asks whether God is capable of willing things other than himself. Thomas, of course, believes he is. It is one of his most basic convictions. All things are good, and good things have a natural tendency not only to maintain and attain good but to spread and diffuse it, so as to reproduce their likeness. If the best of created natures shares the good they are, how much more

---

[26]Tyler Wittman's explanation of Thomas's argument ends in the same place. According to Wittman, Thomas "circumvents" the problem by distinguishing two "logical moments," one involving a consideration of God's will in abstraction from the negative conditioning of simplicity, and then a second moment where simplicity is reintroduced. But the first moment undermines the absoluteness of simplicity, and in so doing loosens the tether that binds God's being and his will; see *God and Creation in Thomas Aquinas and Karl Barth* (Cambridge: Cambridge University Press, 2018), 86-88. So too Anton C. Pegis, *Saint Thomas and the Greeks* (Milwaukee, WI: Marquette University Press, 1939), 52-59. God's perfection as Being means that the universe is radially contingent: "It has no compelling reason for existing and God is driven by no intrinsically compelling reason to produce it." Creation is thus "infinitely imperfect." No created order has a greater claim on God than any other: "All possible worlds are—possible worlds." God acts through his free will, not by a compulsion of nature. From these premises, Thomas can explain how the one, simple God can immediately create a world of multiplicity, without positing any Plotinian or Avicennian mediating principles of beings. God makes a multiple world because he chooses to display the array of his glory. To say otherwise is to limit the power of God to act as he pleases. But this implies a voluntarist gap between God's being and will that belies simplicity, and also implies that creation is arbitrarily related to God's being.

[27]St. Thomas Aquinas, *Summa theologiae*, vol. 5: *God's Will and Providence*, trans. Thomas Gilby (Cambridge: Cambridge University Press, 2006).

is it fitting for God to share his infinite goodness by making a creation as like himself as possible. He wills his goodness as end, and his willing of other beings is folded into that more ultimate and necessary end. His will is moved only by the will to be the goodness he eternally is. As he knows other things in knowing himself, so he wills other things in willing his own goodness (*ST* 1.19.2).

The momentum of this argument is toward the conclusion that, given God's *esse*, creation is inevitable. If natural things at the "highest pitch" diffuse the good they are, and if this "especially" pertains to the divine goodness, and if there is no obstacle to God diffusing his goodness (as there certainly is not), then surely creation follows from the nature of God. God is under no compulsion to create. Yet, given the Goodness he is, he *will* create.

Thomas recognizes the pressure of the argument and follows with a further article demonstrating the freedom of God's will (*ST* 1.19.3). To prove that God is not bound to will what he wills, Thomas introduces a distinction between absolute and hypothetical or "suppositional" necessity.[28] Absolute necessity is true or real by definition: it is necessary, absolutely, that Bart

---

[28]Contemporary theologians replicate Thomas's line of argument. According to Steven Duby, "The faculty of willing in God does not differ from the act of willing as though God could shift from passive potency to act." But this faculty/act has "a twofold object," God as infinite good and created things other than God as recipients of his good (Duby, *Divine Simplicity*, 196). For James Dolezal too, the final end of God's will is always God himself. So God wills and God is also the object of his willing. Willer, will, act of willing are identical. But there is a trick here, since Dolezal speaks of an *ultimate* end, when the question is really about the relation between God's will and the *contingent* things of creation. He introduces Thomas's distinction between "absolutely necessity" in God's will of himself and "suppositional necessity" in willing other things. As Thomas says, God's willing of other things "is not necessary considered absolutely, because the will of God does not have a necessary relation to this willed object." *God Without Parts: Divine Simplicity and the Metaphysics of God's Absoluteness* (Eugene, OR: Pickwick, 2011), 206. Though God's will and wisdom are identical, this does not mean he cannot do otherwise: It is not the case that "the divine wisdom should be restricted to this present order of things." Thomas concludes, "we must simply say that God can do other things than those he has done" (208). Dolezal concludes that God is both free and simple, though we cannot

the bachelor be unmarried. Hypothetical necessity pertains when something is in fact the case. It is not absolutely necessary that Socrates be sitting; he could be standing or walking to the Piraeus or drinking hemlock. But if he *is* sitting, it is hypothetically necessary.

Armed with this distinction, Thomas can clarify the relation between God's willing of himself and his willing of creatures. Willing an end (divine goodness) is not the same as willing the things that lead to that end (diffusion of divine goodness to creatures). The end may be willed absolutely, while the means are willed hypothetically. It is not absolutely necessary, for instance, that I board a boat to cross the ocean, if there are other ways for me to make the crossing. Once I have made the decision to travel by sea, all the requirements of a sea voyage become necessary—a boat, sails or a motor, provisions, etc. Similarly, God wills other things to the end that they might share his goodness, but they are not a necessary means for the attainment of God's absolute will, for he would enjoy his own goodness with or without creatures. Creatures are hypothetically necessary. God need not create. But, given that God *does* will to create, creatures cannot be unwilled, because the will of God is immutable (*ST* 1.19.3).

Cracks are evident on the surface of the argument. For starters, the distinction between absolute and hypothetical necessity introduces a complexity in God's will that compromises his utter simplicity. It will not do to say this is only a distinction from our vantage point. If hypothetical and absolute necessity are identical in God, Thomas has not escaped the objection. Nor does Thomas have an escape hatch with his journey analogy, for there is no evident way for God to attain the excess good of diffusing his goodness to others than by creating others to be beneficiaries of

---

understand how. His own argument backs himself into a corner and he calls time out with an appeal to mystery. This is, I suggest, another fudge.

said diffusion. God would be his goodness without creating, but how could he *diffuse* his goodness without creatures?

The cracks become wider as he answers the objections. In response to the argument that God must be whatever is natural to him, Thomas distinguishes those things God is bound to will by nature from those he wills voluntarily (*non ex necessitate vult, neque tamen innaturale, aut contra naturam, sed est voluntarium*; *ST* 1.19.3). Once again, God's will is unmoored from God's nature, no longer simply identical with his knowing and being. To the argument that God is bound to will what he wills because will is identical to the *esse* that he is, Thomas punts, now using his subtle knife to separate knowledge and will. Divine knowing has a necessary relation to things known, but the same cannot be said of the relation of divine will to things willed. God knows all things as they exist in him; he knows things other than himself through himself, by knowing the ways other things may participate in him. Knowledge thus has absolute necessity. But since created things need not exist in themselves, the will that they exist has only a hypothetical necessity.

Thomas does the same dance here that he does on the question of the eternity of the world. He offers arguments concerning the goodness of God that imply creation is inevitable, then he loosens simplicity to ensure God retains the freedom to have acted otherwise than he did. He introduces distinctions to ease tensions and contradictions, but they function merely as system-saving distinctions, without any extrasystematic reality.

Thomas appears to take God's freedom to create or not as axiomatic, as part of the Christian definition of Creator, and adjusts his theology accordingly. He flexes and stretches concepts to make room for what he knows to be true—namely, that God is not in any way constrained in creating. Yet, in the end, Thomas answers the question, "Can a simple God create?" by dancing away from simplicity in order to flirt with voluntarism.

Thomas is left with the quandary he started with. Either God *must* create because he is his eternal act of creating, in which case he undermines God's freedom to create or not and his freedom to create otherwise. Or God *cannot* create because creation requires the actualization of some potency (at least the actualization of a potency for his will to create to terminate in an actual creation), and the simple God is always already fully actualized, whether or not creation exists. He does not resolve the dilemmas he poses. Instead, his attempted solutions make matters quite a bit worse. To put it starkly: Thomas's doctrine of God cannot get past the first verse of the Bible before slamming into incoherence. Something has gone wrong.

To my mind, the most promising pathway out of the quandary is Thomas's category of "hypothetical necessity," which I will put to use below. For now, however, I examine a second answer to the problem of the freedom of God's act of creation—that of Sergius Bulgakov.

THE ABSOLUTE AND THE ABSOLUTE-RELATIVE

From one angle, Russian Orthodox theologian and philosopher Sergius Bulgakov accepts the force of Thomas's arguments for an inevitable creation.[29] According to David Bentley Hart, Bulgakov "succeeded in describing a genuine and seamless consonance between the claims Christianity makes regarding, on the one hand, the immanent and infinitely sufficient divine life and, on the other hand, the contingency and gratuity of the economy of creation and salvation," while remaining "cognizant of the metaphysical and theological difficulties this poses."[30] At the baseline, this

---

[29]On Bulgakov's theology of creation, see Brandon Gallaher, *Freedom and Necessity in Modern Trinitarian Theology* (Oxford: Oxford University Press, 2016), 95-114.

[30]David Bentley Hart, *Theological Territories: A David Bentley Hart Digest* (Notre Dame, IN: Notre Dame University Press, 2020), 58.

means that the order (*taxis*) of the economic Trinity must be identical to the *taxis* of the immanent Trinity. Moreover, Hart says,
Bulgakov recognizes that "any hint of arbitrariness" in the relation between God and creation is disastrous, both for our understanding of God and for our understanding of creation. If creation
is arbitrarily related to the eternal essence of God, and if God is
understood as choosing among various possible worlds, God is reduced to a "god." Instead of being fully actualized, this "godlet" goes
shopping at a Cosmic Costco of Possible Worlds. In Hart's view,
Thomas's quasi-voluntarism leaves God making choices and operating in the same "ontic" realm as other beings.[31]

If Bulgakov partly agrees with Thomas, he eventually diverges
in dramatic fashion. God is, Bulgakov writes, "absolute in His
proper, divine life, and He does not need the world for Himself."
The creation or noncreation of the universe "is not a hypostatic
or natural necessity of self-completion." On the contrary, God's
"trihypostatizedness fully exhausts the hypostatic self-definition
and closes its circle." With regard to "the life of Divinity *itself*,
the world did not have to be." Creation is not the work of God "in
His hypostatic nature, but in His creative freedom." Yet this is
not to say that creation is not necessary "in some other sense."
Nor does it imply that God "could have not created the world."
On the contrary, "God *needs* the world" and "it could not have
remained uncreated."[32]

---

[31]This is why, Hart argues, Maximus the Confessor denied God possesses a "gnomic"
will that deliberates between choices. If he does, he is not the transcendent source
of all things, but "a" being whose actions "reduce potency to act," just as we do. On
this model, it is even possible to imagine a "god" prior to the Trinity, a god who
chooses to be triune. This theory is not hypothetical: Schelling proposed the existence of an *Urgrund*, an "abyssal freedom" from which the Trinity emerges (*Theological Territories*, 58-59). Jennifer Newsome Martin summarizes Bulgakov's critique of
Schelling in *Hans Urs von Balthasar and the Critical Appropriation of Russian Religious
Thought* (Notre Dame, IN: University of Notre Dame Press, 2015), 171-90.

[32]Sergius Bulgakov, *Lamb of God*, trans. Boris Jakim (Grand Rapids, MI: Eerdmans,
2008), 119-20.

Bulgakov makes these assertions in successive paragraphs. How can it be true both that God "does not need the world for Himself" and that "God *needs* the world"? The answer is in the phrase "for Himself." God does not need the world for his own self-completion. He is fully himself in the perfect triune communion. Creation is a free act because there is no "determinate necessity for Him as a need of Him to develop or complete Himself." Yet the freedom of God is the freedom of love, and love has its own modes of "necessity." God is love, and "it is proper for love to love and to expand in love." Were the love of God confined to the absoluteness of his own triune being, absoluteness would be turned into a "limit of self-love or self-affirmation." God's absoluteness is so utterly absolute that he can extend his love beyond his own limits to love what is other than himself.[33]

It is thus "proper for the ocean of Divine love to overflow its limits," and it would be *improper* for God "not to actualize this possibility," for it is the nature of love to exhaust "to the end all the possibilities of love." If creation were impossible, then there would be a limit on God; if creation is possible, "God's love could not fail to actualize it by creating the world." In short, "God-Love *needs* the creation of the world in order to *love*, no longer only in His own life, but also outside of Himself, in creation." While God's love is fully satiated in himself, yet it has, paradoxically, a kind of "insatiability," by which God "goes out of Himself toward creation, in order to love, outside Himself, not-Himself." God's love is not "limited by His Divinity." The "world could not fail to be created," and yet it is a free act, not bound to any natural necessity but "necessary with the necessity of love, which cannot *not* love." God's love "realizes in itself the identity and indistinguishability of freedom and necessity."[34] There is a

---

[33]Bulgakov, *Lamb of God*, 120.
[34]Bulgakov, *Lamb of God*, 120, emphasis in original.

"self-bifurcation" in the Absolute, as it takes up the relative into itself. The Absolute sacrifices its absoluteness without losing it. Indeed, the Absolute manifests its utter Absoluteness by its capacity to sacrifice and yet retain it, nothing lost. Creation is a metaphysical Golgotha, rooted as it is in the same selfless and self-giving love as the cross.[35]

Given the nonarbitrariness of creation, God's relation to creation is "part of the fullness of the concept of God. Creation cannot be eliminated from this concept as something accidental and inessential, as something that could exist or not exist. It is impossible for it not to exist."[36] Though we may speak of an "Absolute" unrelated to creation, this is only "a conventional abstraction, in which one examines the essence of God." Concretely, "the Absolute simply does not exist, for relation to the world and being for the world belong to the being of God and are inseparable from Him." "God" is a relational term, describing the relation of the Absolute to the world; yet "*the Absolute is God*," and "can be understood only in relation to the world." For the sake of God's grandeur, it is not enough for God to be Absolute, "self-enclosed and all-exclusive." It is "proper for Him to be God, that is, the Absolute-relative, a self-revealing Mystery that the language of logic can express only by an antinomy."[37]

Creation is a union of the Absolute with nothing, the placing of the Absolute in the nothing from which creation was made. Because the Absolute comes into relation to the world as God, the act of creation establishes the reality of God *in process*. Bulgakov puts it dramatically: "In creating the world God thereby flings himself into creation; he seemingly makes himself the creation.

---

[35]Sergius Bulgakov, *Unfading Light: Contemplations and Speculations*, trans. Thomas Allan Smith (Grand Rapids, MI: Eerdmans, 2012), 184-85.
[36]Bulgakov, *Lamb of God*, 121.
[37]Bulgakov, *Lamb of God*, 121.

God is drained into nothing, as he converts it into material for his image and likeness. He gives it full freedom of actualization in creatures, while he himself becomes potential. Ignorant of envy, he wants to live in creatures and *become* in them."[38]

Creation is thus the site of "the maximum cosmological antinomy." The Absolute God who is the fullness of life, to whom nothing can be added, who is unchanging and without need, yet is also Creator who "lives and acts in the world." Because creation is "real by the realness of its Creator," we can say, "God himself becomes in the world and through the world." With regard to himself, God is eternally complete; in regard to the world "God is not complete insofar as the world is not complete." He is not absolute in regard to the world, for he is not yet "all in all," as he will be. Creation's history is not merely cosmogonic but *theogonic*.[39]

Though a relation to the world is essential to a concrete concept of God, the relation is not pantheistic: "The boundary between the Creator and the creation must be preserved unconditionally." If all is God, then there is no divinity. Yet, on the other hand, we cannot reduce the world "solely to an accident inwardly unconnected with God." To "magnify Divinity at the expense of the world" is to "impoverish Divine love." Creation cannot surmount the boundary between Creator and creature, but *God* can, and, in a sense, he *must*. If he were *merely* absolute, "He would be the absolute that does not exist for anything outside itself." But this would amount to saying he does not exist at all, since "to exist is to be for another." As God, he is "the Absolute existing for another—precisely for the world." And thus the "other of Divinity is included in the depths of the divine life" in a panentheism in which "all is in God or for God." To place himself in "extradivine

---

[38]Bulgakov, *Unfading Light*, 196.
[39]Bulgakov, *Unfading Light*, 196-97.

being" is to "repeat Himself, as it were." To extend himself beyond himself is an expression of his omnipotence.[40]

Like Thomas, Bulgakov sees creation as a "pre-eternal creative act": "For Him the act of creation is just as immanent as His divinity." But Bulgakov immediately places this in the context of trinitarian love. An absolute that is not Trinity "can remain alone, enjoying itself in the boundlessness of its egotism." But the trihypostatic (tripersonal) God of Love is not an egotist, and so "For God and in God, His creative activity is just as eternal as His being, as the Holy Trinity itself in its Wisdom." The creation begins, but "*only for the world*; it does not begin for God." The triune God's creative activity "is temporal for itself, it is eternal for God."[41]

While "the Absolute need have no relations," yet the Absolute is God the Creator, and "God can only be understood not in himself alone, but in his relation with the world as well. If God were simply the Absolute, all our theology would be negative theology, saying what God is not. But God is not just the Absolute. He is God, related by his love to the world." Theology can thus be affirmative.[42]

According to Hart, Bulgakov thinks of "creation as a free act falling entirely within the dynamism of the divine life, without . . . compromising divine freedom or creaturely autonomy." He does this in part by positing an "*Ur-kenosis*" within the triune life, a divine self-emptying that constitutes the persons as persons. The Trinity exists as "infinite donation and surrender . . . infinite receiving that is also the eternal constitution of the giver . . .

---

[40]Bulgakov, *Lamb of God*, 121-22.

[41]Bulgakov, *Lamb of God*, 122-23.

[42]Aidan Nichols, "Wisdom from Above? The Sophiology of Father Sergius Bulgakov," *New Blackfriars* (2004): 610. Of course, if God were merely Absolute, theology would be *hyper*-negative, because there would be no theology at all—apart from the knowledge God has of himself.

infinite out-pouring in the other that is the eternal being of God."[43] Because *kenosis* is the essence of divine life, God is not altered by the historical kenosis of the incarnation and cross. Jesus simply *is* God's eternal self-emptying love at work within creation.

SOPHIA

Bulgakov proposes a paradox: As Absolute, God does not need creation for his own self-fulfillment. Yet the triune God is love, and love seeks to extend itself outside itself; as love, he needs creation. He could leave the paradox standing, but instead pursues a resolution. Bulgakov affirms divine simplicity, but for Bulgakov simplicity characterizes the Absolute. He is faced with a version of the dilemma Thomas faces: How does he make the transition from a simple "Absolute" to the "Absolute-relative" that is "God"?

Unlike Thomas, Bulgakov resolves the dilemma by calling a new character onto the stage, "Sophia."[44] He begins his portrayal of Sophia with a consideration of created spirit. Personal spirit is not enclosed in itself but "open for the world; and the world thereby becomes the precondition of the personal spirit as living personality." Person and the world exist in a perichoretic intertwining: Nature is the "not-I that enters into I and lives in it." Created spirit is conditioned by nonspirit.[45]

Analogously, God too exists within a world, the "Divine world in God," which is the nature or common *ousia* of the triune God. Some theologians deny the existence of divine *ousia* "by itself" because they fear it will diminish God's personal character. Bulgakov has the opposite worry. Denying or downplaying the existence of Divinity "impoverishes His being . . . reducing it to

---

[43]Hart, *Theological Territories*, 59.

[44]For background on the development of Sophiology, see Robert F. Slesinski, *The Theology of Sergius Bulgakov* (Yonkers, NY: St. Vladimir's Seminary Press, 2017), 45-47.

[45]Bulgakov, *Lamb of God*, 90-91.

abstract personal consciousness," a purely subjective interplay of persons without objective ontological weight. Though the divine *ousia* "exists only personally," yet it is *not* personal only. Thus, "in God there is not only a Person (and Persons) but also Divinity, which is not a personality, although it belongs to a Person (and Persons) and is totally hypostatized." Divinity is "both personal and impersonal," personal in that it is personalized in the persons, impersonal "by itself."[46]

Bulgakov is not satisfied with the way theologians have handled the one divinity of God. "Substance" (*ousia*) has typically been interpreted "purely as a philosophical abstraction," a concept brought in "to achieve a logical solution of the trinitarian dogma."[47] The creedal confession that the persons are consubstantial is separated from religious experience, shrunk to a piece of impenetrable theological verbiage. Bulgakov turns to Scripture for a richer account. Though the Bible "never alludes to the abstract concept of substance," yet it "does give us revealed teaching on the life of the triune God." The Bible describes not only the persons but their common "glory," and mysteriously refers to a feminine principle of "wisdom." Bulgakov follows these clues to formulate a theology of the *ousia*.[48]

Drawing on German idealism,[49] Bulgakov claims Sophia must be understood not as a set of discrete items, but in its "interior

---

[46]Bulgakov, *Lamb of God*, 101, 103.

[47]Sergius Bulgakov, *Sophia, The Wisdom of God: An Outline of Sophiology* (Hudson, NY: Lindisfarne, 1993), 25.

[48]Bulgakov, *Sophia*, 25. Bulgakov appeals to the biblical notion of glory, which is "not God, but divinity" in offering a biblical rationale for his concept of Sophia (30). Meredith Kline's claim that glory is the visible effulgence of the Spirit is biblically more plausible and far less speculative. See his *Images of the Spirit* (repr., Eugene, OR: Wipf & Stock, 1999).

[49]Bulgakov is influenced by this tradition, yet also sharply critical of it. His most extensive treatment in English is found in *The Tragedy of Philosophy: Philosophy and Dogma*, trans. Stephen Churchyard (Brooklyn, NY: Angelico, 2020), 24-51 and Excurses I and III (on Kant and Fichte).

organic integrity," as an "All-Unity." Wisdom is not "just one divine property among many" but "the foundation of all divine properties" and "the divine nature as containing that All-Unity which is the content of the life of God." This includes all "properties of the divine nature" as well as "the archetypes of all created things." Sophia is thus "the divine 'world' where God lives as the Holy Trinity. It is the divine life."[50]

Sophia is the content of divine life, the "property of all properties," and "the All as unity and unity as All." Divine nature is not just the life of the persons but the "absolute content of the . . . divine life, with all its properties." But Sophia is not abstract, a mere set of properties. She is "nothing other than God's nature, His *ousia*," both as the "power and depth" of God and as the "self-revealing content" of God. Sophia is both the "closed depths, the source of life," as well as "the open depths, life itself." Source and life are identical, "even as Ousia and Sophia are identical." Far from being an abstraction or mere concept, Sophia is an "*ens realissimum*." Bulgakov goes so far as to say "God is Sophia; Sophia is Divine," but he adds that the statements are not reversible: Sophia is not "the God," but "only *theos* or *Theos*."[51] She is "the Pleroma, the Divine world, existent in God and for God, eternal and uncreated, in which God lives in the Holy Trinity." As such, she contains all the Trinity reveals about itself in itself: "It is the Image of God in God Himself, the self-Icon of Divinity."[52] She is the content and life of the trihypostatic God without *being* the trihypostatic God.

Sophia has quasi-personal qualities. She loves and is loved. To say "God is Sophia" is to say that "God, hypostatic love, loves Sophia, and that she loves God with an answering, though not

---

[50]Nichols, "Wisdom from Above?," 608.
[51]Bulgakov, *Lamb of God*, 103.
[52]Bulgakov, *Lamb of God*, 103.

hypostatic love." She does not merely "belong to God" but "*is* God" and "*loves* the trihypostatic God."[53] Love is what binds the persons and also what binds Sophia to the persons, as the principle of coherence and harmony among the archetypes contained within Sophia. This raises a problem: Sophia is not a "someone," so how can Sophia love the trihypostatic God? Nichols suggests Bulgakov uses "love" in a "non-strict sense." The divine ideas internal to Sophia harmonize into an All-Unity, and "harmony is a sign of love." Further, Sophia exists "through giving itself to the divine persons, yielding itself up to be drawn into their personal life," all of which are "the terms of love," specifically "feminine metaphors." Sophia has the character of "bride more than the bridegroom."[54]

Sophia is the entity who allows Bulgakov to bridge the gap between the Absolute and the Absolute-relative. Sophia provides the "sufficient basis" for creation, which means creation is marked by "sophianity." While the trihypostatic God of Love is a "closed, self-sufficient, eternal act of Divine, substantial Love," this love exteriorizes itself. The object of that love is "not only an abstract idea or a dead mirror" but "a living essence, having person, hypostasis"—in a word, Sophia.[55] Because Sophia exists as the object of triune love, that love eternally moves out from the triphypostatic communion of persons. When love moves out in creating the world, Sophia remains the object of that love. Given her ambiguous ontological status, Sophia can have a foot on either side of the Creator-creature divide.

Sophia allows Bulgakov to say creation is not arbitrary, a sheer manifestation of power. Such an idea is blasphemous. God made the world through *Wisdom*—so says Proverbs. And for Bulgakov,

---

[53]Bulgakov, *Lamb of God*, 105.
[54]Nichols, "Wisdom from Above?," 608-9.
[55]Bulgakov, *Unfading Light*, 217.

Wisdom is neither an attribute nor a divine person. To say God made the world in Wisdom is to say "the pre-existent content of divine Wisdom begins to exist outside God, in time, as well as within him, in eternity."[56] As Bulgakov puts it, creation "consists in the fact that God has put forward his own divine world [Sophia] not now as a world existing eternally but as a world in becoming." As it descends from the Absolute to creation, the All-Unity of Sophia proliferates as an "all-multiplicity."[57] Sophia holds the world close to God, and God to the world: There are not two wisdoms, but "one wisdom in two modalities, Uncreated and created."[58] Though there is an "infinite difference" between the divine world and creation, yet "the All in the Divine World, in the Divine Sophia, and the All in the creaturely world, in the creaturely Sophia, are one and identical in content (though not in being). *One and the same Sophia is revealed in God and in creation.*"[59]

For Bulgakov, then, it is possible to say "God created the world out of Himself, out of His essence," by establishing "His proper divine world not as an eternally existing world but as a *becoming* world." This is the positive meaning of creation *ex nihilo*. Sophia alone can accomplish this. The Absolute cannot itself be immersed in creation. The Absolute becomes Absolute-relative, God the Creator, through the mediation of Sophia. Though divine, she is distinct from the divine persons, and therefore is capable of entering "in becoming as another form of being" while remaining "one and the same divine world." In creation, the divine world potentializes into something extradivine, being "submerged in and modified by nonbeing" but also "liberating itself from nonbeing."[60] Once again, this depends on the mediating

---

[56]Nichols, "Wisdom from Above?" 611.
[57]Bulgakov, *Lamb of God*, 127.
[58]Nichols, "Wisdom from Above?," 612.
[59]Bulgakov, *Lamb of God*, 126.
[60]Bulgakov, *Lamb of God*, 126.

ontological position of Sophia, divine yet not identical to the tri-hypostatic person that is God. The triune God cannot be "potentialized." Sophia can and is.

Initially, the Wisdom of God is present merely as the world's potential, a pledge of a sophianic future. Through time, the world moves toward a "fullness of created Wisdom" and "a perfect reflection of the uncreated Wisdom."[61] In the end, creation will reflect "the countenance of the Divine Sophia."[62] Uncreated Sophia will one day be manifested as creation adorned as a bride for the Lamb. Creation's development toward this fulfillment is the "germination of the divine seeds of being in the soil of non-being," which is to say, "the actualization of divine prototypes, of the divine Sophia in the creaturely." In the beginning, they are only seeds, and they come to full fruit because Sophia travels the road of becoming along with creation, now in a state of potentiality but also as "the principle of its actualization and finality."[63] Sophia is the Alpha and Omega of creation, the principle of creation's origin and its eventual divinization.

For Bulgakov, Sophia is a solution to various theological dilemmas.[64] Sophia mediates between the Absolute and the Creator, divine person and divine person, between God and creation, between creation's initial and final state. Yet Sophia's very pervasiveness and plasticity creates problems for Bulgakov. At various points, Bulgakov insists that Sophia is not a fourth hypostasis because she is not a hypostasis at all.[65] But his descriptions of Sophia belie his insistence. Sophia loves and is the object of love, albeit in a nonstrict sense; she is hypostasis even if she is not *an*

---

[61]Nichols, "Wisdom from Above?," 612.

[62]Bulgakov, *Lamb of God*, 127.

[63]Bulgakov, *Sophia*, 75.

[64]Gallaher calls her "a conceptual panacea for all number of philosophical and theological ills" (*Freedom and Necessity*, 54).

[65]Bulgakov, *Sophia*, 35.

hypostasis; she is alive and a most-real *ens*. Bulgakov rejects the idea of a fourth hypostasis on dogmatic grounds, but his denials are sheer dogmatic assertions. Everything he says about Sophia suggests a hypostasis; despite all appearances to the contrary, he declares, she is *not*. We will be excused if we kick a rock and say, "If it acts like a hypostasis, quacks like a hypostasis . . ."[66]

---

[66]In classic Orthodox theology, the divine energies play much the same role as Sophia. Gregory Palamas appeals to the distinction of essence and energies in order to untie the knots surrounding creation. Essence and energies are equiprimordial. *The Triads*, ed. John Meyendorff; trans. Nicholas Gendle (Mahwah, NJ: Paulist, 1983), 3.2.5. Some *works* of God are equally without beginning. Providence needed to exist before creation, "so as to cause each of the created things to come to be in time, out of nonbeing." Divine knowledge existed before the choice of creating (3.2.6). Thus, as Maximus says, "Existence, life, holiness and virtue are works of God that do not have a beginning in time" (3.2.7). Yet, neither the energies nor the works are identical to the ineffable, unknowable essence. They "inhere" in the essence, as "powers of the senses in what is called the common spiritual sense of the soul" (3.2.5). God is everywhere, containing all and not contained by anything, yet "it does not follow that the Divine Nature consists in the fact of being everywhere, any more than our own nature uniquely consists in being somewhere" (3.2.9). Though we name God from his energies, "he transcends all of them." These energies are able to "provide him with a name and manifest him entirely" only because of the "indivisible and supernatural simplicity" of the essence (3.2.7). There are also energies "which have a beginning and an end." Though all are uncreated, "not all are without beginning." This applies specifically to the energies and acts of creation. To these "beginning and end must be ascribed, if not to the creative power itself, then at least to its activity," which is directed toward created things. Otherwise, how would God be said to rest from his work? (3.2.8). Recently, David Bradshaw has proposed the essence/energies distinction as an alternative to Augustinian and Thomist divine simplicity (*Aristotle East and West*, 221-62). Bradshaw affirms divine simplicity, but the energies give him flexibility to avoid Thomist aporias (*Aristotle East and West*, 81-82). As Matthew Levering says, "The uncreated energies make possible a certain kind of divine change." *Engaging the Doctrine of Creation: Cosmos, Creatures, and the Wise and Good Creator* (Grand Rapids, MI: Baker Academic, 2017), 79. Bradshaw offers biblical support for the distinction by pointing to the glory revealed to Moses on Sinai, the glory that, like Bulgakov's Sophia, "both is and is not God" in "The Divine Glory and the Divine Energies," *Faith and Philosophy* 23, no. 3 (2006): 279-98. For a defense of Palamas, see Eric Perl, "St. Gregory Palamas and the Metaphysics of Creation," *Dionysius* 14 (1990): 105-30. David Bentley Hart questions the import of the essence-energies distinction: "I am not at all convinced that Palamas ever intended to suggest a *real* distinction between God's essence and energies; nor am I even confident that the energies should be seen as anything other than sanctifying grace by which the Holy Spirit makes the Trinity really present to creatures. I take the distinction to mean only that God's transcendence is such that he is free to be the God he is even in the realm of creaturely finitude, without estrangement from himself and without the creature being

Like Thomas, Bulgakov's theology is overshadowed by the un-related, simple Absolute. Unlike Thomas, he tries to dispel the shadow by positing a mediating reality, Sophia, who fills the gap between the Absolute and creation and so enables the Absolute to "become" God. Because of his prior commitment to the Absolute who is not-yet-Creator, he feels the need to explain the conditions of possibility for creation. All the necessary ontological flexibility is lodged in Sophia since in himself the Absolute cannot "become" anything. The Absolute wishes to summon the nothing toward its own love. As Love, Divinity "wants the not-itself, the non-Divinity," and goes out of itself in the condescension of creation. In order to achieve this, Divinity establishes a boundary or "border" between God and world that is "itself neither the one nor the other but something completely particular, simultaneously uniting and separating the one and the other." With a nod to Pla-tonic *metaxu*, in-betweenness, Bulgakov identifies this between

admitted thus to an unmediated vision of the divine essence." *Beauty of the Infinite: The Aesthetics of Christian Truth* (Grand Rapids, MI: Eerdmans, 2004), 204. On Gregory's use of the Dionysian concept of an "inferior Deity," see Theodoros Alexo-poulos, "The Problem of the Distinction between Essence and Energies in the He-sychast Controversy. Saint Gregory Palamas' *Epistula III*: The Version Published by P. Chrestou in Light of Palamas' Other Works on the Divine Energies," *Studia Pa-tristica* 96 (2017): 521-33. Aristotle Papankolaou, "Divine Energies or Divine Per-sonhood: Vladimir Lossky and John Zizioulas on Conceiving the Transcendent and Immanent God," *Modern Theology* 19, no. 3 (2003): 357-85, approves Zizioulas for subordinating the energies to the hypostases. Roy Clouser finds continuity between Orthodoxy and Reformation theology, over against the "AAA" tradition of absolute simplicity found in Augustine, Anselm, and Aquinas; Clouser, "Pancreation Lost: The Fall of Theology," in *Divine Essence and Divine Energies: Ecumenical Reflections on the Presence of God in Eastern Orthodoxy*, ed. C. Athanasopoulos and C. Schneider (Cambridge: James Clarke, 2013), 68-95. John Milbank (same volume, 158-209) argues that the Christian confession of creation *ex nihilo* and the Trinity made "me-diation ultimate and pertaining to the Godhead itself" and thus eliminated God's need for a "mediating sphere between divine and non-divine reality" (174). Divine ideas have played a similar role in Western theology; neither creature nor Creator, they hover in the between and provide Platonic resources to explain how the tran-scendent God creates and relates to creation; see Anton C. Pegis, "The Dilemma of Being and Unity," in *Essays in Thomism*, ed. Robert Brennan (Eugene, OR: Wipf & Stock, 2014; first published in 1942), 158-59.

as Sophia.[67] As the between-being, Sophia need not have the attributes of Absoluteness. Creation in and by Sophia is thus "*the isolating of her potentiality from her eternal actuality.*" The "actualization" of Sophia's potency is the content of the process of creation, and this separation of potentiality from actuality is the "creative fertilization of nothing."[68]

One result is to displace the triune God from his unique place as Creator. The Son and Spirit do not participate in creation "hypostatically" but "sophianically," as the dyad of Word and Spirit, through the mediation of Sophia.[69] Sophia thus occupies the space of Plato's demiurge, between the Absolute and the multiple motion of creation.[70] Bulgakov certainly affirms Genesis 1: "In the beginning God created the heavens and the earth." But his sophianic pyrotechnics are not only distracting but damaging, insofar as Sophia occupies theological territory that must be reserved exclusively for the Father who creates through his Word and Spirit.

Sophia is Bulgakov's solution to the same problem that haunts Thomas: How is it possible for an absolute, simple, self-contained, immutable God to create? Bulgakov proposes a paradox: Creation is both unnecessary (as the self-completion of God) and "necessary" (because God is love and love seeks expansion). He cannot, however, leave the paradox as it stands,

---

[67]Bulgakov, *Unfading Light*, 216-17. Since Philo, "the question has arisen of the need for some mediating principle between God and the world." The necessity of a mediator "cannot be denied," because only this can maintain the distinction of God and the world while insisting on creation's participation in God's being. Regarding the Logos as a mediator has led to subordinationist Christologies. The mediator cannot be located in a hypostasis but must be in the nature of God. Given her double-facing character, as both divine and creaturely, existing in two modes as "eternal and temporal," Sophia meets the requirements (Bulgakov, *Sophia*, 74).

[68]Bulgakov, *Unfading Light*, 228.

[69]Bulgakov, *Sophia*, 68-69.

[70]Slesinski hears a "gnostic ring" in Bulgakov's early Sophiology (*Theology of Sergius Bulgakov*, 50).

but introduces Sophia as the bridge between the Absolute and the Absolute-relative that is the Creator. Thomas fudges simplicity and introduces untenable distinctions. Bulgakov fudges with a speculative Sophiology.

Neither Thomas nor Bulgakov can get through the first verse of the Bible without encountering difficulties. Perhaps we should change tack. Perhaps we should take Genesis 1:1 as a foundational premise and move on from there. I propose we should start at the very beginning. It is a very good place to start.

IN THE BEGINNING

That God created the heavens and the earth, all agree. The question is, how? "How" does not refer to "mechanism." In that sense, we both do and do not know how he created: We know he created by Word and Spirit, but how Word and Spirit create from nothing we cannot know. In this context, "How?" is a demand for a coherent account of God in his relation to creation. Specifically, I have been asking, how can an Absolute God—simple, immutable, immobile—create?

As I start afresh, I take up some insights from each of the theologians discussed above. From Bulgakov, I retrieve and radicalize the insight that "Absolute" is no more than a conventional placeholder and that the Absolute-relative is the only God with whom we have to do. I will retrieve a good many other things from Bulgakov in later chapters—without, however, adopting his Sophiology. From Thomas, I borrow the notion that creation exists by a hypothetical necessity—it is necessary because God *has* created. Thomas's theology of creation will also return to the stage at various points in later chapters.

Finally, I will take up a modified version of David Bentley Hart's radicalization of Thomas and Bulgakov. For creatures, Hart observes, all action and every choice are shadowed by "unrealized possibilities" and involve "a collapse of the indeterminate potentiality into determinate actuality." None of that pertains to God. God is not overshadowed by possibility but is an infinite actuality. He does not choose from among possibilities but is the source of all ontic possibility.[71] Any tension between freedom and necessity "simply disappears." God does not choose his nature and his actions from a range of options but "simply is reality as such." Thus, *because* God is infinitely free, "creation inevitably follows from who he is." Hart concedes that "might not have been" is true of creation in itself, as a statement of its absolute ontological contingency. But "might have been otherwise" says nothing about God.[72] In what follows, I agree that "might not have been" is a statement about creation, but I want to reverse Hart's argument. Not: Creation inevitably follows from who God is. Rather: Who God is inevitably follows from the fact that he created.

Let us start, as I say, at the very beginning. The first statement of Scripture is about God the Creator, and thus about God's relation to creation. Strictly speaking, we do not even learn of God's existence until we have read of his act of creation: In the original Hebrew of Genesis 1:1, the verb *created* precedes the name *'elohim*: "In the beginning created *'elohim* the heavens and the earth." The Bible does not start with God-in-himself and then proceed to describe, with embarrassed stutters, how the Absolute creates and relates to what he makes. It begins with God establishing that relation in the act of creating a world other than himself. From his first introduction, the God of the Bible is the

---

[71]Failure to see this is a key flaw in process theology. Hartshorne's conclusion is similar to Hart's: God is "incapable of not creating," but to arrive at this conclusion he posits a realm of possibilities, some of which *must* be actualized. *The Divine Relativity: A Social Conception of God* (New Haven, CT: Yale University Press, 1967), 73-74.

[72]David Bentley Hart, *You Are Gods: On Nature and Supernature* (Notre Dame, IN: Notre Dame University Press, 2022), 115-16.

God who makes, shapes, creates, governs, speaks heaven and earth and all that is in them. In Scripture, there is no God without interplay with creatures, without a created playground.

Scripture thus knows nothing at all about a God who might-or-might-*not* create. Scripture reveals only the God who *has in fact* created. Scripture knows nothing of a God who might have created an infinity of different worlds but only the God who did in fact create *this* heaven and *this* earth. "Creator" is fundamental theology. *Creator*, not *esse*, is the first name of God. Creation is *the* fundamental theological premise.[73]

Karl Rahner complained that theologians elaborated the treatise *de Deo uno* prior to and independently of the treatise *de Deo trino*. My complaint is, perhaps, more foundational: Before the treatise *de Deo creatori*, theologians have placed the treatise *de Deo in se*. But surely we cannot know any such God. "What would God be, absent creation?" we are tempted to ask. It is a question *we* cannot ask because the existence of the questioner indicates that God has in fact created and is not in fact without creation. An inquiry into God-without-creation or God-without-economy is necessarily an inquiry into God-without-*me*.[74] Knowledge is a relation of the knower to the thing known, and if we think away the knower we dissolve any possibility for knowledge. Knowledge

---

[73]Luther's emphasis is similar: "Outside that beginning of the creation there is nothing except the uncovered divine essence and the uncovered God." We can know nothing of God except by the clothing of his works, so an unclothed God is strictly incomprehensible and unspeakable by creatures. See *Lectures on Genesis*, at 1:3, in *Luther's Works*, vol. 1: *Lectures on Genesis, Chapters 1-5*, ed. Jaroslav Pelican, trans. George V. Schick (St. Louis: Concordia, 1958).

[74]Tyler Wittman writes, "Theology's principal material object is God himself considered as God's perfection, intelligible without the economy." Though he goes on to say this is a "passing movement" toward the "genuine material object" of theology, God and all things in relation to the God who is Alpha and Omega, the starting point is off-kilter. We may ask, to *whom* is "God himself . . . intelligible without the economy"? Certainly not to any theologian, for he or she would not exist to judge intelligibility were it not for the economy (*God and Creation in Thomas Aquinas and Karl Barth*, 293).

of God in particular takes the form of communion. Like Adam's knowledge of Eve (Gen 4:1), our knowledge of God is nuptial: How can we the bride know anything of a bridegroom who is not a bridegroom?

A non-Creator is, in the strictest possible sense, a *nonentity*. God-without-creation is an *idol*. No such God exists, because the only God who *is* is the God who created the heavens and the earth. Attempting to know God-without-creation is a double deletion— both of the knower (us, since we are uncreated) and of the object of knowledge (God, since no non-Creator exists). Noticing the absence of both bridegroom and bride, I say, with Shakespeare's Benedick, "This looks not like a nuptial."[75]

Of course, God did not burst into being along with creation. He did not make himself in making heaven and earth. The Bible speaks of the life of God in the "before" when there was no created time. "Before the mountains were born or You gave birth to the earth and the world, even from everlasting to everlasting, You are God" (Ps 90:1-2). "In the beginning was the Word, and the Word was with God, and the Word was God" (Jn 1:1). Jesus speaks of his life of glory with the Father that pre-existed the foundation of the world: "Father, glorify Me together with Yourself, with the glory I had with You before the world was" (Jn 17:5) and "Father . . . You loved Me before the foundation of the world" (Jn 17:24). The Son was known before the foundation of the world (1 Pet 1:20), and the Father loved and chose us in the Son "before the foundation of the world" (Eph 1:4).

None of these passages, however, speak of God as a *non*-Creator, nor as a *potential* Creator. To speak of God's everlasting Godness before the world is to speak of the *Creator* of the world he everlastingly preceded. The Father who shared glory with and loved the

---

[75]*Much Ado About Nothing* 4.1.67.

Son before the world was is the Father who has in fact created through the Word who was toward him, the Word who is also God. The God who chose us before the foundation of the world is the God who created the beings he chose to create and re-create.

When Scripture speaks of God's "absoluteness" or "independence," it does not formulate a "metaphysics which can think divinity, not by contrast with the world, but without it."[76] On the contrary, *every* time Scripture speaks of God's transcendence, it speaks of his lordship *over creation*. Scripture never speaks of God's Godness by speaking of simplicity, or *actus purus*, or *esse ipsum*. It always speaks of the transcendence of the *related* God, the Creator. God is incomparable, Isaiah says, as Lord over nations and Savior of Israel. There is none like him, who knows the end from the beginning (Is 40:22; 45:21; 46:9-10). His dominion is everlasting, Nebuchadnezzar confesses, stretching from generation to generation and extending over all inhabitants of earth (Dan 4:34-35). The God who needs no bulls and goats is the God who owns the world and all is contains (Ps 50:12). The God who has no need of anything is the God who gives life and breath to all living things (Acts 17:25). The "absolute" God is not God without us, but the One in whom we live, move, and exist (Acts 17:28). The aseity, absoluteness, independence, and sovereignty of God are the aseity, absoluteness, independence, and sovereignty of the Creator. The only transcendence Scripture knows of is the transcendence of the Creator. His independence is not the independence of a God-without-world. It is the independence of the Maker and Lord of heaven and earth.

We should not posit a God-without-creation to secure God's independence. *Nor do we need to*. It is enough to say "Creator."[77] To say

---

[76]David Burrell, *Freedom and Creation in Three Traditions* (Notre Dame, IN: University of Notre Dame Press, 1993), 102.

[77]In the Bible, "Creator" rather than "simplicity" is the ontologically sufficient ground for affirming the absoluteness of God; against Dolezal, *God Without Parts*, 6.

"Creator" is to name the God who is the origin of created existence and of all created existents. To say "Creator" is to name the God who freely calls into being things that are not, the God who gives existence to beings other than himself (Rom 4:13).[78] To say "Creator" is to say all that is other than the Creator receives its existence, and its continuing existence, from him. To name the Creator is to name the One who has been from eternity and will be to eternity. "Creator" gives us all the independence, aseity, sovereignty, and divine freedom we need, without introducing distorting extrabiblical categories and concepts, without getting caught in the snags and snarls we have been examining in this chapter and the last.

---

[78]It has become fashionable to translate Gen 1:1 as a dependent clause. Instead of "In the beginning, God created the heavens and the earth," it is rendered as "When God began to create. . . ." *bere'shit* ("in the beginning"), it is argued, is a construct or genitive form, and therefore takes an object: "In the beginning *of* God's creating" (cf. parallel phrases in Jer 26:1; 27:1; 28:1; 49:34). Gen 1:2 is then taken as a description of a preexisting chaos that *'elohim* shapes into a cosmos. Some medieval rabbis understood Gen 1:1 in this sense (Ibn Ezra and Rashi). On this translation, Genesis does not speak of an absolute beginning but only describes what God did whenever it was that he began to shape chaotic stuff into heaven and earth. None of these arguments hold up. The form *re'shit* can be absolute (Is 46:10), and in contexts where the construct precedes a verb, a construct is always unambiguously in the construct. Since it is ambiguous in Gen 1:1, it is *not* a construct. Further, the verb *create (bara')* is in the perfect, an aspect that normally describes action prior to the main action, setting conditions for what follows. The normal *waw*-imperfect narrative form begins in Gen 1:3. If Gen 1:2 were the main clause, the verb would precede the subject; but the noun "earth" precedes the verb "was." Thus, the order indicates a new topic in Gen 1:2; Gen 1:2 is *not* the main clause of a sentence in which Gen 1:1 is a dependent clause. On this, see Umberto Cassuto, *A Commentary on the Book of Genesis,* part 1: *From Adam to Noah* (Skokie, IL: Varda Books, 2005), 18-20; also Gordon J. Wenham, *Genesis 1–15*, Word Biblical Commentary (Waco, TX: Word, 1987), 11-15. Beyond the grammatical arguments, the alliteration of *beresh'it bara'* (the first three consonants of the two words are identical) argues for a conceptual link between "beginning" and "create": God's creating is a beginning. Ancient versions (LXX; Vulgate) take *bere'shit* as absolute, and both the Old and New Testaments assume the same (Is 41:4; 46:9-10; Col 1:18; Rev 3:14; 21:6; 22:13). In John 1, the Word's work in creation and his incarnation are both described by *egeneto*, suggesting that both describe historical acts rather than a "timeless relationship between God and man." Karl Barth, *Church Dogmatics 3/1: The Doctrine of Creation*, ed. Geoffrey Bromiley and T. F. Torrance (London: T&T Clark, 2010), 13, cf. 98. On the whole question, see Nathan J. Chambers, *Reconsidering Creation Ex Nihilo in Genesis 1*, Journal of Theological Interpretation Supplement 19 (University Park, PA: Eisenbrauns, 2020), 133-235.

At the same time, "Creator" is an inherently *relative* term. If "Creator" is the first name of God, then our theology must be, from top to bottom, a theology of the *related* God.[79] The Creator is *internally* related, a speaking communion capable of internal address, a God who says "us" (Gen 1:26). This internal relationality is the condition of possibility for creation. But, as far as theology is concerned, this God is always already related to what is *other* than himself. Creator and creation are joined in mutual relation, a relation we must finally describe as mutually *dependent*.

The dependence is radically asymmetrical. Creation need not have existed. It is utterly dependent on the Creator for its initial and persistent being. It will reach its *telos* only by the power, not of Sophia, but of the Spirit of Jesus. By definition, the God who is Creator in the biblical sense does not depend on the creation for his existence or his glory. He is the source of all, and, as Paul says, needs nothing to sustain his existence as the living God.

Yet, the Creator *does* depend on creation in various senses. There is no creation without God, yet it is also the case that, *once he has created*, there is no God without creation. Given creation, the identity of God depends on creation. He would not be the God of Abraham if Abraham did not exist, and Abraham would not exist had the Creator not created him. He would not be the God of exodus without creating this world, in which Israel, Egypt, Pharaoh, Moses exist, where plagues and signs and wonders take place. He would not be God of resurrection had he not raised Jesus, the Jewish rabbi of Nazareth, from his tomb outside Jerusalem. There is no unrelated *deus absconditus*

---

[79]My point overlaps with Barth's doctrine of election, which he understands as God's *self*-determination to be God-for-us—that is to say, to come among us in the incarnate Son. *Church Dogmatics* 2/2: *The Doctrine of God*, trans. Geoffrey Bromiley (London: T&T Clark, 2004), 3-194. Thus, as Wittman summarizes Barth's position: "God's actuality is unthinkable apart from God's self-posited relation to creatures through Christ" (*God and Creation*, 287; cf. 131, 147).

lurking in the background. What he shows is what he is, for he *is* Creator.

The Creator is in a real, mutually defining relation with creation, though, as we shall see in chapter seven, this real relation with creation is enveloped in God's real relation with God. "Creator" safeguards against the reduction and relativization of God by building a drastically asymmetrical relativity into the foundation. Once we have baked in this asymmetrical reciprocity, we can say without hesitation or qualm that God is responsive to creation. We do not need to posit an in-between entity like Sophia to make sense of the biblical portrait of a God who relates to his creation. Creation need not be, but it *is*, and, given that it is, God *is* related. He is Creator, and so acts and reacts, rejoices in our praise and answers our prayers.

We might think we can establish God's independence of creation with a hypothetical: if the world suddenly disappeared, God would not cease to be. This is false. *Having created*, the Creator revealed in Jesus Christ will see creation through to its completion in glory. If he does not, it is not merely a failure for creation; it is the *Creator's* failure to be Creator. God is love. He loves what he has made. If he were to let go the object of his love, his love would not be love and he would not be the God who is love. His love is immutable, which is to say, utterly faithful, and it is intentional, directed to the creation as it really exists. The flame of Yah burns for his future bride, and he will have her or cease to be the consuming fire. A hypothetically necessary creation is no less irreversible than an absolutely necessary one—necessary also for God to be God.

We may, in retrospect, consider that the gift need not have been given. Indeed, we *must* consider it so, or else it would not be the *gift* of creation. But this retrospection is the reflection of creatures to whom the gift has already been given, and the One who need not have given is the one who *has already given*. Since our very existence is gift, we of course can have no experience or knowledge of a God who has not given the gift of existence. Theology comes too late to know a God *a se* because theology is an activity of creatures, always already recipients of the gift. Here above all, Minerva's owl flies at dusk. Genesis 1:1 thus establishes a firm protocol against speculation.[80]

It also establishes protections against incoherence and trackless wandering. I am not merely dismissing questions. Starting with the Creator offers the only path toward a coherent theology. Christian theology has been haunted by the specter of a nonexistent God who may or may not create. Much labor has been expended to build a bridge between the Absolute and the Absolute-relative, to fill the gap between the unknown not-yet-Creator and the known Creator of heaven and earth. The gap has been filled sometimes by fudge, sometimes by Sophia. But the gap itself is the problem, the source of incoherences, aporia, dilemmas, incoherences which disappear, are rendered solvable, or are at least reframed by making the first statement of the creed our theological starting point. Where no chasm exists, bridge building becomes moot.

For instance: by beginning with the Creator, we dispel worries about the knowability of God, which are *entirely* the fruit of an imagined abyss between the nonexistent non-Creator and the Creator. We ask, Can God be known? Since God knows himself,

---

[80]Why does Genesis start with a *bet*, the second letter of the alphabet, rather than an *aleph*? ask the rabbis. Because the *bet* "is closed at the sides but open at the front," thus teaching us to speculate from "the day that days were created" but not "on what was before that"; quoted in Catherine Keller, *The Face of the Deep: A Theology of Becoming* (London: Routledge, 2002), 157. Theology is incapable of going past the *bet* even if, with Thomas, we define theology as the knowledge God has of himself in which we participate in the beatific vision. As soon as "we" and "participate" are introduced, we are no longer talking about God-in-himself, but about God the Creator. "We" have no other God to talk about.

that question must mean, Can a God be known *by creatures*? The answer to this question is only a puzzle if it means, Can a God who *has not created* be known by creatures?[81] Once we make the implicit explicit, the answer is obvious: Of course not, because if God has not created, there are no creatures to know him. If, by contrast, we ask, Can the *Creator* be known?, the answer is equally obvious: *Of course*, he can be known, because creatures exist only as God addresses them, only as God speaks them into being and sustains them in existence by his continuing address and the continuing breath of the Spirit. To be a creature is be spoken to, and by, the Creator. We can know nothing without knowing God's address. The Creator revealed in Scripture cannot *not* be known (Rom 1:20-21).[82] If we do not acknowledge him as God, it is because we suppress the truth in unrighteousness, not because he lies on the far side of the abyss of creation.

"Creator" marks the difference between Hellenic and biblical theology. Greek metaphysics is a quest for an *archē*, a principle or beginning to serve as anchor and explanation for the ordered cosmos (see chap. 2). To fulfill the role, an *archē* must be wholly unmovable, unrelated and unrelatable, absolute being without a trace of becoming or process. Christian theology has often mimicked the Hellenistic quest, setting out in search of the unrelated God. Genesis 1:1 renders that impossible. The only God who *is* is

---

[81] Apophatic theology is the discipline of "thinking away" every limitation from God, which includes thinking away every claim that God is "an agent with a context and a history, as a presence alongside other presences within a universe of diversity, independence and change." Rowan Williams, *Understanding and Misunderstanding "Negative Theology"* (Milwaukee, WI: Marquette University Press, 2021), 12-13. This seems to be an impossible effort to "think away" ourselves in order to come to a knowledge of the God-without-us.

[82] By the same token, "Creator" marks out the contours of a properly biblical mysticism. It is not a mysticism of ascent beyond being to the ineffably unnamable God. Biblical mysticism points to our selves and our immediate surroundings as the created radiance of the Creator. We cannot escape his presence because we exist only by virtue of his continuous presence.

the *related* God, the God who has created a world that is other than himself and who, in that very act, has related himself to a world other from himself. The quest for an *unrelated* non-Creator is quixotic, for an unrelated God has nothing to do with us. Worse, it is idolatrous, for no such God exists. It is a quest to transcend creation and to be as God.

Setting up Creator as the first name of God softens or eliminates dilemmas of simplicity. In some respects, confessing the Creator as our first theological axiom *strengthens* simplicity. It obviates the handwringing over the use of relative terms for God, which has tormented theologians only because they juxtapose and compare a nonexistent non-Creator to the Creator whose acts are recorded in Genesis.[83] I can say without hesitation that God *is actualized* as Creator, without getting knotted up in claims about an eternal creative act that produces no creatures. We need not posit an eternal act of creating, identical to the *esse* of God, that *does not* and yet *does* terminate in an actual creation other than God.[84] There is no room for worries about a composite of secondary potency/primary actuality, no need to puzzle over God's unenacted capacity to create, because God *is* Creator.

---

[83]Thomas Aquinas on relative terms like *Creator* and *Lord*: "These relations . . . which refer to his effects cannot possibly be in God. . . . They cannot be in him as accidents in a subject, since no accident is in him, as we proved in the first book. Neither can they be God's very substance, because, since relative terms are those which essentially refer somehow to something else, as the Philosopher says, it would follow that God's substance is essentially referred to something else. Now that which is essentially referred to another depends in some way on it, since it can neither exist nor be understood without it. Hence it would follow that God's substance is dependent on something else outside it: thus it would not be of itself necessary being" (*SCG* 2.12). Peter Lombard offers a similar argument: Things that are said of God in time "are said relatively, according to an accident which does not befall God, but which befalls creatures, such as creator, lord, refuge, giver or granter, and suchlike." Peter Lombard, *The Sentences*, book 1: *The Mystery of the Trinity*, trans. Giulio Silano (Toronto: Pontifical Institute of Mediaeval Studies, 2010), 1.30.1. Such accidents are "in the creature, not in the Creator." The name is relative and denotes the relation to the creature, but "it denotes no relation which is in the Creator" (*Sentences* 1.30.7).

[84]As Rosmini does in *Trine Being (Contd.)*, 128-30, par. 1286.

For the same reason, there is no space for questions about God's freedom to create or not create to arise. Because God *did* create. God is free, but in terms of Genesis 1, he freely created and loves *this* world. There is no space for questions about God's immutability to arise with reference to creation either, because there is no question about a transition from non-Creator to Creator. The God revealed in Scripture is immutably the Creator of heaven and earth. The question of God's mutability must be posed on *this* side of "in the beginning," rather than on the "far side." Questions about immutability are questions about the *related* God, the Creator.

Bulgakov is right: We have to do only with the Absolute-relative, never with the Absolute. But we need not posit a Sophia to occupy the metaphysical space for what is not-quite-God to have characteristics of multiplicity, relativity, and mutability that cannot be attributed to God. We need not, with Bulgakov, speak of God's desire or yearning to extend his love to what is not God, which again suggests an unfulfilled potency. We can instead speak of God's realized, actualized, and *fulfilled* yearning to extend his love to what is not God, a love realized and actualized in the creation he has actually created. Confessing "I believe in the God the Father . . . Creator of heaven and earth" keeps the divine persons where they should be—on the front lines of the work of creation. They do not disappear behind the divine-creaturely Sophia (or energies). Creation is the work of the Father who sends forth his Spirit to energize the creative Word he speaks.

My position converges with the most radical claims of Bulgakov and Hart. Is noncreation *possible*? No. To say God might not have created is to set God within a set of possibilities "larger" than God's actuality as the Creator of the heavens and the earth. Or it is to say that, *within* God, possibility is more fundamental than actuality. But that violates a fundamental principle of theology proper, that nothing is more fundamental than God's infinite actuality. God invents creation's possibilities.[85] There is *no possibility* for God *not* to be Creator. He could not *not* have created—not because he is under some external or internal compulsion to create, not because the pressure of his self-diffusive Goodness moves him to create. He could not *not* have created because he *did*. We can say, "God's free will could not be otherwise," because his free will is actualized in the creation of the heavens and earth, light, a firmament, sea and land, plants, animals, and man, Abraham, Isaac, Jacob, and Jesus. Once done, it cannot be undone. Creation is hypothetically necessary, and we do not need to speculate about absolute necessity, because we know of no non-Creator for whom creation might or might not be absolutely necessary.

Is it possible for God to create a world other than the one he did create? No.[86] Because this world is the world he *did* create. There is no need to send God off to shop at the Cosmic Costco of Possible Worlds, even if the Costco is all in his head.[87] We do not have to imagine God filling his shopping cart as he moves from indecision to decision. By the time we are on the scene to speak of and sing

---

[85]My argument has some analogies with Ross, "God, Creator of Kinds and Possibilities: *Requiescant universalia ante res*," in *Rationality, Religious Beliefs, and Moral Commitment: New Essays in the Philosophy of Religion*, ed. Robert Audi and William J. Wainwright (Ithaca, NY: Cornell University Press, 1986), 315-34; and the analysis of Anselm in Jonathan McIntosh, "Speaking of Possibilities: The Theistic Actualize of Anselm's Divine *Locutio*," *Modern Theology* 33, no. 2 (2017): 213-34.

[86]Biblical counterfactuals (God might have started Israel over with Moses; God might have destroyed Nineveh; Peter might have been sifted like wheat) are counterfactuals *within* the existing creation. Scripture never pushes those counterfactuals back to "before the foundation of the world" (God might not have created). Indeed, the presence of the counterfactuals is an argument in favor of "Creator" as the first name of God, because they reveal a God who *responds* to men. Counterfactuals point to the genuine interplay that takes place between God and world. "Interplay" comes from William Desmond, *Being and the Between* (Albany, NY: SUNY Press, 1995), 246.

[87]As, for example, found in Eleonore Stump and Norman Kretzmann, "Absolute Simplicity," *Faith and Philosophy* 2, no. 4 (1985): 353-82. See also Alvin Plantinga, "Actualism and Possible Worlds," *Theoria* 42, nos. 1-3 (1976): 139-60.

to him, whatever choice is involved has already been made. Before we begin, we are already in the world designed to be the stage for the unfolding of the Father's love in the Son and Spirit. As I have said, Hart is correct: "It could have been otherwise" functions only as a reminder of the contingency of creation. "The world need not have been" is true by definition. That is what it means for the world to be a "creation."

My "fundamentalist" proposal to begin with Genesis 1:1 converges with the most baffling claims of Robert Jenson. Jenson, famously, denies the *logos asarkos*, an unfleshed Word.[88] If we imagine he is speaking of God-without-creation, it seems he implies the existence of eternal flesh. If he means God the Creator, then he is simply saying that God is God of *this* world—the world of the patriarchs and Israel, the world created to be the realm of Jesus, the incarnate Son. In that context, denying the *logos asarkos* is merely the negative of affirming an Edwardsian supralapsarianism: The end for which God created the world was to form a bride for the Son and induct her into the divine family.[89] And that is simply to elaborate the truth of creation as such: In the beginning God created *this* world, not another.

Confessing Creator as first theology unravels puzzles surrounding the end for which God created the world. God is, of course, the end of all his actions; he is, in himself, Omega as well

---

[88]His last statement of this question is in Jenson, "Once More the *Logos asarkos*," *International Journal of Systematic Theology* 13, no. 2 (2011): 130-33.

[89]Jonathan Edwards, *Miscellany 702* in *"The Miscellanies," Entries Nos. 501-832* in *The Works of Jonathan Edwards*, vol. 18, ed. Ava Chamberlain (New Haven, CT: Yale University Press, 2000). Self-consciously starting with creation would sharpen Bruce McCormack's revision of Chalcedonian orthodoxy; see *The Humility of the Eternal Son: Reformed Kenoticism and the Repair of Chalcedon* (Cambridge: Cambridge University Press, 2021). McCormack writes, "The preexistent Logos *as such* is a pure postulate, a human invention . . . an 'idol' by any other name." Rather, "*as eternally generated* [the Son] already has a relation to Jesus of Nazareth" (253). Taken as a statement of God-without-creation, this seems to deny God's freedom to create a world without, say, Israel, Rome, execution by crucifixion, etc. But McCormack's statement is exactly correct when taken as a claim about the Creator of *this* world.

as Alpha. But it makes all the difference whether the God who is Omega is a non-Creator or the Creator of the heavens and the earth. The traditional puzzles all arise from theology's oscillation between the one and the other. If we posit a non-Creator, an end that does not include our blessed union with God is perfectly feasible. But that non-Creator does not exist. For the Creator who *is*, it is unthinkable for him to create a world without intending to fold our joy into his. The end for which the Creator creates is "at once God and his creature united in Christ, the *totus Christus*."[90]

Taking Genesis 1:1 as fundamental theology cuts through the debate between "process theology" and "classical theism." To the classical theist, the God of process theism becomes God in the course of creation's history. To the process theist, classical theism elevates God so far beyond creation that it does not affect him at all; he does not even need creatures to be Creator.

But there is a hidden convergence between the two opponents. Process theologians scorn deracinated Thomism (a construct of Thomists as well as process theologians), and Thomism is deracinated because it is haunted by the ghost of a transcendent non-Creator. Yet process theologians theorize about divine relativity while rejecting the rubric under which this relativity is true—the rubric of "given creation."[91] Classical theists, for their part, also

---

[90]Jenson, *Systematic Theology*, 2:19. Jenson extrapolates the argument of Jonathan Edwards. Edwards's premise is that "the glorious attributes of God consist in a sufficient to certain acts and effects." Thus, Jenson argues, "In that God supremely values himself he identically values those acts and effects. But given the nature of this God's triune being, his acts are acts of communication, and their effects therefore knowledge, in the biblical sense that unites cognition and love. Therefore, in supremely valuing himself God supremely values other persons' knowledge and love of himself. But since God is himself the supreme value, to know and love him is to be infinitely blessed. Therefore, in infinitely valuing himself God equivalently values our blessedness." All this arrives at the "dangerous" assertion: "In infinitely valuing us God infinitely values himself" (18-19).

[91]Charles Hartshorne, *The Divine Relativity: A Social Conception of God* (New Haven, CT: Yale University Press, 1967). See the Barthian critique of process theology in Colin Gunton, *Becoming and Being* (Eugene, OR: Wipf & Stock, 2001); also John Feinberg's

refuse to start at the beginning. They set parameters of what can be known and said of God "in himself," boundaries that guide the exploration of God's relation to and involvement with creation: God *must* be thus and thus if he is to be Creator.[92] Classical theism is constructed as a Great Wall against a relative, related God; it is a theology of a non-Creator. In fact, classical theism always *assumes* creation, at least implicitly, because the whole project consists in exploring what may be known of God as origin of created existence and of all created existents. God's relation/relativity to creation is presupposed even as it is suppressed or forgotten. Classical theism is unwittingly an exploration of divine relativity—that is, of the God of creation, the only God who is.

While process theism posits a divine relativity while rejecting creation, classical theism attempts to safeguard against the relativity of God by positing a nonexistent being, a God who may or may not create, a God whose eternal creative act does "not yet" terminate in a finite creation. Both are, in their different ways, haunted by the specter of a non-Creator, who—to reiterate one last time—*simply does not exist*. The debate is interminable because it is shadow boxing, a theatrical battle between those who *share* their most important premises.

The theological stakes here could not be higher, and the cultural stakes are also very high. Theologies that proclaim a "God

---

excellent summary and analysis in *No One Like Him: The Doctrine of God* (Wheaton, IL: Crossway, 2006), 149-79. Hartshorne quite explicitly rejects creation *ex nihilo*, on the Aristotelian grounds that a "first moment" is impossible, since a moment is always a boundary between past and future time. See *The Logic of Perfection* (LaSalle, IL: Open Court, 1962), 123; Gunton, *Becoming and Being*, 103; Alfred North Whitehead, *Process and Reality*, ed. David Ray Griffin and Donald W. Sherburne (New York: Free Press, 1978), 95-96, 342. Whitehead dismisses Genesis as "too primitive" to be relevant and considers the doctrine of creation as a "fallacy" that "infused tragedy" into the histories of Islam and Christianity.

[92] Isaak August Dorner's revised version of immutability makes the same mistake. He begins with a not-yet-Creator and then concludes he must change to bring the world into being. *Divine Immutability: A Critical Reconsideration*, trans. Robert R. Williams and Claude Welch (Minneapolis: Fortress, 1994), 142-43.

beyond God" are among the deep springs of modern atheism. Such theologies raise doubts about God, for a God too transcendent to relate to us is a God who may safely be dispensed with, replaced by immanent processes. The elaboration of a theology of a non-Creator leaves us with the lingering fear that the generous good God of creation, the God who chose Abraham and came to us in Jesus, may not be the real God, God as he is in himself.

CONCLUSION

Here is the thesis that will guide the remainder of this book: All theology rooted in the Bible must be carried out under the rubric, *given creation*. Beginning with Genesis 1 does *not* leave us ignorant of God's nature and character. Over the next two chapters, I will sketch a portrait of the Creator by resorting to an old tradition, a meditation on divine names. We will learn much about the God who is from everlasting to everlasting. We will *not*, however, trick ourselves into thinking we are talking about any God but the Creator. For there is no other.

5

TRIUNE CREATOR

Katherine Sonderegger has recently challenged the twentieth-century obsession with the Trinity, arguing that "the doctrine of the Trinity, however central to the Christian mystery, must not be allowed to replace or silence the Oneness of God" because "God is supremely, gloriously One; surpassingly, uniquely one." For Sonderegger, "the Mystery of the Trinity must in itself be a form of Oneness,"[1] so she presses for a "starting point in the Oneness of God."[2] "One," of course, is said in many ways, but Sonderegger insists that in Scripture the oneness of God is a "metaphysical predicate" that governs and determines "all other predicates, Attributes, Perfections."[3] In his absolute unity, God is beyond all class, conception, and comparison, beyond likeness and number. In his utter and unutterable unity, his being is "an annihilating concreteness."[4] Sonderegger self-consciously follows Thomas Aquinas (or Thomists) in giving systematic priority to *de deo uno* over *de deo trino*.[5] She claims biblical authority for this decision.

---

[1] Sonderegger, *Systematic Theology*, vol. 1: *The Doctrine of God* (Minneapolis: Fortress, 2015), xiv-xv.

[2] Sonderegger, *Doctrine of God*, 8.

[3] Sonderegger, *Doctrine of God*, 25.

[4] Sonderegger, *Doctrine of God*, 25.

[5] For this distinction, see Karl Rahner, *The Trinity* (Freiburg: Herder & Herder, 1997).

Scripture rests on the foundation of Torah, and Torah teaches the oneness of God.[6]

Trinitarian readings of the Old Testament, however, predate the twentieth century,[7] and there is, in particular, a long-standing tradition of teasing out trinitarian traces in the first chapter of the Bible. Augustine's pervasively trinitarian interpretation of Genesis 1 was not the first,[8] but it was the most thorough and influential in the West.[9] At a superficial level, Augustine found more or less explicit references to the three persons in Genesis 1. The opening verses explicitly name God (the Father) and the Spirit, and Augustine argues that the opening phrase, *in principio*, means "in the Son," because Paul calls the Son the *principium* in whom the Father creates (Col 1:18; *qui est principium*).[10] The

---

[6]Sonderegger, *Doctrine of God*, 12-13. John Frame likewise insists we can speak of God without explicit reference to the Trinity, citing the Old Testament as proof. *Doctrine of God: A Theology of Lordship* (Phillipsburg, NJ: P&R, 2002), 15n32. Frame is right if we isolate the Old from the New, but the Old is not, or *should* not be, isolated. Indeed, the Old is illumined *only* in the light of the New, for there is revealed what the Old concealed. As I argued in chapter one, we do not read the Old Testament rightly if we fail to see Jesus on every page (Lk 24:25-26), and if we see Son, we must surely also see his Father and his Spirit.

[7]Augustine devotes many pages of *De trinitate* to Old Testament theophanies.

[8]Irenaeus spoke of creation through the "two hands" of the Father, Son, and Spirit (*Against All Heresies* 4.20.1). Origen, *Homily I on Genesis*: "What is the beginning of all things except our Lord and 'Savior of all,' Jesus Christ 'the firstborn of every creature.' . . . Scripture is not speaking here of any temporal beginning, but it says that the heaven and the earth and all things which were made were made 'in the beginning,' that is, in the Savior." *Origen: Homilies on Genesis and Exodus*, trans. Ronald E. Heine, The Fathers of the Church 71 (Washington, DC: Catholic University of American Press, 1981). See also Ambrose, *Hexaemeron* 1.4.15

[9]Augustine wrote on this topic in several treatises on Genesis, especially *The Literal Meaning of Genesis*, as well as in the latter books of *Confessions*. In quoting from Augustine's Genesis commentaries, I use the translation in *On Genesis*, Works of Saint Augustine: A Translation for the 21st Century, trans. Edmund Hill (Hyde Park, NY: New City Press, 2006). The summary offered here is drawn from various sources, with the help of Scott Dunham, *The Trinity and Creation in Augustine: An Ecological Analysis* (Albany, NY: SUNY Press, 2008); Jared Ortiz, *"You Made Us For Yourself": Creation in St. Augustine's Confessions* (Minneapolis: Fortress, 2016); Gavin Ortlund, *Retrieving Augustine's Doctrine of Creation: Ancient Wisdom for Current Controversy* (Downers Grove, IL: IVP Academic, 2020).

[10]*On Genesis: A Refutation of the Manichees*, 1.2.3; *Literal Meaning of Genesis* 1.6.12. The connection is evident in the Greek as well: The LXX begins with *en archē*, and Paul uses the same word as a title for Jesus in Colossians 1:18 (*hos estin archē*).

remainder of Genesis 1 describes the common work of the persons, but this common work follows the internal *taxis* of the Trinity. "God said" names the Father and his Word,[11] and "God saw" names the Father and the Spirit.[12] Thus, "we recognize the complete indication of the Trinity," the "Word's begetter," the Word himself, and "the holy goodness, by which God is pleased with whatever pleases him on its being perfect in its own small, natural way."[13] There is the speaking Father, the spoken Son, and the hypostatic Goodness and Delight through whom the Father delights in the goodness of creatures formed by his Word.

Beyond these surface indications, Augustine detects a triune deep structure in the creation account, which he sums up with the claim that "the Father made each and every nature through the Son in the Gift of the Spirit."[14] Creation is a single act, performed simultaneously by the triune persons. Like all of God's works outside himself (*opera ad extra*), it is undivided (*indivisa*). Yet, Augustine says, it is possible to analyze this single act as a trinitarian pattern of *creatio*, *conversio* or *vocatio*, and *formatio*.[15]

The Father founds the creation (*creatio*) both by forming the ideas of creation within the Logos and by creating the formless stuff of creation from nothing. He creates "in the beginning" by eternally positing creaturely things as eternal reasons within the *principium* who is the Word.[16] The *fiat* of creation is nothing but the Word, "always adhering to the Father." As *principium*, the Son is the source of creation

---

[11]*Literal Meaning of Genesis* 1.2.4.

[12]*Literal Meaning of Genesis* 1.6.12; see Dunham, *Trinity and Creation*, 64-65.

[13]*Literal Meaning of Genesis* 1.6.12.

[14]*True Religion* 7.13, quoted in Ortiz, "*You Made Us For Yourself*," 9.

[15]See Ortiz, "*You Made Us For Yourself*," 11-14. Ortiz relies on Marie-Anne Vannier, "*Creatio*," "*Conversio*," "*Formatio*" *chez S. Augustin* (Fribourg: Editions Universitaires Fribourg Suisse, 1997). See also Carol Harrison, *Rethinking Augustine's Early Theology: An Argument for Continuity* (New York: Oxford University Press, 2008), 74-114.

[16]*Literal Meaning of Genesis* 4.24.41; Dunham, *Trinity and Creation*, 63. Augustine may have learned this from Ambrose, who makes the same connection in his *Hexameron* 1.4.15.

in its imperfection. Made from nothing, created things strain against
their Creator to remain or return to their original formlessness (*non
autem imitatur hanc Verbi formam, si aversa a Creatore, informis et imper-
fecta remaneat*).[17] If they lose the Father, they lose themselves. Self-
nihilation is a constant threat to things made *ex nihilo*. God will not
leave creation in that condition; he will not lose them, and he will not
allow them to lose themselves.

The Father sends the Word to rescue the imperfect creatures
he produces. Creatures are designed to imitate the Word's adherence to the Father. No imperfect or incomplete thing can
imitate the form of the Word, since, in its becomingness, it is
"unlike that which supremely and originally is." To become what
they truly are, creatures must "turn," each in its own way, to the
being that truly and always *is* (*cum et ipsa pro sui generis conversione
ad id quod vere ac semper est*). Only then does a creature really imitate "the form of the Word which always and unchangingly ad-
heres to the Father." The Word converts fragile beings to the One
Who Is, so that, as it responds to God's call to imitate the Word's
clinging to the Father, the creature "becomes a perfect, complete
creature."[18] By the Word's call, the creature is able to imitate the
stability of God's being. In sum, the creative "Let there be" is

> an incorporeal utterance of God in the substance of his co-eternal
> Word, calling back to himself the perfection of the creation, so that
> it should not be formless, but should be formed, each element on
> the particular lines which follow in due order. By so turning back
> and being formed creation imitates, every element in its own way,
> God the Word, that is, the Son of God who always adheres to the
> Father in complete likeness and equality of being, by which he and
> the Father are one.[19]

---

[17]*Literal Meaning of Genesis* 1.4.9
[18]*Literal Meaning of Genesis* 1.4.9.
[19]*Literal meaning of Genesis* 1.4.9.

By the *creatio* of the Father and the *vocatio* of the Son, created beings are converted into diverse imitations of the Son's communion with the Father.

The Son thus plays a double role:

> His being the beginning implies his being the source of creation as it comes into being from him while still imperfect, while his being the Word implies his conferring perfection on creation by calling it back to himself (*revocatae ad eum*), so that it may be given form by adhering to the creator, and by imitating in its own measure the form which adheres eternally and unchangeably to the Father.[20]

Like the Cappadocians, Augustine believes the Spirit brings all God's works to completion.[21] Confirming the *vocatio* of the Word, the Spirit gives each creature a dynamic orientation toward its *telos* in the Father, a dynamic represented in Genesis 1 by the declaration "It was so." Creatures are completed in their unique existence at creation, but the Spirit's work of perfecting takes place over time, until the creature reaches its full *formatio* as an imitation of the Word. Thus: God (the Father) says, "Let there be" (Son), and this summons is worked out in the "It was so" of the Spirit.

This is quite wonderful.[22] In the universe Augustine describes, everything is oriented toward God, not on account of a

---

[20]*Literal Meaning of Genesis* 1.4.9

[21]Gregory of Nyssa, *On "Not Three Gods"*; Basil of Caesarea, *On the Holy Spirit* 16.38. The paradigm persists into medieval and reformation theology: Bonaventure, *Collationes in Hexaemeron* 11.4-5; Calvin, *Institutes* 1.13.18. Bonaventure offers a variation on the theme: "Every created substance has matter, form, and composition: the original principle of foundation, the formal complement, and the bond. It has substantial existence, power, and operation. And in these the mystery of the Trinity is represented: the Father as the origin (*origo*), the Son as the image (*imago*), and the Holy Spirit as the bond (*compago*)" (*Collationes in Hexaemeron* 2.24).

[22]My main complaint is Augustine's notion (very common, in theologians from Athanasius to Barth) that created things tend toward nihilation. To be sure, every creature depends for its persistence entirely on the continuing work of Word and Spirit. If the Spirit departs, they return to dust. But that is quite different from suggesting that, *while* the Word and Spirit sustain, things strain in the opposite direction,

supernatural addition to its natural essence but in its creature-liness as such. The most basic reality, and aim, of every created thing is, in its becoming, to come to imitate the Word in his adherence to the Father. Things are what they are as they are summoned to the Father, and they are perfected—they become "light" as they are brought to light—by the divine Goodness that is the Spirit. Creatures are theological realities at the core, and eschatological-teleological as well, because they are created for future perfection.[23] Creatures are "deified"—or, more accurately, "logified" or "filiafied"—as they become more perfect imitations of the Son through the *formatio* of the Spirit.[24]

Details of Augustine's interpretations and inferences are debatable. Does *bere'shit* really have christological overtones? Does "God says" refer to the eternal Word who is God? Is the hovering *ruakh* the Spirit, a spirit, a wind, a breath? Is the Trinity really so

---

toward nothing. That posits a kind of negative power in created things, an inherent tendency for creatures to wriggle free from the sustaining power of God, or a gravitational pull from the "nothing." Where would such a negative power come from? It seems to betray a residually mythological understanding of creation—creation as a *Chaoskampf* in which God must battle to keep the primal chaos, *das Nichtige*, at bay. Karl Barth, *Church Dogmatics* 3/1: *The Doctrine of Creation*, ed. Geoffrey Bromiley and T. F. Torrance (London: T&T Clark, 2010), 98-109, makes a proper mess of Gen 1:2. Created things simply *are* nothing except by the creative and sustaining Word; there is no creaturely force that is not a gift from God.

This theory is sometimes used to provide a metaphysical framework of the possibility of sin: Wobbling between Being and nothing, creatures are capable of defying their Creator. But the freedom of creatures to defy the Creator is quite different from an ontological drift from him, for even rebellious creatures are nothing but so many (twisted) imitations of the Word. Sinners are, as Cornelius van Til liked to say, children who slap their Father while sitting on his lap. If creatures tended toward nihilation, sin would be not merely possible but nearly inevitable. Thomas Aquinas says, rightly, that creatures are nothing if left to themselves. But we need to add the corollary: They are *never* left to themselves. The Creator will *not* leave them to their own devices. Once created, a creature's existence is hypothetically necessary.

[23]Dunham, *Trinity and Creation*, 73.

[24]Luther endorses the basic trinitarian thrust of Augustine's account, which he also finds in Hilary of Poitier; Luther, *Lectures on Genesis*, at Gen 1:20, in *Luther's Works*, vol. 1: *Lectures on Genesis, Chapters 1–5*, ed. Jaroslav Pelikan, trans. George V. Schick (St. Louis: Concordia, 1958).

evident in Genesis 1? Is there a trinitarian deep structure to the creation account? I think Augustine is fundamentally right, and in the following pages I will provide fuller, no doubt more tedious, exegetical support. For those who wish to skip the tedium, I state my conclusion at the outset: the Bible *never*, for even a single clause, teaches a strict, monadic monotheism. The Bible *never* teaches that God is simply one, without simultaneously hinting at, however teasingly, plurality within the divine life. The sequence of revelation is *not* from monotheism to trinitarian monotheism because Genesis 1 is already nascently trinitarian.

To ease in, I first explore some formal, literary features of the creation account.[25]

THE LITERARY TEXTURE OF GENESIS 1

Genesis 1:1–2:3 is a repetitive, symmetrical text. The Hebrew text is filled with words repeated seven times or in multiples of seven.[26] The first verse of Genesis has seven words containing twenty-eight (7 x 4) consonants, split neatly in half: The first three words (*bere'shit bara' 'elohim*) contain fourteen letters; the last four words (*'et hashamayim w'et ha'eretz*), which constitute the object, also contain fourteen letters. The second verse of Genesis has fourteen words. Two verses in, and we already see microscopic tracings of the sabbatical structure of the whole.

Sabbatical hints persist through the chapter. *'Elohim* is used thirty-five times (7 x 5) and "earth" (*'erets*) appears twenty-one times (7 x 3). Individual days repeat words in multiples of seven to italicize critical themes. Together "light" and "day" are used seven times in Genesis 1:1-5, which describe the creation of

---

[25]In this volume, I focus on the "first" creation account (Gen 1:1–2:3). I hope in a later volume to explore anthropology, focusing on Genesis 2–3.

[26]Umberto Cassuto, *A Commentary on the Book of Genesis,* vol. 1, *From Adam to Noah* (Varda Books, 2012), 12-15.

light; "water" is used seven times on days two and three (Gen 1:6-13), when *'elohim* moves waters to form a zone of habitation on earth; "earth" is used seven times on day six, which recounts the creation of the living souls that inhabit the land—beasts, cattle, creeping things, and man. "It was good" appears seven times, the seventh a vigorous "*very* good." The heptamerous patterns continue into Genesis 2:1-3, which contains thirty-five words (7 x 5), and Genesis 2:2-3a consists of three sentences of seven words, each of which includes the phrase "the seventh day":

> By the seventh day, *'elohim* completed His work which He had done.
> And He rested on the seventh day from all His work which He had done.
> Then *'elohim* blessed the seventh day and sanctified it.

The creation week is a majestic procession toward Sabbath glory, rest, and joy, and the embedded sabbatical patterns hint that, from the moment of their creation, before they reach Sabbath, things already taste of Sabbath. In a creation characterized by change and becoming, "no being is fully coincident with itself." I am not what I was yesterday, nor what I will be tomorrow. I strain, slip, slide away from earlier versions of myself. And yet, even with this constant internal displacement, "each is itself," and this being-itself is a glory, not a defect. In the midst of becoming, beings truly *are*, even though they are not what they were or will be. Created beings are "promises" of more; yet the fact of their existence is evidence that "the more is there now, already at work."[27] The sabbatical literary patterns of Genesis 1 fill out the content of this "more." Earth, light, day, water exist as promises, specifically of Sabbath. Created good, they give promise of the "very good" of the seventh day. Within

---

[27]William Desmond, *Being and the Between* (Albany, NY: SUNY Press, 1995), 241.

the tumult and turmoil of becoming, each thing is a secret pledge of future rest.

The creation days are structured by repeated phrases arranged in a formulaic sequence:

"*'elohim* said" (Gen 1:3, 6, 9, 14, 20, 24)
"Let there be X" or "Let X do Y" (Gen 1:3, 6, 9, 14, 20, 24)
"It was so" (Gen 1:7, 9, 11, 15, 24, 30)
"*'elohim* saw X was good" (Gen 1:4, 10, 12, 18, 21, 25, 31)
"*'elohim* called" (Gen 1:5, 8, 10)
"Evening and morning, X day" (1:5, 8, 13, 19, 23, 31)

And, as many have noted, the six days of active creation are symmetrically organized in two panels, as *'elohim* first "forms" the formless and then "fills" the zones he forms. First, he creates kingdoms, then he enthrones kings.[28]

Table 5.1. The Panel Structure of Genesis 1:1–2:3

Forming realms	Filling with kings
1. Light/dark, day/night	4. Sun, moon, stars
2. Firmament between waters above/below	5. Fish and birds
3. Separation of waters, plants	6. Land animals, man
Sabbath	

Each pair is a figure of the trajectory of the entire week. Day and night (day 1) are completed with ruling heavenly lights (day 4); the firmament and waters (day 2) are filled with birds and fish (day 5); the land, sprouting with plants (day 3), finally teems with animals and man (day 6). Through the week, *'elohim* prepares a cosmic house for his Sabbath enthronement.

---

[28]Meredith Kline, *God, Heaven, and Har Magedon: A Covenantal Tale of Cosmos and Telos* (Eugene, OR: Wipf & Stock, 2006), 32-39. Herder appears to have been the first to notice the parallel structure of the account; J. G. Herder, *The Spirit of Hebrew Poetry*, 2 vols., trans. James Marsh (Burlington, VT: Edward Sith, 1833), 258.

Several details, however, do not fit this scheme. Genesis 1:1-2, for starters, appears to stand apart from the heptamerous form of the narrative. Many have read Genesis 1:1 as a summary statement or title. "Heavens and earth," it is said, is a merism for "everything," or it means the organized cosmos that comes to be at the end of the six days (cf. Gen 2:1, 4). Citing Isaiah 45:18, some have argued that it is inappropriate for God to create a formless void like the one described in Genesis 1:2. These arguments are not convincing.[29] Opposing terms of a merism retain their distinct meaning. Further, if "heavens and earth" is a merism for everything, "earth" (*'erets*) changes meaning in Genesis 1:2, where it clearly refers to the lower world. That would be an abrupt shift in meaning, especially since *'erets* ends Genesis 1:1 and then is used again immediately as the first word of Genesis 1:2. Such a reading breaks the narrative flow. It is true that "heaven and earth" often refers to the organized cosmos, but the phrase does not *mean* that. Besides, Genesis 1:1 does not even summarize the narrative that follows, which describes the formation of a *three*-story cosmos of heaven, earth, and sea. As to Isaiah 45:18, if *'elohim* does not create the formless void, where does it come from?

It is far better to take Genesis 1:1 as the first act of creation. Grammar favors this. The verb *bara'* is in the perfect, which typically describes action that occurs prior to the main action. Heaven and earth are distinct *regions* of creation. Heaven is *'elohim*'s created dwelling place, the holy temple filled with his glory. It has hosts (Gen 2:1), but Genesis 1 does not indicate when its hosts are made. Presumably, they are made simultaneously with heaven, which appears

---

[29]The following relies on Vern S. Poythress, *Interpreting Eden: A Guide to Faithfully Reading and Understanding Genesis 1-3* (Wheaton, IL: Crossway, 2019), 291-321; and Nathan J. Chambers, *Reconsidering Creation ex nihilo in Genesis 1*, Journal of Theological Interpretation Supplement 19 (University Park, PA: Eisenbrauns, 2020), 211-35.

to come into being fully formed.[30] After Genesis 1:1, the narrator's attention is entirely directed to earth. By contrast to heaven, earth is at first shapeless and empty, "unproductive and uninhabited."[31] Through the six days, *'elohim'*s actions shape the shapeless and fill the empty. Even if Genesis 1:1-2 stands outside the sequence of days, these verses are still part of the creation narrative.[32]

Another anomaly is the two-panel outline: Filling begins on the double-day of day three, when *'elohim* gathers the water to uncover the dry land and also calls plants to spring from the earth. As seed and fruit bearers, plants provide a model for other fruitful things that emerge from sea and land (Gen 1:22, 24). Thus, the first three days include *four* acts of creation, three acts of "forming" and one of "filling." Each act of creation begins with "*'elohim* said":

1 Light (Gen 1:3)

2 Firmament (Gen 1:6)

3 Gathering of waters (Gen 1:9)

4 Plants (Gen 1:11)

There is a mismatch between days and speeches, between days and creative acts.

Yet here too we discover symmetry, for days four to six also form a four-act sequence. Each act is marked by "*'elohim* said," and this second sequence again culminates with a two-act day (day 6):

1' Heavenly lights (Gen 1:14)

2' Waters teem, birds fly (Gen 1:20)

---

[30]See Kline, *God, Heaven, and Har Magedon*, 5-9; Chambers, *Reconsidering*, 217-20. Heaven is often neglected in discussions of Genesis 1, an oversight I hope to rectify in a second volume on cosmology and the metaphysics of creation.

[31]Poythress, *Interpreting Eden*, 304, quoting C. John Collins, *Genesis 1–4: A Linguistic, Literary, and Theological Commentary* (Phillipsburg, NJ: P&R, 2006), 54.

[32]I favor Luther's view that Gen 1:1-2 are part of the account of Day 1, and thus among the works of six days in which God made heaven and earth (Ex 20:11); Luther, *Lectures on Genesis*, at Gen 1:1.

3' Land animals (Gen 1:24)
4' Man (Gen 1:26)[33]

Strikingly, plants are at the climax of each movement. At the end of the first sequence, *'elohim* summons earth to produce seed-bearing grasses and fruitful trees (Gen 1:11-12); at the end of the second, earth becomes a banquet table, spread with the same grasses and trees as food for living souls (Gen 1:29-30).

Yet again, the symmetry is imperfect. If Genesis 1 were organized simply by the seven days, we would expect seven acts of divine speech. If it were organized by eight acts of creation, we would expect eight speeches. Instead, "*'elohim* said" occurs *ten* times, four times on day six alone (Gen 1:24, 26, 28, 29). *'Elohim*'s words at creation anticipate the ten words Yahweh speaks to Israel from Sinai. The Ten Commandments are "creative" words, forming former slaves into a new people of God. Conversely, the ten words of creation are commandments decreed by the Creator enthroned in heaven.[34] *'Elohim* commands, and earth is formed as obedience.

Besides, the forming-filling, kingdom-kings pattern does not capture the entire thrust of the chapter. The two-panel structure takes its cues from Genesis 1:2, where earth is described as "formless and void" (*tohu w'bohu*, the one Hebrew phrase *everyone* should know). If the earth is formless, it needs to be formed; the empty earth needs to be filled. Hence, creation is forming and filling. James B. Jordan points out the obvious: There is a *third* imperfection *'elohim* needs to address—namely, darkness. Day

---

[33]The two four-act sequences run in parallel. Each begins with light—first light itself, then heavenly luminaries; 2 and 2' make reference to the firmament (*raqia*, 1:6-8 [5x], 20). In 3, *'elohim* gathers waters so dry land or "earth" (*'erets*) will appear (Gen 1:9-10), and in 3' he summons land creatures from the *'erets* (Gen 1:24). The parallel between the fourth acts is more opaque, yet it points to resemblances between plants and human beings: Plants spring from earth, as does man (Gen 2:7); plants and man are both created to be fruitful, and so to sustain the creation (Gen 1:11-12, 28).

[34]For development of this parallel, see my *Ten Commandments: A Guide to the Perfect Law of Liberty* (Bellingham, WA: Lexham, 2020), 1-6.

one meets this need, which suggests the possibility of a semi-chiastic relationship between 1:2 and the remainder of Genesis 1. The world that is a) formless, b) empty, and c) dark will be c') lighted, then a') formed, then b') filled. From this hint, Jordan proposes a chiastic outline for the entire creation week.[35]

> A Day 1: Separation of light and darkness.
> > B Day 2: Firmament between heaven and earth.
> > > C Day 3: Elohim speaks twice.
> > > > D Day 4: Light-bearers in the firmament.
> > > C' Day 5: Elohim speaks twice. "Good" in middle. "Be fruitful," "kind."
> > B' Day 6: Man as mediator between heaven and earth.
> A' Day 7: Sabbath, Elohim's rest and enthronement.

This outline captures textual links that the two-panel outline misses. Days three and five echo one another in various ways. Structurally, both include two speeches of *'elohim*. On day three, "*'elohim* said" is used twice (Gen 1:9, 11), and on day five *'elohim* speaks (Gen 1:20) and then "blesses, saying" (Gen 1:22; *waye-varek . . . le'mor*). On both days three and five, *'elohim* judges his work good in the middle of the paragraph, rather than merely at the end (Gen 1:10, 21). Both days refer to "fruit" (Gen 1:11, 22) and both use the phrase "according to its kind/all kinds of" (Gen 1:11-12, 21).[36] The connections between days two and six are more conceptual than verbal, but this chiasm suggests that man is created to be elevated to heavenly places, stationed with the sun, moon, and stars as rulers of earth and keepers of time. The light of day one points ahead to the full glory of the seventh day.[37]

---

[35]Jordan, *Creation in Six Days: A Defense of the Traditional Reading of Genesis 1* (Moscow, ID: Canon, 1999), 211-26.

[36]On *lemiyn*, see A. Rahel Davidson Schafer, "The 'Kinds' of Genesis 1: What is the Meaning of *Min*?" *Journal of the Adventist Theological Society* 14, no. 1 (2003): 86-100.

[37]Augustine anticipates the chiasm: "Does the light of the first day, perhaps, correspond . . . to the resting on the seventh, so that with the two ends of the series

The chapter is more complex than the two-panel analysis implies. Similarly, the days are not as symmetrically repetitive as they may initially appear. Table 5.2 indicates the raggedness of the literary texture.[38]

Table 5.2. Variation in Genesis 1 (based on Richard Middleton)

Day 1	Day 2	Day 3	Day 4	Day 5	Day 6
Elohim said	Elohim said	Elohim said	Elohim said	Elohim said	Elohim said
Let there be light	Let be firmament	Let water gather	Let there be lights	Let waters teem	Let earth bring forth
There was light	Elohim made	It was so	It was so	Elohim created	Elohim made
Elohim saw good	Elohim separated	Elohim called	Elohim made	Elohim saw good	Elohim saw good
Elohim separated	It was so	Elohim saw good	Elohim placed	Elohim blessed	Elohim said
Elohim called	Elohim called	Elohim said	Elohim saw good	Evening/ morning	Let Us make man
Evening/ morning	Evening/ morning	Let earth sprout plants	Evening/ morning		Elohim created
		It was so			Elohim blessed
		Earth sprouted plants			Elohim said: food
		Elohim saw good			Elohim saw very good
		Evening/ morning			It was so
					Evening/ morning

balancing in this way, the pattern could be perfect by weaving the outstanding lights into the middle? But if the first day balances with the seventh, then the second day in its turn should balance with the sixth. In what way, though, is the solid structure of heaven at all like man made in the image of God? Or could it be this, that as the heaven occupies the whole upper part of the cosmos, so too man has been granted the right to lord it over the whole of the lower part?" (*Literal Meaning of Genesis* 2.13.26).

[38]This chart summarizes the analysis of Richard Middleton, "Creation Founded in Love: Breaking Rhetorical Expectations in Genesis 1:1–2:3," in *Sacred Text, Sacred Times: The Hebrew Bible in the Modern World*, ed. Leonard Jay Greenspoon and Bryan F. LeBeau, Studies in Jewish Civilization 10 (Omaha, NE: Creighton University Press, 2000), 47-85.

Some variations are notable. After day two, *'elohim* stops separating, and after the middle of day three he stops naming. There is no execution formula "it was so" on days one or five, and no evaluative statement ("it was good") on day two. Sometimes *'elohim* simply says (day 1); sometimes he says and makes (days 2, 5, 6). Once (day 4), he speaks, makes, and places. After day three, he frequently summons creation to participation in its own filling (days 3, 5, 6). As Richard Middleton has argued, these variations belie the idea that "P" has a rigid, mechanistic, ritualistic mind devoted to a mechanistic, rigid God.[39] Creation is ordered, but it is not ordered with robotic regularity. Creation is an order with difference, each day's work a variation on a theme. Creation's order is more musical than mechanical, more Baroque than Bauhaus.

'Elohim is not a tyrant. His omnipotence is evident, for how else can he form the watery void *ex nihilo* or light, shape, and fill a world by speech? But he does not maintain his omnipotence by hoarding power. He leaves much of the world unnamed. At the Sabbath, *'elohim* ceases, so creation has a chance to stretch its muscles and show its stuff. Even before the Sabbath, the Creator makes room for creatures to act and do. *Most* of the earth's filling is accomplished by creatures of water and earth, rather than directly by the Creator. With regard to filling, *'elohim* imitates earth, for earth is *first* to fill (Gen 1:12). Earth possesses power to sprout plants only by virtue of *'elohim*'s word (Gen 1:11), but, once summoned, earth fills itself, and this occurs *before 'elohim* fills the sea and sky on day five.[40] *'Elohim* is not a control freak who has to do everything himself. He does as he pleases, but it

---

[39]Richard Middleton, "Creation Founded in Love."

[40]Arguably, *'elohim* directly fills creation only with sea monsters (Gen 1:21) and human beings (Gen 1:27), and perhaps birds. All other creatures emerge from created substances, whether water or earth.

pleases him to exercise power by empowering creatures to do divine things.[41]

Much of earth's *forming* is also the work of creatures. "Forming" takes place through separation and naming. *'Elohim* calls light into being, then separates it from the darkness and names the light and the darkness (Gen 1:3-5). At the end of day one, the dance of light and dark gives earth a temporal structure. On day two, he separates the waters above and the waters below, inserting and naming a firmament between (Gen 1:6-8). On day three, he gathers the waters of the earth into one place so earth itself can finally emerge (Gen 1:9), then names earth "earth" and the gathering of waters "sea" (Gen 1:10). This process of separating and naming *is* the process of forming. It *is* the act of creation.

Yet, after day three, *'elohim* stops separating and naming. Once in place, the firmament itself keeps the upper and lower waters separated. God makes and places heavenly lights to "separate the day from the night," to rule day and night, and to mark out seasons, days, and years (Gen 1:14, 16). Perhaps *'elohim* himself shines out in the light of the Spirit.[42] After day four, time's form depends on the labor of creatures. Since at least Augustine,[43] readers of Genesis 1 have puzzled over the apparent contradiction between day one and day four. How can there be a cycle of light and darkness, day and night, when there is no sun or moon? Many have taken this apparent anomaly as evidence that the days of creation are not temporal periods at all.[44] This misses the thrill of one the most dramatic moments of the creation week: On day

---

[41]Luther takes *'elohim* as a hint of Trinity (*Lectures on Genesis*, at Gen 1:26), and observes that judges and rulers are later called *'elohim* because they are authorized to carry out divine tasks (*Lectures on Genesis*, at Gen 1:2).

[42]Paul Beauchamp, *Creation et separation: Etude exegetique du chapitre premier de la Genese* (Paris: Cerf, 2010), 193.

[43]Augustine, *Literal Meaning of Genesis* 1.11.23.

[44]In chap. 7, I argue at length for a temporal understanding of the creation week.

four, the Creator delegates a crucial *act of creation* (separating) to creatures. Sun, moon, and stars are created to carry on *'elohim*'s work.[45] No wonder ancient peoples were tempted to worship heavenly lights.

Ever since, creatures continue to carry on the creative work of separating. In Genesis 2, Yahweh *'elohim* separates portions of the earth into the land of Eden, the garden in the land, and the land of Havilah where there is gold (Gen 2:9, 11). After that, shaping earthly space is left to earthly creatures. Animals mark territories, while human beings establish property boundaries, build city walls, distinguish sacred space from profane. God continues to orchestrate the distribution and boundaries of earth (Acts 17:26), but he orchestrates by enabling creatures to carry on the creative work of separating.

'Elohim also delegates naming, the second aspect of "forming." After *'elohim* names earth and sea on day three, he names no other creatures until he assigns names to selected men and women (Gen 17:5; 32:28). At the end of Genesis 1, *almost everything* is unnamed, and the task of naming passes on to Adam, who names wild beasts, cattle, and birds (Gen 2:19-20), and later his wife and sons. Human beings have been naming creatures ever since, and whatever we name it, "that is its name" (Gen 2:19). God adopts human names for creatures. Terah calls Abram "Abram," and so does Yahweh (Gen 15:1). Hagar's parents called her "Hagar," and that is the name Yahweh uses when he speaks to her (Gen 21:17). Some city founder named Sodom "Sodom," and that becomes Yahweh's name for the city (Gen 18:20). The Lord does not name camels, pigs, rock badgers, rabbits, vultures, kites, ravens, grasshoppers, or crickets; rather, when he speaks of these creatures, he adopts the human labels (Lev 11:1-23). He does not name the

---

[45]Barth, *Church Dogmatics 3/1: The Doctrine of Creation*, ed. Geoffrey Bromiley and T. F. Torrance; London: T&T Clark, 2010), 159-60.

organs of the body, or the parts of a flower, or the constellations and galaxies, or the elements of the periodic table, or the standard forms or instruments of classical music, or the features of architecture. In the beginning, creation is *under*-nominalized, as generous, humble *'elohim* leaves room for creatures to carry on the divinely creative act of naming.

Thomas Aquinas's definition of "creation" as the conferral of *esse* is based on a very partial reading of Genesis 1 (*ST* 1.45.5). Human naming, separating, and ruling are not merely superficial "cultural" transformations or mere acts of maintenance. *'Elohim creates* a habitable world by separating and naming, by forming and filling, and creaturely action continues that creative work. The world does not come into existence from nothing at every moment, but the world is continually proceeding toward its fulfillment through the creative human work of forming and filling, of separating and naming, which entirely relies, of course, on the work of the Father's Word and Spirit. Because the Creator delegates divine powers to creatures, history is a *creatio continuo*.[46]

For Bulgakov, creation is a metaphysical Golgotha, an expression of self-giving love because the Absolute sacrifices its absoluteness to become the Absolute-relative.[47] In Genesis, God is never anything but Creator. He is Absolute-relative from the outset, and the sacrifice of creation is his kenotic gift of divine

---

[46]History moves under the shadow of what Paul Griffith hauntingly calls "the Devastation." *Decreation: The Last Things of All Creatures* (Waco, TX: Baylor University Press, 2014). Looking back, the angel of history, as Benjamin said, sees only mayhem and rising mountains of waste. Human history is a history of wicked separations and misnamings, of deformations and emptyings. There is no apparent fullness of time, but only a continuous depletion. Yet, in its original design, and in its actual accomplishment, humans carry on the Creator's work of form, filling, separating, and naming. Creation and humanity have been and will be restored; the fullness of time has appeared in Jesus and will reach its *telos*.

[47]Sergius Bulgakov, *Unfading Light: Contemplations and Speculations*, trans. Thomas Allan Smith; Grand Rapids, MI: Eerdmans, 2012), 184-85.

power to creatures.[48] It is a sacrifice without loss, an expenditure of power without the least diminution. Yet it *is* sacrifice, for the Creator God of love gives his creation existence and, with existence, a share in his power to do the divine work of lighting, forming, and filling; of making and being fruitful; the divine work of creating. Nor is this merely the work of what we think of as living *spirits*. *Dirt* does divine things, as do the flaming balls of gas we call sun, moon, and stars.

As Richard Middleton observes,

> A close reading of the text depicts God neither as a warrior creating by violence nor as an extrinsic transcendence unilaterally imposing order on the world. Rather, Genesis 1 artfully shattered both ancient and modern rhetorical expectations and, instead, depicts God as a generous Creator, sharing power with a variety of creatures, inviting them (and trusting them—at some risk) to participate in the creative (and historical) process.[49]

Creation is an act of self-effacing, self-giving love. Creation *is* a demonstration of power, but mostly insofar as *'elohim gives* power, insofar as he demonstrates his utter confidence in his own power and glory, unthreatened by the power of others.[50] *'Elohim* has no need to compete with creatures for his rights. Nor does he create beings to do menial tasks. He gives creatures the capacity to perform divine tasks. The power of creation is the power of love.

---

[48]Ferdinand Ulrich sees an analogy between the "self-emptying" of the Son (Phil 2) and the act of creation. See D. C. Schindler, *A Companion to Ferdinand Ulrich's Homo Abyssus* (Washington, DC: Humanum Academic, 2019), 23.

[49]Middleton, "Creation Founded in Love," 67. Middleton's essay is in part a response to the "tehomic" theology of Catherine Keller, *The Face of the Deep: A Theology of Becoming* (London: Routledge, 2002).

[50]Thomas Aquinas agrees. In response to the Kalam Islamic theologians, who claimed to exalt the power of God by insisting on a mono-causal divine occasionalism, Thomas claims that occasionalism actually *limits* the power of God, "for it is due to the power of the cause that it bestows active power on its effects" (*ST* 1.2.105.5). *St. Thomas Aquinas, Summa theologiae*, vol. 29: *The Old Law*, trans. David Bourke (Cambridge: Cambridge University Press, 2006).

As Thomas says, the good is self-diffusive.[51] The literary shape of Genesis 1 indicates that 'elohim is not a "frozen . . . block of absolute essence." Such a "loveless, greedy God" would be "impotent to create," incapable of communicating himself because he is enclosed within himself.[52] "Creation is prodigal, a lavish spendthrift, nothing miserly," writes William Desmond. It "gives and gives; it renews even when it takes into death; it is fire that burns and is rekindled in its burning."[53] It gives because it is the gift of a lavish Creator. Creation is prodigal as the product of a prodigal God, who *is* not by careful retention of himself but by the excess of his self-gift. The Creator, being supremely good, is supremely self-diffusive, the source of all created goodness as he gives of his goodness to all creatures. The Creator, being supremely love, is supremely merciful, and creation is his first mercy.[54]

This theological conclusion is already a nascent confession of the Trinity. For God is unthreatened by the creative powers he gives to creatures because he exists eternally as an unthreatened communion of power and glory. The Father pours the glory of the

---

[51]As Schwöbel points out, self-diffusion and participation can imply an impersonal process or sharing. I understand self-diffusion as a personal exchange of gift, reception, and return gift. See Christoph Schwöbel, "The Eternity of the Triune God: Preliminary Considerations on the Relationship between the Trinity and the Time of Creation," *Modern Theology* 34, no. 3 (2018): 9-10. On this point, we once again see the importance of the starting point we arrived at in chap. 4. Thomas struggles to explain how God can be self-diffusively good without creation. Genesis has no such struggle because the only God it reveals is the Creator, who is, as soon as we meet him, diffusing his good gifts to creation, including the gift of being-created.

[52]Ferdinand Ulrich, *Homo Abyssus: The Drama of the Question of Being*, trans. D. C. Schindler (Washington, DC: Humanum Academic, 2018), 27; see also Schindler, *Companion to Ferdinand Ulrich's Homo Abyssus*, 117. As the very form of God, the Word is "the form of God's richness as love," richness he shares "above all with those who are most vulnerable." This "*communication of richness*" begins with creation *ex nihilo*. David L. Schindler, *The Generosity of Creation* (Washington, DC: Humanum Academic, 2018), 109.

[53]Desmond, *Being and the Between*, 230.

[54]Schindler, *Companion*, 63n29; Schindler cites Stefan Oster's introduction to Ulrich's *Gabe und Vergebung*, though the thought is traceable to Thomas.

Spirit on the Son without reserve; he does not begrudge sharing eternal glory with the Son, nor the Son with the Father. So too, the triune Creator does not begrudge sharing glory and power with creatures. From the very moment, creation is "deified" and on its way to being more fully so. For the Creator is not envious.[55]

I am getting ahead of myself. I have drawn some fairly large conclusions from the formal characteristics of Genesis 1. I am confident they are justified. After all, as Augustine recognized, trinitarian traces are evident all through Genesis 1, traces that become more legible as the chapter continues. Once again, let us start at the very beginning, with the first divine name.

'ELOHIM

The God who creates the world is named by the Hebrew word *'elohim*. In Canaanite usage, the singular *'el* is the name of the creator and father of the gods, sometimes of a warrior god (*'el gibbor*), a judge, or a patriarch. The word *'el* rarely appears in the Hebrew Bible as a name for the God of Israel, though it is sometimes used in combination names such as *'el 'elyon* ("God most high," Gen 14:18) and *'el ro'i* ("a God who sees," Gen 16:13).[56] Instead of *'el*, the God of Israel is *'elohim*, typically thought to be a plural form of *'el* with an added *he-* syllable.[57] In many contexts, the word retains its plural meaning. The same Hebrew word describes

---

[55]See Plato, *Timaeus* 29E. "God is not envious" is a theme of Athanasius's *Discourse Against the Arians* (2.29) and is given a particular gloss in the work of Rowan Williams, who stresses that the Creator is transcendently unimpaired and unthreatened by creatures because he is not in competition with them. See Williams, *On Christian Theology* (Oxford: Blackwell, 2000), 63-78; "Faith in the Modern Areopagus," *Church Life Journal*, February 18, 2021, available online at https://churchlifejournal .nd.edu/articles/faith-in-the-modern-areopagus/.

[56]"*'el*," in G. Johannes Botterweck, Heiz-Josef Fabri, and Helmer Ringgren, eds., *Theological Dictionary of the Old Testament*, 15 vols. (Grand Rapids, MI: Eerdmans, 2011), 1.244-53, 255.

[57]Helmer Ringgren, *'elohim*, *TDOT*, 1:273. This derivation is not without its problems, and *'elohim* may be derived from a root other than *'el*. That does not change the fact that it is a plural form.

both Yahweh, the *'elohim* of the exodus (Ex 20:1) and the "gods" whom Israel is forbidden to place before his face (Ex 20:3; cf. Gen 31:30; Deut 13:2; Is 42:17). Though plural in form, *'elohim*'s grammatical behavior is erratic. In a few cases, *'elohim* of Israel is the subject of a plural verb (Gen 20:13) or modified by a plural adjective (Josh 24:19). In the vast majority of cases, when *'elohim* designates the God of Israel, it takes singular verbs and is modified by singular adjectives. The very first clause of the Old Testament is representative: "God created" is *bara' 'elohim*, a masculine singular verb with a plural subject. The pattern is: "*'elohim* . . . he/his."

Remarkably, the same erratic grammar appears in God-talk in other ancient Near Eastern religions. Plural forms of "god" take singular verbs and adjectives in Canaanite, Ugaritic, Phoenician, a few Aramaic texts, and first-millennium Akkadian.[58] Joel Burnett concludes these cognates of *'elohim* function as a "concretized abstract plural" denoting "deity,"[59] and he concludes the Hebrew term has the same abstract connotation, as the plural "virgins" denotes "virginity" (Lev 21:13; Deut 22:14, 15, 17).[60] Perhaps, he speculates, the plural is used to indicate that the god in question sums up all the conditions, qualities, and attributes inherent in the idea of "God." That is, *'elohim* refers to the fullness of all one expects of an *'el*. Other abstract plurals function in the same way: Abraham is Eleazar's *'adonim* because he embodies all the best qualities of "master" or "lord" (Gen 24:9), and our eyes look to the Lord our God just as servants look to the hand of their "masters" (Ps 123:2).[61] Yahweh is *'adonai*, possibly an archaic plural form of *'adon* (Josh 3:11, 13): He is "Lords Yahweh."

---

[58]Joel S. Burnett, *A Reassessment of Biblical Elohim*, SBL Dissertation Series 183 (Atlanta: SBL Press, 2001), 7-53.

[59]Burnett, *Reassessment*, 53.

[60]Burnett, *Reassessment*, 22.

[61]Burnett, *Reassessment*, 21. Burnett observes that not every plural implies this kind of perfected fullness (22), which is why he prefers to call the plural form an abstract plural.

In some exodus passages, *'elohim* oscillates between singular and plural. "I am Yahweh your *'elohim*, who brought you up from the land of Egypt," is Yahweh's first-person singular declaration from Sinai (Ex 20:2). Yet Yahweh delivers through the destroyer (Ex 12:23), and leads by the *mal'ak ha'elohim* (Ex 14:19) and the pillar of cloud and fire (Ex 13:22; 14:19). In Psalm 78:48-50, God (*'el*, Ps 78:41) enlists a small army of "minor deities" who help Yahweh deliver Israel; Hail, Lightning, Anger, Fury, Death, and Plague are personified as agents or energies of Yahweh. Together with these powers, *'el* is *'elohim* (Ps 78:56). In the song of the sea, further, Miriam leads Israel in praise of Yahweh, and also of his "right hand," his "burning," and his "breath" (Ex 15:6-7, 10).[62] *'Elohim* is "God of gods" because he harnesses all the powers to accomplish his purposes. He is *'elohim* in that he possesses all these powers in himself, for the right hand is his, the fury and anger are his, the burning is the flashing of the God who is himself a consuming fire. Yet with all these indications of plurality, Yahweh remains an "I." He remains Yahweh, Israel's God, who is one (Deut 6:4-5).

Burnett's work offers a roundabout way of taking *'elohim* as an indication of divine plurality. Since Peter the Lombard,[63] Christians have often opted for the shorter route: the plural *'elohim* points directly, if obscurely, to the Trinity. In his *de tribus Elohim*, the Italian Reformer Giralamo Zanchi (Zanchius) claims the term shows there are "three Gods according to the thing," since "there are three persons, each of whom is God." His preferred formula is closer to creeds, as he equates the persons with *'elohim* and the unified substance with Yahweh: "There are indeed plural *Elohim*, but only one *Jehovah*: and that each of these *Elohim* is *Jehovah*."[64]

---

[62]Burnett, *Reassessment*, 87-89.

[63]Lombard, *Sentences* 1.2.4.5.

[64]See the English translation of books 1–3 of Zanchi's treatise at https://nsa.edu/assets /documents/On%20The%20Triune%20Elohim%20Books%201-3.pdf. For an extensive discussion, see Benjamin R. Merkle, *Defending the Trinity in the Reformed*

The Shema provides Zanchi with a key piece of evidence since it employs the plural *'elohim* in a passage emphasizing the oneness of Israel's God. Israel confesses "that Jehovah is one, although we teach that there are plural and distinct Elohim." The Shema provides the "sum of this doctrine, [that] there is only one true and eternal God—truly distinguished three *'Elohim* or 'persons,' Father, Son and Holy Spirit: of which each is God, *Jehovah*, such that there are not many *Jehovahs*, but they are all simultaneously only one *Jehovah*." Since, Zanchi thinks, "Jehovah" derives from the Hebrew verb for "is," it signifies the one essence or being of God, while *'elohim* points to the plurality of hypostases.

This may seem a stretch, but Zanchi's reading of the Shema gains strength in the light of 1 Corinthians 8, described by N. T. Wright as Paul's "redefinition" of the Shema. The echoes of the Shema are evident: In a world of many gods and many lords (1 Cor 8:5), there is "for us" Christians only "one God" (1 Cor 8:4, 6), the Creator. For a Jew like Paul, creational monotheism is "what matters"; it is second nature. It is a shock, then, when Paul revises this central Jewish confession. The Septuagint of the Shema confesses the oneness of both *kyrios* (Lord, YHWH) and *theos* (God, *'elohim*): *kyrios ho theos hēmōn heis estin*. Paul splits the terms: The Father is the "one God" and Jesus is the "one Lord." Paul places Jesus "at the heart" of the Jewish confession of the one God, confessing a "Christological monotheism."[65]

I think Wright is right, but, in the light of Zanchi's argument, "redefinition" is not quite the right word. Rather, Paul offers an

---

Palatinate: The Elohistae, Oxford Theology and Religion Monographs (Oxford: Oxford University Press, 2016), chap. 4. Zanchi's arguments were taken up by many Reformed scholastics. See Richard Muller, *Post-Reformation Reformed Dogmatics*, vol. 4: *The Triunity of God* (Grand Rapids, MI: Baker, 2003). For a recent defense of the argument, see David L. Cooper, *The God of Israel* (Los Angeles: Biblical Research Society, 1973).

[65]N. T. Wright, "One God, One Lord, One People: Incarnational Christology for a Church in a Pagan Environment," https://chamberscreek.net/library/N.%20T.%20Wright/wright1998one.html.

interpretation. The names of God in the Shema *already* hint at unity and plurality; *'elohim* is *already* associated with the Father as Creator (in Genesis 1); the angel-messenger of Yahweh is already identified with Yahweh, and so readily identified with the *kyrios* Jesus (see chap. 6 below). Paul states openly what the Shema had always declared in a veiled manner. In a world of powers, for Israel as for "us," there is one God, *'elohim* the Creator, and one Lord, Yahweh incarnate as Jesus of Nazareth.

Thus, from the first mention of God in Genesis 1, he is named as plural. The author of Genesis 1 is no "strict monotheist" who worships a monadic God. He proclaims instead the works of *'elohim.*

HOVERING SPIRIT

Augustine is correct to discern trinitarian hints in the combination of Spirit and Word. The *ruakh* appears first, in Genesis 1:2, hovering over the formless deep. *Ruakh* can mean "breath," "wind," or "Spirit." Though most English translations retain the traditional translation "Spirit of God," recent commentators and translators have argued for "wind," claiming that "Spirit," especially when capitalized, overly Christianizes an ancient text. Instead, they take *'elohim* as an adjective ("mighty," "divine") or as a genitive of source ("of God"). Thus: "A mighty wind/wind from God hovered on the face of the waters."[66] On this reading, the

---

[66]See H. M. Orlinsky, "The Plain Meaning of *Ruah* in Gen. 1.2," *Jewish Quarterly Review* 48 (1957/1958): 174-82; Claus Westermann, *Genesis 1–11,* trans. John J. Scullian (Minneapolis: Fortress, 1994), 107-8; John Goldingay, *Genesis,* Baker Commentary on the Old Testament Pentateuch (Grand Rapids, MI: Baker, 2020), 28; Gordon Wenham, *Genesis 1–15,* Word Biblical Commentary (Nashville: Thomas Nelson, 1987), 16-17; Joseph Blenkinsopp, *Creation, Un-Creation, Re-Creation: A Discursive Commentary on Genesis 1–11* (London: T&T Clark 2011), 33-34; R. Luyster, "Wind and Water: Cosmogonic Symbolism in the Old Testament," *Zeitschrift für die altestamentliche Wissenschaft* 93 (1981): 1-10; Guy Darshan, "*Ruah 'Elohim* in Genesis 1:2 in Light of Phoenician Cosmogonies: A Tradition's History," *Journal of Northwest Semitic Languages* 45, no. 2 (2019): 51-78; Mischeck Nyierenda, "Theological Interpretation

mighty wind or "fearful storm" does not form the formless earth but, along with the darkness and formless void, is a feature of original chaos.[67]

The arguments for the traditional translation are compelling. The *ruakh* is on *'elohim*'s side of the Creator-creature divide. As Augustine notes, the Spirit is in a position of superiority to the earth,[68] hovering above it, moving as a bird hovers over an egg or protectively over its young (see Deut 32:11). The Spirit carries out the work of *'elohim* himself in giving shape to and filling the formless void. More broadly, "none of the other eighteen occurrences of this phrase [*ruakh 'elohim*] in the OT means anything like 'mighty wind'" (e.g., Ex 31:3; 35:31; Num 24:2; 1 Sam 10:10; 16:15).[69] Exodus 31:3 is especially pertinent. Bezalel is filled with the *ruakh 'elohim* to forge the vessels of the tabernacle, in a context that is closely parallel to Genesis 1, since "the creation of a world [is analogous] to the creation of a shrine."[70] No one thinks Bezalel is filled with a "divine wind." If the phrase means "Spirit of God" in the creation text of Exodus 31:3, it means the same in the

---

and Translation Reception: Translating 'Spirit of God" in Genesis 1.1-2," *The Bible Translator* 64, no. 3 (2013): 284-99; Lynell Zogbo, "Ideology and Translation: The Case of *Ruach Elohim* and *Ruach YHWH* in the Old Testament," in *Current Trends in Scripture Translation*, ed. Philip A. Noss (Reading, PA: United Bible Societies, 2002), 213-21; Jacob Loewen, "Clear Air or Bad Breath?" *The Bible Translator* 34, no. 2 (1997): 213-19.

[67]"Fearful storm" comes from Gerhard von Rad, *Genesis*, rev. ed. (Philadelphia: Westminster, 1972), 49-50.

[68]*Literal Meaning of Genesis* 1.7.13.

[69]Victor Hamilton, *The Book of Genesis, Chapters 1–17*, New International Commentary on the Old Testament (Grand Rapids, MI: Eerdmans, 1990), 111. Hamilton leaves open the question whether *ruakh* should be translated as "wind" or "spirit," but he insists that in either case the *ruakh* comes from God and accomplishes God's purposes.

[70]Hamilton, *Genesis 1–17*, 112. As many have noted, Exodus 25–31 is laid out as a series of seven speeches of Yahweh, which culminates with a reiteration of the Sabbath command (Ex 31:12-17). Bezalel is promised the *ruakh 'elohim* in the sixth speech, corresponding to the sixth day. He is a new and greater Adam, filled with the Spirit to carry out the original Adamic task of forming the materials of creation into a temple for the Creator.

creation text of Genesis 1:2. As to the adjectival theory: *'elohim* is almost never used unambiguously as a superlative (cf. Gen 23:6; 30:8; Jon 3:3). Even if it is a superlative elsewhere, it is not in Genesis 1. After all, *'elohim* is used thirty-five times in the creation account, and everywhere else it clearly means "God." How is a reader expected to distinguish the adjectival *'elohim* in Genesis 1:2 from the thirty-four uses of the noun *'elohim*?

When *ruakh* means "wind," it usually implies destruction rather than creation (Ex 15:10; Is 11:15; 40:7). When it means "breath" or "spirit" it implies energy, vitality, "creating and not uncreating." If the *ruakh* of Genesis 1:2 is a beneficent power, it should be translated as "Spirit" rather than "wind." Finally, the verb *hover* (participle of *rakhaph*) does not describe the movement of wind. Deuteronomy 32:10-11 uses the same verb to describe "how a bird teaches its young to fly."[71] That Deuteronomy passage also echoes Genesis 1:2 by describing the wilderness as *tohu* ("waste" or "formless"). Moses' song evokes the Spirit's work in creation, comparing him not to a rushing wind but to a protective, nurturing eagle who guards, encircles, and cares for its young, "freeing" them to soar.[72]

Later passages that speak of creation by word and Spirit/breath draw from Genesis 1:2 (Job 33:4; Ps 33:6). Of these, Psalm 104:27-30 is one of the most relevant. The psalm as a whole blesses Yahweh for his work of creation. He lays the foundation of the earth and covers it with a garment of water (Ps 104:5-6). When he rebukes the waves, the waters retreat and the

---

[71]Hamilton, *Genesis 1–17*, 115.

[72]In addition to Hamilton, see Henri Blocher, *In the Beginning: The Opening Chapters of Genesis* (Downers Grove, IL: InterVarsity Press, 1984), 68-69; C. John Collins, *Genesis 1–4: A Linguistic, Literary, and Theological Commentary* (Phillipsburg, NJ: P&R, 2006), 45n17; Edward J. Young, *Studies in Genesis 1* (Phillipsburg, NJ: P&R, 1999; first published in 1964), 36-42; William McClellan, "The Meaning of *Ruah 'Elohim* in Genesis 1, 2," *Biblica* 15, no. 4 (1934): 517-27.

mountains rise (Ps 104:7-9). Earth is watered by springs, which quench the thirst of beasts, donkeys, birds (Ps 104:10-13) and cause grass to grow for cattle and trees and vines for mankind (Ps 104:14-17). God tends and feeds the beasts in the remotest parts of the mountains and forests (Ps 104:18-23). Psalm 104:27-30 sing of creation's dependence on God. He feeds all flesh, and when he hides his face, they are "dismayed." Each creature's breath (*ruakh*) is a gift from God, and when he takes it away, they return to the dust (Ps 104:29). But when he sends out his own *ruakh*, creatures are newly created (*bara'*) as he renews the face of the ground (*'adamah*). *Bara'* is a relatively rare verb, and is used in conjunction with *ruakh* in only two passages, Genesis 1:2 and Psalm 104:30. The latter is clearly speaking of Yahweh's Spirit, not "wind," as his active creative power. The Psalmist provides an inner-biblical interpretation of Genesis 1:2, emphasizing the Spirit's role in the work of creation.

Elsewhere in Scripture, the Spirit is the source of sound, including the sound of music. Yahweh confronts Adam and Eve in the deafening *ruakh* of the day (Gen 3:8). The Spirit falls on Saul when he meets a band of prophetic minstrels, and he prophesies in song (1 Sam 10:1-13). Filled with the Spirit who abandoned Saul, David plays the harp to drive an evil spirit from the king (1 Sam 16:13-23). Be filled with the Spirit, Paul says, so that you may sing Psalms and spiritual songs and make melody in your heart (Eph 5:18-19). The Spirit's advent is accompanied by music, for he is both the visual and audible glory of God. So too in Genesis 1. Before the Word resounds, the Spirit, hovering like a winged bird, has established the basso continuo of creation. *'Elohim* the Creator, creating by and through his Spirit, is God most musical.[73]

---

[73]"God is a great fugue," writes Robert Jenson, *Systematic Theology*, vol. 1: *The Triune God* (Oxford: Oxford University Press, 1997), 236. And, of course, see Jeremy Begbie, *Theology, Music, and Time* (Cambridge: Cambridge University Press, 2000).

He is not envious, and so he joyfully sings a creation that can, and will, join in to harmonize on his eternal song.[74] This too is a form of deification.

The Spirit is the passion, the source and center of the emotional life of the Creator. He arouses judges to battle frenzy, regrets creating humanity (Gen 6:3, 6), delights in his Servant (Isa 42:1), yearns over wayward Ephraim (Jer 31:20), and rejoices over Israel's return (Jer 32:41). The Spirit hovers, birdlike, over the liquid earth (cf. Deut 32:10-11). *'Elohim* spreads the wing of the Spirit over the formless waters, as Yahweh later stretches the wing of his Spirit-robe over Israel, still squirming in her blood and afterbirth (cf. Ezek 16:6). By the Spirit, *'elohim* claims and forms earth as a bride. Before He utters his first fiat, the Creator is to the creature as bridegroom to bride.

Creation by the Spirit is an act of divine passion, a fulfillment of divine yearning. He creates by a Word charged with the Love that is the Spirit and creates a world that is itself charged with the passion of the Spirit. The Creator's yearning is not like our yearning. He does not long for what he lacks. His longing is the longing of infinite fullness, undiluted joy, sheer bliss, not the longing to have what is absent but longing to share what is superabundantly present. Pseudo-Dionysius says the highest name of God is "the Good," which he equates with *erōs*. Dionysius knows it is a daring move, but he cites Scripture and the Fathers in defense and argues that *erōs* is a better name for God than *agapē* because, in D. C. Schindler's words, "*eros* brings out the ecstatic, self-transcending, and . . . 'other-affirming' character of love."

---

[74]Jenson once again: In the eschaton, "the point of identity, infinitely approachable and infinitely to be approached, the enlivening *telos* of the Kingdom's own life, is perfect harmony between the conversation of the redeemed and the conversation that God is. In the conversation God is, meaning and melody are one. The end is music." *Systematic Theology*, vol. 2: *The Works of God* (Oxford: Oxford University Press, 1999), 369.

To say the Spirit is *erōs* is to say he is *"moved by His beloved." Erōs* implies reciprocity. If he is *erōs*, God is not merely an *object* of love, but "is himself a lover."[75]

Creation by the Spirit of *erōs* gets to the heart of the "Christian difference": God is not a remote First Cause or inaccessible origin but "enters *also into the middle* . . . and comes in pursuit of his creatures." To speak of divine *erōs* is already implicitly to speak of incarnation. And *erōs* helps us grasp the paradoxical depths of the Creator-creature relation. God does not undergo temporal change, but neither is he simply static. He possesses "'a supra-temporal fullness of life,' an eternal 'ever more.'"[76] That is to say, "God, precisely as perfect goodness, does not wish to be good only in himself . . . but wishes to have his (own) goodness only *in* and *with* his other." This goodness is none other than God's own goodness, yet "he (freely) wishes to have his goodness, to be perfectly good, only in and through the mediation of his other, the world that is his creation."[77]

---

[75]D. C. Schindler, "Mediation: The Distinguishing Mark of Christianity," *Communio* 48 (2021): 23; see also Schindler, "The Redemption of Eros. Philosophical Reflec tions on Benedict XVI's First Encyclical," *Communio* 33 (2006): 375-99. Thus Dionysius: "We may be so bold as to claim also that the Cause of all things loves all things in the superabundance of his goodness, that because of this goodness he makes all things, brings all things to perfection, holds all things together, returns all things. The divine longing is the Good seeking good for the sake of the Good. That yearning which creates all the goodness of the world preexisted superabundantly within the Good and did not allow it to remain without issue. It stirred him to use the abundance of his powers in the production of the world." *Divine Names* 708B in *Pseudo-Dionysius: The Complete Works*, trans. by Colm Luibheid (Mahwah, NJ: Paulist, 1987).

[76]Schindler, "Mediation," 23-24. The quoted phrases are from von Balthasar. See also Thomas Traherne: From all eternity, the God of Israel "wanted like a God. He wanted the communication of His divine essence, and persons to enjoy it. He wanted Worlds, He wanted Spectators, He wanted Joys, He wanted Treasures. He wanted, yet He wanted not, for He had them." His eternal desire is the "very ground and cause of infinite treasure. . . . Want is the foundation of all His fulness." *Centuries of Mediation*, 1.41-42 in Bertram Dobell, ed., *Centuries of Meditation* (New York: Cosmo Classics, 2007). Traherne's claim is coherent provided we do not imagine a non-Creator yearning for a creation, but the Creator whose wants are fulfilled.

[77]Schindler, "Mediation," 24-25.

Here again it is crucial to start at the very beginning. If God is a not-yet Creator or non-Creator, it is hard to speak of divine "yearning" without turning God into a dependent, whose desire is fulfilled only in the creation he has not yet begun to create. If, as in Genesis, God is simply Creator, the God who is already Bridegroom to bride, the yearning of the Spirit is always already satisfied, though it is no less genuine yearning for that. An Absolute cannot be *erōs* without risking his absoluteness. Only the Creator Spirit can *be erōs*.

We are putting the pieces together. The "Creator" of Genesis 1 is, at least, *'elohim* (already plural) and the Spirit of *'elohim*. Can we find a third?

GOD SAID

No sooner has *'elohim* breathed his breath over earth than the breath is vocalized as Word (Gen 1:3). The Creator speaks the Word by the breath of the Spirit. That is, the speech by which God creates is impassioned speech, the anointed, Pentecostal speech of the Spirit. That God creates by Word is one of the most obvious and distinctive biblical claims about creation (Ps 33:6; 148:5; Jn 1:1-5; 2 Cor 4:6; Heb 11:3). There are vague parallels in Egyptian and Babylonian myth, but nothing truly comparable.[78] Given the centrality of this confession in Scripture, it is remarkable how little attention the tradition has paid to this theme and how undeveloped it is in theology and biblical scholarship. I will return

---

[78]Westermann, *Genesis 1–11*, 111-12. See also the critical comments in Barth, *Church Dogmatics* 3/1, 112-13. Of the Memphian account, Barth comments, "What this creator first does with his mouth when he brings forth his children She and Teen is something very different form creative utterance." He "spits" out his children, and then engages in a masturbatory "auto-procreation" with his own shadow, which suggests that the "spitting" was sexual to begin with. In the *Enuma Elish*, Marduk demonstrates his creative power by decreasing and remaking a garment, but this is, as Barth says, "merely a kind of preliminary and probationary witchcraft." "Creation" itself is a combat, where "there is no trace of a mighty utterance by Marduk."

more fully to this point in chapter six. For now, I briefly summarize the biblical case for seeing the Son of God in the speaking
of *'elohim*.

Genesis 1:3 plunges Augustine into an interrogative mood: In
what way did God speak? Did he speak in time "or in the eternity
of the Word"? If in time, could God have spoken without change?
How could he speak words without a temporal, created medium?
Did God speak audibly, as the Father did at Jesus' baptism? If so,
what language did he use? Who was there to hear his words?
Whom did he address? Augustine concludes that the "voice of
God" refers to "the intelligible meaning of the audible utterance,
Let light be made, and not the audible utterance itself." If it is "intelligible" rather than "audible," the speech can be eternal and
changeless, belonging "to the very nature of the Word," who is
co-eternal with God.[79]

Augustine notwithstanding, I take "Let there be light" to be
an actual utterance, as the divine voice simultaneously resounds
from heaven to earth and creates a medium for sound. God
speaks with the voice of a trumpet (Ex 19:16, 19; 20:18), a
thunder-voice that splits cedars and drives does into labor (Ps
29:3-9). The cosmos begins with a great sound, not a Big Bang
but a Big "Be!"

Yet Augustine is also correct to recognize that the Word of
'elohim is the living Word, a second identity within the Creator.
The two are hardly incompatible. After all, the Word who becomes flesh spends a lot of his life talking. How do we know
'elohim speaks the Word that is toward (*pros*) *'elohim* and is *'elohim*?
John tells us (Jn 1:1-3). He begins "in the beginning" (*en archē*),
identifies the spoken Word with the divine Word made flesh in
Jesus, speaks of the light that shines in the darkness (Jn 1:4-5, 9)

---

[79]*The Literal Meaning of Genesis* 1.2.4-6. Basil agrees (*Hexameron* 2.7; 3.2).

and the creation of a new-Adamic community of the "children of God" (Jn 1:12). All this is set in a sequence of seven (or eight) days (Jn 1:19, 29, 35, 43; 2:1) that culminates with a sabbatical (and third-day) wedding at Cana, where Jesus turns the water in the man-sized waterpots into wine (Jn 2:1-11). John's prologue does not merely allude to Genesis 1. It is an apostolic *interpretation* of the creation account.[80]

There are other hints of triune life in John's reading of Genesis 1. The Word was God and "with [*pros*] God" (Jn 1:1-2). How *pros*? It seems a throwaway preposition, but Bulgakov says it indicates "the Holy Spirit as the hypostatic love of the Father and the Son." The Word is the one by whom all things are made, but the reference to creation alludes also to the work of the Spirit, through whom creation "received reality and life." "In him was life," John continues (Jn 1:4). *What* life? Bulgakov again finds a veiled reference to the Spirit: John "refers to the Life-giving Spirit, who reposes upon the Son and, with Him, constitutes the Dyad of the self-revelation of the Father, while abiding 'in him.'" The light (Jn 1:9) is Christ, but "in the ecclesiastical literature it also frequently refers to the Holy Spirit." The incarnate Son reveals the glory of the Father and comes with the fullness of grace and truth, and these too are manifestations of the Spirit, who is the Glory, the agent of glorification, and the Grace that rests on the Son. The Prologue is not simply a "logology" but "a complete trinitarian theology, including a pneumatology, though the latter is expressed almost tacitly, in a mere breath."[81] John comes to his pneumatological Christology through a reading of Genesis 1.

---

[80]Peder Borgen, "Logos Was the True Light: Contributions to the Interpretation of the Prologue of John," *Novum Testamentum* 14, no. 2 (1972): 115-30.

[81]Sergius Bulgakov, *The Comforter*, trans. Boris Jakim (Grand Rapids, MI: Eerdmans, 2004), 161-62.

As noted above, Augustine sees a reference to the Son in the opening phrase of Genesis, *bere'shit*, "in the beginning" (LXX, *en archē*). That may seem a stretch, but in this, Augustine has an ally in the apostle Paul. In his "Christ hymn" in Colossians 1, Paul explicitly identifies Jesus as the *archē* (Col 1:18), in a context where Jesus is the agent of creation (Col 1:16, 19-20). As N. T. Wright has pointed out, Paul's various titles for Jesus unpack the possible meanings of *bere'shit*. The Hebrew preposition *b-* can mean "in," "through," or "to" (in Greek, *en*, *dia*, or *eis*), each of which describes Christ's role in creating: "By [*en*] Him all things were created . . . all things have been created through [*dia*] Him and for [*eis*] Him" (Col 1:16). The noun *re'shit*, translated in Greek as *archē*, can mean firstborn, supreme, firstfruits, head, beginning, all titles Paul gives to Christ.[82] What appears to be Augustine's weakest trinitarian argument is actually quite strong, for the Word spoken by *'elohim* (Jn 1:1) is also the *archē* in, through, and for whom he creates the heavens and the earth.[83]

Thus, the first verses of Genesis reveal a God who takes a plural name. In shadowy form, the first verses also reveal the persons who are this God—*'elohim* who creates and speaks, his Spirit who shapes and fills, and the Word of *'elohim* who summons light, gives pattern to the heavenly lights, and calls living souls from

---

[82]N. T. Wright, *Colossians and Philemon*, Tyndale New Testament Commentaries (Downers Grove, IL: IVP Academic, 2008), 71-79. Wright relies on C. F. Burney, "Christ as the arche of Creation," *Journal of Theological Studies* 16 (1965): 160-76, who concludes "Christ fulfills every meaning which may be extracted from *Reshith*" (176).

[83]In other contexts, *bere'shit* introduces the reign of a king: "In the beginning of the reign of Jehoiakim" (Jer 26:1: *bere'shit mamlekut yehoyaqiym*; see Jer 27:1; 28:1). The beginning of heaven and earth is also the establishment of a reign and a realm. *'Elohim* sets boundaries, issues laws, pronounces judgment ("it was good"). King *'elohim* builds his cosmic palace to house his image, the princely son Adam. See Gerald Bowyer, "Elohim's Dynasty: Kingdom and Co-Regency in the Hebrew Text of Genesis 1–3," (Unpublished Licentiate Thesis, Collegium Augustianum, 2016), 6-24. As we shall see in chap. 6, there might also be a hint of a throne shared by divine rulers, *'elohim* and the Word he speaks as "let be."

earth and sea. We discern a trinitarian exterior. Can we infer anything of the inner life of this Creator?

LET US MAKE

Given this background in the opening verses of Genesis 1, it is hardly surprising that *'elohim* should speak to himself as plural before he creates man. Trinitarian interpretations of Genesis 1:26 have been common since the early centuries. Justin, Irenaeus, Basil, Chrysostom, Augustine, Luther, Calvin, Zanchi, and Barth all interpret "let us" as divine self-consultation.[84] There are, of course, alternative interpretations.[85] Of late, the most popular is that *'elohim* addresses the angelic hosts who assist him in the creation of man. That interpretation suffers from crippling flaws.

We know from various Scriptures that the angels were made at the beginning, and that they form a joyful chorus at the foundation of the earth (Gen 2:1; Job 38:7).[86] But it is one thing to recognize the divine council as spectators of the creation week and another to say they participate in creating.[87] Further, Scripture nowhere indicates that man is made in the image of angels, nor that angels are made in the image of God. Rather, *man*

---

[84]Justin the Martyr, *Dialogue with Trypho* 62; Irenaeus, *Against All Heresies* 4.20.1-3; Basil, *Hexaemeron* 9.6; Gregory of Nyssa, *On the Making of Man* 16.5; Augustine, *Literal Meaning of Genesis* 3.19.29; Chrysostom, *Homilies on Genesis* 8.1; Luther, *Lectures on Genesis*, at Gen 1:26; Calvin, *Commentary on Genesis*.

[85]Some suggest it is a polytheistic residue, but that seems unlikely in a text so thoroughly purged of mythical elements. Others have suggested it is a "plural of majesty," but there is little evidence for such royal grammar in the Old Testament. For discussion, see D. J. A. Clines, "The Image of God in Man," *Tyndale Bulletin* 19 (1968): 53-103; Gerhard Hasel, "The Meaning of 'Let Us' in Gn 1:26," *Andrews University Seminary Studies* 13, no. 1 (1975): 58-66.

[86]Angels play an outsized role in Augustine's literal interpretation of Genesis 1, but he inserts them for his own philosophical reasons. They are *not* in the text.

[87]At the extreme, Keller, *The Face of the Deep*, 172-78, moves from the plural *'elohim* to the conclusion that "the turbulent swarm of godhood has always transgressed any possible boundaries between the One Original Creator and the many derivative creatures" (178).

is alone the created image of God. Within Genesis 1, the grammar works against the angelic-council interpretation. After the plural "Let Us make," the narrator describes the execution of the plan with singular verbs: "God (*'elohim*) created man in *His* own image (*betsalmo*), in the image of God *He* created (*bara'*) him; male and female *He* created (*bara'*) them" (Gen 1:27). "Our" image (Gen 1:26) becomes "His image" (Gen 1:27). If "we" plan to create man, why do "they" not do the creating?[88] Whoever is included in the "us" of Genesis 1:26 is included in the *'elohim* and the "he" of Genesis 1:27. If the divine council is the "us," they inexplicably fall back into the role of spectators, a "mere entourage," when the planned act is executed.[89] Barth is correct: It will not do to say Genesis 1:26 is a mere "consultation" with the divine council. It is a summons to "an act . . . of creation, in concert with the One who speaks."[90] If an angelic swarm does not do the creating, they must not have been summoned.

---

[88]Luther finds a trinitarian hint in the interplay of singular and plural: "Here both appear: 'Let Us make' and 'He made,' in the plural and in the singular; thereby Moses clearly and forcible shows us that within and in the very Godhead and the Creating Essence there is one inseparable and eternal plurality. . . . These Makers are three separate Persons in one divine essence" (*Lectures on Genesis*, at Gen 1:26).

[89]Barth, *Church Dogmatics* 3/1, 190. Luther also rejects the angelic interpretation of "us," which he characterizes as an opinion of the Jews. Luther, *Lectures on Genesis*, at Gen 1:26.

[90]Barth, *Church Dogmatics* 3/1, 189-90. Randall Garr attempts to elude the force of this point by calling attention to uses of the first person plural cohortative in which a single member of a group executes the group's decision: "The addressee of a directive and the subject of its execution may be grammatically different." None of the examples, though, are truly comparable to Genesis 1:26-27, where a speaker calls unnamed addressees to participate in something but then carries out the plan on his own. In Deuteronomy 1:22-23, the "let us" includes a plan to delegate the action to "men" who will serve as spies. David calls on his courtiers with "Let us rise"; the execution formula states "the king left," but the narrator immediately adds "and all his household" (2 Sam 15:14-17). Garr claims that the imperative in 2 Sam 11:16b is "addressed to a group" but carried out by Joab alone. "Deliver Uriah" is plural, but it occurs in a letter written for Joab's eyes only. If 1 Sam 27:5-6 were truly parallel to Gen 1:26, the latter would read, "Find someone to make man in our image"; if 2 Sam 21:6 were parallel, Gen 1:26 would say, "Let man be made in our image." See *In His Own Image and Likeness: Humanity, Divinity, and Monotheism* (Leiden: Brill, 2003), 41.

Christopher Kou has offered a decisive objection to the "divine council" theory, rooted in an understanding of "image of God."[91] "In the image" means "as image." Man himself, male and female, *is* the image of God, not a creature formed in conformity with some other image. In the Old Testament, "image" (*tselem*) frequently refers to an idol (cf. Num 33:52; 2 Kings 11:18), an icon or statue of a god, placed within the god's house to symbolize the god's or goddess's presence and to assert his or her authority. Likeness (*demut*) is more abstract, often referring to a similarity between or among objects (cf. 2 Chron 4:3; Ezek 1:5, 10). Though the words have overlapping semantic domains, they are distinct enough to justify the patristic distinction: Man *is* the image, but may lose his likeness to God, as a defaced statue that no longer bears any resemblance to Abraham Lincoln is still an image of Abraham Lincoln.

In Genesis, man the Creator's image is a living icon, set within the cosmic temple as the climax of creation. As image, Adam represents *'elohim* in the world, stakes *'elohim*'s claim on the world, rules *'elohim*'s world as his prince. Given what an image *is*, it cannot be an image of a *creature*. The whole point of an image is to be a visible representation of the invisible *God*. Were Adam made in the image of angels, he would be an idol, an icon of beings that are not-God. As Kou concludes, of all the possible views of "let us," the divine council view is the one that is simply "impossible."[92]

---

[91]Christopher Kou, "God's Statue in the Cosmic Temple: *Tzelem* and *Demut* in Genesis and the First Person Plural Cohortative of Gen 1:26 in Light of Sanctuary Setting and Christological Telos," *Journal of the Evangelical Theological Society* 66.1 (2023): 11-31. The following paragraphs sum up Kou's argument.

[92]Barth makes a similar point: "If we wish to speak of a plurality of Elohim in this connexion, we cannot dispute the fact that in ascribing to them an active part in creation, and calling their image the image of God, we give to the term its most proper sense, and thus endow them with the attribute of true deity" (*Church Dogmatics* 3/1, 190). Attributing deity to angels is what experts call a serious theological problem.

The plural of Genesis 1:26 is a plural of "fullness" or "duality"[93] that points to the fullness of life in the triune communion. It is possible that *'elohim* addresses the Spirit, introduced in Genesis 1:2, and is the only other active divine agent on the scene. On this reading, man is made in the image of *'elohim* and his Spirit. Given the association of Spirit and glory elsewhere in the Old Testament, the text points to man as a manifestation of the glory of *'elohim*.[94] Genesis 1:26 reveals more explicitly what we already suspect from Genesis 1:1: That the Creator is somehow plural, somehow capable of being speaker to himself as other, somehow capable of being an "us" or a "we," while remaining a "he."

Though rare, plural divine pronouns are found elsewhere in the Bible. After the fall, the Lord warns that Adam has "become like one of Us" (Gen 3:22), which suggests that the "us" of Genesis 1:26 may open to include human counselors. Before Yahweh descends to inspect the tower on the plain, he says, "Come, let Us go down," mocking the "let us" of the builders (Gen 11:4, 7). In an overtly trinitarian context, Jesus speaks of his Father and himself as a "we" and an "us." He asks the Father to make the disciples one "even as We are" (Jn 17:11, 22) and asks that the disciples be given a place "in Us" (Jn 17:21). Father and Son are a "we" by virtue of their perichoretic union, a communion spacious enough for creatures. Their "we-ness" is the form of their oneness.

While Genesis 1 presents "a God who is the one and only God," without competitor or rival or consort, Barth writes, this one God "is not for that reason solitary, but includes in Himself the differentiation and relationship of I and Thou."[95] This I-Thou is a *necessary* inference from "let us." A divine Speaker (*'elohim*) speaks,

---

[93]See Clines, "The Image of God in Man"; Hasel, "The Meaning of 'Let Us' in Gn 1:26."
[94]See Meredith Kline, *Images of the Spirit* (Eugene, OR: Wipf & Stock, 1999).
[95]Barth, *Church Dogmatics* 3/1, 190.

and that divine Speaker addresses another or others. If, as we have concluded, the other(s) cannot be creatures, the Speaker must be addressing divine Hearer(s). If we take "us" seriously, Speaker and Hearer cannot be simply identical; *'elohim* cannot be a solitary God talking, Gollum-like, to himself. Addresser and Addressee(s) are distinct, yet both are *'elohim*. And this God who contains both Speaker(s) and Hearer(s) within himself also acts as a singular "he" and speaks as a singular "I" (Gen 1:29).[96]

We can, in fact, tease out a rudimentary trinitarian theology: The Creator is internally differentiated, *linguistically* differentiated, such that a divine "I" can speak to divine Other(s) as a communal "We," summoning the Other(s) to collective action. The Creator of Genesis 1 includes a conversation of Speaker(s) and Hearer(s). By the axiom of simplicity, what God does is who God is. The God who converses as Speaker and Hearer, as One to Another, must *be* a conversation.[97] The Logos, John informs us, is

---

[96]Barth brings his discussion to this confident conclusion: "An approximation to the Christian doctrine of the Trinity . . . is both nearer to the text and does it more justice than the alternatives suggested by modern exegesis in its arrogant rejection of the exegesis of the Early Church. . . . If we think that what is said here about the Creator can finally and properly be understood only against the background of the Christian doctrine of the Trinity, we have at least the advantage of being able to accept everything that is said quite literally and without attenuation in this or that respect. We can take seriously not only plurality in the being of God, but also the 'Let us' as a summons to a real divine act, and the 'our' image as the true image of God. . . . Those who are not prepared to think of God's triunity must ask themselves whether they can really do the same." More punchily: *Only* a trinitarian reading of Genesis 1:26-27 accounts for what is on the page (*Church Dogmatics* 3/1, 190). Garr's form-critical analysis of *habah* cohortatives highlights similar features (*In His Own Image and Likeness*, 42-43). In each case, a speaker formulates a directive to take some initiative in a dynamic situation; the core argument of the speaker is "an event" (38). The situation is addressed jointly by the speaker and (a) distinct addressee(s). The addressee(s) tacitly or overtly consent(s) to the action, and the plan is executed by an agent, whether identified or unidentified. In Genesis 1:26-27, all these components are dimensions of *'elohim*'s intra-divine consultation and united divine action.

[97]Schwöbel, "Eternity of the Triune God," 9-11, cites Luther in support. This rules out the Dionysian ascent to the silence beyond language; see *Mystical Theology* 1033C. See also Matthew Bates, *The Birth of the Trinity: Jesus, God, and the Spirit in the New Testament and Early Christian Interpretations of the Old Testament* (Oxford: Oxford

with God-as-God, a Word "both spoken by and to God, and is the God who speaks and hears." He is one being with the Father and Spirit, and so "is himself the Word that the Father speaks and the Spirit enlivens." By the Spirit, the Father and Son realize a "mutuality that is perfectly free-speaking."[98] Again by the axiom of simplicity, God is his attributes. Thus this conversation and communication of equal divine persons is beauty: "to be God is to be enjoyable." To be the triune conversation is to be justice, "the perfect harmony of triune communal life." In its harmony, it is beautiful with the beauty of music: "God's beauty is the actual exchange between Father, Son, and Spirit, as this exchange is perfect simply as exchange, as it *sings*."[99]

As Creator, this God does not hoard the conversation he is to the original circle of "us." He is not envious. Father, Son, and Spirit do not monopolize one another as interlocutors. *'Elohim* addresses a world that exists by virtue of that very address. And the very content of his self-consultation, the plan deliberated in the "let us," is the creation of man in his own image and likeness. To man as male and female, he gives dominion, sharing divine vitality as he has with the earth, sea, plants, trees, birds, fish, and land creatures. Because he gives to this creature the gift of speech, he opens out the conversation that is the life of *'elohim* to include a created partner, a being who can both hear and speak back, a prophetic creature to whom *'elohim* both speaks and listens. Since the conversation of *'elohim* is a perfect harmony of voices, since the conversation rises to music, so the triune song opens out to include the voices of singing creatures, ultimately all creatures—the trees that clap their hands, the hills filled with

---

University Press, 2016), who shows how patristic prosopological interpretation gave insight into the inner-trinitarian conversation.
[98]Jenson, *Systematic Theology*, 1:223.
[99]Jenson, *Systematic Theology*, 1:225.

music, and, above all, the harmonies and riffs added by creation's chief singer, man.

Genesis 1 opens up the rich inner life of *'elohim* without any compromise of his unity as the one Creator. Genesis 1:26-27 contains a hint of the axiom, *opera ad extra indivisa sunt* ("the works of God outside himself are undivided"), for the God who speaks to himself within himself, as an I addressing one or more Thous, is the God who acts as a singular "He" and addresses man as a singular "I." And this points to the triunity of God's personhood. Created personalities, being unihypostatic, exist in multiple modes only outside ourselves. Unless I am mentally disturbed or an English monarch, my saying "we" implies reference to more beings than "I." When I say "he," I direct attention toward an other who is outside myself. This is one of the ways created existence and personality are limited and conditioned. His plurality notwithstanding, *'elohim* speaks and acts as a single subject. *'Elohim*'s internal conversation hints at what Bulgakov calls God's "trihypostatic personality." He is a unified subject, the one living God, whose "personal consciousness of self unites all the modes of the personal principle." The one Creator contains the rich relationality of "I, thou, he, we and you" in himself. A fully realized personality is "trihypostatic personality, in which the personal unity is revealed in the reality of three hypostatic centers."[100]

Contrary to Sonderegger and other theologians who stress the unity of God, the Creator's unity is *never* naked or bare unity. In contrast to Greek metaphysics, the Christian problematic is not one of harmonizing "one" and "many." The Greek dilemma is pre-solved. Trinitarian Christianity disturbs the simple contrast of one and many by redefining unity as a harmony of difference and difference as the dynamic of unity. Unity is only manifest

---

[100]Sergius Bulgakov, *The Lamb of God*, trans. Boris Jakim (Grand Rapids, MI: Eerdmans, 2008), 94-95.

and realized in multiplicity.[101] Within a trinitarian ontology, unity "ceases to be anything hypostatically real in contrast to difference" and instead becomes an apprehension of "harmony displayed in the order of the differences." Unity is "both a dynamic happening and a complex relationship."[102] The "harmony of the Trinity is . . . not the harmony of a finished totality but a 'musical' harmony of infinity."[103]

Being trihypostatic, God is not actualized statically, "as the unipersonal self-consciousness of the separate, isolated I in itself, reposing in its self-givenness," but dynamically, "as the eternal act of trinitarian self-positing in another," the self-positing that is love: "The flames of the divine trihypostasis flare up in each of the hypostatic centers and are then united and identified with one another, each going out of itself into the others, in the ardor of self-renouncing personal love."[104] In the name 'elohim and the conversation he is, we already gain a glimpse of this God of love, manifested in his creative work, for the only God who *is* is the God who has flared out not only in each of the "I's" that constitute the "us" of 'elohim, but in the artificial glory of a creation other than himself.

Communion in love is the form of the highest being, a love that is active and infinitely mobile in its eternal processions. Substantial love is the reality deep down things.[105] Even Thomas Aquinas thought *relatio* the weakest of Aristotle's categories, but he had forgotten himself. From the moment of creation, relation is elevated into the life of God, no longer weak and no longer a

---

[101]On the Christian disruption of the Greek problem of one and many, see David Bentley Hart, *The Beauty of the Infinite: The Aesthetics of Christian Truth* (Grand Rapids, MI: Eerdmans, 2004), 180-81.

[102]John Milbank, *Theology and Social Theory: Beyond Secular Reason* (Oxford: Blackwell, 1990), 428.

[103]Milbank, *Theology and Social Theory*, 424.

[104]Bulgakov, *The Lamb of God*, 94-95.

[105]Piero Coda, *Ontologie trinitaire: Penser et vivre à la lumière de la Trinité* (Nouvelle Cité, 2020), 85.

"category." A trihypostatic God, the God who is himself a conversation, sets the rhythm of Being, the rhythm of "giving that gives itself," the rhythm of love according to which all created things are called to sing and dance.[106]

CONCLUSION

Let me gather up some stray threads from the previous chapters. "How can God create?" I asked. By that I meant, "Can we give a coherent account of creation?" We cannot, if we start our theology with a nonexistent non-Creator. We cannot, if we forget or neglect the Trinity. A God who is utterly and only one, a God who is simply simple, cannot be eternally actualized as God. His justice, kindness, love, and fruitfulness cannot be operative, for all these are operative only in relation to an other. A monad has, at best, *potential* to create, which is also potency to display mercy, kindness, justice, love, and holiness. In itself, as Athanasius said, a single Unoriginated is fruitless, barren, silent, a light without radiance. And that means, if he can create at all, he will depend on the creation for his actualization as God. He cannot be Lord of creation because he is locked in a symmetrically dependent relation with the creation.

I have argued that the only God is the God who is actualized as Creator. Genesis 1 begins to reveal the truth about that Creator. He is actualized as Creator because he is plural in himself, as *'elohim*, his Spirit, and his Word, the one God who can converse as I and Thou and Us, who can act as He. Only this God can be fully himself for himself, and fully himself in and for creation. Only the God who is an eternal inner communion and conversation can take on external relationships without ceasing to be what he is. Only this God can be in a *real* but asymmetrical relation to the

---

[106]Klaus Hemmerle, *Theses Towards a Trinitarian Ontology* (Brooklyn, NY: Angelico, 2020), 35.

creation. Only this God can create and fully commit himself to what he has made, even to the point of entering the world and suffering death to preserve it, while ever remaining Lord.

This leads, one last time, back to simplicity. We could strip simplicity down to basics: God has no physical parts; though he has distinct attributes and properties, they are all perfectly harmonious. That is well within the bounds of orthodoxy. But I suggest we go further and retain a strong, though revised, simplicity. Confessing *'elohim* as the triune Creator provides the tools we need to retrieve and purify simplicity. Simplicity must be thoroughly, consistently trinitarian. Trinity must qualify simplicity, not simplicity Trinity.[107]

God, let us say, is *actus purus*. But then we ask, *How* is he so? *What* act is the *actus purus* by which God is God? When discussing the Trinity, Thomas acknowledges that the act by which God is God is the triune act of begetting and being-begotten, of breathing and being-breathed. But he does not see it through. Robert Jenson is more rigorous when he argues the identity of essence and existence is reversible. If God's essence is *to be*, so his *esse* is what stands where essence would be—if he had essence. And that *esse* is the eternal vibrant life and love of *'elohim* and his Word and his Spirit; the communion in love of Father, Son, and Spirit; the eternal chorus of the triune persons. Such is the *essence* of God. To say "God" or "deity" or "divine nature" is simply to say "Father, Son, and Spirit" in other terms.[108] The life of God *is* God, and that life is the life of three persons, a life of generation and procession,

---

[107]The Trinity *alone* saves simplicity. If there is no "eternal going out" and "eternal return," then God would be nothing but "rigid dead substance or equally lifeless law." Without distinction and difference, a simple God "could not know or will himself," for "there would be conceivable no reflection in himself, no transparency for himself, and no blessedness." A simple God can *be* and can be the *living* God only if he is Trinity. See Isaak August Dorner, *Divine Immutability: A Critical Reconsideration*, trans. Robert R. Williams and Claude Welch (Minneapolis: Fortress, 1994), 137.

[108]Jenson, *Systematic Theology*, 1:213-14.

a life of eternal communion. That life *is* justice, holiness, wisdom, power, goodness, and truth, all actualized in the infinitely mobile, infinitely lively, inexhaustibly energetic life of triune love, all actualized in relation to a contingent creation.

6

METAPHYSICS OF GENESIS

Augustine cites Exodus 3:14-15 ninety-some times in his writings,[1] often citing the name "I am" (Heb. *'ehyeh*) as support for speaking of God as "Being." In Augustine's Latin translation, Psalm 122:3 reads, "*cuius participatio eius idipsum*"; in English, Jerusalem "shares the selfsame." Augustine takes *idipsum* as a reference to God and, as Andrea Dalton Saner puts it, proceeds to interpret it in several stages. *Idipsum* means God is "Being-Itself," though Augustine immediately admits he cannot understand what that means: "How can I say anything about it, except that it is Being-itself?"[2] Having set the apophatic groundwork, Augustine puts the name in narrative context with a paraphrase of Moses' encounter at the burning bush:

> What is That Which Is if not he who, when he wished to give Moses his mission, said to him, I AM WHO AM (Ex 3:14)? What is That Which Is if not he who, when his servant objected, "So you

---

[1]Alexandra Parvan and Bruce L. McCormack, "Immutability, (Im)passibility and Suffering: Steps towards a 'Psychological' Ontology of God," *Neue Zeitschrift für Systematische Theologie und Religionsphilosophie* 59, no. 1 (2017): 8n8; Emilie Zum Brunn, *St. Augustine: Being and Nothingness* (New York: Paragon, 1988), 119, lists forty-seven "commentaries" on Ex 3:14 in Augustine's writings.

[2]*Enarrations on the Psalms*, at 121.5, quoted in Andrea Dalton Saner, "YHWH, the Trinity, and the Literal Sense: Theological Interpretation of Exodus 3:13-15" (PhD thesis, Durham University, 2013), 89.

are sending me. But what shall I say to the sons of Israel if they challenge me, Who sent you to us?" (Ex 3:13), refused to give himself any other name than I AM WHO AM? He reiterated, "Thus shall you say to the children of Israel, HE WHO IS has sent me to you" (Ex 3:14). This is Being-Itself, the Selfsame: I AM WHO AM. HE WHO IS has sent me to you. You cannot take it in, for this is too much to understand, too much to grasp.[3]

Clearly, in using *idipsum* as a divine name, Augustine does not intend to depict God as a frozen block of being. *Ego sum qui sum* is the God of Israel and exodus, also, Augustine goes on to say, the God who comes to us in Jesus, who "is rightly understood by this name, I AM WHO AM, inasmuch as he is in the form of God."[4] Though existing in the form of God as "Being-Itself," he makes it possible for us to share in Being by becoming "a participant in what you are." At the end of Augustine's exposition, the veil is lifted. The ungraspable God is brought near, not from below but

---

[3]*Enarrations on the Psalms*, at 121.5, quoted in Saner, "YHWH, the Trinity, and the Literal Sense," 89-90.

[4]Though critical of Augustine, Parvan and McCormack ("Immutability, [Im]passibil-ity and Suffering," 9-10) also call attention to the christological turn in Augustine's argument. Augustine, they say, identifies *two* names at the burning bush. Initially, God reveals himself as "I AM" (Ex 3:14), which is the name of Being, the self-subsistent, eternal, simple, immutable, impassible, fully actualized, perfect God. If this were all we knew of God, we would not know that he is related to us in any way, much less related as one of us. But God reveals a second name in Exodus 3:15, "YHWH . . . the God of Abraham, the God of Isaac, and the God of Jacob." At times, Augustine says God reveals his second name only because the first is incomprehen-sible to human beings. But he also offers a thicker rationale. Augustine sees the sec-ond name as already a foreshadowing of incarnation. Unless God takes flesh, he can-not fully be the God of Abraham, Isaac, and Jacob, and thus "does not have his full name." God's Being is not wholly exhausted by the name of Being; for he also bears the name of incarnate love for man. Augustine thus implies that "incarnation says something about the immutable being that God is." If God wanted to be only what he is for himself, we would be nothing: "God wants *to be* not only what he is for himself but that which he is *for us* too." To this we can add: In a sermon, Augustine imagines Moses in fear "to discover himself so unlike facing the transcendent Essence." To comfort him, the Lord adds his covenant name, which speaks of God's nearness. The two names are not in contradiction, since a God who is Being itself "shall never be missed by men" (Sermon 7.7, quoted in Brunn, *Being and Nothingness*, 115).

from above, not by mystical ascent but by loving humiliation, because "the Word was made flesh so that flesh might participate in the Word."[5]

Thomas Aquinas likewise makes overt metaphysical use of Exodus 3, citing the passage to give an affirmative answer to the question, "Is HE WHO IS (*qui est*) the most appropriate name for God?" Thomas adds three supporting arguments. The meaning of a name should express the form of the thing named. In naming God, that principle is not strictly operative, since *qui est* "does not signify any particular form, but rather existence (*esse*) itself." Yet the name is appropriate, because, as Thomas has already proven, in God essence and existence are identical. Further, the name is suitable precisely because of its open-ended lack of determination.

---

[5]*Enarrations on the Psalms*, at 121.5, quoted in Saner, "YHWH, the Trinity, and the Literal Sense," 90. Jean-Luc Marion claims that by this move Augustine shifts the center of gravity from ontology to charity and soteriology; see *In the Self's Place: The Approach of Saint Augustine* (Stanford, CA: Stanford University Press, 2012), 300-302. Marion complains that translators metaphysicize Augustine's use of *idipsum*, often rendering it as "Being itself" (298, quoting Aime Solignac). In Marion's view, *idipsum* actually marks the *difference* between Augustine and Aquinas. Rather than using *ipsum esse* or *idipsum esse*, Augustine prefers the unmodified *idipsum*: "that itself [*idipsum*] which is God, whatever that might be" (*De trinitate* 2.18.35). To Marion, *idipsum* does not function as a metaphysical term at all but is more like a demonstrative pronoun: "that itself" verbally gestures toward the thing without making any claim about the nature of the thing indicated. Instead of translating what Augustine wrote, translators translate "an implicit text" that says *ipsum esse*, not *idipsum*. For Marion's Augustine, God is different from creation not because he is Being but because of the particular *way* God is, as the immutable one. Thus, Augustine frequently expounds *idipsum* by reference to immutability; e.g., "You are the thing itself, *quia non mutaris*" (*Confessions* 9.4.11). Translating *idipsum* as if it were a metaphysical concept bypasses Augustine's intention, substituting a "metaphysical concept of Being . . . for a radically biblical and decidedly apophatic denomination." *Esse* is precisely what Thomas's *ipsum esse* and Augustine's *idipsum* "do *not* have in common." In fact, Marion argues, *idipsum* "emerges from a tradition more ancient, because biblical, than the *ipsum esse*. . . . *Idipsum* is not equivalent to *ipsum esse* but resists it in advance and dismisses it" (299). Augustine thus refuses to "think God as Being—so as to not make Being a god" (306). But surely Thomas is not the first to think Being and immutability are convertible, since the God who immutably *is* must by that fact be *ipsum esse*. It is hardly a surprise to find Marion reading Augustine as a proto-Marion, thinking "God without Being." I am doubtful Marion's Augustine is the Augustine of history. Brunn confirms that Augustine defines "God-Being" as immutability, but notes that "Augustine does not get tired of repeating that God 'is' because he is immutable" (*Being and Nothingness*, 105).

Determinate names pick out an aspect of a thing, and "add some nuance of meaning which restricts and determines the original sense." Not *qui est*. This name "fixes on no aspect of being but stands open to all and refers to him as an infinite ocean of being." Finally, *qui est* is suitable because it is a present-tense name, and so "especially appropriate to God whose being knows neither past nor future."[6]

Though Thomas does not overtly link the revelation of the name to its textual context, his observation that *qui est* is an *open* name (*indeterminate ad omnes*) makes room for narrative unfolding and unveiling. The God who says "I am" in sending Moses is also the God who says "I am" when he pummels Pharaoh with plagues, splits the sea, speaks from Sinai. None of these actions exhausts his boundless life. Whatever comes, whatever Israel needs, "He Who Is" *is*, and so is up to it. Without change, he unchangeably gives whatever Israel needs him to give at any particular moment. Just because he is an ocean of being, *qui est* can be infinitely specified with determinate predicates; just because he is simple, Thomas says, he is able to enter into an infinite variety of relations with creatures. Jesus says, I am bread, I am light, I am the good Shepherd, I am the door, but "I am" shines through them all. Jesus can say all these truly because Jesus is the incarnation of the God of unbounded existence. "Being is said in many ways," Aristotle said,[7] and because God is Being, each of the many ways of speaking being speak of him.

---

[6]*ST* 1.13.11; in Herbert McCabe, ed., *St. Thomas Aquinas, Summa theologiae*, vol. 3: *Knowing and Naming God* (Cambridge: Cambridge University Press, 2006). For recent defenses of this interpretation of YHWH, see Saner, "YHWH, the Trinity, and the Literal Sense"; Janet Martin Soskice, "Aquinas and Augustine on Creation and God as 'Eternal Being,'" *New Blackfriars* 95 (2014): 190-207; Michael Allen, "Exodus 3 after the Hellenization Thesis," *Journal of Theological Interpretation* 3, no. 2 (2009): 179-96; Matthew Levering, "Contemplating God: YHWH and Being in the Theology of St. Thomas Aquinas," *Irish Theological Quarterly* 67 (2002): 17-31.
[7]*Metaphysics* 1003ª33.

The equation of God's name with Being is, according to Etienne Gilson, the cornerstone of Christian metaphysics. It is a "metaphysics of Exodus" (distinguished from a metaphysics *in* Exodus) that possesses "inexhaustible metaphysical fecundity."[8] The equation of the one God with "Being-Itself" is, quite literally, a metaphysics inspired by Exodus.[9] No Greek philosopher reaches this conclusion. Plato believed "divinity belongs to a class of multiple beings, perhaps even to all beings whatsoever." Aristotle "understood that God is, of all beings, the one that deserves the name of being par excellence," but, being a polytheist, he was constrained to regard "divinity" as an "attribute of a class of beings." The unmoved mover possesses this attribute in the highest degree, but he remains one of the "beings." And, besides, for Aristotle, the first name of God was not "Being" but "Thought." Aristotle certainly contributed to the idea of the Christian God, but Gilson thinks the surprising thing is "that having gone so far along the right road he should have failed to follow it to the end." In comparison with the "gropings" of pagan philosophy, the Bible is "straightforward" and its results are "startling."[10] Paul Ricoeur sums up Gilson's argument: "Without the book of Exodus, philosophers would have never reached the idea that Being is the proper name of God and that this name designates God's very essence."[11]

Impressive as this tradition is, the link between the biblical record of God's name and the philosophical concept of *esse* is more tenuous than it appears. After I examine some of the exegetical

---

[8]Etienne Gilson, *The Spirit of Mediaeval Philosophy* (New York: Charles Scribner, 1940), 51. See also Etienne Gilson, "Maimonide et la Philosophie de l'Exode," *Mediaeval Studies* 13 (1951): 223-25.

[9]See Etienne Gilson, *The Christian Philosophy of Thomas Aquinas* (Notre Dame, IN: Notre Dame University Press, 1994).

[10]Gilson, *Spirit of Mediaeval Philosophy*, 44-51.

[11]Andre LaCocque and Paul Ricoeur, *Thinking Biblically: Exegetical and Hermeneutical Studies* (Chicago: University of Chicago Press, 1998), 352-54.

complications, I will return to Genesis 1 to sketch a trinitarian "metaphysics of Genesis" that surpasses and sublates the metaphysics of Exodus. Instead of establishing the primacy of *esse*, the divine name reinforces the primacy of "Creator."[12]

"I AM" IN EXODUS

Neither Augustine nor Thomas knew the wild ways of Hebrew verbs, whose aspects are underdetermined and so more fluid than those of most Western languages. *'Ehyeh* can be translated in past, present, or future tense. It is not, as Thomas assumes, equivalent to *ego sum*, but might be either "I was" or "I will be."[13] Further, as Ricoeur points out, the Hebrew verb *hayah* has a range of senses, from the static "to be," to the dynamic "happen" or "become" (e.g., Ex 4:3, 9). One of the most common clauses in Hebrew narrative, *wayehi*, means "and it happened" (e.g., Ex 4:24). God's self-identifying statement, *'ehyeh 'asher 'ehyeh*, might be translated as "I happen as I happen" or "I become what I become," and the short form *'ehyeh* might be "I become." The verb aspect also has modal possibilities: I can, desire, ought to be what I can, desire, ought to be. Nothing demands that the first *'ehyeh* have an identical meaning to the second. "I am as I was," "I will be as I am," "I will be as I ought to be," or "I will become what I desire to be" are all perfectly legitimate translations. The *idem per idem* construction suggests a protean indeterminacy that the fixed present-tense "I am that I am" obscures.[14] YHWH, with its

---

[12]Contra Tyler Wittman, *God and Creation in Thomas Aquinas and Karl Barth* (Cambridge: Cambridge University Press, 2018), 292-93, who appeals to Exodus 3 to establish God's intrinsic perfection, apart from creation, as the first logical moment in theology.

[13]Victor P. Hamilton, *Exodus: An Exegetical Commentary* (Grand Rapids, MI: Baker Academic, 2011), 61-68.

[14]Jean-Pierre Sonnet, "*Ehyeh asher ehyeh* (Exodus 3:14): God's 'Narrative Identity' among Suspense, Curiosity, and Scripture," *Poetics Today* 31, no. 2 (2010): esp. 334-37. Hillel Ben-Sasson pointedly says, "The meaning of the verb *hyh* in the Bible does not readily lend itself to the present tense. As a verb that denotes both action

admittedly obscure relationship with the verb *hayah*, has the same range and flexibility.

Most uses of *'ehyeh* in the Hebrew Bible are properly rendered with future tenses.[15] The Lord utters *'ehyeh* in Genesis 31:3, when he instructs Jacob to "return to the land of your fathers and to your relatives," promising "I will be with you" (*'ehyeh 'immak*). *'Ehyeh* has a future sense in other parts of Exodus: "*'ehyeh* with you," Yahweh assures Moses when he first commissions him to Egypt (Ex 3:12); "*'ehyeh* your mouth," Yahweh assures Moses before sending him to speak to Pharaoh (Ex 4:12, 15); "*'ehyeh* your God," Yahweh says as he lays out his plans for exodus and covenant (Ex 6:7).

Later biblical writers were well aware of this temporal flexibility. In the Apocalypse, John uses the phrase "He who is and who was and who is to come" (*apo ho ōn kai ho ēn kai ho erchomenos*) in the opening greeting, as part of a trinitarian blessing (Rev 1:4).[16] The "seven Spirits" and Jesus Christ are explicitly named (Rev 1:4-5), so the tensed phrase must refer to the Father. The suspicion that this is a translation or interpretation of YHWH or *'ehyeh 'asher 'ehyeh* is confirmed by other uses of the phrase in Revelation. "'I am [*egō eimi*] the Alpha and the Omega,' says the Lord God, 'who is and who was and who is to come, the Almighty" (Rev 1:8), echoing Yahweh's declarations made through the prophet

---

and a state, *hyh* does not describe a static being." In Exodus 3, the form points to an "uncompleted action in the past, present, or future." *Understanding YHWH: The Name of God in Biblical, Rabbinic, and Medieval Jewish Thought* (New York: Palgrave Macmillan, 2019), 45. On the relation with *'ehyeh* and *YHWH*, see Cornelis den Hertog, *The Other Face of God: "I Am That I Am" Reconsidered* (Sheffield: Sheffield Academic, 2012), 50-59.

[15]Saner, "YHWH, the Trinity, and the Literal Sense," 123.

[16]The fact that this is a name rather than a description is indicated by the case. Governed by the preposition *apo*, the articles and participles should be in the genitive, but the entire phrase is in the nominative, treated as an indeclinable name. For further reflection, see my *Revelation 1–11*, International Theological Commentary (London: T&T Clark, 2018), 87-88.

Isaiah (Is 41:4; *'aniy YHWH ri'shon v'et 'acharoniym 'aniy-hu*; in the LXX, the final clause is translated as *egō eimi*). The Lord's announcement is a riff on the name revealed at the burning bush and on Sinai. Finally, John hears the living creatures thundering the Sanctus in the heavenly liturgy: "HOLY, HOLY, HOLY IS THE LORD GOD, THE ALMIGHTY, WHO WAS AND WHO IS AND WHO IS TO COME" (Rev 4:8). It is the song of the seraphim of Isaiah 6, who sing the Sanctus to YHWH *tze'baoth*, "Yahweh of hosts."

In the Apocalypse, in short, the name is tensed, and multiply so. The God and Father of Jesus is not *qui est* but *qui est et qui erat*. John does not name a God who simply *is* but a God with a past, a God who can be spoken of with "was," a God who can be spoken of as having a "will be," a God with a future. Or, to be specific, a God who is *qui venturus*, who is not merely a persistence of present-tense being but a God who will *come*. The action of advent has entered into the name of God (as the name "Jesus" is introduced into Paul's revised Shema in 1 Cor 8). Past faithfulness and future advent are folded into the *name* of God, and so we must say more: It is not merely that we may speak of God's past and future; it is not merely that the God of present being transcends time; it is that past and future are of the being of God. This clashes with traditional conceptions of "Being," which has been used precisely to rule out tensed predication of God. The name unveiled in Revelation points in the opposite direction, indicating that divine being is nothing but "divine eventfulness."[17] The God of the Bible transcends time by encompassing rather than escaping it (see chap. 7 below).

---

[17]Robert Jenson, *Systematic Theology*, vol. 1, *The Triune God* (Oxford: Oxford University Press, 1997), 212. Jenson points to Thomas as "the great exemplar and standard" in revising the concept of divinity to make such predications possible. I believe that is largely true, but as I have stressed throughout this book, Thomas's revision of "being" is incomplete, in his failure entirely to work through the implications of trinitarian theology and the doctrine of creation with maximal consistency.

Fixing on "Being" as the meaning of *'ehyeh* and YHWH is more the achievement of the Septuagint than of the Hebrew Bible. The LXX translates "I am who I am" as *egō eimi ho ōn*, "I am the existing/being One" or "I am the being." The masculine *ho ōn* is closer to the personalism of the Hebrew than the common philosophical neuter, *to on*, but Philo fused the two variations to draw the conclusion that at the burning bush God reveals his *existence* and, by immediate implication, his immutability.[18] The Vulgate follows the LXX by using *ego sum qui sum* and *qui est*, thus encouraging Augustine and Western theology to follow Philo in linking YHWH to *ho ōn/ego sum*.

In short, Thomas is mistaken to emphasize the present tense of the name. *'Ehyeh 'asher 'ehyeh* can just as well be translated as "I will be who I will be," with the sense, "Wait and see! For the moment, I remain hidden, but you will discover who I am at some future time."[19] At the beginning of Exodus, the name remains open ended. We cannot know what it means until we read the whole story.

The Pentateuchal habits of naming point in the same direction. YHWH is one of fifty-two wordplay names in the Pentateuch. These wordplays typically do not reveal some hidden "essence" of the person but memorialize his or her birth, anticipate a future achievement, or sometimes both. Noah is named *noach* because his father Lamech hopes he will bring rest (*nacham*) from labor on the cursed ground (Gen 5:29). Perez is so named because he breaches a breach (*parats perets*), breaking through to beat his twin brother Zerah in their race down Tamar's birth canal

---

[18]Ricoeur, *Thinking Biblically*, 338.

[19]Austin Surls, "Making Sense of the Divine Name in the Book of Exodus: From Etymology to Literary Onomastic" (PhD dissertation, Wheaton College, 2015); Sonnet, "*Ehyeh asher ehyeh* (Exodus 3:14)"; Merold Westphal, "The God Who Will Be: Hermeneutics and the God of Promise," *Faith and Philosophy* 20, no. 3 (2003): 328-44.

(Gen 38:28-29). Moses' name points back to his origin from the
waters and forward to his future as one who draws others from
the water (Ex 2:10). We might say these names have ontological
weight in defining the "essence" of the person named, so long as
we recognize "essence" is not a stable substrate underlying the
person's life story but the realization of a character unveiled over
the course of the person's history.[20] In the context of the Pentateuch, we do not expect the name YHWH to provide a *definition*
of "divine nature" that underlies God's words and actions. Rather,
we expect the name to summarize a history. YHWH, we expect,
indicates something about where he came from and anticipates
what he will do.

Consistent with this, Exodus 3 does no more than *begin* the revelation of YHWH. *'Ehyeh* ("I will be" / "I am") first appears in
Exodus 3:12 when Yahweh assures the hesitant Moses, "I will be
with you." When he speaks again, two verses later, identifying
himself as *'ehyeh 'asher 'ehyeh*, his promise of future presence and
help is still reverberating. "I will be what I will be" is, contextually,
the most immediate meaning, with modal overtones: "I can/may/
want to be what I can/may/want to be."[21] The open-endedness of
the phrase highlights "God's freedom in history and thwarts the
magic or idolatrous power attached to a graspable or manageable
divine name."[22] The name reveals God's transcendence, not by
indicating his self-subsistence as Being so much as YHWH's determination of his own actions, his lordship over the creation,
and his always surprising constancy. In the following chapter,
'ehyeh has the same thrust. "I will be with your mouth," he tells
Moses (Ex 4:12), and then again, "I will be with your mouth and
[Aaron's] mouth" (Ex 4:15). Throughout, God reformulates the

---

[20]See Surls, "Making Sense of the Divine Name," 40-66.
[21]Sonnet, "*Ehyeh asher ehyeh*," 335.
[22]Sonnet, "*Ehyeh asher ehyeh*," 336.

promise embedded in the name, in order to orient future action and shape Moses' expectations about how he will assist. Clearly, the name does not pick out a God above the fray of Israel-in-Egypt, but the God who acts decisively, triumphantly, on Israel's behalf.

We thus need the entire book of Exodus to grasp the meaning of the name. When Moses first confronts Pharaoh, the latter says he does not know Yahweh (Ex 5:2), so Yahweh sends plagues to make his name known to Israel and the Egyptians (e.g., Ex 7:5). The theme comes to a climax in Exodus 33–34. After the golden calf, Yahweh reveals his glory and proclaims his name to Moses on the very mountain where he first called Moses from the burning bush. The name is not simply "I am who I am," but "YHWH, YHWH *'Elohim*," gracious, compassionate, slow to anger, full of *hesed* and truth, who forgives sin and yet punishes the guilty (Ex 34:6-7). *That* is the divine being revealed in the name "I am who I am," defined *not* as "Being-Itself" but as the God of Israel and the just and merciful Lord of nations.[23]

Beyond exegesis, there are theological reasons why we cannot rightly say, "God is Being," without immediately adding, "God is Trinity" or "Being is triune." If God equals Being, "*not*-being" has no place in our speech about or concepts of God. If God equals Being, we must say "is" and only "is"—God is his attributes, God is his essence, God is, God is, God is. All that is in God is God—so

---

[23]Surls, "Making Sense of the Divine Name," 219-52. Augustine claims God "did not say: I am the Lord God, almighty, merciful, righteous" but instead "doing away with all the attributes that could have been useful for naming him and designating him as God, he answered that he was called Being itself" (*Enarrations on the Psalms* 134.6, quoted in Brunn, *Being and Nothingness*, 106). Regarding Exodus 3, Augustine is of course correct, but he is wrong when Exodus 3 is read, as it must be, within its larger context. For a concise and balanced theological reading of Exodus 3, see Pierre Coda, *From the Trinity: The Coming of God in Revelation and Theology* (Washington, DC: Catholic University of America Press, 2020), 122-28. Note also Ps 145:8-9, which moves immediately from a quotation of the proclamation of the name ("gracious and merciful; slow to anger and great in *hesed*") to a confession of the Creator's goodness to creation: "Yahweh is good to all, and His mercies are over all His works."

goes the axiom. Trinitarian theology, by contrast, *necessarily* says "not" in order to make distinctions among the persons and their relations. Relations are referred to another, and so relations entail negation. The Father is God, yet the Father *is not* the Son; the Son is God, yet the Son *is not* the Father; the Spirit is God, yet the Spirit *is not* the Son or the Father. Which is to say: Fatherhood is "in God," yet God *is not* purely and exclusively Fatherhood, since he is also Son and Spirit. Sonship is "in God," yet God *is not* purely and exclusively sonship. Unless we say "not," we cannot name the triune God.

More abstractly stated: To affirm the Trinity, we must affirm the reality of "nonbeing" in God.[24] A simple and unified being, Aristotle said, is continuous, without ragged intervals of time, space, or "not."[25] If so, the Trinity is not Being simply, because the persons are distinguished by uncreated distances and absolute intervals that can only be rendered by negations. This is emphatically *not* a denial of the unity of God. We need not, as I indicated above, discard simplicity. Rather, we specify the triune shape of his unity and simplicity. The "not" of personal distinction is incorporated into the perfect perichoretic union of the Trinity. If the triune God is Being, he is Being who has sublated nonbeing. Within the triune life, nonbeing is not merely opposed to Being; rather, the not-being of personal relations drives the infinite dynamism of triune existence. Without the not-being of personal difference, God would not be the *living* God.[26]

---

[24]Coda, *From the Trinity*, 494. As Coda points out, Augustine affirms the reality of this "relative nonbeing" within the triune communion: "In order to affirm logically and ontologically, in the rigor of theological discourse, the real distinction and otherness of the three in the one divine essence, [Augustine] clearly stated that the one is not the other, each one however being the one true God." See also Coda, *Ontologie trinitaire: Penser et Vivre á la lumière de la Trinité* (Nouvelle Cité, 2020), 86, 109-17.

[25]E.g., *Physics* 185^{b}5-8; *Metaphysics* 1016^{a}1.

[26]Coda, *From the Trinity*, 495: "Nonbeing is not of itself the alternative and external dimension of being, but the very motor of its internal movement."

In the end, the equation of God's biblical name with "Being" does not stand up to exegetical or theological scrutiny. Yet, I hasten to add, none of this is intended as an argument against metaphysics as such. What I propose is a *"revisionary metaphysics."* We have already begun this revision with our musings on *'elohim* in chapter five, a name that opens into a trinitarian theology proper. Can we perhaps do something similar with another divine name, YHWH? In what follows, I assume with the Western tradition that the names *'ehyeh 'asher 'ehyeh* and YHWH have ontological weight. They reveal truth about God's being and, since God is the Creator, about created existence. These names do not, however, point to "Being" as the first name of God. Remembering the lessons and limits of the metaphysics of Exodus, I propose we start afresh with a metaphysics of Genesis, a metaphysics of creation in which "I am" and YHWH are, most fundamentally, names of the Creator. Let us, once again, start at the very beginning.

"TO BE" IN GENESIS 1

At the burning bush, Yahweh explains his name by reference to *hayah*, the Hebrew verb "to be": *'ehyeh 'asher 'ehyeh*, usually translated as "I AM WHO I AM" (Ex 3:14) and *'ehyeh shelachaniy*, "I AM has sent me." From Exodus 3, we discover that the Tetragrammaton YHWH is a form of or a pun on *hayah*.[27] The link between YHWH and "to be" is not new news to Moses. It is evident already in Genesis 1:1–2:3. The Creator of Genesis 1 is identified as *'elohim*, not YHWH, yet *YHWH 'elohim* is identified as the one who "made earth and heaven" (Gen 2:4). By the time YHWH first appears, Genesis has preintroduced the name by repeated use of the verb "to be." The introduction of YHWH in Genesis 2:4 is the climax of an emerging theology of divine and created being.

---

[27]See Ben-Sasson, *Understanding YHWH*, 47-56.

Hayah is first used in Genesis 1:2: "The earth was (*haytah*) formless and void." It is a third-person feminine form to match the feminine noun, "earth" (*'erets*). All other uses of the verb in 1:3-2:3 are masculine, singular or plural. They group together into neat bundles. *'Elohim* speaks "be" seven times, six times in a jussive form ("let there be" [*yehiy*] or "let them be" [*hayu*]; Gen 1:3, 6 [2x], 14 [2x], 15) and once as an imperfect ("they shall be" [*yihyeh*]; Gen 1:29). Six times the verb appears in the phrase "it was so" (*yehiy*; Gen 1:7, 9, 11, 15, 24, 30), once in the parallel phrase "it was light" (Gen 1:3; also *yehiy*). Each of the six days ends with the formula, "there was (*yehiy*) evening and there was (*yehiy*) morning, X day" (Gen 1:5, 8, 13, 19, 23, 31), for a total of twelve uses in closing formulae. In sum, the masculine forms of the verb are sorted into numerically significant groups: Two sets of seven, each of which breaks down, like the creation week, into a six plus one; one set of twelve (6 x 2).

Overall, *hayah* is used twenty-seven times in Genesis 1:1–2:3, which is three times three times three, perhaps another shadowy reference to the tripersonality of *'elohim* and a trace of the triadic structure of the creation. Within the set of twenty-seven, though, is a set of twenty-six. Apart from Genesis 1:2, the verb is always masculine. As James Bejon pointed out, the twenty-six masculine forms contain *only* consonants of YHWH: *yhy* (23x), *hyw* (2x), or *yhyh* (1x).[28] Twenty-four times, the creation account uses a form of *hayah* that begins with *yh*, the first two consonants of YHWH and the consonants of Yah, the short form of Yahweh. Twice, the form includes *all three* unique consonants YHWH, though not in order (Gen 1:14-15, the plurals, "let them be").

Pause. Take a breath. Here is the punch line: Each letter of the Hebrew alphabet has a numerical value, and ancient writers and

---

[28]In personal communication.

readers sum up letters in a word so as to assign a numerical value, known as a gematria. The gematria of YHWH is 26 (y = 10; h = 5; w = 6; 10 + 5 + 6 + 5 = 26). That is to say, the creation account repeatedly uses the verbal root of YHWH; these forms include only consonants of YHWH and they are used a YHWH number of times. Though Genesis 1 does not utter YHWH, the name is hiding just under the surface of the text. *Ta da!*

Even the exception proves the rule. The one use of *hayah* that includes a consonant *not* found in YHWH is the first, the description of the initial condition of earth: "Earth was (*haytah*) formless and void, and darkness over the face of the deep" (Gen 1:2). Genesis 1:2 describes a state of "nonbeing," the formless and dark emptiness that precedes the first of *'elohim*'s fiats. Before he speaks *yhy*, the world is *not hayah*. Before *'elohim* first whispers "let be," the world exists, but its condition does not resemble the being of *YHWH 'elohim*. The one use of *hayah* that does not verbally resemble YHWH is the not-*hayah* of unformed earth. Through the creation week, *'elohim* speaks and acts so that the unbeing of the earth comes to resemble YHWH.

It may seem a tenuous connection, until we recognize how often twenty-sixfold patterns appear as a structuring and literary device in the Hebrew Bible. Yahweh promises to show Moses his glory (Ex 33) in a speech of twenty-six words: "17 in verses 21–22 and 9 in verse 23."[29] Psalm 1 has a fifteen-word core that describes the righteous man (Ps 1:3), and the core is encompassed by sections that contain twenty-six words each. The psalm's numerical arrangement depicts the righteous man nestled in YHWH's twenty-sixfold protective presence.[30] In

---

[29]Caspar J. Labuschagne, *Numerical Secrets of the Bible: An Introduction to Biblical Arithmology* (Eugene, OR: Wipf & Stock, 2016), 91. Seventeen is the numerical value of *kabod*, "glory," often a substitute for YHWH.

[30]Caspar J. Labuschagne, *Numerical Features of the Psalms and Other Selected Texts*, on Psalm 1, available at https://www.labuschagne.nl/ps001.pdf. The numerology has

Psalm 23, "the three words in the phrase *kiaatta immadi*, 'for you are with me' (Psalm 23:4), are situated in the mathematical center of the text, with 26 words preceding them and 26 after them."[31] Psalm 32 has a similar organization, with a central word ("in a time," *le'et*, Ps 32:6) surrounded on each side by fifty-two (2 x 26) words. When the doxology of Psalm 72 is included, the word total for the Psalm is 156, or 6 x 26.[32] Isaiah 59:1-14 divides into two paragraphs (Is 59:1-8, 9-14), each of which contains a number of words that is a multiple of twenty-six (Is 59:1-8 contain 104 words, or 4 x 26; Is 59:9-14 have 78, or 3 x 26; the total is 182, or 7 x 26).[33]

Twenty-sixfold patterns organize larger patches of text. Some editions of Genesis contain a note that indicates the total number of verses in the book, 1,534 (59 x 26).[34] There are eleven divine monologues in the Pentateuch, seven in Genesis 1–11 (Gen 1:26; 2:18; 3:22; 6:3, 7; 8:21-22; 11:6-7), four more in the remainder of the Pentateuch (Gen 18:17-19; Ex 3:17, 13:17; Deut 32:20-27). Altogether, these monologues contain 289 words, the square of 17, the numerical value of *kabod* ("glory"). The total number of words in the introductory formulae to these soliloquies (e.g., "God said"; "YHWH God said"; "YHWH said") is twenty-six.[35] That is, there is a YHWH-number of words indicating "God speaks."

James Bejon has discovered numerous patterns in Exodus 3–15:

> The word "heart/intent" (Hebrew *lev/levav*) occurs 26 times in our text, and the word "hand/power" (*yad*) occurs 52 times (twice 26). . . . And, midway through our text, we (unexpectedly) find

a double reference, since 52 (2 x 26) is the gematria of *'ashre*, "blessed," the first word of the psalm. Significantly, *'ashre* appears twenty-six times in the Psalter.

[31]Labuschagne, *Numerical Secrets*, 11.

[32]Labuschagne, *Numerical Features*, on Psalm 72, available at www.labuschagne.nl/ps072.pdf.

[33]Labuschagne, *Numerical Secrets*, 76.

[34]Labuschagne, *Numerical Secrets*, 8.

[35]Labuschagne, *Numerical Secrets*, 64.

ourselves presented with a genealogy (6.14–25), the focal point of
which is Moses and Aaron's mother, Jochebed . . . , whose name
combines the name YHWH . . . and the root *K-B-D*. . . . (Jochebed's
line is the most extended of Exodus 6's.) Furthermore, Jochebed
happens to be the 26th individual listed in 6.14–25's genealogy,
and the birth of her two sons marks the rise of the world's 26th
generation. Appropriately, then, in the 26th generation of creation, YHWH reveals his twenty-six-valued name to mankind.[36]

Outside the Pentateuch, the Song of Songs uses "my beloved"
(*dodi*) twenty-six times, numerically linking YHWH with the
bridegroom and indicating a conscious allegorical dimension to
the Song.[37]

The creation account itself makes use of the twenty-sixfold
pattern. Altogether, the divine speeches in Genesis 1–2 contain
104 words (4 x 26). The total number of words in divine speech
formulae using *'amar* (*'elohim* says) in Genesis 1–2 is twenty-six.
The pattern continues in the following chapters. In Genesis 3, the
total number of words in the divine speech formulae amounts to
twenty-six, and the divine speeches in Genesis 3–4 contain a total
of 208 words (8 x 26).[38]

Given this evidence, which could be greatly expanded, it is inconceivable that the twenty-six masculine forms of *hayah* in
Genesis 1 is accidental. Exodus later links YHWH with *hayah*, but
an attentive reading of Genesis 1 already discloses the connection.
By the time we first hear the Name openly, the text has insistently
whispered YHWH's name and number. The pianissimo melody
of Genesis 1 comes to a sudden fortissimo in Genesis 2:4, with the

---

[36]James Bejon, "YHWH, the Exodus, and the Number 26," Thoughts on Scripture,
November 3, 2021, https://jamesbejon.substack.com/p/yhwh-the-exodus-and-the
-number-26.

[37]Edmee Kingsmilll, *The Song of Songs and the Eros of God: A Study in Biblical Intertextuality* (Oxford: OUP, 2010).

[38]Labuschagne, *Numerical Secrets*, 78.

dramatic revelation that *'elohim*'s gifts of existence are in fact gifts of himself, for his name is a form of "to be."

Commentators have often distinguished the "power name" *'elohim* (Gen 1) from the "covenant name" YHWH (Gen 2).[39] Different theologies, and different concepts of creation, are sometimes extrapolated from the distinct names. *'Elohim* speaks creation from a majestic distance; he is the sovereign God, high and lifted up, who dwells in unapproachable light. YHWH's style is more intimate. He forms man from the dust (Gen 2:7), plants a garden and makes trees sprout from the ground (Gen 2:8-9), places the man in the garden (Gen 2:15), speaks a command (Gen 2:16), resolves the flaw of Adam's solitude (Gen 2:18-22), pulls a rib from Adam to build a woman (Gen 2:21-22), plays matchmaker by introducing the woman to the man (Gen 2:23-24), "walk[s] in the garden" (Gen 3:8), and provides skins (Gen 3:21). His proximity is discomfiting, for he comes to scrutinize the man

---

[39]In his 1611 study of Genesis and Exodus, Andrew Willet wrote, "As *Elohim* is a name of power and justice, given unto God in the creation: so now *Iehovah* a name of mercy, is attributed unto God, the whole worke being finished, because therein his mercy appeared: or rather now after God had made his worke full and complete, he is also set forth in his full and complete titles." *Hexapla in Genesin & Exodum*, 21, quoted in Goldingay, *Genesis* (Grand Rapids, MI: Baker Academic, 2020), 56; full text of Willet at https://quod.lib.umich.edu/e/eebo/A15408.0001.001?view=toc. Cassuto offers a similar distinction: "The Tetragrammaton occurs when Scripture reflects the concept of God, especially in His ethical aspect, that belongs specifically to the people of Israel; *'Elohim* appears when the Bible refers to the abstract conception of God that was current in the international circles of the Sages, the idea of God conceived in a general sense as the Creator of the material world, as the Ruler of nature, as the source of life." YHWH expresses a "direct and intuitive notion of God that is characteristic of the unsophisticated faith of the multitude," while *'elohim* conveys a more philosophical concept. Or, YHWH presents God "in His personal character, and in direct relationship to human beings or to nature," while *'elohim* speaks of "a Transcendent Being, who stands entirely outside nature, and above it." *'Elohim* had to be used in Genesis 1, since that chapter shows God as Creator and "Master of the world" who has no "direct relationship" with nature. YHWH had to be the name in Genesis 2–3, since here "God appears as the ruler of the moral world," laying a specific command on man, requiring an account of his actions, and entering into "direct relationship with man and the other creatures." *A Commentary on the Book of Genesis*, vol. 1: *From Adam to Noah* (Varda Books, 2012), 86-87.

(Gen 3:8-9), to issue curses (Gen 3:14), and finally to expel them from Eden (Gen 3:23). Very roughly: *'elohim* is to Plato's Forms as YHWH is to the demiurge.

To be sure, each name has its own distinct import, but they are not at all in tension, for the names are revealed together.[40] Genesis 1 has already introduced the covenant name YHWH, albeit in disguise. The "transcendent" God of power (*'elohim*) speaks fragments of the name YHWH as he speaks the world into being. If YHWH names God as covenant Lord, in intimate though commanding communion with the creation, the Creator of Genesis 1 is already revealed as covenant Lord, already the God of generous love. Breathing out his Spirit, *'elohim* speaks, shapes a firmament of light, summons the earth to produce grasses and fruit trees, makes and places lights in the sky, calls on the sea to teem with fish and the land to bustle with cattle, beasts, and creeping things, deliberates over the creation of man, and invites man and all land animals to receive life from the banquet of the earth. He acts with power, but, as much as the *YHWH 'elohim* of Genesis 2, he is the good Creator who opens his hand to satisfy the desire of every living soul—because *'elohim* is also YHWH.

The hints of YHWH in Genesis 1 help close the gap critical scholars perceive between Genesis 1 and Genesis 2.[41] When it

---

[40]As John Frame has argued in many connections, a biblical understanding of transcendence does not contradict immanence but entails it. See "God and Biblical Language: Transcendence and Immanence," available at https://frame-poythress .org/god-and-biblical-language-transcendence-and-immanence/.

[41]In closing the gap between Genesis 1–2, the pattern of uses of *hayah* weakens one plank of the documentary hypothesis. According to the Graf-Wellhausen scheme that inexplicably remains popular among biblical scholars, the Pentateuch is the product of four sources or schools: Yahwist (J), Elohist (E), Deuteronomist (D), and Priestly (P). Scholars have used various indicators to disassemble the text into its supposed sources, including stylistic features. As the names of the documents/ schools suggests, one of the key indicators is the divine name. Genesis 1 is typically assigned to P on stylistic grounds, though it could be assigned to E by virtue of its exclusive use of the name *'elohim*. *No* critical scholar classifies Genesis 1 as a "Yahwist" document. Yet the author of Genesis 1 clearly knows the name YHWH.

names the Creator *YHWH 'elohim*, Genesis 2:4 does not suddenly introduce an unknown character or an unanticipated name. It brings into clear focus a God of whom we have had fleeting glimpses. Twenty-seven times *hayah*, the root of YHWH, is repeated, until we reach the twenty-eighth (4 x 7) that makes the name explicit. The numerology is, once again, significant. Twenty-eight factors into four and seven, the first the biblical number of spatial extent (four corners of earth, four winds of heaven, four points of the compass), and the second, obviously, the number of the temporal stretch of creation's coming-to-be. As a spatio-temporal manifold, as a cross of reality stretched on temporal and spatial axes, creation is itself a "28." *Hayah* denotes, at least, existence, and the existence of creation as a totality is summed up in the twenty-eighth use of *hayah*, the name YHWH. In YHWH, all that is in heaven, earth, and under the earth, all that is made over the week of days, everything visible and invisible, coalesces and coheres.

Why the disguise? Why the tease? Why not name the Creator *YHWH 'elohim* from the start? Why does YHWH hide, peek out, then fully declare his name? I can only speculate by showing how the disguise fits into Genesis 1. The creation week as a whole moves from darkness to light, evening to morning, from disguise to disclosure. At the outset, the earth is shrouded in darkness and robed with water. *'Elohim* dispels the darkness on day one, but the earth does not rise from beneath the veil of water until day three. Creation is prepared for man, but man does not appear until the sixth day. It is fitting for YHWH's name to be disclosed last rather than first, for he is the God who not only initiates but completes creation. He is not only Alpha-*'elohim* but also Omega-YHWH.

Thus, the delayed revelation of the name reinforces the eschatological tilt in the creation week. Creation is not complete until the work of the sixth day, after which *'elohim* ceases and enters his rest. The name YHWH is not fully disclosed until the week is complete. With Augustine as guide, we can extrapolate the shape of history from the shape of the creation week: God's name is finally disclosed only in the fullness of time, when the Son anointed by the Spirit reveals the Father, when the Son returns in answer to the cry of the Spirit and the Bride. God unfolds the interior communion of his life of love only in the incarnation and in the *totus Christus* of head and body.[42] Indeed, the full disclosure of God awaits the new heavens and new earth, for God will not be enthroned as God of a fully glorified creation until the world is fully glorified. Perhaps YHWH is throne name, the name *'elohim* assumes at his entry into Sabbath rest. Israel's history mimics YHWH's own pattern of delayed identification, for Israel emerges "late" in human history, as Israel's God is named "late" in the creation account.

Genesis 1 puts me in mind of the *Odyssey*, where Odysseus is named only at the very end of the proem. The technique is thematic for the entire epic because Odysseus is throughout the hidden hero, who comes in disguise and discloses himself at the last moment, which is the right moment. YHWH is the original hidden hero.[43]

---

[42]This is a major theme of the Apocalypse. See my *Revelation 1–11*, 101-6.

[43]The conclusion that YHWH names the Creator has strictly grammatical support. As David Noel Freedman, William Albright, and others have argued, YHWH is a masculine singular hiphil form of *hayah*, with the sense of "He who causes to be." At the burning bush, Yahweh assures Moses he will deliver Israel with the declaration, "I will cause to be what I will cause to be," that is, I will bring about what I have determined to bring about, the rescue of Israel. See Freedman, "The Name of the God of Moses," *JBL* 79, no. 2 (1960): 151-6; Albright, *From the Stone Age to Christianity: Monotheism and the Historical Process* (Baltimore: Johns Hopkins, 1940) 197-99; Albright, "Contributions to Biblical Archaeology and Philology," *JBL* 43, nos. 3/4 (1924): 370-8; Paul Haupt, "Der Name Jahwe," *Orientalistische Literaturzeitung* 5 (1909): 211-14. On this reading, Paul's claim that Abraham trusted the God who "calls the not-beings as beings" (*kalountos ta me onta hos onta*; Rom 4:17) is a precise rendition of Yahweh.

THE SPOKEN GOD

Let me repeat a numerological connection that might have gotten lost in the arithmetic barrage: Seven times, *'elohim* speaks *hayah*. In the breath of the Spirit, *'elohim* haltingly discloses his second name by his utterances: *yehiy* (Gen 1:3), *yehiy . . . yehiy* (Gen 1:6, 2x), *yehiy* (Gen 1:14), then *hayu* (Gen 1:14), *hayu* (Gen 1:15), then the imperfect *yihyeh* (Gen 1:29), so resonant with *Yah, Yah.* In speaking the creation into being, *'elohim* speaks his own name, the name hidden from the foundation of the world. YHWH names the Creator, but we can be more specific: YHWH is the content of *'elohim*'s utterance. YHWH is the *spoken* God by whom the speaking God speaks the world. Genesis 1–2 thus anticipates the logic of John 1.

Table 6.1. The Divine Name in Genesis and John

Genesis 1:1, 3, 6; 2:4	John 1:1, 3
In the beginning	In the beginning
'elohim said, let there be (*yehi*)	was the Word
and it was so	all things came into being through Him
YHWH *'elohim*	the Word was God

As we saw in chapter five, Genesis 1 reveals a God who speaks and a God who hears ("let us," Gen 1:26), a God who is an eternal communicative, conversational communion. Genesis 1 additionally discloses the God who speaks and a God who is spoken. When *'elohim* says "let be," he does not merely speak words of power that form light, a firmament, lights of the heavens. He speaks *himself* as that creative Word. The creative Word is no mere demiurgic agent of the Creator. The creative Word is God himself as spoken. The act by which God creates—saying *yehi*, "let be"— is the same act by which he is God, for God is named both *'elohim* and YHWH. God is because he is *internally* creative, speaking the eternal Word.[44] Along with John 1, this provides an exegetical basis for the longstanding conviction that the Father's generation of the Son is the ground and prototype for the creation of the world. The Word spoken by the Father before the beginning is the very Word who speaks as he is spoken in the beginning.

YHWH is, in brief, the name of the Second Person of the Trinity. The New Testament confirms this repeatedly,[45] by recording that *Jesus*, Word and Son, speaks *egō eimi*, the Greek equivalent of *ehyeh*.[46] This name is especially prominent in John's Gospel. Several times, Jesus uses the name absolutely, without a predicate. Jesus assures the disciples straining against the storm, "*egō eimi*; do not be afraid" (Jn 6:20). In his debate with the Jews at the Feast of Booths, Jesus uses the phrase repeatedly: "unless you believe *egō eimi*, you will die in your sins" (Jn 8:24); "when you lift up the Son of Man, then you will know *egō eimi*" (Jn 8:28); "before Abraham was born, *egō eimi*" (Jn 8:58).[47] Jesus predicts the future experiences of the disciples, so that when his words come to pass they will know "*egō eimi*" (Jn 13:19). During his arrest, his "*egō eimi*" knocks the soldiers to the ground (Jn 18:5-6, 8).

---

[44]John Milbank, *Theology and Social Theory: Beyond Secular Reason* (Oxford: Blackwell, 1990), 430, channeling Eriugena.

[45]I could also fill out my argument by attending to the interplay of difference and identity between YHWH and *mal'akh-YHWH* ("angel of YHWH") in various passages of the Old Testament (e.g., Gen 16:7-16; 22:9-22). In these passages, YHWH is the name of the *sent* God. To be sure, in some passages YHWH does double duty, naming both the *mal'akh* and the God to whom he prays (Zech 1:12-21).

[46]The Father speaks *egō eimi* only once in the Gospels, in Mt 22:32, where Jesus quotes "God" as the speaker of the Ex 3:6. Every other use of *egō eimi* in the Gospels is in the mouth of the *Son*.

[47]The debate in John 8 begins and ends with *egō eimi*. Jesus instigates the battle by saying, "*Egō eimi* the Light of the world" (Jn 8:12), and the conflict intensifies from a verbal combat to violence when he claims, "before Abraham was born, *egō eimi*" (Jn 8:58). The whole debate is about Jesus' identification of himself with YHWH. See David Mark Ball, *I Am in John's Gospel: Literary Function, Background and Theological Implications*, Journal for the Study of the New Testament Supplement Series (London: Continuum, 1996), 81.

In a few cases, Jesus says *egō eimi* with an implied predicate. "Are you the Christ?" Caiaphas asks. Jesus answers, *egō eimi*, implying "I am the Christ" (Mk 14:61-62). In some passages, another clause is added to or nested between "I" and "am." When the Samaritan woman speaks of the Christ, Jesus answers "*egō eimi* who speak to you" (Jn 4:25-26), and the Great Commission merges Immanuel with "I am": "*egō* with-you *eimi*" (Mt 28:20). John famously uses *egō eimi* in conjunction with symbols that explicate Jesus' character, being, and mission. *Egō eimi* bread, light, the door, the good shepherd, the resurrection and the life, the way and truth and life, the vine, seven declarations that roughly follow the sequence of the exodus narrative. As Augustine recognized, *Jesus* is the *ego sum qui sum* revealed at the burning bush.

A number of studies have linked Jesus' *egō eimi* to the Hebrew *'anu hu*, "I am he," prominent in the late chapters of Isaiah.[48] Isaiah directly echoes the song of Moses (Is 47:8, 10) and frequently says there is no God but Yahweh (Is 44:6, 8; 45:5, 6, 18; 46:9). Idols are formed or molded, but Yahweh is the "I am he" who was before all gods and will continue when no other gods are before him (Is 43:10). Isaiah links *'ani hu* with *'ani* (or *'anokiy*) YHWH. In Isaiah 45:18, Yahweh the Creator of heaven and earth declares *'ani YHWH*, "I YHWH."[49] Yahweh's Servant comes so Israel "will know *'ani hu*" (Is 43:10); that is, so they will know "*'anokiy 'anokiy YHWH*," the Savior (Is 43:11). As in the first exodus, so in Isaiah's second exodus: Yahweh does what he does

---

[48]See the reviews of the literature in Ball, *I Am in John's Gospel*, 33-36; Catrin H. Williams, *I am He: The Interpretation of 'ani hu' in Jewish and Early Christian Literature*, Wissenschaftliche Untersuchungen Zum Neuen Testament 2 (Reihe: Mohr Siebeck, 2000), chap. 1. The phrase is used only once in the Pentateuch (Deut 32:39), where Yahweh declares his uniqueness and his authority over life and death.

[49]Some scholars have doubted that *ani hu* should be linked to Yahweh's "I will be who I will be" in Exodus 3:14 (Williams, *I am He*, 52-54). I think otherwise. See the thorough analysis of Steven Rudd at "Jesus Echoes the 'I AM' statements of Jehovah in the Gospel of John," https://www.bible.ca/trinity/trinity-i-am.htm.

so Israel and the nations will know his name. Given the second exodus context, it is natural for Isaiah to evoke the Name revealed at the burning bush. *'Ani hu* is a variation on the *'ehyeh* ("I am") of Exodus 3:14, and Jesus' *egō eimi* echoes both "I am" of the first exodus and the "I am he" of the second.[50]

Notably, Isaiah sometimes links *'ani hu* or *'ani YHWH* with creation. Isaiah 45:18 is modified chiasm:

A Thus says YHWH,
>   B who created (*bara'*) the heavens
>>   C (He is the *'elohim* who formed the earth and made it, He established it
>   B' and did not create (*bara'*) it a waste place (*tohu*, cf. Gen 1:2),
>>   C' but formed it to be inhabited),
A' I am YHWH (*'ani YHWH*), and there is none else.

Bara' and *tohu* take us back to Genesis 1:1-2. Genesis 1 never mentions Yahweh, yet Isaiah knows Yahweh as the God of Genesis 1. He is justified in reading Genesis 1 as an account of the doings of Yahweh not only because Genesis 2:4 identifies the Creator *'elohim* with YHWH, but also because Genesis 1 *already* identifies the "let be" by which the world is spoken with the God whose name is "I am/will be" and whose number is twenty-six. Isaiah 48:12-16 likewise identifies the God who says *'ani hu* as the Creator, the "first and last" who founded earth and heaven with his hands and with his hands will shape it from glory to glory.

We reach the same conclusion by tracking *kyrios* ("Lord") in the LXX and New Testament. *Kyrios* is the standard Greek

---

[50]Rudd points to parallels between Old Testament "I am he" and John's "I am" passages:

Is 41:10: "Do not fear, for *'ani* with you," and Jn 6:20: "*Ego eimi*; do not be afraid." Is 52:6: "*'ani hu* . . . who is speaking," and Jn 4:25-26: "*Ego eimi* who speak[s] to you." Deut 32:39: "*'ani hu* . . . who puts to death and gives life," and Jn 11:25: "*Ego eimi* the resurrection and the life." These links are strengthened further when we factor in the LXX, where *'ani hu* is consistently rendered as *ego eimi* (Is 41:4; 43:10; 48:12 [2x]). Jesus might as well be quoting the Greek translation of Isaiah.

translation of YHWH. *YHWH 'elohim* in Genesis 2:8 becomes *kyrios ho theos*, the same phrase as Exodus 3:15. In the New Testament, *kyrios* is regularly used as a title for Jesus. Typically, the Father is *ho theos*, and Jesus is *kyrios* (e.g., 1 Cor 8:6). The New Testament triune formula is God, the Lord, and the Spirit. Once again YHWH is taken as the name of the Second Person.

Jesus' *ego eimi* sayings are typically taken as proof that Jesus is divine. Fair enough. But we can press and invert the point. If *ego eimi* is the Greek way of saying *'ani hu*, and *that* is a way of identifying God as YHWH, then *Jesus* is YHWH. YHWH is not a general name for the one God, but specifically a name for the *Second* Person. YHWH is the name of the God uttered by *'elohim* who brings heaven and earth into being. YHWH is the spoken God.

METAPHYSICS OF GENESIS

Our meditation on the name YHWH has led us back from a "metaphysics of Exodus," which focuses on God's eternal act of being, toward a "metaphysics of Genesis," which refocuses attention on God as the boundless source, origin, and giver of existence to everything that is other than God. This encourages us to leave behind vestiges of a theology of God-without-world (often implicit in the metaphysics of Exodus) and move toward a theology of God the Creator. *'Elohim* speaks *yehi*, and *'elohim is YHWH*. YHWH names the God who speaks and is spoken, who in his speaking and his being spoken, *gives* being. To name *'elohim* as *YHWH* is to speak of the God who "calls not-beings as beings" (Rom 4:17; *theou tou . . . kalountos ta me onta hos onta*). I argued in chapter four that "Creator" is the first name of God. Now I can reinforce that conclusion: Even when God is named in terms of being—as *'eheyh* or *YHWH*, he is *still* named as Creator. "To be" is, for God, to be Creator.

This is not, to repeat, an abandonment of metaphysics but a paring purification, carried out with the fiery sword of the written Word. A metaphysics of Genesis abides contentedly under the rubric, "given creation," the rubric under which *all* Christian theology operates. Even the name traditionally used to express God's independence of creation—YHWH, *esse*, Being— names the Spoken God by whom the Creator speaks the heavens and the earth. There is no God but the God who has created.

Nor, once again, is God's unity an undifferentiated oneness. From the first chapter of the Bible, we are introduced to a God who is both God *and* God-again, both God and Another, the Speaking God who speaks the Spoken God by the breath of the Spirit. To pursue a metaphysics or ontology of Genesis is to pursue a trinitarian ontology. We may continue to speak of God as "Being" if we wish, so long as we do not forget that this is identical to saying "triune Creator."

We can tease out other dimensions of the metaphysics of Genesis. The Creator creates by the Word that is God, and creation by word is creation in freedom. The God who speaks the world into being is a person, Lord, Advocate, and Guardian of his and every people, a "living Person . . . who knows and wills and speaks." Creation exists in and as co-respondent to God's utterance, and is "wholly referred to it for its existence, its survival and sustenance."[51] To be is to be included in the conversation God is. This creating Word, which is YHWH, is an irruption of grace and compassion, as God reaches out to "rescue" the formless darkness; the creating Word thus anticipates the incarnation, for God is "God with us" from the first utterance, and the cosmos exists "in no other way than by the Word of God."[52] As

---

[51]Barth, *Church Dogmatics* 3/1: *The Doctrine of Creation*, ed. Geoffrey Bromiley and T. F. Torrance London (T&T Clark, 2010), 110.
[52]Barth, *Church Dogmatics* 3/1, 111.

God creates by speaking, so every creature participates in God as it hears, receives, and obeys that Word. The Word does not keep creatures at a distance: "How could [the world] be more closely bound to God than by the fact that it is by His Word?" The world is as close as can be, for "the Word of God is not less than God Himself."[53] Creation is not a first address of God but a further address, a modulation in God's eternal self-utterance. Creation is a rhetorical act, the outward address of the eternally speaking God.[54]

As noted above, the God who creates by Word is God insofar as he speaks himself. For God, to be is to speak. He is eternally, inherently, necessarily communicative. *'Elohim* is God in that he speaks YHWH. God is "I am" in that he speaks "I am." He "will be" in that he speaks "will be." God is God as he speaks an eternal "let be."[55] God *knows* himself as God only as he eternally speaks himself as Word, only as he, together with the Word, breathes the Spirit who searches the depths of God. He is God only as Speaking and Spoken God are united in loving communication by the Spirit. To put it in terms anachronistic to Genesis, God is God only as the Father speaks the Son, only as he eternally breathes out the "let be" that is the eternal begetting of the Son and the procession of the Spirit. God is God not by retaining life and love and joy, but by their eternal bestowal.

---

[53]Barth, *Church Dogmatics* 3/1, 116. As we have seen, Barth endorses the patristic habit of finding a glimpse of the Trinity in Genesis 1: The author "has equated the utterance of God, which is as such His 'expression,' with God Himself." After all, if "God alone creates," and if the Word "creates," then "His Word is God Himself—the one God." The Word is in God before he utters it, but as he "becomes" Creator in speaking the Word, the Word becomes "the instrument of His creation" while remaining his equal. Whether he remains in himself, or speaks creation, he never ceases to be God, the Speaker and the Word.

[54]David Bentley Hart, *The Beauty of the Infinite: The Aesthetics of Christian Truth* (Grand Rapids, MI: Eerdmans, 2004), 181.

[55]*Uno eodemque Verbo dicit seipsum et quaecumque fecit*; "By one and the same Word He speaks both Himself and whatever He has made" (Anselm, *Monologion*, 33, quoted in Barth, *Church Dogmatics* 3/1, 115).

The bestowal is mutual, for the Speaking God is himself only by virtue of the Spoken God, and the Spoken God exists only as the Speaking God speaks. YHWH the Spoken God cannot be except as *'elohim* speaks, and *'elohim* cannot be the Speaking God except as he utters YHWH. Further, the Speaking God cannot speak apart from the suspiration of his Breath, nor can the Spoken God be spoken except through the Spirit through whom the Speaking God speaks. Which, translated, means: The Father is not Father except as he generates the Son; nor is the Son the Son except as he is generated by the Father. Nor can the Father generate, or the Son be generated, except through the infinite fertility of their shared Spirit. God is not God without the vitality of eternal processions. Which means, once again, God is God not by retaining life and love and joy but by their eternal bestowal *and return*, only by the eternal *circulation* of glory.

Because the Creator *is* Word, he is immediately, eternally, necessarily the manifest God.[56] The living God is not in transcendent isolation beyond disclosure, because he is himself disclosure. The Speaking God who is God's own disclosure is the One through whom all comes to be (Col 1:16-17). The Spoken God, the Word, is, to use Thomas's language, the exemplar, the efficient cause, and the final cause of all that is. YHWH is the pattern of each created being, and the *typos* in which the harmonious pattern of all things coheres.[57]

---

[56]David Bentley Hart, *The Hidden and the Manifest: Essays in Theology and Metaphysics* (Grand Rapids, MI: Eerdmans, 2017), 137-64.

[57]We can mix in some of the overtones of Heraclitus, for whom *logos* is the harmony of things. In his perfect harmony with *'elohim* and the Spirit, the Spoken God is the exemplar of perfect unity in difference. Spoken as the "let be" of creation, he is the strong "unapparent harmony" who creates all apparent harmony. The Spoken God is perfectly tuned to the Speaking God by the Spirit, and so he tunes the differences of creation so they harmonize with himself and with each other. As Heraclitus puts it, "Difference and agreement are to the cosmic *harmonia* as a back-tensed tuning is to a bow and lyre." See Eva Brann, *The Logos of Heraclitus* (Philadelphia: Paul Dry Books, 2011), 42-43, 73.

We must speak of the perfections or attributes of God within this context. The creation account records actions—creating, hovering, speaking, making, placing, blessings, inviting—from which we may *infer* attributes. A God who creates from nothing is a God of power. A God who constructs an intricately ordered cosmos is a God of wisdom and justice. A God who forms a world that is "very good" is good in himself and holy. The Creator is, as the Westminster Shorter Catechism has it, a God of wisdom, power, holiness, justice, goodness, and truth.[58] All the actions of *'elohim* that exhibit these perfections are actions he performs through his breath and speech. God's perfections are not the actions of an undifferentiated God, but of the God who speaks "let be" and energizes all things by the life of his hovering Spirit. God is wisdom in that he speaks wisdom by the breath of his Spirit of wisdom; he is truth in that he speaks truth in the Spirit of truth; he is just in that he speaks rightly by the Spirit who clothes the Word with justice; he is good in that he discloses, diffuses, and gives himself in the lyric of his Spiritual song. God is the God that he is, with his perfections, because he is *'elohim*, YHWH, and the Spirit; the Speaking God, the Spoken God, and the Spirit who empowers the speaking to be spoken. Because it offers a trinitarian reshaping of ontology, the metaphysics of Genesis sublates the metaphysics of Exodus.

It is a metaphysics open to incarnation. The name *YHWH 'elohim* combines the Speaking *'elohim* with the Spoken *hayah/* YHWH. *YHWH 'elohim* is the "us" who, with the Spirit, conspires to create man. Genesis 2 uses this double name as God comes close to form humanity and humanity's environment. *YHWH 'elohim*, the Speaking-Spoken God, fashions the man from dust, plants the garden east in Eden, causes trees to grow, places the

---

[58]Westminster Shorter Catechism, q. 4.

man in the garden, issues commands, performs surgery on the sleeping man, builds the woman, and plays matchmaker by bringing the woman to the man. Under the name *'elohim*, God speaks and makes the heavens and the earth, operating "at a distance" through the power of his eternal Voice. Under the name *'elohim YHWH*, God and his Voice engage with creation, digging in the *'adamah*, molding the dust, giving life with the intimacy of a kiss.

In New Testament terms, the Father and Son, in one unified action, fashion, plant, place, build. And there is no reason not to take Genesis 2 quite literally in this regard. If the Son of the Father can become flesh, live a human life, suffer weakness and frailty, die a human death, and rise in glory to bring our humanity to the throne of God, then the Son of the Father can surely take form to fashion, plan, place, and build. Does *YHWH 'elohim* have hands to muck about in the dusk? Jesus did. Why not the Spoken God who acts as one with the God who speaks him? Does *YHWH 'elohim* actually, physically plant trees? Perhaps the Son takes a subincarnate yet physical form to engage directly with earth. Why not?

'Elohim is because he speaks the "let be" that is YHWH. God is God as the God who speaks and is with his Word. Which is to say, at further level of abstraction, God is insofar as he extends and communicates himself in and as Another, and again Another. Nothing, not even God, *is* by retaining its being, life, and power in itself. God is himself by self-transcendence, "identical with Himself in going beyond Himself, in giving away."[59] The

---

[59]In a move reminiscent of Karl Barth, Klaus Hemmerle begins his *Theses Towards a Trinitarian Ontology* by reflecting on revelation. God's word precedes human words, since he creates speaking beings by his word. Yet God's word also *follows* human words. If God wants to make himself known to human beings, he must speak humanly. When he speaks in human language, his word is preceded by our words. God's word "answers" human words already spoken. By speaking our language, the

self-revealing God is a God of self-giving love. God gives himself to us in his Son, and this self-gift is not a mere role God happens to play. His self-gift is his eternal life and being as Father, Son, and Spirit. The essence of God is this reciprocal self-giving.[60]

Being, including especially divine Being, is often characterized as what persists in a world of change, what is unalterably itself. Being is what fully *preserves* Being. An ontology of Genesis insists instead on the primacy of love. Love does not retain but *endures* through self-gift, through manifestation, through dispossession. Love is *action*, an outgoing from the self to the Other. God is love, and the love God *is* is what it is only as it extends itself. An ontology of Genesis confirms the activist ontology of Thomas Aquinas, for whom God is most essentially the *act* of being. In the trinitarian version of this insight that we came to in chapter five, the act by which God *is* is the active, infinitely energetic life of the Trinity. For a divine metaphysics of Genesis, the verb is the "new substantive."[61]

In the triune fugue, there is real development, as the Father begets the Son and together they breathe out the Spirit. The Father unfolds himself in his self-gift to the Son, knows and is himself in the Word he speaks and hears, and together they reach the consummation of joy in the passion of the Spirit. Thus the triune God transcends the distinction of potentiality and actuality, because he is an "eternally self-rejuvenating" triune life. He is eternally actualized because he is eternally producing himself

---

God who spoke first humbles himself, takes second place, and even allows his word to be mangled and distorted. But God's word could not reach its hearers at all without passing through this humiliation. God's word communicates—God's word *is* God's word—only as it passes through a process of "both relinquishment and elevation." *Theses Towards a Trinitarian Ontology*, trans. Steven Churchyard (Brooklyn, NY: Angelico, 2020), 14-17.

[60]Coda, *Ontologie trinitaire*, 82-84; Antonio Rosmini, *Theosophy*, vol. 3: *Trine Being (Contd.)* (Durham, NC: Rosmini House, 2011), 182-84, par. 1320.

[61]Hemmerle, *Theses*, 35.

in the processions of the Son and Spirit.[62] That this development is eternal, always already realized, does not alter the fact that it is genuine *development*. The Creator's immutable being *is* this eternal becoming.[63] His being is the lush movement of eternal music.

To round off: In a metaphysics of Genesis, to be God is to be Creator. It is a metaphysics of God-with-world. And, crucially, we must add that, according to the metaphysics of Genesis, to be Creator is to be the Creator who by his Breath speaks and who by his Breath is spoken, the God who is by his speaking, breathing, and being spoken.

MIRROR OF YHWH

A metaphysics of Genesis is a metaphysics of the Creator, also of the creation. With regard to the latter, it is a metaphysics of the *word*.[64] As Hamann would put it, what in the metaphysics of

---

[62]Dorner, *Divine Immutability: A Critical Reconsideration*, trans. Robert R. Williams and Claude Welch (Minneapolis: Fortress, 1994), 137, 139.

[63]Once again, there is an overlap with Darth, who describes the processions as an *ad intra* "becoming." See Wittman, *God and Creation*, 147. See also, in a different idiom, John Milbank, who denies God is simply *actus purus* because, if God is merely actualized, his actualization becomes a limit and God becomes finite. There is in God "a kind of surplus to actuality," such that "no priority can be given either to pure *actus* or pure *virtus*." In the Trinity "infinite realized act and infinite unrealized power coincide" in God's "circular 'life,' that is more than stasis" (*Theology and Social Theory*, 423).

[64]Remarkably, recent treatments of the doctrine of creation barely mention the fact that God creates by word. Simon Oliver mentions "God's creative word," but it is subordinated to his (correct) argument about the peacefulness of the act of creation. Later, Oliver (again, rightly) emphasizes that the eternal Word, the Second Person, creates. Other than that, Simon says virtually nothing about the role of God's speech in creation. *Creation: A Guide for the Perplexed* (London: Bloomsbury, 2017), 13, 39. Recent work on creation emphasizes the creation's "participation" in God. That is sometimes characterized as participation in the Word, but in these writers "Word" is not understood as actual utterance but as the Second Person or as a metaphysical principle, rather than as the spoken word. It is a curious lacuna in contemporary discussions of creation. Three twentieth-century Protestant theologians have stressed the significance of creation by word: Bonhoeffer, *Creation and Fall*, Dietrich Bonhoeffer Works 3, ed. Martin Ruter and Ilse Todt, trans. Douglas Stephen Bax

Exodus is Being, Genesis prefers to call "Word."[65] Creation by word distinguishes Genesis from all ancient myths that depict a god creating from his own substance or "natural fecundity."[66] God creates in "complete freedom," bound to the world only insofar as he "binds the world to Himself by His Word." Creating by the Word that is God, *'elohim* remains "wholly God, wholly the Creator, wholly Lord" even while creating something other than himself. A Creator who creates by word is neither distant from creation nor continuous with it. He is "in the world *in the word*."[67] Creation by word is a barrier against pantheism.

A metaphysics of the word prioritizes the audible over the specular. Classical metaphysics, in both its pagan and Christian varieties, is a philosophy of the eye. It need not have been. There is no inherent reason why *eidos*, the shape of what is seen in the mind's eye, should be taken as paradigmatic for all knowledge or existence. There is no inherent reason why ultimate realities should not rather be imagined as *logoi* or *rhemata*. For some thinkers, the metaphysics of sight—including certain versions of the metaphysics of Exodus—had certain advantages, most importantly to secure existence and knowledge from the corrosions of time: "Beings are fully reliable objects of knowledge just insofar as they simply appear in the present tense of consciousness without inner reference to past or future, as objects in space appear to sight."[68] If, however, created existence is a "coming to word," it is slipperier, ultimately impossible to pin down.[69] For no

---

(Minneapolis: Fortress, 2004); Robert Jenson, *Systematic Theology*, vol. 2: *The Works of God* (Oxford: Oxford University Press, 1999); and Barth, *Church Dogmatics* 3/1.

[65]Hamann wrote, "What in your language is Being, I prefer to call the Word," quoted in John R. Betz, "Enlightenment Revisited: Hamann as the First and Best Critic of Kant's Philosophy," *Modern Theology* 20, no. 2 (2004): 291-301.

[66]Bonhoeffer, *Creation and Fall*, 40.

[67]Bonhoeffer, *Creation and Fall*, 40-41 (emphasis original).

[68]Jenson, *Systematic Theology*, 1:210.

[69]Once again, I note a partial convergence with Aquinas. For Thomas, creation implies that things are unfathomable to creatures. See Pieper, *Silence of St. Thomas*, 57-67.

utterance can be uttered all at once, and every utterance confronts us with unrealized future possibilities. Every time we
speak, we cut channels through time; every word we speak bears
the trace of promise. If God speaks and is Word, there is no safe
place where we can hide from history. If we live in a verbal world,
there is no arresting the flow of time, for verbal flow is the form
of created existence.

God's word is a commandment, an expression of his will, and
so, Augustine to the contrary, God's word is not "a symbol, a
meaning, or an idea," but "a spoken word."[70] God's words are
imperatives: "God commands the world to be, this command is
obeyed, and the event of obedience is the existence of the world."
God creates by an "agency of the same sort as the *torah* by which
he creates Israel," an agency that holds as much in the present as
in the past since "the world is no less dependent on God's creating
word in any moment of its existence than it was at the beginning."[71]
God does not *just* command. The Creator is also the God of
promise, and so created beings are "promises" of more, promises
of future continuation, actualization, flowering.[72] The Creator's
speech sometimes functions as a pattern for making ("God
said . . . and made").[73] He delegates tasks. He blesses and

[70]Bonhoeffer, *Creation and Fall*, 41-42. The lack of continuity between God and the
world excludes, in Bonhoeffer's view, all efforts to reason from creation to God. He
dismisses the *via eminentiae*, the *via negationis*, and the *via causalitatis* and insists
human beings know God only in his revelation. I think Bonhoeffer overstates the
contrast. Genesis 1 does suggest an "analogy of being," a resemblance between the
Creator who speaks and is YHWH and the creation that comes to be by the Creator's
"let be." Bonhoeffer echoes Luther, who also insists the words of creation are imperatives. Luther, *Lectures on Genesis*, at Gen 1:3, in Jaroslav Pelican, ed., *Luther's
Works*, vol. 1: *Lectures on Genesis, Chapters 1–5*, trans. George V. Schick (St. Louis:
Concordia, 1958).
[71]Jenson, *Systematic Theology*, 2:7-9.
[72]William Desmond, *Being and the Between* (Albany, NY: SUNY Press, 1995), 241.
[73]Basil discerns two persons in the combination of "he spoke" and "he made," illus-
trating the principle that "Everywhere, in mystic theology, history is sown with the
dogmas of theology." *Hexameron* 6.2, in Blomfield Jackson, trans., *The Hexameron*
(Columbia, SC: Create Space, 2014), originally published in *Nicene and Post-Nicene*

evaluates and, at the end of Genesis 1, invites all creatures to a banquet. Creation takes the shape it does, has the powers it possesses, because of the variety of the Creator's speech acts.

'Elohim speaks hayah seven times in Genesis 1, but the verb is used much more often with direct reference to the creation. The sequence of Genesis 1–2 is thus: 'elohim speaks hayah; the world comes to hayah; it is revealed that 'elohim is hayah/YHWH. Created things receive their existence (hayah) from 'elohim's verbal yehiy (let be), and their hayah is a reflex of 'elohim's own existence as YHWH. Genesis 1–2 thus justifies Thomas's conclusion that created things resemble the Creator by virtue of their existence; the gift of creation is the gift of being. The Creator speaks "let be" and is YHWH, and the things that the Creator creates "be." Genesis 1 reveals an analogy of being that takes the form of a Thomist verbal ontology.

Through his speaking, the God who bears the name YHWH "repeated Himself in creation" and "reflects Himself in nonbeing." Creation is "the divine 'ecstasy' of love, which is the creative 'let there be' addressed outward, to the emerging extradivine being."[74] This ecstasy is God himself in Word and Spirit, who is by the breathy utterance of his own "let be," who is God in being also YHWH. In creating, this God of love extends the ecstasy of the love he is beyond himself to create and then embrace what he creates. He extends the ecstasy he is in order to mirror his own ecstasy in creatures.

Creation's being is itself a mirror of the Creator's, and creation also mimics the *form* of the Creator's existence. Created being is, of course, receptive being, in imitation of the receptivity of the

---

Fathers, Second Series 8, ed. Philip Schaff and Henry Wace (Buffalo, NY: Christian Literature Publishing, 1895).

[74]Sergius Bulgakov, The Lamb of God, trans. Boris Jakim (Grand Rapids, MI: Eerdmans, 2008), 126-27. Bulgakov is, of course and unfortunately, describing the action of Sophia.

Son and Spirit in their procession from the Father, and the receptivity of the Father who is Father insofar as he has a Son. Because creation comes from God's Word, it is knowable and intelligible.[75] Resulting from speech, creation *is* speech (Ps 8; 19).[76] It signifies. The order of created causes is also an order of signs. Creation's order is linguistic and musical. Creation has the kind of meaning speech has, which means that knowing creation is a *hermeneutical* adventure. Poetry is the human "genre" that best matches the sort of world we live in, and science does best when it becomes like poetry—or, better, when it recognizes that it is already poetic through and through.

Things are as they resemble the God who speaks and is spoken. Things are as they speak themselves, for there is no interval between created being and its manifestation. A creature's essence is not hidden under a thick surface of phenomenal appearance. Existence as such is manifest existence—in the Creator, and so in the creature.[77] Things are what they are, they become what they will be, by extending themselves beyond themselves; they are what they are in exceeding themselves. In traditional Thomist terms, substances manifest themselves in their accidents, by

---

[75]Thomas Aquinas says the same, though roots the intelligibility of things in God's knowledge rather than his speech. See Josef Pieper, *The Silence of St. Thomas* (South Bend, IN: St. Augustine's, 1957), 55. The difference is negligible, however, because for Thomas knowledge has a quasi-linguistic structure, in that "coming-to-know" involves the emanation of a mental word.

[76]Luther writes that the entire creation is nothing but "the Word of God uttered by God, or extended to the outside." Thus everything is a word of God: "Sun, moon, heaven, earth, Peter, Paul, I, you, etc.—we are all words of God, in fact only one single syllable or letter in comparison with the entire creation." Human beings speak and assign names, but God's words "are realities, not bare words" (*Lectures on Genesis*, at Gen 1:5).

[77]Thomas Aquinas comes to an analogous conclusion with his insistence that existing is an act, which he extrapolates from Aristotle's instruction to learn the nature of a thing by noticing "how it interacts with the world about it." As David Burrell puts it, "In one fell swoop, then, Aquinas keeps us from regarding the nature of a thing as some inaccessible substratum and also directs us to the existing nature as the source of a thing's power to act." *Freedom and Creation in Three Traditions* (Notre Dame, IN: University of Notre Dame Press, 1993), 33.

which the substance is itself and is a presence in the world to and among others.[78] Composite things exist by their self-transcending excess, and in this they are the mirror, not the negation, of the triune God.

As David L. Schindler observes, this means that objective reality has its own interiority, which is a participation in and echo of God's *word*. Objects are also *subjects*; *everything* speaks to us, because everything is created by and as a word of the Creator.[79] Every thing exists for the sake of "generous communication," and thus, before we begin to observe it, is already "apt for true relation and community with humans."[80] Reality is radically symbolic and sacramental: "All beings bear reference *from within* themselves to a *transcendent meaning* that is *from another*."[81] Everything has a "fundamental word-like character," which implies that human beings are fundamentally "listeners": "The human being is meant to be in relation with things, indeed to be in relation with all created reality, to see and hear creatures first as they are given, rather than to manipulate or instrumentalize them. The word-like nature of things in their inner reality as creatures demands this priority of *listening* to things *spoken*—and thus as *given*."[82] Set in a speaking world, human beings are created to be *contemplative*—and also to speak back to love and command creation.

As the first creature, light is paradigmatic. God is light in that the Father eternally shines in the radiance that is the Son

---

[78]D. C. Schindler, *A Companion to Ferdinand Ulrich's Homo Abyssus* (Washington, DC: Humanum Academic, 2019), 45-47.

[79]Schindler, *The Generosity of Creation* (Washington, DC: Humanum Academic, 2018), 102.

[80]Schindler, *Generosity of Creation*, 99.

[81]Schindler, *Generosity of Creation*, 103-7.

[82]Schindler, *Generosity of Creation*, 100. Schindler makes these points in the context of examining the modern battle between "objectivism" and "subjectivism." The battle arises, he argues, precisely because reality has been rendered mute by mechanistic science. Ideas are not impositions on a merely material reality; on creationist grounds, material reality is already ideal, already meaningful and communicative.

(Heb 1:3) and the diffusion of the Spirit. Divine light exists, as Athanasius insisted, only by extending itself beyond its source, for "Light source without radiance" is just another name for "darkness." So too created light. As soon as light exists, it shines, manifesting itself as light. Every other thing comes to be under its beneficent reign. There is no interval between being and manifestation, existence and appearance. Exteriors are not fixed boundaries separating interior from other. Inner and outer are foldings and unfoldings. In the universe created by YHWH *'elohim*, to exist at all is to radiate a glory that shows and speaks. As product of *'elohim*'s "let be," created things are sensible and knowable in their luminosity. As Thomas Aquinas puts it, "The measure of the reality of a thing is the measure of its light."[83]

'Elohim speaks in order to make and give, and he creates a world in which every thing speaks itself in order to create and give. He speaks "let be light" and "there *is* light." The existence of light is a created resemblance of the speech of *'elohim*, who is YHWH. Light exists to *give* light to everything else. Light lends itself to everything it illumines, for everything that comes into the light is light (Eph 5:13). Light enables everything to mimic the self-illumination that is light, which itself mimics the self-manifestation of the Creator. Light also sets the example of generosity for all other creatures. Light gives order and shape to days, for light and its withdrawal keep the time of "evening and morning," which "are" (*hayah*) each of the six days. God calls plants to rise from the earth, "and it was (*hayah*) so" (Gen 1:11). Once in existence, plants are given, and give themselves, for food (Gen 1:29). *'Elohim* speaks,

---

[83]A comment on 1 Tim 6:4, quoted in Pieper, *Silence of St. Thomas*, 56. There is biblical grounding for Robert Gosseteste's "metaphysics of light." See his *On Light*, trans. Clare C. Riedl (Milwaukee, WI: Marquette University Press, 1978). John Milbank finds a similar theme in Augustine: for Augustine, nothing is inertly *there* in self-enclosed isolation, prior to its self-expression. "The Confession of Time in Augustine," *Maynooth Philosophical Papers* 10 (2020): 20.

makes, and places the lights of the heavens, but they exist in order to take over the divine vocation of separating, signifying, and ruling the day and night (Gen 1:14-15). Things are as gifts of God, as expressions of the radical generosity of the Creator, each bearing within itself and its actions and energies the trace of its generous Maker. The Creator is Love, and love is the reality deep down things.[84]

For the Creator, love is the very "rhythm of Being."[85] The rhythm is the perfect rhythm, harmony, and eternal melody of the Trinity. The Father gives himself wholly to the Son: "The Father loves the Son and has given all things into His hand" (Jn 3:35), and again "All things the Father has are Mine" (Jn 16:15). And yet, by that very act, the Father *retains* all, for he is Father only by giving all to the Son, because he is nothing but Father of the begotten Son.[86] And so too the Son is himself only by his return gift of filial homage to the Father; and the Spirit is himself by retaining his own but by spreading the glory he is over the Father and Son. God is not persistently himself by stingy retention; self-gift is the mode of retention and persistence and eternally realized excess and self-transcendence.

---

[84]Schindler, *Companion*, 23-24.

[85]Hemmerle, *Theses*, 35. That rhythm is triple. Language provides an apt illustration (45-47). Language exists only in the action of communicating, and communication is a process constituted with a triple origin: The speaker initiates speech and is responsible for it, yet he could not speak without language and he would not speak unless there were a listener to hear and respond. The "poles" of speaker, language, and listener are equally basic. In fact, the poles do not exist at all outside their mutual relationships. Speakers do not exist independently of the language they speak and the hearers they address, nor does language exist without speakers and hearers, nor hearers without speakers speaking language. Yet the poles do not collapse into each other. Speaker, language, and listener remain distinct, even though they exist only in relationship to each other in the process of conversation. Hemmerle discovers the same triadic structure in play: I am fulfilled as a player by playing, but I cannot play without a game and other players. Relationship and process are not eddies on the surface of an immutable underlying substance. In a trinitarian ontology, process and relationship go all the way down—and all the way up, because God himself is the original rhythm of eternal love.

[86]Piero Coda, *Ontologie trinitaire*, 83-84.

Made by the God whose life is marked by reception, creation's existence is receptivity. Made by the God whose triune life is an eternal round of self-gifts, everything exhibits the form of self-gift. To be is to be embedded in a round of exchange, receiving from God and/in others, giving to God and/to others. Things are not, as some versions of "Being" might suggest, most fully themselves when they are at rest, unchanging, alone. Beings exist and fulfill themselves not by holding back, but by giving ahead: "Everything fulfills itself and brings that which is its own most to perfection by entering into its relatedness, into its being-beyond itself, into its self-having as self-giving, into its character as to and for each other."[87] God *is* by extending himself in Another, in Word and Spirit, and so too created things are by extending themselves, in relation to other things, by becoming other than themselves in time, by speaking themselves more fully with each passing moment. For created things as for God, "self-having [is] self-giving." Things are what they are, they possess themselves, in action, motion, process, relation, only in the movement of love.

Our inner life is ours only as it extends outward, touches and receives, and incorporates the outer life into the inner. Our inner life exists only as we communicate outward, as we reproduce ourselves in the world, among others. Life is life only as it extends forward. Life is life only as it is *more* life. Time is time only in its continuation. Language is only language as it continues to speak. When language ends, there is only silence. Stopped time is no

---

[87]Hemmerle, *Theses*, 52. Against his intentions, David Bentley Hart's description of the fragility of existence identifies analogies with triune life: "Nothing has its actuality entirely in itself"—not even the Father, whose Fatherhood is inconceivable without the Son; everything "must always receive itself from beyond itself, and then only by losing itself at the same time"—as the Son is by receiving all from the Father and by a returning self-gift to the Father; he speaks of the "ontological indigence of becoming" but fails to identify these features of created becoming as figures of the triune processions. Hart, *The Experience of God: Being, Consciousness, Bliss* (New Haven, CT: Yale University Press, 2013), 92.

longer time. Life without more life is death.[88] Created existence *is* only as it continually goes beyond what it is. Every being is itself in the ecstasy of being-beyond-itself. In all this, creaturely becoming is not a defect in created existence, but a mirror of trinitarian "becoming." Which is another name for triune love.

Created things are events, their existence finally a product of their accumulated actions and happenings. This is not to say they are not identifiable things. It is to specify the shape of their thingness. The happenings that are created things take place in relation to the Creator and other creatures. That relationality does not dissolve the uniqueness of particulars but, again, specifies the shape of their particularity. But the actions and happenings that make us what and who we are forever elude us. We cannot control the consequences of what we say or do. We speak and act and then try to catch up to grasp what we have done or said. Far less are we capable of bringing what happens *to* us under control. The elusiveness of our actions and happenings points to a transcendence inherent in created existence, a transcendence without which our lives entirely lack meaning. As Maurice Blondel puts it, "God acts in this action, and that is why the thought that follows the act is richer by an infinity than that which precedes it."[89]

In addition, we constantly surpass ourselves in a horizontal self-transcendence. Our actions "constitute our identity," yet they inevitably "'add' to us, go out from us, and even escape and elude us."[90] We are what we are only as we surpass what we are. We cannot know what we shall be, and so cannot know what we are. Human action thus always takes the form of sacrifice. With each

---

[88]Hemmerle, *Theses*, 37, 41.

[89]Blondel, *Action: Essay on a Critique of Life and a Science of Practice*, trans. Oliva Blanchette (Notre Dame, IN: University of Notre Dame Press, 1984), 371, quoted in John Milbank, *Theology and Social Theory*, 210.

[90]Milbank, *Theology and Social Theory*, 211.

word and act, I birth a new, unforeseen self from my old; each day, my today-self looks with surprise at the unfamiliar yesterday-self who had not yet done, thought, or said what I have. Yet this self-immolation is the path of self-discovery and self-fulfillment, for I become who I am only by transcending who I was.

Successiveness is the truth of created reality. Creation consists of "different appearances, which are the interactions which take place between humans and between human and other beings." There is no "deeper reality of essences or substances underlying the 'series' of phenomenal appearances" in their infinitely inter-twined relations. For Blondel, to ask the question of Being is to ask about the meaning of the whole series of interacting things, moments, events, happenings. We *cannot* explain theoretically what holds the series together. We see only part of the chain, and can never identify a sufficient reason why one link would be added rather than another. As I am what I am by constantly sur-passing myself, so reality is what it is as a "constant creative self-surpassing" that can never be fully anticipated.[91]

Creation is left radically dependent, wholly vulnerable. There is no self-same material underlying the chain; nothing in nature holds it together. Created reality *just is* the temporal chain of events and actions, which reaches always beyond itself toward the Creator and toward its own fulfillment. It holds together only in and by the Creator, only as it mimics the eternal outgoing and in-coming that is the life and being of the Creator. '*Elohim* is '*elohim* only by extending himself as another, the Spoken God, YHWH. Or, in New Testament terms, the Father is Father only by an eternal active extension beyond himself in the begetting of the Son and the breathing of the Spirit. It is only in *this* God that our actions, lives, and identity have coherence. His triune

---

[91]Milbank, *Theology and Social Theory*, 212.

faithfulness is the condition of possibility for my ability to tell my life, or the life of the world, as *a* story.[92]

CONCLUSION

Within a trinitarian metaphysics of Genesis, long-standing dilemmas of philosophy are dissolved or resolved. Take, for example, the opposition of inner and outer, a fundamental crux at least since Descartes: How does the inner mind touch the world outside? If being is the rhythm of self-giving love, the dichotomy disappears. Mind comes to its perfection as mind not by isolating itself in its own *cogito*, but by reaching beyond itself into the external world and accepting the outer world into itself. In the happening that is the rhythm of being, inner and outer, which seem to be polar opposites, are in a mutually dependent relationship, yet without being absorbed into each other. We become ourselves in extending beyond ourselves. We discover life by losing it, for, to repeat, life is only as it is more life.[93] The structure of human experience is homologous with the structure of reality, for creation as a whole exists only in its existence as a series of moments and appearances. There is simply "no deeper reality of essence of substances," by virtue of "its own creative self-surpassing."[94]

Sin defies the self-depletion that is the form of existence for both Creator and creation. Sin bids for autonomy, for self-containment. In sin, we strive to be as independent as God, but since God is *not* independent in the way we imagine, our striving for godlikeness estranges us from him and from our calling to genuine godlikeness. Sin seeks to arrest our self-surpassing in more, and only later do we realize that the achievement of static, self-contained being is death. Striving for autonomy, we become

---

[92]Jenson, *Systematic Theology*, 1:222.
[93]Hemmerle, *Theses*, 41.
[94]Milbank, *Theology and Social Theory*, 212.

precisely *unlike* the God who is *'elohim*, YHWH, and the Spirit; Speaker, Spoken, and Spirit. We are of all creatures most miserable, unless we are burst open by the Spirit who replicates the self-giving of Jesus in us. For in Jesus, we are restored to true creaturehood, which is identical to true godlikeness. We are restored to godlike dependence, godlike becoming, to the self-giving that is the only possible form of self-having, to the humility that is the form of glory.

A metaphysics of Genesis is a trinitarian ontology according to which creation is created to sing in harmony with the triune song of Love, which is a transcendent choral solo, an eternal fugue. A metaphysics of Genesis is not a deductive system. We cannot arrive at trinitarian insights from a purely immanent investigation of creation. The trinitarian shape of reality is *revealed*, and it can be seen only by those who enter into the rhythm, who follow the music. A trinitarian ontology of love implies an epistemology of love, for reality is known only to lovers whose existence is a song of love.

7

GOD SPEAKING AND GOD SEEING

William Desmond has called attention to a "major temptation" that has plagued the Western tradition of metaphysics. Metaphysics is the mind's quest to make intelligible sense of things. To be intelligible, a thing must be determinate. It must possess a measure of fixity. The fluxes and flows of becoming seem *un*intelligible, just because they are not fully determinate: "becoming happens because an unfinished process has to be further determined; and hence there is always a constitutive indeterminacy in any process of becoming, or in any being marked by process."[1] Time is not only unintelligible. It is terrifying because it is a medium of death. Even if we never died, each moment of our lives would die. As soon as it comes to be, it passes away. We may retain this or that for more than a moment, but nothing lasts forever—not our first kiss, not the aroma of spring, not youth, not the satisfactions of accomplishment, not the memory of past pleasures and pains. Vapor of vapors, all is vapor.

Enter the temptress, who seduces metaphysics into imagining and pursuing a something or a nothing that escapes vaporization.

---

[1] William Desmond, *Being and the Between* (Albany, NY: SUNY Press, 1995), 239.

If there were such an unmovable anchor, it would be fully intelligible because it would be "completely determined" and "beyond all becoming."[2] Bewitched, intoxicated metaphysics turns from the becoming of temporal existence—the only existence we *know*—to the determined and intelligible fixity of eternity. Eternity is construed as the opposite of time—simple, one with itself, changeless, resting in itself, while time is multiform, mutating, a restless bloomin' buzzin' welter of confusion. Time is succession; eternity is a perfectly realized, successionless present. A dualistic understanding of time and eternity, of God and becoming, serves as a "buffer . . . against the terrors of time."[3]

It does not work. Wraiths slip past the barrier to terrorize us. Dualism and the flight to eternity it encourages hold terrors of their own, because in the flight, one must leave behind and negate time. Time itself becomes a negative of eternity, leaving becoming radically ungrounded. The dualism of time and eternity entrenches our withdrawal from time and our fear of its corrosions. By the same token, dualism puts being with its determination, intelligibility, stability, and permanence out of reach, precisely because it sunders the relation of time and eternity. Dualism's "solution" undoes the problem it set out to resolve. Metaphysics starts out trying to understand the relation of time and eternity, becoming and being, God and creation, and ends by saying no such relation exists.[4]

Theology has often fallen prey to this metaphysical temptation.[5] "What is the relation between time and eternity, not in creation, which is encompassed by time in virtue of its becoming,

---

[2]Desmond, *Being and the Between*, 239.
[3]Desmond, *Being and the Between*, 239-40.
[4]Desmond, *Being and the Between*, 239-40.
[5]This has been a defining theme in the work of Robert Jenson, most succinctly in "The Triune God," in *Christian Dogmatics*, ed. Carl E. Braaten and Robert W. Jenson (Minneapolis: Fortress, 2011), 1:79-192.

but in the eternal God Himself?" asks Sergius Bulgakov. "Does time exist for eternity?"[6] Many theologians answer, No: "The simplest and most widespread . . . opinion is that time simply does not exist for God, since His eternity makes time totally transparent and dissolves it." For these theologians, "time exists only for the creature, as a kind of illusion owing to the creature's limited condition; it does not exist for God, for whom there is only eternity."[7]

Thus, it is argued, God is timeless not only because he is ever-lasting but because there is no succession in his life, no before and after in his knowledge, his actions, his being.[8] Creatures live from

---

[6]Sergius Bulgakov, *The Lamb of God*, trans. Boris Jakim (Grand Rapids, MI: Eerdmans, 2008), 132.

[7]Bulgakov, *Lamb of God*, 133.

[8]On Thomas's view of time and eternity, see David Burrell, *Freedom and Creation in Three Traditions* (Notre Dame, IN: University of Notre Dame Press, 1993), 101-10; also the revisionary Thomist account of immutability in W. Norris Clarke, *Explorations in Metaphysics: Being God Time* (Notre Dame: University of Notre Dame Press, 1994), 183-210. In *ST* 1.10.1, Thomas characterizes eternity as everlastingness and a lack of succession or, positively, an "instantaneous whole." The latter refers to Boethius's classic definition, usually understood as a denial of successiveness: "Eternity, then, is the complete, simultaneous and perfect possession of everlasting life; this will be clear from a comparison with creatures that exist in time. Whatever lives in time exists in the present and progresses from the past to the future, and there is nothing set in time which can embrace simultaneously the whole extent of its life: it is in the position of not yet possessing tomorrow when it has already lost yesterday. In this life of today you do not live more fully than in that fleeting and transitory moment. Whatever, therefore, suffers the condition of being in time, even though it never had any beginning, never has any ending and its life extends into the infinity of time." In *The Consolation of Philosophy*, vol. 6, rev. ed., trans. Victor Watts (London: Penguin, 1999). Some features of Boethius's definition, however, press in a different direction. An eternal being is *alive*. The point of contrast between what "lives in time" and what is eternal is that the former does not, and the latter does, embrace the whole of its life at once. *My* self slips away into the past, my future self has not yet arrived. An eternal being may experience past and future, but if he does, he will lose nothing to the past nor gain anything in the future. For Boethius, eternity is not, arguably, timelessness or absence of succession, but a transcendence of time that *includes* successiveness without loss. See Christoph Schwöbel, "The Eternity of the Triune God: Preliminary Considerations on the Relationship between the Trinity and the Time of Creation," *Modern Theology* 34, no. 3 (2018): 3. Richard Sorabji notes that Boethius is motivated in part by a desire to avoid determinism. If God *foresees* what I will do, what I will do is as fixed as the past. Instead, God "sees what we are doing contemporaneously with our doing it." God's knowledge is infallible, but it is not *prior*

moment to moment, each moment slipping away to make way for the next. *Nothing* in God, however, comes to be, nothing is lost. He did not anticipate me writing this sentence in late spring 2022, and he will not need to remember it next February. In my past, late spring 2022 was already "present" to God; in my future, it will still be "present" to him. God has complete, simultaneous and perfect possession of all he is, and all that was, is, ever will be. To say he does X today and Y tomorrow is a vulgar, mythological usage, suitable to sluggish children and fundamentalists. Adults speak of God in the present tense only: "God is X" or, more strictly still, "God is." God's life is, as Augustine says, a *stans nunc*, a "now" frozen in place and standing still, a now that does not slip away or reach ahead. Even that is not adult enough, though, since *nunc* must not be taken in a temporal sense. We must, strictly, speak of eternity paradoxically, as a timeless present, which makes it very difficult to speak of it at all.

The question of the relation of time and eternity melds into the broader question of God's ongoing relation to creation as such. Thus, to explain how temporal and relative terms can be said of God, Thomas moves into a more fundamental issue, relations. There are three: real, rational, and mixed. God's relation to creation is of the third kind. Creation is really related to God, but God is not really related to creatures. Because "God is altogether outside the order of creatures . . . it is clear that being related to God is a reality in creatures, but being related to creatures is not a reality in God."[9] To say God is not "really related" to creation does *not* mean he is not related at all. "Real relation" is narrowly construed, referring to a relation of causal dependence or a relation

because it is timeless. *Time, Creation, and the Continuum: Theories in Antiquity and the Early Middle Ages* (London: Duckworth, 2002), 254-55.

[9]St. Thomas Aquinas, *Summa theologiae*, vol. 3: *Knowing and Naming God*, trans. Herbert McCabe (Cambridge: Cambridge University Press, 2006), 1.13.7.

between terms that exist on the same ontological plane. God is related to creation in all sorts of other ways, but he is not caused by creation; we should not imagine that God exists in the same field of reality as creation. Thomas's denial that God's relation to creation is "real" is another way of speaking of God's transcendence.[10] Even with these qualifications, Thomas's denial is misleading, for it implies a transcendence that conflicts with immanence, which is not genuine transcendence (see chap. 1 above).

The relation of eternity and time thus lurks behind all other questions about God's relation to creation. Immutability, impassibility, simplicity, immobility, are all, like eternity as a successionless now, prophylactics against time. They inoculate God against the threat of temporal coming to be and passing away. For the metaphysical tradition, the basic question is, In a world of flux, is there anything that endures?[11] And the theological answer has often been, Yes, if we can but escape time.

Following this path to its end is fatal to Christian theology. If time is nothing to God, if God's eternity is defined in simple

---

[10]David Burrell, *Aquinas: God and Action*, 3rd. ed. (Eugene, OR: Wipf & Stock, 2016), 44, 9-55. On Thomas's theory of relations, see also Frederick Bauerschmidt, *Thomas Aquinas: Faith, Reason, and Following Christ* (Oxford: Oxford University Press, 2013), 114-19; R. T. Mullins, *The End of the Timeless God* (Oxford: Oxford University Press, 2016), 119-26; Tyler Wittman, *God and Creation in the Theology of Thomas Aquinas and Karl Barth* (Cambridge: Cambridge University Press, 2018), 112-16; Matthew R. McWhorter, "Aquinas on God's Relation to the World," *New Blackfriars* 94 (2012): 1-17. Norris Clarke, a Thomist, complains that Thomists have not done an adequate job of explaining how a God without a real relation to the world "can be said to be truly involved in a personal dialogue with us, in a mutual love relationship." Positively, he suggests there is a "relation of personal consciousness" in God toward the world, such that "God is truly other, different, in his consciousness, because of his relations with us" (*Explorations in Metaphysics*, 195-56; cf. 185). I doubt many Thomists will be convinced because Clarke's position introduces a distinction between God's real and intentional being that is inimical to simplicity. I am unconvinced because Norris Clarke posits an "intentional consciousness" in God that functions as a mediating reality between God's "real being" and creation. If God *is* Creator, if Creator is first theology, no such mediator is necessary.

[11]Klaus Hemmerle, *Theses Towards a Trinitarian Ontology* (Brooklyn, NY: Angelico, 2020), 35.

opposition to time, Bulgakov insists, we lose "the entire Bible," which "represents a total rejection of this point of view." Scripture is about "God's works in the world," and if we dismiss it all as anthropomorphism, we "undermine the entire content of our faith" and "transform the living, merciful, salvific God, the Creator and All-Mighty, into the static absolute of Hinduism." If only eternity exists for God, "the most difficult thing of all is to understand and accept the Incarnation."[12] Lose the incarnation, and you lose everything. No Christian theologian can allow that God is incapable of entering time to live and die and rise as man.

We are faced with a dilemma. Can we make do without the prophylactics? Can we formulate a theology of the *related* God, the Creator, that does not collapse into a theology of a related *god*? Can we affirm God's temporal involvement in time without allowing him to dissipate into time? I believe the answer is yes, and Genesis 1 provides the key. Once again, I start at the very beginning.

TIMELESS CREATOR?

Creation is one of the traditional places where Desmond's metaphysical temptation makes its appearance. It is one of the primary sites of a clash between the biblical text and an assumed (often Hellenically inspired) concept of God. Augustine provides a paradigmatic instance. He frequently uses utterances as paradigmatic instances of temporality. Before we speak, the entire utterance is in the future. As we speak, more and more of the utterance disappears into the past, and less and less of the utterance remains in the future. We use up the ribbon of time as we speak. Our actual speaking is the present knife-edge between past and future. With this model in the background, Augustine cannot get past Genesis 1:3 without running into challenges: "And God said."

---

[12]Bulgakov, *Lamb of God*, 133.

To Augustine's ear, the claim that "God speaks" immediately raises the question of temporality and change. If God spoke in time, then the utterance necessarily involves change. How can an unchanging God utter the opening words of the creation account, "Let there be light"?

Augustine wants to know whether these words were uttered in time or "in the eternity of His Word"?[13] He raises the question because God "clearly, is not subject to change."[14] Thus, if God spoke words, he must have done so through a mutable created medium, as he did when he said "This is my beloved Son" at the baptism of Jesus.[15] Augustine's point here is not about the audibility of the Creator's voice, though he does raise that question. The puzzle is how an unchangeable God could begin a set of words and pass through that set of words in a temporal sequence without employing a temporal medium to do so.

The thought that the Creator employs a created medium raises a further problem. When the Father speaks at the baptism of Jesus, creation was already well in place. The unchangeable God could speak by unchangeably exciting created media to form an audible utterance.[16] But when the Creator speaks "Let there be light," there are no created media to put to use. If there were, then light would not be the first thing created.[17] Augustine ponders whether Genesis 1:1 may provide an answer. Heaven and earth already exist, so Augustine asks, "Could some voice have been produced in a temporal process involving change through some heavenly created being, to say, Let light be made?" If so, "then it

---

[13] Augustine, *Literal Meaning of Genesis* 1.2.4, in *On Genesis*, trans. Edmund Hill, Works of Saint Augustine 1/13 (Hyde Park, NY: New City, 2006).

[14] Augustine, *Literal Meaning of Genesis* 1.2.4.

[15] Augustine, *Literal Meaning of Genesis* 1.2.5.

[16] It is not clear that this resolves Augustine's objection. After all, even though speaking through created media, the Father spoke audible words. If it is true, the Father speaking means he began an utterance, spoke, and ended the utterance.

[17] Augustine, *Literal Meaning of Genesis* 1.2.4.

was this bodily light that we perceive with our bodily eyes which was made, when God said through a spiritual creature (which God had already made when he made heaven and earth in the beginning), *Let light be made.*"[18] He ultimately dismisses this conclusion, and opts for the theory that the "light" of Genesis 1:3 is not, after all, "bodily light" but the spiritual knowledge of angels.

The entire paragraph is written in the interrogative mood. Augustine makes no assertions about how God might have spoken, "Let there be light." He only raises puzzles and muses on them. But the subterranean momentum of his argument has a quite different trajectory. He does not think the Creator actually uttered the sentence "Let there be light," whether from himself or through a created agent. That becomes clear from the scornful *reductio*:

> Did the voice of God, saying Let light be made, also make an audible sound . . . ? And if that is the case, what language was this voice speaking . . . , since there was no diversity of languages yet, something that came about later on at the building of the tower after the flood? What was the one and only language in which God spoke the words, "Let light be made"? And who was there, who needed to hear and understand, to whom this sort of utterance would be addressed? Or is this an altogether absurd and literal-minded, fleshly, train of thought and conjecture (*absurda carnalisque cogitatio est atque suspicio*)?[19]

Augustine clearly does think these questions are absurd and carnal. His alternative is not to *deny* the divine voice but to discard the notion of an *audible* divine utterance in favor of the idea that the "voice of God" is the "intelligible meaning" of the utterance. Intelligible meanings belong to the nature of the eternal Word himself. Citing John 1, Augustine argues that if all things were

---

[18]Augustine, *Literal Meaning of Genesis* 1.2.4.
[19]Augustine, *Literal Meaning of Genesis* 1.2.5.

made by the Word, then surely light was one of the things made. Augustine solves the puzzle of an unchangeable eternal God who speaks a temporal utterance trinitarianly: "God's saying *Let light be made* is something eternal, because the Word of God, God with God, the Son of God, is co-eternal with the Father." Through this eternal utterance, "a time-bound creature was made."[20]

Augustine's stuttering over Genesis 1:3 is not an isolated case. He has already stuttered over Genesis 1:2. God, he says, creates the formless void *and* the things made from it simultaneously. Formless matter, Augustine says, is not "prior in time to things formed from it." Rather, form and matter "are both created simultaneously together, both the thing made and what it was made out of." Formless matter is prior *as source* but *not* prior in time, just as a voice, the "basic material for words," is prior as source but not in time to an act of speech.[21] Genesis 1 depicts the formless void as being prior in time because we cannot speak simultaneously of simultaneous things: "One thing had to be mentioned before the other, although God made each of them . . . simultaneously."[22] Augustine concludes:

> What came first in the making solely as source comes first also in time in the telling. If two things of which neither is in any way prior to the other cannot be named simultaneously, how much less can their stories be told simultaneously! So then, there is no doubt at all that this formless basic material, almost the same as

---

[20] Augustine, *Literal Meaning of Genesis* 1.2.6. Augustine later (1.3.6) presents a version of this same argument, which brings the trinitarian considerations more fully into view. Later (1.4.9), he asks why the text does not say the "unformed basic material" of the world was spoken into being, and answers in a similar vein: "Because it is by the Word, always adhering to the Father, that God eternally says everything, not with the sound of a voice nor with thoughts running through the time which sounds take, but with the light, co-eternal with himself, of the Wisdom he has begotten." But "imperfection or incompleteness" does not mimic the form of the Word, because it is unlike the Word that supremely *is*.

[21] Augustine, *Literal Meaning of Genesis* 1.15.29.

[22] Augustine, *Literal Meaning of Genesis* 1.15.29.

nothingness though it be, was still made by none but God, and was simultaneously created with the things that were formed from it.[23]

Behind this claim is once again Augustine's conviction about God's eternity. God is not measured in time, and neither are his *works* measured by time.[24] We should put away the "literal-minded, fleshly way of utterances in time." Moses writes as he does because "the very Wisdom of God took our weakness upon herself and came to gather the children of Jerusalem under her wings."[25] Genesis 1 is accommodated to childish minds.[26]

It is not difficult to answer Augustine's "absurd" and "childish" questions. As Augustine himself admits, God *can* speak audibly, so why not at the beginning? Perhaps God created a medium of sound simultaneously with his first utterance. If that displaces light from its position as first creation, so be it; it carries the tantalizing implication, explored briefly in chapter six, that sound, voice, or perhaps music is a more ontologically basic than light. Audibility is more fundamental than visibility, because Word is the source of light, the medium of visibility. By the time light first dawns, earth has already been filled with the divine voice. Creation consists not so much of *phenomena* as of *legomena*.[27]

---

[23] Augustine, *Literal Meaning of Genesis* 1.15.29. Augustine, it seems, distracts himself by a semi-technical meaning of the word "form." In metaphysical terms, the form-less void of Gen 1:2 *is* formed. Genesis does not describe the pure potency of prime matter, but "earth" and a "deep," with structure—Spirit above, waters below, earth under the waters. The form it lacks is not the form of Aristotelian substances, but the three-tiered shape *'elohim* gives it during the first three days of the creation week.

[24] Augustine, *Literal Meaning of Genesis* 1.18.36.

[25] Augustine, *Literal Meaning of Genesis* 1.18.36.

[26] Theologians can say "there is no before and after in God" only when they have, momentarily, forgotten what they believe about God's triunity. On the one hand, none of the persons are "before or after another" (Athanasian Creed). On the other hand, there is a *taxis* in the immanent Trinity, such that the Father is "before" the Son, as the generator of the Son.

[27] The terms are from Robert Jenson, *Systematic Theology*, vol. 2: *The Works of God* (Oxford: Oxford University Press, 1999), 36. I hope to follow up on these suggestions in a second volume. For now, see the stimulating work of Ted Goia, *Music: A*

Time would be more basically the time of utterance than the visual sequence of darkness and light. All this puts me in mind of Ben Jonson's evocative synesthetic plea (echoed and elaborated by J. G. Hamann and Eugen Rosenstock-Huessy): "Speak, that I may see thee!"

Augustine's question about the language spoken by the Creator arises even more acutely in Genesis 2–3, where *YHWH 'elohim* speaks *to* Adam in the garden. The account implies the existence of a primordial language shared between the Creator and the creature.[28] Or is Genesis 2 also describing communication of intelligible meaning without audible words? If it is what it appears to be—verbal communication in human language—why not assume Hebrew was the original language, as Augustine himself proposes elsewhere?[29] Is Genesis 2 also "childish"? At what point, if ever, does the Bible's childishness come to an end?

In the face of Augustine's bafflement, Genesis displays nary a twitch of a furrowed brow. It blithely records *'elohim* speaking and doing and acting, all within the temporal framework of a week of days. We can make the point from another angle: Given the way Genesis speaks about creation, how does Augustine know Genesis is accommodated to childish understanding? He must have access to an "adult" theology, but where does it come from? I suspect Augustine would point to Scriptures that teach God is eternal and argue: If God is "eternal," then "God said and made through six days" must be a figure. But why does he not instead

Subversive History (New York: Basic, 2019), chaps. 1–2; the various works of Victor Zuckerkandl, especially *Sound and Symbol: Music and the External World*, trans. William Trask (Princeton, NJ: Princeton University Press, 1969); also John Milbank, "Confession of Time in Augustine," *Maynooth Philosophical Papers* 10 (2020): 9-20.

[28]Strangely, Augustine does not re-ask the question about language or audibility in his discussion of Genesis 2, where it seems even more pertinent.

[29]Augustine, *City of God*, 16. See Josef Eskhult, "Augustine and the Primeval Language in Early Modern Exegesis and Philology," *Language and History* 56, no. 2 (2013): 98-119.

adjust his understanding of eternity in the light of Genesis 1? Is it possible that one of the aims of Genesis 1 is to depict *how* the eternal God is eternal?[30]

The power of Desmond's "metaphysical temptation" is most obvious in theologians who, like Augustine, insist on the absoluteness of God and his independence from creation. In reaction, however, some theologians have found it preferable to permit God to be swallowed and digested into temporality. Some argue that God undergoes change at the moment of creation. God exists in a timeless eternity *until* he creates the world, and then becomes temporal.[31] Inspired by Hegel, others argue that God is realized as God through history. History is God's coming-to-Trinity, as for Hegel history is the coming-to-consciousness of the *Geist*.[32]

Abstract as it may seem, this debate can be focused with a practical question: Is prayer a rational activity? To the absolutists, we ask: Should we ask God to do things, and is it rational to expect a *response*? To relativists: Is God sufficiently independent of time and history to direct it toward his ends?

---

[30]John Milbank has argued that Augustine develops an innovative temporal ontology in which time is more fundamental than space, and the music and dance of temporality is more ontologically basic than distinctions of form and matter, soul and body, being and nonbeing (Milbank, "Confession of Time," 1-52). Even on this attractive reading, Augustine still sets eternity and time too much in opposition, and he does so because he operates with an implied fundamental theology of the *un*related non-Creator.

[31]R. T. Mullins sums up the view of the Oxford temporalists: There is a metaphysical "dead time," a time without change, prior to creation, but "after creation, God's life contains a before and after just like every other endurant being. Further, in creating a world with uniform laws of nature God creates a world with a temporal metric." More elaborately: "God is temporal prior to creation. However, God's life is unchanging and unmetricated. God undergoes an intrinsic change in the act of creating the universe. The endurant God takes on succession in His life. This means that God will lose moments of His life as they slip into the nonexistent past, and God must wait for anticipated future moments to become present before He can live them." "Is God the Prisoner of Time? Yeah, but so What?" *Journal of Analytic Theology* 2 (2014): 165-66.

[32]For a somewhat dated but still useful survey of the contemporary discussion, see John Feinberg, *No One Like Him: The Doctrine of God* (Wheaton, IL: Crossway, 2006), 375-436.

Polemical bombs are tossed back and forth, to little effect.[33] "God is not a 'god,'" shout the absolutists. "God is personal, interactive in time," shriek the relativists. "God is not subordinate to creation!" say the absolutists. "Do you ever pray?" ask the relativists. We should become suspicious whenever a debate seems intractable. Intractability is usually a sign that, beneath the pyrotechnics and theatrics and tribal sloganizing, the contestants are unwittingly playing for the same team. Here, I think the suspicion eminently justified. Absolutists and relativists seem diametrically opposed, but they share a common premise. Augustine's puzzlement arises from his attempt to meld together the *un*related God of his inherited theology with the related Creator of Genesis 1. Some relativists, in their turn, assume a God unrelated to anything outside himself who *changes into* a Creator God who is related to creation. Other relativists assume divine relativity *without* creation. In their different ways, each side pursues knowledge of the not-yet-Creator.

I have already ruled out that inquiry. The only God *we* can know is the God who *has* created and who is related to the temporal world. As I have insisted, this is not a mere epistemological limitation. We cannot know any God but the Creator because the only God who *is* is the God who has created. "Creator" is his first title. It is pointless to try to determine how *un*related God is, related to time. An unrelated God *cannot* be related. What we need to know is how the *Creator* is related to the time of creation. And to know that, we must, once again, start at the very beginning. It is a very good place to start.

I have already made a beginning by insisting that the Creator is the triune God whose act of creation is an extension outward of his inner life of love, by arguing that all created things exist by

---

[33]I am making the same argument here that I made in chap. 4's discussion of classical theism and process theology. In this context, the debate is specifically focused on God's relation to time, which is in fact the main bone of contention.

their extension outward from themselves into relation with others because God is by virtue of his mutual relations, by observing that life is life only as it is more life, including even the life of God. These moves have shifted the center of gravity of our metaphysics, from the question of *stasis* through change toward a metaphysics of creative love, which says, "love alone remains."[34]

All this remains to be filled out with further exploration of Genesis 1, which introduces a God capable of hearing prayer, a God whose answers to prayer are truly answers and not prerecorded messages.

TIME IN GENESIS 1

What is time? It depends on whom you ask. Plato famously described time as "a moveable image of Eternity," whatever he might have meant by that.[35] For Aristotle, time is a measure of movement and change, or perhaps, an order within movement and change.[36] In this, Aristotle appears to anticipate modern cosmology, which treats time as a reality that confronts us, will we or not, as a "feature of [the world's] architecture."[37]

Augustine comes close to saying time is nothing.[38] The past no longer exists, the future is not yet, and the present disappears before you can point to or speak of it. The problem is worse than it seems: The present exists *only* as it slips away into the past; it exists only in its erasure. How then can it be said to exist at all? Augustine avoids saying time is "nothing" by turning inward to

---

[34]Klaus Hemmerle, *Theses Towards a Trinitarian Ontology* (Brooklyn, NY: Angelico, 2020), 35.

[35]Plato, *Timaeus* 37D. See Simon Oliver, *Philosophy, God, and Motion* (London: Routledge, 2013), 8-28.

[36]Aristotle, *Physics* 217^b-224^b. For the argument that Aristotle thinks of time not as a measure but as an order, see Ursula Coope, *Time for Aristotle: Physics IV, 10-14* (Oxford: Oxford University Press, 2005).

[37]Jenson, *Systematic Theology*, 2:34.

[38]Augustine, *Confessions* 11.14-18.

the soul. The timeless, eternal being of God determines the fundamental meaning of Being. The existence of everything else is defective because it is temporal. I am not a *full* being because my entire existence is not present in the present. The basketball-player-me is long gone, making way for the aging-theologian-me.[39] Within creation, however, there *is* one "finite image of the infinite Presence"—the soul.[40] Time is the soul's "distension"—its "spreading-out"—between memory and anticipation. Even in the soul, past and future are not present as past and future. I remember and anticipate *now*, and so the soul is the site where past and future are transmuted into modes of the present, as the present presence of the past and the present presence of the future. Time is not "out there" but "in here," in souls made of the kind of spiritual stuff that enables them to resemble the eternal present of God.

Genesis 1 offers an alternative portrait of time, one that harmonizes the external and internal dimensions of time and thoroughly bypasses Desmond's metaphysical temptation. In Genesis, there is no ontological dualism. Nothing opposes God; creation is not combat, but a call that brings not-beings into being. The darkness, formlessness, and emptiness of Genesis 1:2 are immaturities,

---

[39]Jenson suggests Augustine runs down *cul de sacs* in part because he is captive to impossible spatial metaphors. He assumes Plato's concept of "the turning wheel of time with the geometric still point of eternity at its center," yet, as a Christian, he believes time is linear, so straightens out the Platonic circle into a line. Though time is linear, Augustine continues to think of eternity as equidistant from every temporal point. Much confusion arises from "this oxymoronic root metaphor, of a point perpendicular to a straight line yet equidistant from all points on it" (*Systematic Theology*, 2:32).

[40]Jenson, *Systematic Theology*, 2:30. It is not clear that Augustine intends to offer a metaphysics of time. And, Jenson's reading needs to be qualified by Milbank, "The Confession of Time in Augustine." Milbank argues that, far from psychologizing time, Augustine's musical ontology harmonizes the external, objective flow of time with the internal experience of distension. Even if Jenson does not get Augustine right, he captures the way *Confessions* 11–13 is often read, as a meditation on the soul's experience of time. See J. L. A. West, "St. Augustine on Human Temporality and Divine Eternity," *Faith and Reason* 26, no. 2 (2001): 1-7.

incompletions, peacefully transmuted to perfections during the creation week, not by battle but by the peaceable utterance of God's word accompanied by the fluttering rhythm of his Spirit. The Creator does not have to negotiate with primordial energies or powers. He is not forced grudgingly to permit "formless emptiness" to retain a circumscribed place in his world. Unlike the gods of ancient myths, he is not a second-generation deity who achieves a partial, tenuous victory over the raging Titans or bloodthirsty Erinyes. He is the Creator, Lord, and Giver of life and being.

Because there is no ontological dualism, neither is there any dualism of time and eternity. The Creator is not set over-against creation as the timeless negative of created temporality. Rather, *'elohim* is Creator of time and, being Creator, is necessarily related to time.

After speaking light into existence, *'elohim* separates day and night (Gen 1:3-5). "Separating" (*badal*) is a distinct divine act from "saying" (*'amar*), though perhaps we are to understand that God separates by speaking (cf. Gen 1:6). Light invades the darkness, and God acts within the earthly realm to separate the two. After separating, he names the now-separate entities: Light is *yom*, darkness *layil*. These now-separated, now-named entities are placed into an orderly sequence of evening and morning, which together form a *yom*. The evening-morning rhythm, the separation and ordering of darkness and light, is as much a creature as light itself. As Creator, he is not subject to that rhythm, yet he conforms to it. Having created light and ordered the sequence of darkness and light, the Creator dances to the rhythms of the times, doing *this* now and *that* later. God is Creator of days; he is also Creator *in* days. He is Lord of days, also Lord *in* days.

At the end of day one, God judges the alternation of light and darkness "good." At that point, earth is still formless and empty, still a watery deep. Yet the creation of light and the ordering of days is work enough for day one; God considers it good to dispel the darkness and establish a temporal sequence of evenings and mornings. On days two and three, however, a lighted-but-formless world is no longer good enough, even though it is a product of his own work. On day two, he separates the waters above and below and inserts a firmament between, lending shape to the formless waters. In the first act of day three, he adds a further boundary to separate the waters below to permit dry land to emerge. At the end of a day and a half of hydraulic engineering, he "saw that it was good" (Gen 1:10). For a day, a lighted-but-shapeless world is good; but over the following two days, *'elohim* makes it better yet, giving form to the waters and making a world that is both lit and shapely. Each day surpasses the last. The Creator's mercies are new every morning. *'Elohim* shapes and fills a world *through a sequence of time*, and it is a *progressive* sequence.[41]

Augustine's instantaneous understanding of creation does not merely clash with the biblical text, but with the implied ontology of the text. Augustine is right about the import of the narrative: Genesis 1 previews the whole of history, moving toward eternal Sabbath. In detail, however, his reading of Genesis 1 is at odds with this profound insight. In Augustine's implicit ontology, stuff and all-things-made-of-stuff are created instantaneously. As soon as there is anything, there are *formed* anythings, identifiable somethings, land, plants, stars, fish, birds, and animals. Creation is front-loaded, as all comes to be in one Big Blap of creative power. Genesis 1, by contrast, tilts toward the future; it is *back*-loaded. First there is formless darkness; then light; then God moves

---

[41]Luther hints at this with his observation that the "crude" light of the first day is "perfected" by the creation of the heavenly lights. *Lectures on Genesis*, at Gen 1:14, in *Luther's Works*, vol. 1: *Lectures on Genesis, Chapters 1–5*, ed. Jaroslav Pelican, trans. George V. Schick (St. Louis: Concordia, 1958). Luther also connects the creation as house building for Adam with Christ's promise to prepare mansions for his disciples, a sign that "the first state of this world [is] a type and figure of the future world" (*Lectures on Genesis*, at Gen 1:11).

waters about; then plants spring up; then fish and birds and animals and man, male and female. Initially, the world is empty, then it is filled; first it is shapeless, then shaped; first it is dark, then illumined in glory. Creation comes to be itself as the days pass. What is *first* is not determinative, but what is *last*.[42] The contours of biblical history are already evident in the Bible's first chapter: The last Adam, not the first, determines the character and destiny of the human race; new rather than old Jerusalem is the form of the final creation. The creation week sets a trajectory for an eschatologically oriented cosmos. The *first* creation comes to be as a "final" creation, the product of a sequence of days that constitute the first week. First things come to be *as* last things. The days of creation set the trajectory for the history of creation, which moves from glory to glory.

Each thing becomes more richly itself through the course of the week, as its powers and potencies are realized. On day one, light can do nothing but play off the ripples and waves of the watery deep. On day three, light illumines land and initiates evaporation ("dry land"), while the sprouting plants display, for the first time, light's magical power to catalyze photosynthesis. With plants come new colors, and light discovers, for the first time, its power to shine greenly. When light is concentrated in sun, moon, and stars on day four, its governance of time is complicated by new rhythms of months, years, and seasons. On day six, light enables earth-dwelling living souls to see and live. Light is not most itself at the instantaneous moment of the first fiat. Light becomes itself only as it is realized in relation to other developing features of creation. Even now, we do not yet know what light shall be, because light will not be *entirely* fulfilled as light until it overcomes the darkness once and for all, when it yields to the light of the

---

[42]See my *Deep Comedy: Trinity, Tragedy, and Hope in Western Literature* (Moscow, ID: Canon, 2006).

Lamb (Rev 21:23; 22:5). Time is not a defect, nor corrosive of created existence. Time is glory, the gifted opportunity for each thing to become more fully itself by entering into more richly intertwined relations with what is not itself. Time gives each thing, and the whole creation, the capacity to diffuse the goodness it is more widely.

In Genesis, time is the rhythmic dance of created existence.[43] The dance has its measures and steps, but time is not a mere measure of motion. Rather, the lively motions of creation, especially of light and darkness, constitute time.[44] What we call "time" is an abstraction.[45] We never touch flowing "time," never locate the temporal container that is more or less filled up with events. We experience events and changing things and measure those changes by more regular changes (e.g., a clock). But at no point do we experience the empty form "time." In particular, time as "flow" is abstracted from space. Bergson and his followers complain that measured time breaks up the continuous stream by subordinating it to space. Sunrise and sunset, however, are spatial movements; mechanical clocks measure time by the spatial movements of gears. For Bergsonians, we have not reached time until we have detached it from spatial measures. Genesis 1 cheerfully refers to *periods* of time, integrating the spatial movements of the heavens with the rhythm of time into a music of space-time.

---

[43]Poythress, *Interpreting Eden: A Guide to Faithfully Reading and Understanding Genesis 1–3* (Wheaton, IL: Crossway, 2019), 214-21.

[44]Milbank, "Confession of Time," claims that, for Augustine, time is "radically identified with creation as a natural speaking flow" (20). Augustine's is an "ontology of motion and of motion as life" (20). Time is "ontologically fundamental" (16). It is not a blemish. Creation is, on the contrary, beautiful precisely because it is temporal, beautiful with the beauty of music (21). If this is indeed Augustine's view, it is odd he did not recognize how neatly it suits Genesis 1.

[45]Sacha Stern, *Time and Process in Ancient Judaism* (Oxford: Littman Library of Jewish Civilization, 2007), 3, 18-20. Stern argues that the Bible and ancient rabbinic theology offers a theology of "process" without the concept of "time."

Genesis 1's presentation of time is radically anti-presentist, opposed to Augustine's notion that the lightning flash of "now" is the only time that truly exists. Neither A- nor B-theories capture the time of Genesis.[46] Creation's movement is articulated into periods, "bodies," or "melodies" of time.[47] Time does not flow smoothly, without disruptions, intervals, beginnings and endings. Each day dies in darkness and, each morning, it is called to life again. Sun, moon, and stars mark the beginnings and ends of seasons (*mo'edim*) and years, as well as days (Gen 1:14-16). The heavens form a clock, ticking out days, nights, months, years, cycles of seasons and festivals. The clock is not an extrinsic measure but intrinsic to the motion it segments into parts.

For Genesis 1, time is human time because it is knowable, experienced time. Because we mark days by sunrise and sunset, months by the moon's phases, years by the sun's march through the Zodiac, we are conscious participants in time. And this makes it possible "to live a life which is not merely dreamy and vegetative, but which is marked by a wakeful consciousness of time and history." Genesis presents time as a created gift that enables us to claim days as *our* days, time as our time; in the concrete time of Genesis 1, we are able to decide, act, and be fruitful.[48]

---

[46]The contrast of two theories comes from J. Ellis McTaggart, "The Unreality of Time," *Mind* 17 (1908): 457-73.

[47]The phrase "body of time" comes from Eugen Rosenstock-Huessy, "Time-Bettering Days," *Rosenstock-Huessy Papers,* vol. 1 (Argo, 1981). God sets the pattern for human shaping of time, for we too form bodies of time with our speech and our judgment. "I declare you man and wife" initiates a time of the marriage, which is intended to end with the death of one of the spouses and the accompanying pronunciation of "good." God sets the pattern not only for initiating periods of time, but also for delight in and appreciation of creation, which we mirror as the image of God. Thanks to my son Jordan Leithart for this suggestion.

[48]Karl Barth, *Church Dogmatics 3/1: The Doctrine of Creation,* ed. Geoffrey Bromiley and T. F. Torrance (London: T&T Clark, 2010), 160-61.

Days, months, seasons, and years are the *explicit* temporal rhythms in Genesis 1, but there are many *implicit* rhythms. Time *thickens* as the creation week progresses:[49]

- God's rhythm of work and rest, not only for the week but on each day; *'elohim* ceases at each sunset.
- Rhythms of the waters; e.g., tides (day 2? Or day 4, with creation of moon?).
- Rhythms of plants (day 3), the daily opening and closing of flowers, periodic blossoming and fruit production.
- Rhythms of sea creatures and birds (day 5), both as individuals and as species, over days and seasons.
- Rhythms for land animals (day 6).
- Human rhythms (day 6).

Instead of abstracting "time" from the complex, overlapping rhythms of the world, Genesis foregrounds the rhythms themselves. The time of Genesis is the layered, multiply rhythmic, multi-melody time of polyphony.[50]

Temporal rhythms are inherent in things. To be a particular thing is to exist according to a particular rhythm. Trees have their own arboreal, Ent-like temporality; animals live by their diurnal, nocturnal, or crepuscular rotations; to the created cycles of human existence, we add a thousand modes of "artificial" temporality—the time of the wedding, the time of the game, the time of ritual commemoration, the time of love, the time of the feast, the elusive, threatening time of the deadline. Each created kind and each individual thing is spoken and sung by the Speaking God, and each kind and each individual thing *is* its being spoken and

---

[49]Poythress, *Interpreting Eden*, 255.
[50]See Jeremy Begbie, *Theology, Music and Time* (Cambridge: Cambridge University Press, 2000).

being sung. Things persist through time, but not because of any underlying substratum or prime matter. Creation has no immutable dance floor. It is nothing but dancing, all the way down and all the way up.

We are tempted to think technical measures of time are more basic, fundamental, and true than everyday natural or cultural rhythms. The modulations of experienced time merely play on the surface of "real" time. Science and technical gadgets get at the realest real, which is the material real. Scripture presents a different picture. God created and oversees the "artificial" rhythms of human life as well as the mechanically fixed rhythms by which we measure time. In an ultimate sense, both have the same status as creations of God. Time is, most fundamentally, personal time, because it is articulated, sculpted, composed by the Word of a trihypostatic person. The sun rises at his word, the moon's phases are in obedience to his commands, trees and grasses grow when he summons them, he opens wombs, turns man to dust, and says "Return" to the sons of men.

The personal character of time is essential to making sense of biblical language and religious experience. As Richard Sorabji points out, the idea that God's knowledge is timeless implies there are certain things God cannot know. He can know, "Their hour of need is May 10, 2024," but he cannot know, "Their hour of need is *now*," since "now" refers to "his *own* location in time," a location he cannot have if he is timeless in every respect.[51] We might say it does not matter: If God knows that my hour of need is May 10, 2024, he will come to my aid just then, right when I need it. But, as Sorabji notes, the dated proposition lacks the "action- and emotion-guiding force" of "now."[52] The date makes God's action less personal, as if God consults his internal

---

[51]Sorabji, *Time, Creation, and the Continuum*, 258.
[52]Sorabji, *Time, Creation, and the Continuum*, 259.

timetable and responds to *it* more than to me and my need. Many argue God does not *respond* at all since he is eternally the God who knows the hour of need is May 10, 2024—which is even more obviously impersonal.[53] We should opt for the theory that best expresses God's personal relation to creation in the time he personally created and shaped.

I will return to these considerations below, but first I need to clear away a major objection to the preceding paragraphs.

THE DAYS OF CREATION

Some will object: There is no theology of time in Genesis 1 because there is no time at all.[54] The objection takes various forms. If, as Augustine believed, creation was instantaneous, the creation account includes no time and does not teach us anything about God's relation to it. If the days are a mere literary device, there is no temporal sequence. Some argue the temporal structure is mere scaffolding for the author's ideological and polemical aims. Placed in ancient Near Eastern context, it is obvious that Genesis 1 is a Hebraic version of the ancient concept of creation as the construction of a cosmic temple.[55]

---

[53] According to David Burrell, Thomas insists on God's personal involvement in time. Eternity, Thomas says "takes in the whole of time" (*ST* 1.14.13). Burrell explains that this happens "by way of God's creative intent working itself out temporally, and not by any impersonal image like a duration embracing all of time." Eternity embraces all of time, but "it does so in the divine intent." *Freedom and Creation in Three Traditions* (Notre Dame, IN: Notre Dame University Press, 1993), 109.

[54] Not everyone doubts it. Basil, Ambrose, Bede, Luther, Calvin, and Turretin all believed the days were ordinary created days. For a survey of premodern and early-modern interpretations, see Robert Letham, "'In the Space of Six Days': The Days of Creation from Origen to the Westminster Assembly," *Westminster Theological Journal* 61 (1999): 149-74. Michael B. Roberts, "Geology and Genesis Unearthed" *Churchman* 112 (1998): 225-55, documents adjustments in the understanding of the creation account in the half-century before Darwin.

[55] See B. C. Hodge, *Revisiting the Days of Genesis: A Study of the Use of Time in Light of Its Ancient Near Eastern and Literary Context* (Eugene, OR: Wipf & Stock, 2011). John Walton has deployed some of these arguments to defend a novel concept of "creation" itself: Genesis 1 is not about the origin of the universe, but about God's arrangement of a preexisting cosmos into a temple; it is not about origin but about

None of these arguments convince. What if one of the key things that distinguishes the God of Israel from idols is his relation to time? What if the target of the polemic is Desmond's metaphysical temptation? Grant that Genesis 1 has poetic features; is there any reason to assume a poem cannot record a series of actual events? If poetry and history are opposites, much of what is normally taken as biblical history (the exodus, the exile and return, the incarnation) slips through our fingers. Besides, Genesis 1 is generically closer to prose history than to poetry.[56] If, as Augustine claims, the writer of Genesis wanted to say everything happened instantaneously, he had the linguistic resources to do so (cf. *be'et hahiw'*, "at that time" in Deut 9:20; 2 Kings 8:22).

Much ink has been spilled over the meaning of "day." *Yom* is used fourteen times in Genesis 1:1–2:3, in several senses. Initially, it refers to light or the light portion of an evening-morning compound (Gen 1:5). The refrain at the end of each day defines the "day" in terms of the cadence of labor and rest. *'Elohim* works during the "day" of each day but ceases each night, anticipating the Sabbath of the seventh day.[57] Finally, the word is used

---

assignment of function. See *The Lost World of Genesis One: Ancient Cosmology and the Origins Debate* (Downers Grove, IL: IVP Academic, 2009). This is unconvincing. The contrast between being and function is an artificial one. The sun exists to light earth; man exists to rule. Things are created to fill roles; things are in order to do. Walton's argument assumes a quite modern conception that elides final causality from the definition of a thing. Walton's argument also depends on the assumption that the mere identification of a supposed parallel between Genesis and ancient Near Eastern myth is sufficient to interpret Genesis itself. Suppose that all mythologies were about assigning function; it still needs to be demonstrated that Genesis presents the same sort of cosmogony.

[56]C. John Collins, *Genesis 1–4: A Linguistic, Literary, and Theological Commentary* (Phillipsburg, NJ: P&R, 2006), 44, describes Genesis 1 as an "exalted prose narrative."

[57]"Evening and morning" is often taken as a Hebraism describing the day as beginning in darkness and moving toward light. There is something to that paradigm. The creation week as a whole moves from darkness to light, as does redemptive history, moving from the lunar old covenant to the sunrise of the new. Yet the phrase itself *completes* the account of each day: God's speech and making + God's seeing and evaluating + evening and morning = a day. Thus, it seems, evening falls after God's

in the prepositional phrase "in the day (*beyom*) that YHWH
'elohim made earth and heaven" (Gen 2:4). How long is the time
period in view in Genesis 1:3–2:3? Genesis 1 answers the
question straightforwardly, defining the days of creation as
evening-morning composites—that is, as ordinary created
days.[58] Creation's days are *'elohim*'s work days, but, since his
work sets the pattern for the labor of his image, his work days
are the same as ours. Taking the days as normal created days
best fits the setting of Genesis 1, the syntax of *yom*, and the references to the creation days elsewhere in the Old Testament.[59]

Genesis 2:5 is often invoked as evidence against a temporal
reading of the days of creation. That text purportedly gives a
"naturalistic" explanation for the absence of plant life; there were
no plants because it has not rained and because there is no man
to cultivate the ground. Thus, it is argued, "ordinary providence"
is operative in the creation week. If that is so, the days of creation
cannot be ordinary days since, for example, it would take far
longer than a portion of a day for the waterlogged earth to become
dry land (Gen 1:9-10). Further, Genesis 2 appears to reverse the
order of Genesis 1: In the latter, plants spring up without human
assistance while in Genesis 2, plants sprout only after man is

---

evaluation and the "morning" is the morning of the following day. See Robert V.
McCabe, "A Defense of Literal Days in the Creation Week," *Detroit Baptist Seminary
Journal* 5 (2000): 105-9.

[58]The "day-age" theory suggests that the days are genuinely temporal but represent
longer periods of time. It is now discredited, partly because of its own internal
incoherence; if it is hard to imagine evenings and mornings for three days before
the sun is created, it is surely much harder to imagine millennia between the creation of light and the making of the heavenly rulers. At least, though, the day-age
theory recognized that Genesis 1 records a temporally ordered sequence of actions
and events.

[59]In addition to McCabe, "In Defense of Literal Days," see Gerhard F. Hasel, "The
'Days' of Creation in Genesis 1: Literal 'Days' or Figurative 'Periods/Epochs' of
Time?" *Origins* 21, no. 1 (1994): 5-38; Andrew E. Steinmann, "'*echad* as an Ordinal
Number and the Meaning of Genesis 1:5," *Journal of the Evangelical Theological Society*
45, no. 5 (2002): 577-84.

made. Genesis 1 places the creation of plants on day three, while Genesis 2 implicitly places it on day six.[60]

This line of argument misconstrues the relationship between day three and Genesis 2:5. On day three, 'elohim summons specific plants from the earth, the "firstfruits" plants that consist of grasses and trees, which produce seeds/grains and fruit. Grain-bearing grasses and fruit-bearing trees are proto-sacramental plants, which later become the staples of Israel's daily diet and, more importantly, the staples of Israel's *liturgical* festivity. The field shrubs (*siach*) and herbs (*'eseb*) that have not yet sprouted in Genesis 2:5 are not the same as the grasses and fruit trees of day three. Genesis 2 focuses in detail on events of day six, particularly the creation and commissioning of Adam. The scope of the chapter is limited by that context. The *'erets* of Genesis 2:5 is not the "whole earth" that emerges from the waters on day three, but a more circumscribed "land," perhaps Eden where God will plant his garden (Gen 2:8).[61] Yahweh's goal is to prepare land for the garden to flourish under the care-taking of man, the living soul.

Genesis 2:5 thus does not establish the principle that "ordinary providence" is at work during the creation week. Instead, Yahweh 'elohim, having formed and filled the earth in the previous six days, prepares a specific land whose care he will delegate to man. Eden *will* depend on rain from heaven and the horticultural efforts of Adam and Eve, but it will do so only after the creation week is complete. One can make perfect sense of the sequence by assuming God completes his "supernatural" activity and begins to turn the world over to "natural" cycles.[62]

---

[60]See Meredith Kline, "Because It Had Not Rained," *Westminster Theological Journal* 20 (1958): 146-57. Collins presents a related argument from Genesis 2:4-7 in *Genesis 1–4*, 126-28.

[61]Collins, *Genesis 1–4*, 125.

[62]See further, Poythress, *Interpreting Eden*, 80-87; Edward J. Young, *Studies in Genesis 1* (Phillipsburg, NJ: P&R, 1964), 58-65; Jordan, *Creation in Six Days: A Defense of the Traditional Reading of Genesis 1* (Moscow, ID: Canon, 1999), 51-70.

There is no good reason to doubt that Genesis 1 asserts just what it appears to assert: The world comes to be through a series of creative acts that constitute a history. Creation is that history, and the history creation *is* is a history with a trajectory and *telos*.[63] Biblical history is an avant-garde drama that includes the building of the stage and set as one of its main plot threads.

BETWEEN GOD AND GOD[64]

'Elohim creates the rhythm of days, months, seasons, and years. Having created, he dances to creation's beat. He creates light on day one, heavenly lights on day four; the firmament on day two and birds to fly across the face of the firmament on day five; dry land on day three and creatures of land on day six. Taking Genesis 1 with childish simplicity, we conclude the Creator's life with creation involves a succession of moments and days in irreversible sequence. And, to repeat, of a non-Creator's relation to time we know nothing because there is literally nothing to know.

The most dramatic indication that *'elohim* lives with creation in a succession of moments is the "say-see" sequence that structures most of the creation days. Creation's coming-to-be is framed by daily interactions between *'elohim* and *'elohim*. Every day begins with God speaking and most end with God seeing and evaluating the day's work as "good."[65] Day one begins with *'elohim*'s "Let there be light" (Gen 1:3) and ends with *'elohim* seeing the light is good (Gen 1:3). On day three, God speaks to divide the waters below so dry land can appear and judges that to be good

---

[63]Jenson, *Systematic Theology*, 2:14.

[64]The following sections repeat and rework my "God of Days, God in Days: An Exercise in Biblical Dogmatics," *Criswell Theological Journal* 15.1 (2017): 35-46.

[65]"God saw" appears seven times in the chapter (Gen 1:4, 10, 12, 18, 21, 25, 31). The verb *ra'ah* is used again in Gen 2:19, where Yahweh God brings animals to "see" what Adam calls them. Each creature receives the name Adam assigns, which implies that God sees and approves. For the first time, God sees the action of a human being and judges it good. He sees Adam's seeing and calls it good.

(Gen 1:9-10), then speaks to the now exposed earth to spring up with plants and judges that also to be good (Gen 1:11-13). Most days are microchronic mirrors of the week, which begins with God's speaking and ends with God seeing that all is very good (Gen 1:31).[66] Like the week, each day ends with divine delight; each day anticipates the satisfactions of Sabbath. Each day begins with speech and ends with beauty.[67]

On certain days, *'elohim* speaks and then *makes* (Gen 1:6-7, 20-21). Here the created product is not an immediate result of God's speech. The word of *'elohim* functions instead more like a pattern or plan that *'elohim* follows in producing what was spoken. *'Elohim* speaks himself as Word. YHWH is the name of the Spoken God who is the exemplar of all things, and the Spirit executes and actualizes the pattern of the Word. Through the Spirit, the "let be" (*yehi*) of *'elohim*, which is *'elohim* in the guise of YHWH, gives being (*hayah*) to a new creature.

Day four introduces a further complication. God speaks ("Let there be lights"), makes, and then places or gives (*natan*) the lights he has designed and made in the firmament (Gen 1:14-17). There is a close analogy to the construction of the tabernacle.[68] God speaks and shows the pattern to Moses, Moses makes or

---

[66]The term *microchron* comes from James B. Jordan, *From Bread to Wine: Creation, Worship, and Christian Maturity* (Monroe, LA: Athanasius, 2019).

[67]As Basil points out, "good" (*kalon*) means beautiful (*Hexameron* 2.7).

[68]There are multiple connections between the creation account and the later construction of the sanctuary. Yahweh's instructions for the tabernacle are laid out in seven speeches, each marked by the introductory clause, "Yahweh spoke to Moses, saying" (Ex 25:1; 30:11, 17, 22, 34; 31:1, 12). The last speech (Ex 31:12-17) reiterates the Sabbath command, and the section concludes with "when He had finished speaking" (*kekalloto ledaber*; Ex 31:18), an echo of Genesis 2:1 (*wayekullu*). The tabernacle is a microcosm, built according to seven speeches that replicate the seven days of creation. Each speech provides instructions for Moses to build according to the *tabnit*, the pattern he sees and hears on the mountain (Ex 25:9). He receives a spoken image of the laver (Ex 30:17-21), for instance, and later makes it (Ex 38:8). See L. Michael Morales, *The Tabernacle Pre-Figured: Cosmic Mountain Ideology in Genesis and Exodus* (Leuven: Peeters, 2012).

assigns the making to skilled workmen, and finally Moses places (*natan*) all the items of tabernacle furniture within the tent (Ex 40:6, 7, 8, 18, 20, 22, 30, 33). In Exodus, the tasks are distributed in three directions: Yahweh is architect and his word the blueprint, Spirit-filled workmen and women make according to the pattern (Ex 31:1-5; 36:1-2), and Moses gives the made work to Yahweh's dwelling.[69] In Genesis 1, *'elohim* himself performs all the distributed tasks. *'Elohim* commands *'elohim*, and, having made the lights *'elohim* commands, *'elohim* gives them to the sky. There is, once again, an implied distribution of tasks: The command *'elohim* speaks is *'elohim* himself as YHWH the Spoken God, and the Spoken God carries out the command he is by the power of the Spirit of *'elohim*. *'Elohim*'s speaking initiates a new phase of creation's evolution toward glory. Each time he speaks, he plants seeds springing up in fresh fruitfulness.

What *'elohim* initiates with speech, he completes with "sight." In the Bible, "seeing" is a figure for judgment. Eyes are organs of evaluation. The Lord's eyes test the sons of men (Ps 11:4). When the day of Yahweh comes, he cuts off Israel's food "before our eyes" (Joel 1:16), and his eyes destroy sinful nations from the face of the earth (Amos 9:8). His eyes are open to the temple (2 Chron 6:40), so he can see and respond to the prayers of his king (2 Kings 19:16) and his prophet (Dan 9:18). With his seven burning eyes, Jesus is the perfect judge, from whom nothing is hidden (Rev 1:14; 2:18; 19:12). In Genesis 1, *'elohim* sees the work of each day to judge the quality of the work done and to test, with burning eyes, the condition of the day's products. *'Elohim*'s evaluation is a *self*-evaluation. Throughout the creation week, God judges God. Each day is thus a microchron of cosmic history, which begins with

---

[69]There is an intriguing parallel here with the *Timaeus*, where the demiurge looks to the pattern of the Forms in shaping the world.

the utterance of God and culminates in final judgment, when the Father will rejoice in the completed work of his Son and Spirit.

It is possible to conceive this divine self-approval narrowly: The one person of *'elohim* initiates each day's work and, at the end of each day, commends his *own* performance. "Atta boy, *'elohim*," he says, awkwardly twisting to pat himself on the back. That is conceivable, but, given the signs of divine plurality throughout the chapter, it is more likely that the *'elohim* who makes and the *'elohim* who evaluates are distinct. At the end of each day *'elohim* evaluates and commends the work of his spoken Word and his Spirit, who hovers over the waters. At the end of the day, the seeing God judges and commends the performance of the Spoken God he speaks and the Breath by which he speaks.

Augustine suggests there is a trace of the "holy goodness" of the Spirit in God's approval of his works. The Spirit is the one by whom "God is pleased with whatever pleases him."[70] The Spirit who is the Love of the Trinity hovers "over" the waters, in order to indicate God's love is not "needy," nor "subjected to the things it loves," nor acts "out of the compulsion of his needs." His love is lordly, the sovereign, needless Spirit who is love. He overshadows the deep to display the "abundance of his charity." When God judges creation good, he judges out of the "same genial courtesy." The Spirit hovers so that creation might be, and, by the Spirit, God pronounces it good so that it might abide in its existence.[71]

The reasoning is tricky but Augustine links the judgment that the world is "good" with the completing work of the Spirit. That earth, firmament, plants, stars and sun, fish and birds, animals and man *are* is the gift of the Word; that they are *good* is the product of the perfecting work of the Spirit. From this angle, the concluding pronouncement that closes each day is a commendation

---

[70]Augustine, *Literal Meaning of Genesis* 1.6.12.
[71]Augustine, *Literal Meaning of Genesis* 1.7.13–1.8.14.

of the Spirit as well as the Word. Or, as Augustine suggests, *'elohim* rejoices in the work of the Spoken God in the joy of the Spirit.[72]

Genesis 3 supports Augustine's intuition about the Spirit's agency in the assessment of creation. After Adam and Eve eat the forbidden fruit, they hear the voice of *YHWH 'elohim* walking in the garden. It is the advent of the one God—the Speaking God, *'elohim*, and YHWH, the living Word he speaks. And this doubly named God arrives "in the Spirit [*ruakh*] of the day" (Gen 3:8), the first use of *ruakh* since Genesis 1:2. It is a "primal parousia," a prototype of final judgment, a theophany of the Creator robed as Judge in the glory of his Spirit.[73] *YHWH 'elohim* judges and condemns in and through the Spirit as he judges and commends in the Spirit throughout the week of creation. Or, to reach far ahead: The Spirit's role in God's judgments is evident in Revelation, for the seven burning eyes of the Lamb are the seven Spirits of God (Rev 5:6).[74]

The saying-seeing structure thus implies three conclusions relevant to our inquiry: first, the Creator acts and reacts within the time of creation; second, *God* structures, shapes, and segments time; and, third, the God who segments and unifies time is the Speaking God, the Spoken God, and their Spirit.

We can begin to put these pieces together by resorting, once again, to trinitarian categories. There is, as Robert Jenson says, a "whence" and a "whither" in the triune life whose poles can neither be disconnected nor collapsed into each other.[75] The Creator's creative saying

---

[72]Luther agrees. "God saw it was good" speaks of the preservation of creation, which is the work of the Spirit: "The creature could not continue in existence unless the Holy Spirit delighted in it and preserved the work through this delight of God in his work" (*Lectures on Genesis*, at Gen 1:20).

[73]See Meredith Kline, "Primal Parousia," available at https://meredithkline.com /klines-works/articles-and-essays/primal-parousia/.

[74]See further my *Revelation 1–11* (London: T&T Clark, 2018), 261-62.

[75]Jenson, *Systematic Theology*, vol. 1, *The Triune God* (Oxford: Oxford University Press, 1997), 338-39; see also Schwöbel, "Eternity of the Triune God," 6-7.

and seeing is irreversible because it is the irreversible order of relation among the triune persons. The sequence of his sculpting and singing manifests the sequence of processions that constitute the Creator's triune life. God is as the paternal Source who produces a Second and then, through the Second, a Third.

This triune pattern is also the archetype of which created time is the ectype. *Persons* carve out bodies of time, and time is most fundamentally the product of divine art. Like all creatures, the rhythms of time have their ultimate *ratio* in the Creator. His lively inner glory provides the pattern, the *tabnit*, for created glory. The *taxis* of whence and whither that is the life of God orders created time in its own likeness. Time's order is determined by persons, above all by the ordered life of the triune persons. Hence, the movement of time through past, present, and future mirrors the eternal, and eternally realized, becoming and unfolding of the triune Source, Radiance, and Diffusion.

We can fill out the picture by reference to Antonio Rosmini's Thomistic treatment of the trinitarian "principle" and "termini." The Father is the originating source of which the Son and Spirit are the ends. The two "emanate" from the Father, and this is what makes the Father Father. The Father is actualized as Father ("is in act") in his generation of the Son and his spiration of the Spirit. Son and Spirit are truly *other* than the Father, precisely because they are terms rather than principles. The essence of God is source and end, Alpha and Omega. The Son and Spirit *must* be "something different" from the Father, and the Father/Principle would not be or be perfect "if it did not, of itself, produce the terms that as terms are different from it."[76]

Yet, these others cannot be "outside" the Father; if they were, the Father would be imperfect. Thus, even while giving himself

---

[76]Rosmini, *Theosophy*, vol. 3: *Trine Being (Contd.)*, trans. Terence Watson (Durham, NC: Rosmini House, 2011), 281-82, par. 1383.

wholly away, the Father retains everything he gives, insofar as the Son and Spirit, while other than the Father, remain "in" him. The Father is completed as Father by the emanation of Son and Spirit; they are his own Wisdom and Goodness. Because the Father gives himself to the Son and Spirit, they are also essentially Wisdom and Goodness, *communicated* and received Wisdom and Goodness, Wisdom and Goodness as terms rather than as principle. The Father's self-gift to the Son and Spirit is also what actualizes the divine essence. This essence is, Rosmini says, both "in the principle" and also "communicated" to the Son and Spirit. The essence is "put in act" by the same act by which the distinct persons are put in act. The essence of God is what it is because of the Father's generation of the Son and the spiration of the Spirit. The essence of God is not some "fourth thing" lurking behind the persons. The essence is enacted and actualized in the Father's gift to the Son and Spirit (and, I would add, in the return gift to the Father).

The upshot is: God is *actus purus,* not statically, as if he just is what he always is. He is *actus purus* in the dynamic of the Father's self-gift to the Son and Spirit. He is fully actualized not because he is purely principle, an absolute origin; he is fully actualized because he is eternally principle and terms, because he is source and supplement, Alpha and Omega. The *actus* of *actus purus* is not simply actualization but an actual *act*—the generative self-gift of the Father that terminates as the Son and Spirit. That difference of principle and term is the whence and whither of triune life, which is the source of the temporal structure of creation.

It is thus misleading to say, as Bulgakov does, that temporal becoming is an unstable mix of being and nonbeing, striving for liberating from nonbeing.[77] In both its being and its nonbeing,

---

[77]Bulgakov, *Lamb of God*, 127: "Becoming is being that is submerged and modified by nonbeing in all its cells, but it is also being that is liberating itself from nonbeing."

and both its flows and its interruptions, its moments and its distinction of moments, time mirrors God's energetic life. As we have noted, "not" is essential to the life of God and our speaking of it, for the Father is *not* the Son, the Son is *not* the Spirit, and the Spirit is *not* the Father. "Not" marks the "interval," the nonspatial but absolute distance between person and person. This absolute difference is simultaneously an absolute intimacy of mutual perichoretic indwelling, but the perichoretic communion depends on the absolute difference, since an undifferentiated God is merely a union and not a *com*-union at all. With the intervening "not" between person and person, God is an ordered procession of Father, Son, and Spirit, so that the life of the Trinity is marked by difference between Light, Radiance, and enveloping Diffusion, by the sequence of Source, Flow, and the hovering Spirit who unites Source and Flow.[78] God begins as Father, moves as Son, completes as Spirit; God exists as "past," as "present," as "future."

For just this reason, and for this reason only, the Creator is capable of creating while remaining entirely and utterly himself. Viewed from the creature's perspective, *ex nihilo* implies "the absolute gratuitousness of its coming to be." From God's side, it means that creation is an act of God's self-denying love, by which he "without alienation from himself, expropriates that which is most proper to him, being itself, in order to make a gift of it gratuitously to the other than himself." Just as the Father eternally gives himself wholly to the Son, so the Trinity eternally gives up having an exclusive hold on the divine property of existence,

---

[78]Coda, *From the Trinity*, 497. "Creation," Coda goes on to say, "has its root in this trinitarian 'nonbeing,' this infinite 'nonbeing' of love of which only God is capable." Creation *ex nihilo* does not simply mean "nothing preexisted creation but God," though it does mean that. It also means God creates in "an act of pure love, an act with which he himself makes himself nothing, with respect to creation, so that creation might be."

calling creatures to exist: "The *ex nihilo* of the act of creation is the fullness with which God communicates himself, and nothing less, to that which is not himself." Creation's history is "nothing other than the created image, extended in space and time, of that nothing/all of the love which in God the Trinity is the Word/Son of the Father, his eternal wisdom: *nothing* because he receives his being from the love of the Father; *all* because the infinite fullness of the Father is fully reflected and expressed in him." In sum, "The nothingness of love is the trinitarian grammar with which the book of creation is written."[79]

The life of the triune God is not a "sheer point of presence" but "a life among persons" that is "constituted in a structure of relations." Within the triune life, the Father begets, the Son is begotten, the Spirit is breathed out by the Father through the Son. The "whence" and "whither" in God is a "'past' and 'future,' which is identical with the distinction between the Father and the Spirit."[80] The difference is not measurable, as created time is. Nothing of the source (Father) slips away; nothing encroaches from the future. Yet the difference is absolute. We are not permitted to merge the future (Spirit) into the past (Father) or present (Son). We are not permitted to absorb the persons into some fourth thing, a purely present divine essence above all personal-temporal distinction.

We must take a step further. Created time does not merely *mirror* the whence-whither, saying-seeing *taxis* of the persons. Created time is *enclosed within* the eternal *taxis* as it unfolds in creation. We experience time, Augustine said, as a "distension" of the soul, as we are stretched between memory and desire, between past and future on the knife-edge "nothing" of the present moment. Time is a dimension of our experiencing anything at all;

---

[79]Coda, *From the Trinity*, 497-99.
[80]Jenson, *Systematic Theology*, 2:35.

our experience of time accompanies experience as such. For that very reason, time also comes to us as something outside ourselves, as an infinitely complex but measurable common rhythm that allows us to formulate train schedules, keep appointments, set hours of prayer. Time is a distension of soul because it is, more fundamentally, a "'distension' in the life of God," by which he acts the "enveloping horizon of all events that are not God."[81] Time accompanies all created experience because we are participants in God's life "and so experience this metric as a determining character also of our existence as persons."[82] Time confronts us as an objective, "architectural" feature of the world because it is the distension of the eternal Trinity in time.

Creation is God's act of "accommodating" what is other than God. God makes room for creatures within the mutual gifts and counter-gifts, the whence and whither, of triune life. His hospitality is the gift of existence, which is the gift of time. As the triune God stretches himself out in creating the heavens and earth, this structure remains: the Father initiates, the Son executes, the Spirit completes. Given the irreversible origin-supplement structure of divine life, the creatures God accommodates naturally live from whence to whither, as the triune God of whence and whither envelops created time. Time is not a moving image of motionless eternity. Created time is a moving image of the dynamic, structured, infinitely mobile life of the Father who begets the Son, from whom the Spirit proceeds. It moves because it *shares* the infinite and infinitely mobile life of God. God's actions in time are not irreversible because he is a prisoner of time.

---

[81]Jenson, *Systematic Theology*, 2:35.

[82]Jenson, *Systematic Theology*, 2:34. Jenson draws on Barth and, behind him, on Isaak Dorner, who argues that the reciprocity in the triune relations, by which divine possibility is constantly surmounted by his eternal actuality, is "manifested in the world as time." *Divine Immutability: A Critical Reconsideration*, trans. Robert R. Williams and Claude Welch (Minneapolis: Fortress, 1994), 140.

Time is irreversible because it is enclosed within the irreversible eternal ordered life of the Trinity.[83]

Genesis 1 anticipates the prepositional trinitarianism of Romans 11:36: "From Him and through Him and to Him are all things." Also the implied trinitarianism of Paul's Mars Hill sermon: We live, move, and have being in time because we live, move, and having being in the God who is Beginning, Middle, and End (Acts 17:28). We live, move, and have being in time because creation is enclosed within and suspended between the Father's initiating *fiat* and the Spirit's final glorification of the bride, which is the Creator's distension in creation.[84] Our lives exist between the Father's speaking and the Spirit's delight, between the initiating word and the divine judgment that all is good. All that moves in time dances in the steps of the temporally ordered communion of Father, Son, and Spirit, as the whence and whither of created time mirror and share in the eternal life of God.

Deep calls to deep: This is the theological order of the creation week. God speaks and *then* God sees and commends the products of God's speaking. The Father speaks the Son, whose word is completed in the Spirit, and *then* in the Spirit the Father expresses his delight in their work. The "this, then that" procession is not illusion, not merely the created refraction of successionless divine eternity. God does "this, then that" in time because he is the Father who begets the Son and breathes the Spirit. God does

---

[83]Because God is not "purely present," because he is as much past and future as present, we can, against Augustine, find a theological ground for past and future. We can affirm the full reality of past and future without folding them into the present. The Trinity gives us the ontological ground to say the past is real *as past*, the future *as future*. It gives us ground for saying God knows past as it truly is, as past, and future as it truly is, as future, precisely insofar as he knows himself (Dorner, *Divine Immutability*, 151).

[84]Klaus Hemmerle, *Theses*, 31-32, notes that with the incarnation the "God above us encounters and answers the God who is among us, who catches, supports, and accepts us." Thus are we "between God and God." My argument is that this evangelical suspension of creation within God is operative from the moment of creation.

"this, then that" because the triune succession stretches out to house and embrace created time. One final step will bring God's relation to time into clearer focus. It will bring us to a related Creator without dissolving him in time.

CREATION BETWEEN GOD AND GOD

God is not envious: Creation's powers are real powers. Creation carries out divine tasks. Yet, even when we exercise our own powers, even when we are at our most "independent," we are simply employing the gifts of the creative Word, YHWH, the God who gives being, by the power of the Spirit who is Lord and Giver of life. Our independent existence is nothing but obedience to the command of the Creator. We possess "our own" only in the mode of gift, a gift once and continuously regiven.

Day three of the creation week is crucial in filling out our understanding of God's relation to time and temporal processes, because it marks a shift from monergistic creative activity to a synergism of *'elohim* and creation.[85] During the last half of the creation week, the Creator creates by empowering creation to bring forth new things and to do divine things. Earth brings forth the vegetation not because *'elohim* says "Let there be vegetation" but because *'elohim* says "Let the *earth* sprout vegetation" (Gen 1:11-12). Waters teem because he says "Let the *waters* teem with swarms of living creatures" (though the *tannanim* are created [*bara'*] directly by God, 1:21). Creatures spring from earth like plants because *'elohim* says "Let the *earth* bring forth living creatures" (Gen 1:24). Man, made in the image of God, is another special creation (*bara'*), but we learn in Genesis 2 that the

---

[85]Barth, *Church Dogmatics* 3/1, 152, quotes Calvin: "Let everyone know that the sun is not the source of living things. The mercy of God opens the earth; the favor of God makes its fruit burst forth," and "God acts through creatures, not because he has need of another's help, but because it pleases him to do so."

creation of man as male and female is the product of a sequence of actions—forming *'adam* from the *'adamah*, then the woman from the man. These mediated, synergistic acts of creation are included in the summary statement of Genesis 2:1-3. Even though earth sprouts plants, plants are among *'elohim*'s works, among the things "which he had done," the works "*'elohim* created and made" (Gen 2:2-3). *He* made them, albeit through the agency of Word-empowered earth and water. All of creation's powers are gifts of the Word, yet they are *creation's* powers.[86]

Earth and water do not produce plants by their own power, "left to themselves." It is an absurd qualification. Even as a hypothetical, "left to themselves" is nonsense. There *is* no earth or water *at all* except by the continuing speaking of the Creator. As Herbert McCabe put it, the Creator is not related to the creation as a sculptor who shapes and then leaves his statue; the Creator is to the creation as singer to a song.[87] And there is no ongoing song except as the singer continues to sing. If he stops, there is no song to examine "in itself." Even from the perspective of the Creator, "left to itself" is nonsense. Just by creating the watery earth, he commits himself to maintain it in being and to accompany it through every moment and to bring it to its final end. "Let be . . . let be . . . let be" is the consistent word of *YHWH 'elohim*. Since earth is made to be fruitful, God's continuous gift of existence is also a continuous gift of fruitfulness because it is God's continuous gift of earthiness to the earth.

Creation is involved in its own completion, but that involvement is overarched by, embedded between, God's word of command and his subsequent assessment and judgment. Creation's self-formation originates from God's word and moves

---

[86]The following sections repeat and rework my "God of Days, God in Days: An Exercise in Biblical Dogmatics," *Criswell Theological Journal* 15.1 (2017): 35-46.

[87]Herbert McCabe, *God Still Matters* (London: Continuum, 2005), 226-27.

toward God's word. God says to the land "sprout plants" and then "sees" that it is good; he speaks to the waters to teem, and judges that the resulting teeming is good. God's originating speech enables the creation's liveliness, and God's concluding speech evaluates creation's fruit. Creation's action is enclosed within God's saying and God's seeing, one prospective and one retrospective, one enabling and the other evaluative. Creation's time of action is the room created by the Word that will be perfected in the Spirit, and all creation's infinite varieties and actions exist within that opening.

What happens in the creation week is what continues to happen every week since. Every moment of creation's history initiates a new future, as the Speaking God speaks creation's being through the Spoken God. Grasses yield grain and trees bear fruit only by growth and fruition over a period of time. Yet Scripture tells us that *God* feeds the animals and birds who eat these grasses and fruits (Ps 104:28). The grain on the voluptuous fields of northern Idaho is as much a result of God's speaking and doing as the first grain plants that sprang up on the third day of creation. That grain too is a product of divine Word that empowers created earth, water, and light to turn seeds to more seeds. *YHWH 'elohim* says "let the earth sprout" again and again, and again and again it does. Today's sunrise, your rising, your heartbeat and breath and the incalculable biochemical interactions that maintain your life and the life of all things—all of it, at every moment, is the product of the word of the Creator. Philosophers do not know it, but creation's "permanence is entirely the result of the power of the Word of God."[88]

As we have seen, the rhythm of created time is the rhythm of triune life. There is a "fit" between the eternal becoming within

---

[88]Luther, *Lectures on Genesis*, at Gen 1:9.

God and the becoming of creation. God initiates and completes within that created rhythm; his initiation and completion enclose the actions and happenings of creation. God acts within the confines of evenings and mornings, and, at the same time, evenings and mornings occur within the say-see action of God. God indwells time because time indwells God.[89] God is really responsive to the events that take place within the creation (he *sees* and pronounces good), including the actions of creation itself (e.g., the sprouting of plants, the teeming of seas). Yet his real responsiveness does not subvert his Lordship because, in responding to the events of creation, he is ultimately responding to his own initiative. God's responses to creation are responses to his own speaking and being spoken.

Creation matures from glory to glory through the creation week. Each created thing displays new powers as it enters into new relations with other creatures. Light illumines, then energizes plants, then, coagulated into heavenly lights, gives life and sight to earth's creatures. As the creation unfolds, so the Creator's glory radiates more fully.[90] On day one, the Creator's glory is manifest in light; on day two, it is manifest in both light and the separation of waters; on day four, he fixes light in heavenly lamps and thus manifests is glory more fully. He is Lord of light, then Lord of light and waters, then Lord of waters and light and land. Earth sprouts and makes God the God of plants. Water teems and makes God the God of fish and the great monsters of the sea. Animals emerge from earth, and God becomes Lord of the cattle, beasts, and creeping things. And so it continues to the present

---

[89]See my treatment of the perichoretic relation of past, present, and future in *Traces of the Trinity* (Grand Rapids, MI: Baker Academic, 2015), 49-62. Basil notes that the original darkness is not called "night." Light shone out in the darkness, and thus day comes first and night is merely the opposite of day. Thus we measure time by days, not nights (*Hexameron* 2.8).

[90]Dorner, *Divine Immutability*, 145.

and into the future. Men found the University of Paris, and God becomes the God of the University of Paris. My wife gives birth to a son, and God becomes his God. God was not Lord of fish before there were fish, nor Lord of the University of Paris before its founding. Each day, each moment, unveils a new facet of his infinite glory.

God "has his history in our history."[91] Bulgakov is right: Biblical cosmogony is also theogony, the history of the Creator's coming to his own fullness. The Creator is in a real, mutually defining relation to creation. Crucially, we affirm this *only* because creation is enclosed and encompassed by the eternal, real, mutual relations of Father, Son, and Spirit. Ultimately, *God* makes *himself* Lord of plants, fish, birds, animals, the University of Paris, my son. All of these "God-making" creatures are products of divine speech, objects of the divine judgment of the Seeing God. God's glorification in and through creation, his life in and with the world, is a manifestation in creation of the ever-completed, ever-unfolding life of God. He is glorified in creation as the Spoken God delights the Seeing God, and the Seeing God adorns the Word.

Say-see is the structure of God's entire history with humanity. From the first moment, creation's history is a history of speech. In creating, Barth writes, God speaks "in time," and this "sets the creation in relation and connexion with all the divine utterances which will later constitute the nerve and substance of the biblical history." Like every later utterance, God's first words carve a pathway into the future. By saying "let be," God sets a "boundary" against the initial condition of darkness and emptiness and initiates a new future of light, ultimately endless light. Every subsequent "thus saith the Lord" is an echo of the first creation fiat. As God speaks in parts through Moses and the prophets, "History

---

[91]Hemmerle, *Theses*, 32.

is made, i.e., something old is again and again shown to be old, and something new to be new." When God speaks, the old "has the accent of judgment upon it" while the new "has the accent of the grace of God." Every word is a decree of the Judge of all the earth. This distinguishing Word is the continuous "evening and morning" of time, the "movement of the hand of the divine clock." God's history of fragmented speech gives way finally to the final word of the incarnate Son. In this utterance, *the* new thing appears that "antiquates everything that has gone before." By this new Word, the Word "makes the world created by it its own" and the world "is made a partaker of the Word of God by which it was created; a partaker of its triumphant vitality, of its holiness and glory."[92]

Each particular body within biblical time has the same shape. Yahweh calls Abraham from Ur, a speaking that will not be closed with a final seeing until the end of all things. He leads Israel from Egypt and delivers commands, and Israel's fate turns on what the Seeing God sees in Israel. By his word, the Speaking God raises Assyria as his ax; weighing and inspecting, the Seeing God grinds Assyria to powder. He calls Nebuchadnezzar to be his servant, then closes the time of Babylon with a catastrophic judgment. In speaking Torah and the prophetic word, the words of Jesus and the apostles, the Speaking God speaks the Spoken God again and again. Each new word of the Speaking God is a fresh articulation of the Spoken God, each fresh speaking opening new avenues into the future, giving birth to a new body of time.

This model allows us to address all the other dilemmas and impasses we have encountered. Genesis 1 provides an implied theology of God's eternity. God is eternal in that he is Alpha and Omega, in that he both embraces and inhabits time, in that he is

---

[92]Barth, *Church Dogmatics* 3/1, 114-15.

immanent in time just because he is transcendent. He is eternal as triune, the Father initiating, the Son executing, the Spirit completing so the Father can declare his approval. God is eternal in that he initiates every body of time by his Word and closes off each body of time in the delight of the Spirit. God is eternal not in that he is immune to time or estranged from it. God is eternal in that created time is suspended between the Father's Saying and Seeing, enclosed within the triune life of the Saying and the Seeing God, housed in the distension of triune being. Thus the Creator remains absolutely, faithfully, immutably the triune God he is, his life remains absolutely the life of Source, Order, and Completion, even as he acts in and reacts to the creation, even as he does new things and becomes new in time.

For the same reasons, Genesis 1 answers dilemmas of impassibility. Impassibility is just the question whether God is dependently responsive to the changes of creatures. On the model of Genesis 1, he is so, but only because the creation is absolutely dependently responsive to his initiating Word. The Word summons good fruit from the vineyard that is Israel; when that fruit appears, the Seeing God sees and delights in it, and his delight *is truly a response* to the good fruit Israel produces because it is truly God's response to God. The Word summons good fruit from the vineyard that is Israel; when in its freedom it uses his gifts to produce rotten grapes instead of the wine of righteousness, the Seeing God is filled with just wrath at Israel's abuse of her gifts. His wrath is *truly a response* to Israel's infidelity.

Genesis 1 offers a resolution to the dilemmas of immutability. The Creator is persistently himself just in his changing responses to creation. He is never other than the God he is, the living communion of Father, Son, and Spirit. His involvement in time is precisely the perichoretic communion of Father, Son, and Spirit opened up to include the whence and whither of created time.

When, in response to the word of the prophet, Israel turns from her sins to produce delightful fruit, the Seeing God turns from wrath to joy, his changing response to Israel encompassed by his approval of the Spirit's stirring in the heart of his people. He has truly changed in response to Israel's change, though, because Israel's change of heart is entirely a gift from the Word of grace, he has changed in response to his own action.

We have discovered a Creator who answers prayer. The Spirit moves us to pray; we pray in the name of the Son; the Father responds—*truly responds*—and answers our prayer, commending the Spirit and Son even as he answers our requests and meets our needs. The Spirit provokes, and we quench the Spirit in our refusal to pray, and the Father does not answer; we have not because we ask not.

We do not need the prophylactics that protect God from contamination by time. God does not need them. He is perfectly capable of being wholly himself, Creator and Lord, while acting in time, doing *this now* and *that then*, becoming Lord of plants and then Lord of animals, responding to creatures who are and do only by the continuous speaking of the Speaking God and the continuous anointing of the hovering Spirit. He can say all this without the least threat to his status as Creator, as source of all, because all his acting and doing and responding occurs within the whence and whither of his own triune life. He is in a real relation to creation because his relation to creation is embedded in his relation with himself.[93]

---

[93]Barth says something similar—not surprisingly, since I am dependent here on Jenson, himself a Barthian: "The creature needs the *Creator* to be able to live. It thus needs the *relation* to Him. But it cannot create this relation. *God creates it* by His own presence in the creature and therefore as a relation of Himself to Himself." *Church Dogmatics 1/1: The Doctrine of the Word of God*, trans. Geoffrey Bromiley et al. (London: T&T Clark, 2010), 108. For Barth and for me, "real relation" implies mutuality but not "causal dependence" or "ontological equality." My use of the phrase is similar to that of late medieval nominalists, who do not make "belonging to the same

CONCLUSION

All created action, all moments and periods and bodies of time, all created experience is suspended between God's saying and his seeing. There is no foundation beneath; there is no safety net. There does not need to be, because the Creator's commitment to his creation is infinitely more secure than any flimsy metaphysical scaffolding or crane we might erect to hold creation aloft.

We can follow Bulgakov's lead, without resorting to his speculative Sophiology. According to Scripture, "God lives in the world and with the world, in an interrelationship." He not only acts within the world but "is also defined on the basis of the world" when he repents, rejoices, becomes angry, laments. To dismiss all of this is "to replace the fiery words of Holy Scripture with the scholasticism of the seminarians."[94] In short, Christianity requires us to "presuppose the reality of time, not only for the world, but also for God, with the one reality conditioning the other." He participates "in the becoming of the world" since he becomes "God not for Himself but for the world together with the becoming of the world."[95] Following Genesis 1, we can say all that without reducing God to a god, because we are speaking, from beginning to end, about the triune Creator and none other.

"God crowns his own gifts," Augustine says of our promised rewards.[96] God passes judgment, but the judgment he passes is

---

ontological order" a criterion of "real relation." In this, the nominalists were followed by Reformed scholastics like Turretin and Alsted. See Wittman, *God and Creation*, 245-47, 286-87. Though I reject his conclusions in general, I agree with Charles Hartshorne's observation that "everything that influences God has already been influenced by him." *The Divine Relativity: A Social Conception of God* (New Haven, CT: Yale University Press, 1967), 30.

[94]Orthodox that he is, Bulgakov can think of no insult more vicious than "scholastic."

[95]Bulgakov, *Lamb of God*, 133.

[96]Paraphrased from Augustine, *On Grace and Free Will* 6.15.

not based on creaturely merit. It is ultimately an approval of the gifts and doings of the Son and Spirit. Augustine's aphorism is an ontological principle. It is the structure of creation's history with God, which is God's history with creation. God is responsive to creation, just because he is responsive to himself, for "All very good" is nothing but a jubilant echo of "Let be."

CONCLUSION

"We believe in God the Father Almighty, Maker of heaven and earth, and of all things visible and invisible. . . . And in one Jesus Christ . . . by whom all things were made. . . . And we believe in the Holy Spirit, the Lord and Giver of Life." We so believe because we are told: "In the beginning, God created the heavens and the earth."

This *credo* provides the starting point for all theology. There is no Author's Introduction prior to Genesis 1:1, no Foreword from a leading authority. We start with Creator, or we will be forever surrounded with bottomless pitfalls.

The Creator is the triune God—*'elohim*, his Spirit and his Word; *'elohim*, YHWH, and the Spirit of *'elohim*; the Speaking God, the Spoken God, and the Spirit. In extending the love he is in creation, he generously gives creatures power to do divine things. Creation is other than God, but it is glory as God is glory; it is Godlike—deified—from the beginning, destined to be fully deified in the end. The Creator is the God who speaks "let be" and is what he speaks. He is the God who speaks "let be" and so gives creatures an existence that images the outgoing and self-giving existence he is. The Creator is the Speaking and Seeing God, who initiates every moment and every extended body of time and who closes every moment and body of time with his scrutinizing judgment. Within his life there is a whence and a whither, and so he can and does enclose created time, making it his time with us. He is in creation, even as creation exists in him.

Of the Creator we say, "He was, is, and comes." And, "In him we live and move and have our being." And, "From him and through him and to him are all things."

Behold your God. There is no other.

BIBLIOGRAPHY

ANCIENT, MEDIEVAL, AND REFORMATION SOURCES

Ambrose. *Hexameron*. Translated by John J. Savage. Washington, DC: Catholic University of America Press, 2004.

Anselm. *Monologion. Anselm of Canterbury: The Major Works*. Edited by Brian Davies and G. R. Evans. Oxford: Oxford University Press, 2008.

Aquinas, Thomas. *On the Eternity of the World*. Translated by Cyril Vollert, Lottie H. Kendzierski, and Paul M. Byrne. Milwaukee, WI: Marquette University Press, 1983.

———. *On the Power of God*. Translated by Richard J. Regan. Oxford: Oxford University Press 2012.

———. *Summa Contra Gentiles*. Translated by Laurence Shapcote. Green Bay, WI: Aquinas Institute, 2018.

———. *Summa theologiae, Volume 2: Existence and Nature of God*. Translated by Timothy McDermott. Cambridge: Cambridge University Press 2006.

———. *Summa theologiae, Volume 3: Knowing and Naming God*. Translated by Herbert McCabe. Cambridge: Cambridge University Press, 2006.

———. *Summa theologiae, Volume 5: God's Will and Providence*. Translated by Thomas Gilby. Cambridge: Cambridge University Press, 2006.

———. *Summa theologiae, Volume 6: The Trinity*. Translated by Ceslaus Velecky. London: Blackfriars, 1965.

———. *Summa theologiae, Volume 8: Creation, Variety and Evil*. Translated by Thomas Gilby. Cambridge: Cambridge University Press, 2006.

———. *Summa theologiae, Volume 10: Cosmogony*. Translated by William A. Wallace. Cambridge: Cambridge University Press, 2006.

———. *Summa theologiae, Volume 29: The Old Law*. Translated by David Bourke. Cambridge: Cambridge University Press, 2006.

Aristotle. *Metaphysics*. Translated by C. D. C. Reeve. Indianapolis: Hackett, 2016.

———. *On Sophistical Refutations. On Coming-to-be and Passing Away*. Translated by E. S. Forster. Cambridge, MA: Harvard University Press, 1955.

———. *Physics*. Translated by C. D. C. Reeve. Indianapolis: Hackett, 2018.

Augustine. *On Christian Teaching*. Translated by R. P. H. Green. Oxford: Oxford University Press, 2008.

———. *City of God*. Translated by R. W. Dyson. Cambridge: Cambridge University Press, 1998.

———. *Confessions*. Translated by Henry Chadwick. Oxford: Oxford University Press, 2009.

———. *On Grace and Free Will*. Translated by Peter King. Cambridge: Cambridge University Press, 2010.

———. *Homilies on the Gospel of John, 1-40*. Translated by Edmund Hill. New York: New City Press, 2009.

———. *The Literal Meaning of Genesis*. Translated by Edmund Hill. Hyde Park, NY: New City Press, 2006.

———. *The Trinity*. Translated by Edmund Hill. Hyde Park, NY: New City Press, 2012.

Basil. *Hexameron*. Translated by Blomfield Jackson. Columbia, SC: Create Space Publishing, 2014.

Boethius. *Consolation of Philosophy*. Translated by Victor Watts. London: Penguin, 1999.

Bonaventure. *Collationes in Hexaemeron*. Translated by José De Vinck. Paterson, NJ: St. Anthony Guide Press, 1970.

Calvin, John. *Institutes of the Christian Religion*. Translated by John T. McNeill. Louisville: Westminster Press, 1960.

———. *Commentary on Genesis*. Translated by John King. Edinburgh: Banner of Truth, 1965.

Chrysostom. *Homilies on Genesis*. Translated by Robert C. Hill. Washington, DC: Catholic University of America Press, 1986.

Pseudo-Dionysius. *The Complete Works*. Translated by Colm Luibheid. Mahwah, NY: Paulist Press, 1987.

Edwards, Jonathan. *"The Miscellanies," Entries Nos. 501-832* in *The Works of Jonathan Edwards*, Vol. 18. Edited by Ava Chamberlain. New Haven: Yale University Press, 2000.

Gregory of Nazianzen. *Five Theological Orations*. Translated by Charles Gordon Browne and James Edward Swallow. Buffalo, NY: Christian Literature Publishing, 1894.

Gregory of Nyssa. *Dogmatic Treatises*. Translated by Henry Wace. Grand Rapids: Eerdmans, repr. 1972.

Gregory Palamas. *The Triads*. Translated by Nicholas Gendle. Mahwah, NJ: Paulist Press, 1983.

Grosseteste, Robert. *On Light*. Translated by Clare C. Riedl. Milwaukee, WI: Marquette University Press, 1978.

Irenaeus. *Against All Heresies*. Translated by John Keble. Edinburgh: Cross-Reach, 2018.

Justin Martyr. *Dialogue with Trypho*. Translated by Thomas B. Falls. Washington, DC: Catholic University of America Press, 1965.

Kirk, G. S. and Raven, J. E. eds. *The Presocratic Philosophers: A Critical History with a Selection of Texts*. Cambridge: Cambridge University Press, 1957.

Luther, Martin. *Lectures on Genesis*. Translated by George V. Schick. St. Louis: Concordia, 1958.

Origen. *Homilies on Leviticus*. Translated by Gary Wayne Barkley. Washington, DC: Catholic University of America Press, 1990.

———. *Homilies on Genesis*. Translated by Ronald E. Heine. Washington, DC: Catholic University of American Press, 1981.

Peter the Lombard. *Sentences*. Translated by Giulio Silano. Toronto: Pontifical Institute of Mediaeval Studies, 2010.

Philoponus. *Against Proclus*. Translated by Michael Share. London: Bloomsbury, 2004.

Plato. *Phaedrus*. Translated by Harold N. Fowler. Cambridge, MA: Harvard University Press, 1925.

———. *Phaedo*. Translated by Benjamin Jowett. Amherst: Prometheus, 1988.

———. *Timaeus*. Translated by R. G. Bury. Cambridge, MA: Harvard University Press, 1929.

———. *Sophist*. Translated by Christopher Rowe. Cambridge: Cambridge University Press, 2015.

Plotinus. *Enneads*. Translated by Lloyd P. Gerson. Cambridge: Cambridge University Press, 2019.

SECONDARY SOURCES

Acar, Rahim. *Talking about God and Talking about Creation: Avicenna's and Thomas Aquinas's Positions*. Leiden: Brill, 2005.

Albright, William Foxwell. *From the Stone Age to Christianity: Monotheism and the Historical Process*. Baltimore: Johns Hopkins, 1940.

———. "Contributions to Biblical Archaeology and Philology," *JBL* 43, nos. 3/4 (1924): 370-8.

Alexopoulos, Theodoros. "The Problem of the Distinction between Essence and Energies in the Hesychast Controversy. Saint Gregory Palamas' *Epistula III*: The Version Published by P. Chrestou in Light of Palamas' Other Works on the Divine Energies," *Studia Patristica* 96 (2017): 521-33.

Allen, Michael. "Exodus 3 after the Hellenization Thesis," *Journal of Theological Interpretation* 3, no. 2 (2009): 179-96.

Anatolios, Khaled. "Personhood, Communion, and Trinity in Some Patristic Texts," in Anatolios, ed., *The Holy Trinity in the Life of the Church*. Grand Rapids: Baker, 2014.

Anscombe, Elizabeth. "A New Theory of Forms," *The Monist* 50, no. 3 (1966): 403-20.

Athanasopoulos, C. and Schneider, C., eds., *Divine Essence and Divine Energies: Ecumenical Reflections on the Presence of God in Eastern Orthodoxy*. Cambridge: James Clarke, 2013.

Ayres, Lewis. *Nicaea and Its Legacy: An Approach to Fourth-Century Trinitarian Theology*. Oxford: Oxford University Press, 2007.

Ball, David Mark. *I Am in John's Gospel: Literary Function, Background & Theological Implications*. JSNT Supplement Series. London: Continuum, 1996.

von Balthasar, Hans Urs. *The Glory of the Lord: A Theological Aesthetics, Volume 1: Seeing the Form*. San Francisco: Ignatius, 1983.

———. *Theo-Logic: Theological Logical Theory, Volume II: The Truth of God*. Translated by Adrian J. Walker; San Francisco: Ignatius, 2004.

Barfield, Raymond. *The Ancient Quarrel Between Philosophy and Poetry*. Cambridge: Cambridge University Press, 2011.

Barrett, Jordan P. *Divine Simplicity: A Biblical and Trinitarian Account*. Minneapolis: Fortress, 2017.

Barth, Karl. *Church Dogmatics, I.1: Doctrine of the Word of God*. Translated by Geoffrey Bromiley. London: T&T Clark, 2004.

———. *Church Dogmatics, I/1, Sections 8-12: The Doctrine of the Word of God*. Translated by Geoffrey Bromiley, et al. London: T&T Clark, 2010.

———. *Church Dogmatics, 3.1: The Doctrine of Creation*. Translated by Geoffrey Bromiley and T. F. Torrance. London: T&T Clark, 2010.

Bates, Matthew. *The Birth of the Trinity: Jesus, God, and the Spirit in the New Testament and Early Christian Interpretations of the Old Testament*. Oxford: Oxford University Press, 2016.

Batnitzky, Leora. *Idolatry and Representation: The Philosophy of Franz Rosenzweig Reconsidered*. Princeton: Princeton University Press, 2000.

Bauerschmidt, Frederick. *Thomas Aquinas: Faith, Reason, and Following Christ*. Oxford: Oxford University Press, 2013.

Bavinck, Herman. *Reformed Dogmatics, Volume 2: God and Creation*. Translated by John Vriend; edited by John Bolt. Grand Rapids: Baker, 2004.

Beauchamp, Paul. *Creation et separation: Etude exegetique du chapitre premier de la Genese*. Paris: Cerf, 2010.

Begbie, Jeremy. *Theology, Music, and Time*. Cambridge: Cambridge University Press, 2000.

―――. *Redeeming Transcendence in the Arts: Bearing Witness to the Triune God*. Grand Rapids: Eerdmans, 2018.

Bejon, James. "YHWH, the Exodus, and the Number 26," Thoughts on Scripture, posted November 3, 2021, https://jamesbejon.substack.com/p /yhwh-the-exodus-and-the-number-26.

Ben-Sasson, Hillel. *Understanding YHWH: The Name of God in Biblical, Rabbinic, and Medieval Jewish Thought*. New York: Palgrave Macmillan, 2019.

Betz, John R. "Enlightenment Revisited: Hamann as the First and Best Critic of Kant's Philosophy," *Modern Theology* 20, no. 2 (2004): 291-301.

Blenkinsopp, Joseph. *Creation, Un-Creation, Re-Creation: A Discursive Commentary on Genesis 1-11*. London: T&T Clark 2011.

Blocher, Henri. *In the Beginning: The Opening Chapters of Genesis*. Downers Grove, IL: InterVarsity Press, 1984.

Blondel, Maurice. *Action: Essay on a Critique of Life and a Science of Practice*. Translated by Oliva Blanchette. Notre Dame: University of Notre Dame Press, 1984.

Bonhoeffer, Dietrich. *Creation and Fall*. Dietrich Bonhoeffer Works, 3. Translated by Douglas Stephen Bax. Minneapolis: Fortress, 2004.

Borgen, Peder. "Logos Was the True Light: Contributions to the Interpretation of the Prologue of John," *Novum Testamentum* 14, no. 2 (1972): 115-130.

Botterweck, G. Johannes, et al., eds., *Theological Dictionary of the Old Testament*. 15 volumes. Grand Rapids: Eerdmans, 2011.

Bowyer, Gerald. "Elohim's Dynasty: Kingdom and Co-Regency in the Hebrew Text of Genesis 1-3." Unpublished Licentiate Thesis, Collegium Augustianum, 2016.

Boys-Stones, G. R. and Haubold, J. K., eds., *Plato and Hesiod*. Oxford: Oxford University Press, 2010.

Bradshaw, David. *Aristotle East and West: Metaphysics and the Division of Christendom*. Cambridge: Cambridge University Press, 2007.

―――. "The Divine Glory and the Divine Energies," *Faith and Philosophy* 23, no. 3 (2006): 279-98.

Brann, Eva. *The Logos of Heraclitus*. Philadelphia: Paul Dry Books, 2011.

―――. *The Music of the Republic: Essays on Socrates' Conversations and Plato's Writings*. Philadelphia: Paul Dry Books, 2011.

Brisson, Luc. *How the Philosophers Saved Myths: Allegorical Interpretation and Classical Mythology*. Translated by Catherine Tihanyi. Chicago: University of Chicago Press, 2004.

———. *Plato the Myth Maker*. Translated by Gerard Naddaf. Chicago: University of Chicago Press, 1998.

———. "Why Is the Timaeus Called *Eikôs Mythos and Eikôs Logos*?" in Collobert, et al., eds., *Plato and Myth*.

Broadie, Sarah. Nature and Divinity in Plato's Timaeus. Cambridge: Cambridge University Press, 2011.

———. "Theological Sidelights from Plato's Timaeus," *Proceedings of the Aristotelian Society* 82 (2008): 1-17.

Brunn, Emilie Zum. *St. Augustine: Being and Nothingness*. New York: Paragon, 1988.

Bulgakov, Sergius. *The Lamb of God*. Translated by Boris Jakim. Grand Rapids: Eerdmans, 2008.

———. *Sophia, The Wisdom of God: An Outline of Sophiology*. Hudson, NY: Lindisfarne Press, 1993.

———. *The Tragedy of Philosophy: Philosophy and Dogma*. Translated by Stephen Churchyard. Brooklyn, NY: Angelico Press, 2020.

———. *Unfading Light: Contemplations and Speculations*. Translated by Thomas Allan Smith. Grand Rapids: Eerdmans, 2012.

Bulzan, Daniel. "Apophaticism, Postmodernism and Language: Two Similar Cases of Theological Imbalance," *Scottish Journal of Theology* 50, no. 3 (1997): 261-87.

Burnett, Joel S. *A Reassessment of Biblical Elohim*. SBL Dissertation Series 183. Atlanta: Society of Biblical Literature, 2001.

Burney, C. F. "Christ as the arche of Creation," *Journal of Theological Studies* 16 (1965): 160-76.

Burrell, David B. *Aquinas: God and Action*. Third edition. Eugene, OR: Wipf & Stock, 2016.

———. *Freedom and Creation in Three Traditions*. Notre Dame: Notre Dame University Press, 1993.

———. *Exercises in Religious Understanding*. Notre Dame: University of Notre Dame Press, 1974.

Burkert, Walter. *The Orientalizing Revolution: Near Eastern Influence on Greek Culture in the Early Archaic Age*. Cambridge, MA: Harvard University Press, 1998.

———. "Logic of Cosmogony" in Buxton, ed., *From Myth to Reason? Studies in the Development of Greek Thought*.

Buxton, R. G. A., ed. *From Myth to Reason? Studies in the Development of Greek Thought*. Oxford: Clarendon Press, 1999.

Capra, Andrea. "Plato's Hesiod and the Will of Zeus: Philosophical Rhapsody in the *Timaeus* and the *Critias*," in Boys-Stones and Haubold, eds., *Plato and Hesiod*.

Carone, Gabriela Roxana. "Creation in the Timaeus: The Middle Way," *Apeiron* 37 (2004): 211-26.

Cassuto, Umberto. *A Commentary on the Book of Genesis, Part I: From Adam to Noah*. Skokie, IL: Varda Books, 2005.

Chambers, Nathan J. *Reconsidering Creation Ex Nihilo in Genesis 1*. Journal of Theological Interpretation Supplement #19. University Park, PA: Eisenbrauns, 2020.

Clarke, W. Norris. *Explorations in Metaphysics: Being God Person*. Notre Dame: Notre Dame University Press, 1994.

Clines, D. J. A. "The Image of God in Man," *Tyndale Bulletin* 19 (1968): 53-103.

Clouser, Roy. "Pancreation Lost: The Fall of Theology," in Athanasopoulos and Schneider, eds., *Divine Essence and Divine Energies: Ecumenical Reflections on the Presence of God in Eastern Orthodoxy*.

Coda, Piero. *From the Trinity: The Coming of God in Revelation and Theology*. Washington, DC: Catholic University of America Press, 2020.

Coda, Piero. *Ontologie trinitaire: Penser et vivre à la lumière de la Trinité*. Bruyères-le-Châtel: Nouvelle Cité, 2020.

Cohoe, Caleb. "Why the One Cannot Have Parts," *Philosophical Quarterly* 67 (2017): 751-71.

Collins, C. John. *Genesis 1-4: A Linguistic, Literary, and Theological Commentary*. Phillipsburg, NJ: P&R, 2006.

Collobert, Catherine, et al., eds. *Plato and Myth: Studies on the Use and Status of Platonic Myths*. Leiden: Brill, 2010.

Coope, Ursula. *Time for Aristotle: Physics IV, 10-14*. Oxford: Oxford University Press, 2005.

Cooper, David L. *The God of Israel*. Los Angeles: Biblical Research Society, 1973.

Cornford, Francis. *Plato and Parmenides*. London: Kegan, Paul, Trench, Trubner, & Co., 1939.

———. *Plato's Cosmology: The Timaeus of Plato*. Indianapolis: Hackett, [1937] 1997.

———. *Principium Sapientiae: A Study of the Origins of Greek Philosophical Thought*. Edited by W.K. Guthrie. New York: Harper, 1965.

———. *From Religion to Philosophy: A Study in the Origins of Western Speculation*. Minneola, NY: Dover, [1957] 2004.

Darshan, Guy. "Ruah 'Elohim in Genesis 1:2 in Light of Phoenician Cosmogonies: A Tradition's History," *Journal of Northwest Semitic Languages* 45, no. 2 (2019): 51-78.

de Lubac, Henri. *Mediaeval Exegesis: The Four Senses of Scripture, Volume 1.* Grand Rapids: Eerdmans, 1998.

Desmond, William. *Art, Origins, Otherness: Between Philosophy and Art.* Albany, NY: SUNY Press, 2003.

———. *Being and the Between.* Albany, NY: SUNY Press, 1995.

Detienne, Marcel and Vernant, Jean-Pierre. *The Cuisine of Sacrifice Among the Greeks.* Chicago: University of Chicago Press, 1986.

Dolezal, James E. *All That Is in God: Evangelical Theology and the Challenge of Classical Christian Theism.* Grand Rapids: Reformation Heritage Books, 2017.

———. *God Without Parts: Divine Simplicity and the Metaphysics of God's Absoluteness.* Eugene, OR: Pickwick, 2011.

Dolin, Jr., Edwin F. "Parmenides and Hesiod," *Harvard Studies in Classical Philology* 66 (1962): 93-98.

Dorner, Isaak Augustus. *Divine Immutability: A Critical Reconsideration.* Translated by Robert R. Williams and Claude Welch. Minneapolis: Fortress, 1994.

Drozdek, Adam. *Greek Philosophers as Theologians: The Divine Arche.* London: Routledge, 2007.

Duarte, Shane. "Aristotle's Theology and its Relation to the Science of Being qua Being," *Apeiron* 40, no. 3 (2007): 267-318.

Duby, Steven J. *Divine Simplicity: A Dogmatic Account.* London: T&T Clark, 2016.

———. *God in Himself: Scripture, Metaphysics, and the Task of Christian Theology.* Downers Grove, IL: InterVarsity, 2019.

Dunham, Scott. *The Trinity and Creation in Augustine: An Ecological Analysis.* Albany, NY: SUNY Press, 2008.

Eskhult, Josef. "Augustine and the Primeval Language in Early Modern Exegesis and Philology," *Language and History* 56, no. 2 (2013): 98-119.

Feinberg, John. *No One Like Him: The Doctrine of God.* Wheaton, IL: Crossway, 2006.

Fornari, Guiseppe. *Dionysus, Christ, and the Death of God, Volume I: The Great Mediations of the Classical World.* East Lansing: Michigan State University Press, 2021.

Frame, John. *Doctrine of God. A Theology of Lordship.* Phillipsburg, NJ: P&R, 2002.

———. "God and Biblical Language: Transcendence and Immanence," in Montgomery, John W., ed., *God's Inerrant Word*. Minneapolis: Bethany House Fellowship, 1974.

Frankfort, Henri. *The Intellectual Adventure of Ancient Man: An Essay on Speculative Thought in the Ancient Near East*. Chicago: University of Chicago Press, 1946.

Freedman, David Noel. "The Name of the God of Moses," *JBL* 79, no. 2 (1960): 151-6.

Gallaher, Brandon. *Freedom and Necessity in Modern Trinitarian Theology*. Oxford: Oxford University Press, 2016.

Garr, Randall. *In His Own Image and Likeness: Humanity, Divinity, and Monotheism*. Leiden: Brill, 2003.

Gavrilyuk, Paul. "Plotinus on Divine Simplicity," *Modern Theology* 35, no. 3 (2019): 442-51.

Gerson, Lloyd. *God and Greek Philosophy*. London: Routledge, 1994.

———. *Plotinus*. London: Routledge, 1994.

———. "Plotinus' Metaphysics: Emanation or Creation?" *Review of Metaphysics* 46, no. 3 (1993): 559-74.

Gigon, Olof. *Der Ursprung Der griechischen Philosophie: Von Hesiod bis Parmenides*. Basel: Benno Schwabe, 1945.

Gilson, Etienne. *Being and Some Philosophers*. Second edition. Toronto: Pontifical Institute of Medieval Studies, 1952.

———. *The Christian Philosophy of Thomas Aquinas*. Notre Dame: Notre Dame University Press, 1994.

———. "Maimonide et la Philosophie de l'Exode," *Mediaeval Studies* 13 (1951): 223-225.

———. *The Spirit of Mediaeval Philosophy*. New York: Charles Scribner's, 1940.

Goia, Ted. *Music: A Subversive History*. New York: Basic Books, 2019.

Goldingay, John. *Genesis*. Baker Commentary on the Old Testament Pentateuch. Grand Rapids: Baker, 2020.

Grasso, Elsa. "Myth, Image and Likeness in Plato's *Timaeus*" in Catherine Collobert, et al., eds., *Plato and Myth*.

Griffith, Paul. *Decreation: The Last Things of All Creatures*. Waco, TX: Baylor University Press, 2014.

Gunton, Colin. *Becoming and Being*. Eugene, OR: Wipf & Stock, 2001.

Hadot, Pierre. *Plotinus, or, The Simplicity of Vision*. Chicago: University of Chicago Press, 1998.

———. *What Is Ancient Philosophy?* Translated by Michael Chase. Cambridge, MA: Belknap Press, 2004.

Haecker, Ryan. "Splitting the Difference: Contradiction and the Trinity in Plato's 'Sophist,'" *Macrina Magazine*, January 15, 2022, available at https://macrinamagazine.com/issue-9-contradiction/guest/2022/01/15/splitting-the-difference-contradiction-and-the-trinity-in-platos-sophist.

Halbertal, Moshe and Margalit, Avishai. *Idolatry*. Translated by Naomi Goldblum. Cambridge, MA: Harvard University Press, 1994.

Hamann, J. G. *Aesthetica in nuce,* in Kenneth Haynes, ed. *Hamann: Writings on Philosophy and Language*. Cambridge: Cambridge University Press, 2007.

Hamilton, Victor. *The Book of Genesis, Chapters 1-17*. NICOT. Grand Rapids: Eerdmans, 1990.

———. *Exodus: An Exegetical Commentary*. Grand Rapids: Baker, 2011.

Hankey, Wayne. *God in Himself: Aquinas' Doctrine of God as Expounded in the Summa theologiae*. Oxford: Oxford University Press, 2004.

Harrison, Carol. *Rethinking Augustine's Early Theology: An Argument for Continuity*. New York: Oxford University Press, 2008.

Hart, David Bentley. *The Beauty of the Infinite: The Aesthetics of Christian Truth*. Grand Rapids: Eerdmans, 2004.

———. "Christ and Nothing," *First Things* (October 2003).

———. *Experience of God: Being, Consciousness, Bliss*. New Haven: Yale, 2016.

———. *The Hidden and the Manifest: Essays in Theology and Metaphysics*. Grand Rapids: Eerdmans, 2017.

———. "Providence and Causality: Divine Innocence," in Francesca Aran Murphy and Philip G. Ziegler, eds. *The Providence of God*. London: T&T Clark, 2009.

———. *You Are Gods: On Nature and Supernature*. Notre Dame: University of Notre Dame Press, 2022.

Hartshorne, Charles. *The Divine Relativity: A Social Conception of God*. New Haven: Yale, 1967.

Hasel, Gerhard. "The Meaning of 'Let Us' in Gn 1:26," *AUSS* 13, no. 1 (1975): 58-66.

———. "The 'Days' of Creation in Genesis 1: Literal 'Days' or Figurative 'Periods/Epochs' of Time?" *Origins* 21, no. 1 (1994): 5-38.

Haupt, Paul. "Der Name Jahwe," *Orientalistische Literaturzeitung* 5 (1909): 211-14.

Havelock, Eric A. "Parmenides and Odysseus," *Harvard Studies in Classical Philology* 63 (1958): 133-43

Hazony, Yoram. *The Philosophy of Hebrew Scripture*. Cambridge: Cambridge University Press, 2012.

Hector, Kevin. "Apophaticism in Thomas Aquinas: A Re-Formulation and Recommendation," *Scottish Journal of Theology* 60, no. 4 (2007): 377-93.

Hemmerle, Klaus. *Theses Towards a Trinitarian Ontology*. Brooklyn, NY: Angelico Press, 2020.

Henninger, Mark Gerald. "Aquinas on the Ontological Status of Relations," *Journal of the History of Philosophy* 24, no. 4 (1987): 491-515.

———. *Relations: Medieval Theories 1250-1325*. Oxford: Clarendon Press, 1989.

Herder, J. G. *The Spirit of Hebrew Poetry*. Two Volumes. Translated by James Marsh. Burlington: Edward Sith, 1833.

den Hertog, Cornelis. *The Other Face of God: "I Am That I Am" Reconsidered*. Sheffield: Sheffield Academic Press, 2012.

Hinlicky, Paul. *Divine Complexity: The Rise of Creedal Christianity*. Minneapolis: Fortress, 2011.

———. *Divine Simplicity: Christ the Crisis of Metaphysics*. Grand Rapid: Baker, 2016.

Hodge, B. C. *Revisiting the Days of Genesis: A Study of the Use of Time in Light of Its Ancient Near Eastern and Literary Context*. Eugene, OR: Wipf & Stock, 2011.

Howell, Brian. *In the Eyes of God: A Contextual Approach to Biblical Anthropomorphic Metaphors*. Eugene, OR: Pickwick, 2013.

Howland, Jacob. *The Republic: The Odyssey of Philosophy*. Toronto: Twayne, 1993.

Jenson, Robert W. *The Knowledge of Things Hoped For: The Sense of Theological Discourse*. Eugene, OR: Wipf & Stock, 1969.

———. "Once More the *Logos asarkos*," *International Journal of Systematic Theology* 13, no. 2 (2011): 130-3.

———. *Systematic Theology, Volume 1: The Triune God*. Oxford: Oxford University Press, 1997.

———. *Systematic Theology II: The Works of God*. Oxford: Oxford University Press, 1999.

———. *Theology as Revisionary Metaphysics: Essays on God and Creation*. Eugene, OR: Cascade, 2014.

———. "The Triune God," in Braaten, Carl E. and Jenson, Robert W. eds. *Christian Dogmatics, Vol. 1*. Minneapolis: Fortress, 2011.

Johnson, Dru. *Biblical Philosophy*. Cambridge: Cambridge University Press, 2021.

Johnson, Jeffery D. *The Failure of Natural Theology: A Critical Appraisal of the Philosophical Theology of Thomas Aquinas*. Conway, AR: Free Grace Press, 2021.

Jordan, James B. *Creation in Six Days: A Defense of the Traditional Reading of Genesis 1*. Moscow, ID: Canon Press, 1999.

———. *From Bread to Wine: Creation, Worship, and Christian Maturity*. Monroe, LA: Athanasius Press, 2019.

Keller, Catherine. *The Face of the Deep: A Theology of Becoming*. London: Routledge, 2002.

Keller, Evelyn Fox. *A Feeling for the Organism*. New York: Times Books, 1984.

Kerr, Fergus. "God in the Summa theologiae: Entity or Event," in Hackett, Jeremiah and Wallulis, Jerald, eds. *Philosophy of Religion for a New Century: Essays in Honor of Eugene Thomas Long*. Dordrecht: Springer, 2004.

Kilby, Karen. "Aquinas, the Trinity and the Limits of Understanding," *International Journal of Systematic Theology* 7, no. 4 (2005): 414-27.

Kingsmill, Edmee. *The Song of Songs and the Eros of God: A Study in Biblical Intertextuality*. Oxford: Oxford University Press, 2010.

Kline, Meredith. "Because It Had Not Rained," *Westminster Theological Journal* 20 (1958): 146-57.

———. *God, Heaven, and Har Magedon: A Covenantal Tale of Cosmos and Telos*. Eugene, OR: Wipf & Stock, 2006.

———. *Images of the Spirit*. Eugene, OR: Wipf & Stock, 1999.

———. "Primal Parousia," available at https://meredithkline.com/klines-works/articles-and-essays/primal-parousia/.

Knoll, Manuel. *Antike griechische Philosophie*. Berlin: De Gruyter, 2017.

Kou, Christopher. "God's Statue in the Cosmic Temple: *Tzelem* and *Demut* in Genesis and the First Person Plural Cohortative of Gen 1:26 in Light of Sanctuary Setting and Christological Telos," *Journal of the Evangelical Theological Society* 66.1 (2023): 11-31.

Labuschagne, Caspar J. *Numerical Secrets of the Bible: An Introduction to Biblical Arithmology*. Eugene, OR: Wipf & Stock, 2016.

———. *Numerical Features of the Psalms and Other Selected Texts*. Available at www.labuschagne.nl/psalms.htm/.

LaCocque, Andre and Ricoeur, Paul. *Thinking Biblically: Exegetical and Hermeneutical Studies*. Chicago: University of Chicago Press, 1998.

Lakoff, George and Johnson, Mark. *Metaphors We Live By*. Chicago: University of Chicago Press, 2003.

———. *Philosophy in the Flesh: The Embodied Mind and its Challenge to Western Thought*. New York: Basic Books, 1999.

Leithart, Peter J. *Deep Comedy: Trinity, Tragedy, and Hope in Western Literature*. Moscow, ID: Canon Press, 2006.

―――. *The Ten Commandments: A Guide to the Perfect Law of Liberty*. Bellingham, WA: Lexham Press, 2020.

―――. *Traces of the Trinity*. Grand Rapids: Baker, 2015.

―――. *Revelation 1-11*. International Theological Commentary. London: T&T Clark, 2018.

Letham, Robert. "'In the Space of Six Days': The Days of Creation from Origen to the Westminster Assembly," *Westminster Theological Journal* 61 (1999): 149-74.

Levering, Matthew. *Engaging the Doctrine of Creation: Cosmos, Creatures, and the Wise and Good Creator*. Grand Rapids: Baker, 2017.

―――. "Contemplating God: YHWH and Being in the Theology of St. Thomas Aquinas," *Irish Theological Quarterly* 67 (2002): 17-31.

Lindbeck, George. *The Nature of Doctrine: Religion and Theology in a Postliberal Age*. 25th anniversary ed. Louisville, KY: Westminster John Knox, 2009.

Lloyd, G. E. R. *Polarity and Analogy: Two Types of Argumentation in Early Greek Thought*. Indianapolis: Hackett, 1992.

Loewen, Jacob. "Clear Air or Bad Breath?," *The Bible Translator* 34, no. 2 (1997): 213-9.

Long, D. Stephen. *The Perfectly Simple Triune God: Aquinas and His Legacy*. Minneapolis: Fortress, 2016.

Lundin, Roger et al. *The Promise of Hermeneutics*. Grand Rapids: Eerdmans, 1999.

Luyster, R. "Wind and Water: Cosmogonic Symbolism in the Old Testament," *ZAW* 93 (1981): 1-10.

Markos, Louis. *From Plato to Christ: How Platonic Thought Shaped the Christian Faith*. Downers Grove, IL: InterVarsity, 2021.

Marion, Jean-Luc. *Being Given: Toward a Phenomenology of Givenness*. Stanford: Stanford University Press, 2002.

―――. *In the Self's Place: The Approach of Saint Augustine*. Stanford, CA: Stanford University Press, 2012.

Martin, Jennifer Newsome. *Hans Urs von Balthasar and the Critical Appropriation of Russian Religious Thought*. Notre Dame: University of Notre Dame Press, 2015.

Maspero, Giulio, "Life as Relation: Classical Metaphysics and Trinitarian Ontology," *Theological Research* 2 (2014): 31-52.

McCabe, Herbert. *God Still Matters*. London: Continuum, 2005.

McCabe, Robert V. "A Defense of Literal Days in the Creation Week," *Detroit Baptist Seminary Journal* 5 (2000): 97-123.

McClellan, William. "The Meaning of *Ruah 'Elohim* in Genesis 1, 2," *Biblica* 15, no. 4 (1934): 517-27.

McCormack, Bruce. *The Humility of the Eternal Son: Reformed Kenoticism and the Repair of Chalcedon*. Cambridge; Cambridge University Press, 2021.

McEvilley, Thomas. *The Shape of Ancient Thought: Comparative Studies in Greek and Indian Thought*. New York: Allworth Press, 2002.

McIntosh, Jonathan. "Speaking of Possibilities: The Theistic Actualize of Anselm's Divine *Locutio*," *Modern Theology* 33, no. 2 (2017): 213-34.

McTaggart, J. Ellis. "The Unreality of Time," *Mind* 17 (1908): 457-73.

McWhorter, Matthew R. "Aquinas on God's Relation to the World," *New Blackfriars* 94 (2012): 1-17.

Meek, Esther. *Loving to Know: Covenant Epistemology*. Eugene, OR: Cascade, 2011.

Merkle, Benjamin R. *Defending the Trinity in the Reformed Palatinate: The Elohistae*. Oxford Theology and Religion Monographs. Oxford: Oxford University Press, 2016.

Middleton, Richard. "Creation Founded in Love: Breaking Rhetorical Expectations in Genesis 1:1-2:3," in Greenspoon, Leonard Jay and LeBeau, Bryan F. eds. *Sacred Text, Sacred Times: The Hebrew Bible in the Modern World*. Studies in Jewish Civilization 10. Omaha, NE: Creighton University Press, 2000.

van de Mieroop, Marc. *Philosophy Before the Greeks: The Pursuit of Truth in Ancient Babylonia*. Princeton: Princeton University Press, 2016.

Milbank, John and Pickstock, Catherine. *Truth in Aquinas*. London: Routledge, 2001.

Milbank, John. *Theology and Social Theory: Beyond Secular Reason*. Oxford: Blackwell, 1990.

———. *Word Made Strange: Theology, Language, Culture*. Oxford: Blackwell, 1997.

———. "Christianity and Platonism in East and West," in Athanasopoulos and Schneider, eds. *Divine Essence and Divine Energies: Ecumenical Reflections on the Presence of God in Eastern Orthodoxy*.

———. "The Confession of Time in Augustine" *Maynooth Philosophical Papers* (2020).

Morales, L. Michael. *The Tabernacle Pre-Figured: Cosmic Mountain Ideology in Genesis and Exodus*. Leuven: Peeters, 2012.

Most, Glenn. "From Logos to Mythos," in Buxton, ed., *From Myth to Reason? Studies in the Development of Greek Thought*.

Mourelatos, A. P. D. "Heraclitus, Parmenides, and the Naive Metaphysics of Things," in Lee, E. N., et al., eds. *Exegesis and Argument: Studies in Greek Philosophy Presented to Gregory Vlastos*. Phronesis suppl. 1. New York: Humanities Press, 1973.

Muller, Richard. *Post-Reformation Reformed Dogmatics, Volume 4: The Triunity of God*. Grand Rapids: Baker, 2003.

Mullins, R. T. "Divine Perfection and Creation," *Heythrop Journal* 57 (2016): 122-34.

——. *The End of the Timeless God*. Oxford: Oxford University Press, 2016.

——. "Is God the Prisoner of Time? Yeah, but so What?" *Journal of Analytic Theology* 2 (2014): 160-85.

——. "Simply Impossible: A Case against Divine Simplicity," *Journal of Reformed Theology* 7 (2013): 181-203.

Nichols, Aidan. "Wisdom from Above? The Sophiology of Father Sergius Bulgakov," *New Blackfriars* 85 (2004): 598-613.

Northrup, Mark D. "Hesiodic Personifications in Parmenides A 37," *Transactions of the American Philosophical Association* 110 (1980): 223-32.

Nyierenda, Mischeck. "Theological Interpretation and Translation Reception: Translating 'Spirit of God' in Genesis 1.1-2," *The Bible Translator* 64, no. 3 (2013): 284-99.

Oliver, Simon. *Creation: A Guide for the Perplexed*. London: Bloomsbury, 2017.

——. *Philosophy, God, and Motion*. London: Routledge, 2013.

Orlinsky, H. M. "The Plain Meaning of Ruah in Gen. 1.2," *Jewish Quarterly Review* 48 (1957/58): 174-82.

Ortiz, Jared. "You Made Us For Yourself": *Creation in St. Augustine's Confessions*. Minneapolis: Fortress Press, 2016.

Ortlund, Gavin. *Retrieving Augustine's Doctrine of Creation: Ancient Wisdom for Current Controversy*. Downers Grove, IL: IVP, 2020.

Owens, Joseph. "The Conclusion of the Prima Via," in Catan, John R., ed. *St. Thomas Aquinas on the Existence of God: The Collected Papers of Joseph Owens*. Albany, NY: SUNY Press, 1980.

Pabst, Adrian. *Metaphysics: The Creation of Hierarchy*. Grand Rapids: Eerdmans, 2012.

Pannenberg, Wolfhart. *Systematic Theology, Volume 2*. Translated by Geoffrey W. Bromiley. London: T&T Clark, 2004.

Papankolaou, Aristotle. "Divine Energies or Divine Personhood: Vladimir Lossky and John Zizioulas on Conceiving the Transcendent and Immanent God," *Modern Theology* 19, no. 3 (2003): 357-85.

Parvan, Alexandra and McCormack, Bruce L. "Immutability, (Im)passibility and Suffering: Steps towards a 'Psychological' Ontology of God," *NZSTh* 59, no. 1 (2017): 1-25.

Pavlos, Panagiotis. "Christian Insights into Plotinus' Metaphysics and His Concept of Aptitude (*elitedeiotes*)," *Akropolis* 1 (2017): 5-32.

Pegis, Anton C. "The Dilemma of Being and Unity," in Brennan, Robert ed. *Essays in Thomism*. Eugene, OR: Wipf & Stock, (1942) 2014.

———. *Saint Thomas and the Greeks*. Milwaukee, WI: Marquette University Press, 1939.

Pellikaan-Engel, Maja E. *Hesiod and Parmenides: A New View on their Cosmogonies and on Parmenides' Proem*. Amsterdam: Hakkert, 1978.

Pender, E. E. "Chaos Corrected: Hesiod in Plato's Creation Myth," in Boys-Stones and Haubold, eds., *Plato and Hesiod*.

Perl, Eric. *Thinking Being: Introduction to Metaphysics in the Classical Tradition*. Leiden: Brill, 2014.

Pieper, Josef. *The Silence of St. Thomas Aquinas*. Translated by John Murray and Daniel O'Connor. South Bend, IN: St. Augustine's Press, 1957.

Plantinga, Alvin. "Actualism and Possible Worlds," *Theoria* 42, nos. 1-3 (1976): 139-60.

Polanyi, Michael. *Personal Knowledge: Towards a Post-Critical Philosophy*. Chicago: University of Chicago Press, (1958) 2015.

Polkinghorne, John. *Science and the Trinity: The Christian Encounter with Reality*. New Haven: Yale, 2004.

Poythress, Vern. *Interpreting Eden: A Guide to Faithfully Reading and Understanding Genesis 1-3*. Wheaton, IL: Crossway, 2019.

———. *The Mystery of the Trinity: A Trinitarian Approach to the Attributes of God*. Phillipsburg, NJ: P&R, 2020.

Platter, Jonathan Marc. *Divine Simplicity and the Triune Identity: A Critical Dialogue with the Theological Metaphysics of Robert W. Jenson*. PhD, University of Cambridge, 2020.

Preller, Victor. *Divine Science and the Science of God: A Reformulation of Thomas Aquinas*. Princeton: Princeton University Press, 1967.

Prior, William J. "The Concept of Paradeigma in Plato's Theory of Forms," *Apeiron* 17 (1983): 33-42.

Radde-Gallwitz, Andrew. *Basil of Caesarea, Gregory of Nyssa, and the Transformation of Divine Simplicity*. Oxford: Oxford University Press, 2009.

Rahner, Karl. *The Trinity*. Herder and Herder, 1997.

Ratzinger, Joseph. "Concerning the Notion of Person in Theology," *Communio* 17, no. 3 (1990): 439-54.

Rigali, Mario. "Hesiod in the Timaeus: The Demiurge Addresses the Gods," in Boys-Stones and Haubold, eds., *Plato and Hesiod*.

Roberts, Michael B. "Geology and Genesis Unearthed," *Churchman* 112 (1998): 225-55.

Roecklein, Robert. *Plato versus Parmenides: The Debate over Coming-into-Being in Greek Philosophy*. Lanham: Lexington Books, 2011.

Rosenstock-Huessy, Eugen. "Time-Bettering Days," *Rosenstock-Huessy Papers, Volume 1*. Norwich, VT: Argo, 1981.

Rosenzweig, Franz. *Kleinere Schriften*. Berlin: Schocken, 1937.

Rosmini, Antonio. *Theosophy, Volume 3: Trine Being (Contd.)*. Durham: Rosmini House, 2011.

Ross, James F. "God, Creator of Kinds and Possibilities: Requiescant universalia ante res," in Audi, Robert and Wainwright, William J., eds. *Rationality, Religious Beliefs, and Moral Commitment: New Essays in the Philosophy of Religion*. Ithaca, NY: Cornell University Press, 1986.

Rudd, Steven. "Jesus Echoes the 'I AM' statements of Jehovah in the Gospel of John." Available at https://www.bible.ca/trinity/trinity-i-am.htm.

Rutherford, R.B. *The Art of Plato: Ten Essays in Platonic Interpretation*. Cambridge, MA: Harvard University Press, 1995.

Saner, Andrea Dalton. *YHWH, the Trinity, and the Literal Sense: Theological Interpretation of Exodus 3:13-15*. PhD thesis, Durham University, 2013.

Schafer, A. Rahel Davidson. "The 'Kinds' of Genesis 1: What is the Meaning of *Min*?" *Journal of the Adventist Theological Society* 14, no. 1 (2003): 86-100.

Schaffer, Jonathan. "Monism: The Priority of the Whole," *Philosophical Review* 119, no. 1 (2010): 31-76.

Schindler, D. C. *A Companion to Ferdinand Ulrich's Homo Abyssus*. Washington, DC: Humanum Academic Press, 2019.

———. "Mediation: The Distinguishing Mark of Christianity," *Communio* 48 (2021): 6-29.

———. "The Redemption of Eros: Philosophical Reflections on Benedict XVI's First Encyclical," *Communio* 33 (2006): 375-99.

Schindler, David L. *The Generosity of Creation*. Washington, DC: Humanum Academic Press, 2018.

Schmitz, Kenneth. *The Gift: Creation*. Milwaukee, WI: Marquette University Press, 1982.

Schwöbel, Christoph. "The Eternity of the Triune God: Preliminary Considerations on the Relationship between the Trinity and the Time of Creation," *Modern Theology* 34, no. 3 (2018): 345-55.

Scolnicov, Samuel. *Plato's Parmenides*. Berkeley: University of California Press, 2003.

Sedley, David. *Creationism and Its Critics in Antiquity*. Berkeley: University of California Press, 2007.

———. "Hesiod's *Theogony* and Plato's *Timaeus*," in Boys-Stones and Haubold, eds., *Plato and Hesiod*.

Shapin, Stephen. *Never Pure: Historical Studies of Science as if It Was Produced by People with Bodies, Situated in Time, Space, Culture and Society, and Struggling for Credibility and Authority*. Baltimore: Johns Hopkins University Press, 2010.

Sheldrake, Rupert. *The Science Delusion*. London: Coronet, 2012.

Slesinski, Robert F. *The Theology of Sergius Bulgakov*. Yonkers, NY: St. Vladimir's Seminary Press, 2017.

Solmsen, Friedrich. "Hesiodic Motifs in Plato," in von Fritz, Kurt, et al. *Hesiode et son influence*. Geneve: Vandoeuvres, 1960.

Sonderegger, Katherine. *Systematic Theology, Volume 1: The Doctrine of God*. Minneapolis: Fortress, 2015.

Soskice, Janet Martin. "Aquinas and Augustine on Creation and God as 'Eternal Being,'" *New Blackfriars* 95 (2014): 190-207.

Sonnet, Jean-Pierre. "*Ehyeh asher ehyeh* (Exodus 3:14): God's 'Narrative Identity' among Suspense, Curiosity, and Scripture," *Poetics Today* 31, no. 2 (2010): 331-31.

Sorabji, Richard. *Time, Creation, and the Continuum: Theories in Antiquity and the Early Middle Ages*. London: Duckworth, 2002.

Spaemann, Robert. *Essays in Anthropology: Variations on a Theme*. Eugene, OR: Cascade, 2010.

Sparks, Kenton. *Sacred Word, Broken Word: Biblical Authority and the Dark Sayings of Scripture*. Grand Rapids: Eerdmans, 2012.

Stead, Christopher. *Philosophy in Christian Antiquity*. Cambridge: Cambridge University Press, 1994.

Steinmann, Andrew E. "'*Echad* as an Ordinal Number and the Meaning of Genesis 1:5," *Journal of the Evangelical Theological Society* 45, no. 5 (2002): 577-84.

Stern, Sacha. *Time and Process in Ancient Judaism*. Oxford: Littman Library of Jewish Civilization, 2007.

Stewart, J.A. *The Myths of Plato*. London: Macmillan, 1905.

Stout, Jeffrey. *Ethics After Babel: The Languages of Morals and Their Discontents*. Princeton: Princeton University Press, 2001.

Stump, Eleonore and Kretzmann, Norman. "Absolute Simplicity," *Faith and Philosophy* 2, no. 4 (1985): 353-82.

Surls, Austin. *Making Sense of the Divine Name in the Book of Exodus: From Etymology to Literary Onomastic*. PhD dissertation, Wheaton College, 2015.

Thom, Paul. *Logic of the Trinity: Augustine to Ockham*. New York: Fordham University Press, 2012.

Torrance, T. F. *The Christian Doctrine of God*. London: T&T Clark, 1996.

Traherne, Thomas. *Centuries of Meditation*. Edited by Bertram Dobell. New York: Cosmo Classics, 2007.

Tran, Jonathan. "Linguistic Theology: Completing Postliberalism's Linguistic Turn," *Modern Theology* 33, no. 1 (2016): 47-68.

Turescu, Lucien. *Gregory of Nyssa and the Concept of Divine Persons*. Oxford: Oxford University Press, 2005.

Turner, Denys. *The Darkness of God: Negativity in Christian Mysticism*. Cambridge: Cambridge University Press, 1998.

———. "Tradition and Faith," *International Journal of Systematic Theology* 6, no. 1 (2004): 21-36.

Ulrich, Ferdinand. *Homo Abyssus: The Drama of the Question of Being*. Translated by D. C. Schindler. Washington, DC: Humanum Academic Press, 2018.

Van Riel, Gerd. *Plato's Gods. Ashgate Studies in the History of Philosophical Theology*. London: Routledge, 2013.

Vannier, Marie-Anne. "Creatio," "Conversio," "Formatio" chez S. Augustin. Fribourg: Editions Universitaires Fribourg Suisse, 1997.

Vernant, Jean-Pierre. *Myth and Society in Ancient Greece*. Translated by Janet Lloyd. New York: Zone Books, 1990.

Vlastos, Gregory. "Creation in the Timaeus: Is it a Fiction?" in Graham, Daniel W., ed. *Studies in Greek Philosophy, Volume II: Socrates, Plato and Their Tradition*. Princeton: Princeton University Press, 1995.

———. *Plato's Universe*. Las Vegas: Parmenides Publishing, 2006.

von Rad, Gerhard. *Genesis*. Revised edition. Philadelphia: Westminster Press, 1972.

Walton, John. *The Lost World of Genesis One: Ancient Cosmology and the Origins Debate*. Downers Grove, IL: IVP Academic, 2009.

Wassmer, Thomas. "The Trinitarian Theology of Augustine and His Debt to Plotinus," *Harvard Theological Review* 53, no. 4 (1960): 261-68.

Wenham, Gordon J. *Genesis 1-15*. Word Biblical Commentary, Volume 1. Waco: Word, 1987.

West, J. L. A. "St. Augustine on Human Temporality and Divine Eternity," *Faith and Reason* 26, no. 2 (2001): 1-7.

West, M. L. *The East Face of Helicon: West Asiatic Elements in Greek Poetry and Myth*. Oxford: Clarendon, 1999.

Westermann, Claus. *Genesis 1-11*. Translated by John J. Scullian. Minneapolis: Fortress, 1994.

Westphal, Merold. "The God Who Will Be: Hermeneutics and the God of Promise," *Faith and Philosophy* 20, no. 3 (2003): 328-44.

Whitehead, Alfred North. *Process and Reality*. Edited by David Ray Griffin and Donald W. Sherburne. New York: Free Press, 1978.

Williams, Catrin H. *I am He: The Interpretation of 'ani hu' in Jewish and Early Christian Literature*. Wissenschaftliche Untersuchungen Zum Neuen Testament 2. Reihe. Tübingen: Mohr Siebeck, 2000.

Williams, Rowan. "Faith in the Modern Areopagus," *Church Life Journal* (February 18, 2021), available at https://churchlifejournal.nd.edu/articles/faith-in-the-modern-areopagus/.

———. *On Christian Theology*. Oxford: Blackwell, 2000.

———. *Understanding and Misunderstanding "Negative Theology."* Milwaukee, WI: Marquette University Press, 2021.

Wittman, Tyler. *God and Creation in Thomas Aquinas and Karl Barth*. Cambridge: Cambridge University Press, 2018.

Wright, N. T. *Colossians and Philemon*. Tyndale New Testament Commentaries 12. Downers Grove, IL: IVP Academic, 2008.

———. "One God, One Lord, One People: Incarnational Christology for a Church in a Pagan Environment," available at https://chamberscreek.net/library/N.%20T.%20Wright/wright1998one.html.

Yaffe, Martin D. "Myth and 'Science' in Aristotle's Theology," *Man and World* 12 (1979): 70-88.

Young, Edward J. *Studies in Genesis 1*. Phillipsburg, NJ: P&R, [1964] 1999.

Zachhuber, Johannes. *The Rise of Christian Theology and the End of Ancient Metaphysics: Patristic Philosophy from the Cappadocian Fathers to John of Damascus*. Oxford: Oxford University Press, 2020.

Zuckerkandl, Victor. *Sound and Symbol: Music and the External World*. Translated by William Trask. Princeton: Princeton University Press, 1969.

Zogbo, Lynell. "Ideology and Translation: The Case of Ruach Elohim and Ruach YHWH in the Old Testament," in Noss, Philip A. eds., *Current Trends in Scripture Translation*. Reading: United Bible Societies, 2002.

NAME INDEX

Albright, William Foxwell, 230n43
Anaxagoras, 39-40
Anscombe, Elizabeth, 56n78
Anselm, 69, 71n10, 74n20, 146n66, 160n85
Aristotle, 32n9, 33n12, 36, 41n33, 42n38, 52n66, 59, 67, 69, 70n10, 71, 72-73, 74, 79, 80, 87, 88, 90, 91, 98, 101-5, 106, 109-10, 118, 119, 122, 214, 268
Athanasius, 92, 108, 185n55, 207, 248
Augustine, 11-13, 25, 45n46, 70, 125, 146n66, 166-71, 178n37, 180, 189-90, 196-98, 199, 210-11, 212n5, 215, 220n23, 230, 244, 248n83, 258, 260-67, 268, 269nn39-40, 271, 273n44, 274, 277, 278, 284-85, 289, 291n83, 300, 301
Avicenna, 70n10, 82n49, 84
Barth, Karl, 3, 69, 154n79, 170n22, 195n78, 199, 200, 202n92, 203, 237n53, 242n63, 290n82, 292n85, 296, 299n93
Barth, Markus, 17n35
Basil, 85n56, 199, 244n73, 282n67, 295n89
Bates, Matthew, 204n97
Bauerschmidt, Frederick, 125n21
Bavinck, Herman, 13, 14, 15
Begbie, Jeremy, 9n18
Bejon, James, 225-26
Ben-Sasson, Hillel, 215n14
Berossus, 43n40
Blondel, Maurice, 251-52
Boethius, 45n46, 92, 123, 257n8
Bonaventure, 13n27, 69, 169n21
Bonhoeffer, Dietrich, 244n70
Bradshaw, David, 121n10, 145n66
Brann, Eva, 42n36, 44n42, 58n83
Brisson, Luc, 52n65

Broadie, Sarah, 62n97
Bulgakov, Sergius, 69, 122, 133-48, 182, 245n74, 256-57, 260, 287, 296, 300
Bultmann, Rudolf, 17n35
Burkert, Walter, 41n33
Burnett, Joel S., 187
Burrell, David, 93, 94-95, 96n80, 277n53
Calvin, John, 16, 199, 292n85
Cassuto, Umberto, 227n39
Chesterton, G. K., 26-27
Chrysostom, John, 199
Clarke, Norris, 259n10
Clouser, Roy, 146n66
Coda, Piero, 58n84, 221n24, 288n78
Cohoe, Caleb, 76n27
Cornford, Francis, 36n18, 49n60, 52n67, 61n94, 65n106, 104n103
Curry, Steph, 108-9
Derrida, Jacques, 30
Desmond, William, 38n23, 65n107, 77, 184, 255, 266, 278
Dolezal, James, 130n28
Dorner, Isaak Augustus, 72n12, 111n110, 163n92, 290n82
Drozdek, Adam, 52n66, 105
Duby, Steven, 117n1, 130n28
Edwards, Jonathan, 162n90
Eliot, T. S., 4
Eunomius, 85n56, 108
Feinberg, John, 266n32
Frame, John, 9n18, 166n6, 228n40
Frankfort, Henri, 32n9
Freedman, David Noel, 230n43
Gallaher, Brandon, 144n64
Garr, Randall, 200n90
Gavrilyuk, Paul, 73n17, 74n20, 78n39
Gerson, Lloyd, 33n11, 37nn20-21, 75n24, 75n26, 80n45, 83-84
Gilson, Etienne, 82n48, 214

Grasso, Elsa, 52n65
Gregory of Nazianzus, 5-6, 70n10
Gregory of Nyssa, 85n56
Gregory Palamas, 145n66
Griffith, Paul, 182n46
Grosseteste, Robert, 248n83
Hamann, J. G., 242-43, 265
Hamilton, Victor, 190n69
Hart, David Bentley, 9n19, 111n111, 133,
    134n31, 138, 145n66, 148-49, 159,
    250n87
Hartshorne, Charles, 162n91, 300n93
Hector, Kevin, 6n11, 106n106
Heidegger, Martin, 30
Hemmerle, Klaus, 240n59, 291n84
Heraclitus, 35n15, 41n33, 57
Herder, J. G., 173n28
Hesiod, 31n6, 35, 42, 43n40, 46-47,
    48-50, 61
Hinlicky, Paul, 112n113
Homer, 31, 35, 41-42, 43, 44
Howell, Brian, 15n30
Hugh of St. Victor, 123
Iamblichus, 72
Irenaeus, 166n8, 199
Jenson, Robert, 22, 29, 68, 161, 162n90,
    193nn73-74, 208, 217n17, 256n5,
    269nn39-40, 285, 290n82
John of Damascus, 123
Johnson, Jeffery D., 108n108
Jonson, Ben, 265
Jordan, James B., 177
Justin Martyr, 199
Kant, Immanuel, 30, 70
Keller, Catherine, 200n87
Kepler, Johannes, 65n107
Kerr, Fergus, 99n85
Kilby, Karen, 89n65
Kline, Meredith, 140n48
Knoll, Manuel, 31n6
Kou, Christopher, 201
Levering, Matthew, 145n66
Lincoln, Abraham, 201
Lindbeck, George, 17n35
Lombard, Peter, 158n83
Long, D. Stephen, 86, 88n64, 93n69,
    100n87, 112
Luther, Martin, 150n73, 170n24,
    175n32, 180n42, 199, 200nn88-89,
    246n76, 271n41, 285n72

Maimonides, 9n20, 16
Marion, Jean-Luc, 2, 212n5
Martin Jennifer Newsome, 134n31
Maximus the Confessor, 134n31,
    145n66
McCabe, Herbert, 293
McCormack, Bruce, 161n89, 211n4
McIntosh, Jonathan, 160n85
Middleton, Richard, 178, 179, 183
Milbank, John, 68, 77n34, 88n63,
    146n66, 242n63, 248n83, 266n30,
    269n40, 273n44
Mullins, R. T., 266n31
Newton, Isaac, 65n107
Nichols, Aidan, 142
Oliver, Simon, 242n63
Origen, 166n8
Oster, Stefan, 184n54
Ovid, 79n39
Pabst, Adrian, 57n81
Pannenberg, Wolfhart, 82n48, 128n25
Papanikolaou, Aristotle, 146n66
Parmenides, 36-39, 40, 41n33, 46n48,
    53, 55, 56-57, 59, 60, 73, 74n20
Parvan, Alexandra, 211n4
Pascal, Blaise, 65n107
Pegis, Anton C., 51n64, 57n79, 84n55,
    129n26
Perl, Eric, 80n43, 145n66
Philo, 147n67, 218
Philoponus, 119-21
Pieper, Josef, 71n10
Plato, 30, 31, 34n14, 38, 39, 40-41,
    42, 43, 44-47, 48n53, 49-55, 56n78,
    57-59, 60n88, 61n91, 62-64, 65n107,
    66, 67, 72, 75, 77, 78, 98, 109, 214,
    268
Plotinus, 45n46, 57n79, 67, 71, 72,
    73-77, 78-84, 87, 88, 90, 91, 93
Polkinghorne, John, 16-17
Porphyry, 72
Poythress, Vern, 19n38, 20
Preller, Victor, 6n11
Proclus, 82n48, 118-19, 120
Pseudo-Dionysius, 6, 7, 17n36, 21n40,
    45n46, 194
Radde-Gallwitz, Andrew, 84n56
Rahner, Karl, 112n112, 150
Ricoeur, Paul, 214
Roberts, Michael B., 277n54

Rosenstock-Huessy, Eugen, 265, 274n47
Rosenzweig, Franz, 9n20
Rosmini, Antonio, 127n23, 286-87
Ross, James F., 160n85
Saner, Andrea Dalton, 210
Schelling, Friedrich, 134n31
Schindler, D. C., 184n54, 194
Schindler, David L., 247
Schwöbel, Christoph, 184n51
Sedley, David, 46n47, 62n97
Shakespeare, William, 151
Sheridan, Mark, 13n26
Siger of Brabant, 122n12
Slesinski, Robert F., 148n70
Socrates, 40, 42, 43, 44, 45, 63n99, 94
Solmsen, Friedrich, 48n55
Sonderegger, Katherine, 165, 205
Sorabji, Richard, 257n8, 276
Spaemann, Robert, 15n31
Spinoza, Baruch, 17n35
Stern, Sacha, 273n45
Stout, Jeffrey, 1
Thales, 31n6, 33
Thiselton, Anthony, 2n3
Thomas Aquinas, 6nn11-12, 13n27, 14, 30, 69, 70, 71, 81n48, 82-101, 104, 106-13, 114, 116, 117n1, 121-33, 134, 138, 146, 156n80, 158n83, 170n22, 182, 183n50, 184, 207, 208, 212-13, 215, 217n17, 218, 238, 241, 243n69, 245, 246n75, 246n77, 248, 257n8, 259, 277n53
Torrance, T. F., 122
Traherne, Thomas, 194n76
Tran, Jonathan, 7n14
Turner, Denys, 6n12, 7
Ulrich, Ferdinand, 183n48
Van Riel, Gerd, 52n66
Van Til, Cornelius, 70, 170n22
Varro, Marcus Terentius, 30
Vernant, Jean-Pierre, 31n6
Vlastos, Gregory, 63n100
von Balthasar, Hans Urs, 113
Walton, John, 277n55
Whitehead, Alfred North, 162n91
Willet, Andrew, 227n39
Williams, Rowan, 185n55
Wittman, Tyler, 129n26, 150n74, 154n79, 215n12
Wright, N. T., 188-89
Zachhuber, Johannes, 29n2
Zanchi, Giralamo, 188, 189, 199
Zizioulas, John, 146n66

SUBJECT INDEX

Absolute, the, 136-37, 138, 139, 142, 143, 146-47, 148, 182-83
Absolute-relative, 139, 142, 143, 159, 183
absolutists, 266-67
accidents, 246
accommodation, 14, 15, 16-22
act, 99, 100, 107, 251-52
actualization/actuality, 118-21, 126, 133, 146, 149, 158, 160, 207-8, 241-42, 287
Adam, 181, 201
analogy, 88, 95-97, 244n70, 250n87
angels, 199-200
'ani hu, 233-34
anthropomorphism, 9n20, 13-16, 49n60
aporia, methodological, 3
archē, 32-37, 40, 49, 52, 57-58, 63-64, 72-73, 80, 83-84, 90, 157, 198
asymmetry, 154-55
autonomy, 253-54
becoming, 34, 57-58, 60, 251
beginning, the, 148, 149, 163
being
    archē, 36, 37n20
    becoming, 251
    Being-itself, 36, 210
    and beings, 37, 88
    Creator, 235-36
    diversity, 57
    esse, 90-91
    and the Forms, 56
    and function, 278n55
    and God, 90-91, 128, 210-14, 217, 220-22, 235-36, 241
    homogenous, 36
    idipsum, 210-11
    and images, 55-56
    love, 206-7, 241, 249

not-being/Nonbeing, 37-38, 56, 58n84, 221, 287-88
the Other, 56
ousia, 80
Parmenides, 53
persistence, 241
Plotinus, 80
and reason, 37
receptive, 245-46
the Same, 53-56
self-gift, 250-51
and theology, 36n18
Thomas, 83
Timaeus, 51n64, 60
and time, 53, 217, 269, 287-88
to on, 53-55, 60
and Trinity, 221
truth and falsehood, 38
and unity, 51n64, 56-57
and will, 128
YHWH, 222
Bezalel, 190-91
boundary, 66, 88, 146, 296
breath (ruakh), 192
capacity, 119-20
cause
    and analogy, 96, 97
    creation, 124n19, 126
    efficient, 96, 98, 101-3, 106
    final, 96, 103-4
    Forms, 60
    God, 96-98, 101, 104, 106, 124n19, 126
    natural, 127, 128n25
    unmoved mover, 103-4
    voluntary, 127, 128n25
chasm, 46-47
chiasm, 177-78
Christianity, 29, 66-71, 214
classical theism, 23, 162, 163

communion, 56-57, 60, 62-63
composition, 73n17, 75, 88-89, 92-95, 247
condescension, 21-22
cosmic order, 32-33
cosmogony, 45n46, 46, 52, 57, 296
cosmos
    and *archē*, 32-33, 35, 49, 157
    and Creator-creature boundary, 66
    copy, 61
    and demiurge, 46n46, 61, 64
    eternal, 122
    Forms, 57, 60, 62
    and God, 15
    and mind, 40
    sphere, 53, 64
    Timaeus, 50, 51, 54, 57, 66
    unmoved mover, 72
covenant, 20
created reality, 252-53
created spirit, 139
creation account, 171-85, 223, 226
creation by word, 242-43
creation *ex nihilo*, 29, 143, 288-89
creation week, 64n103, 172, 177, 181, 229-30, 272-75, 291, 292, 294, 295
credo, 303
darkness, 177, 180-81, 229, 270-71
day-age theory, 279n58
days of creation, 173-74, 176, 179, 180, 223, 270-74, 277-84
demiurge, 40-41, 46-49, 54, 59-65, 147
desire, 104
dialogues of Plato, 41n34
divine council, 200-201
divine world, 139, 141, 143.
    See also God; world
documentary hypothesis, 228n41
dualism, 77, 256, 269-70
earth, 179-80, 181, 229
ecstasy, 76
'ehyeh, 215-16, 218, 219-20, 224. *See* being
eidos, 61, 62
election, 154n79
elements, 48, 50-51
emanation, 81
energeia, 79-80, 81
energies. *See* God
equivocity, 77

Er, 44
'eretz, 174
eschatology, 229-30
esse, 90-91, 96n80, 108, 117, 208-9
essence, 81, 83, 113, 145n66, 287
eternal creation, 120-29
eternity, 41, 53, 57, 58, 256-57, 259-66, 270, 297-98
etymology, 48-49
evil, 47
existence, 80-81, 83, 107, 113, 251
Fabergé egg, 34, 38
fire, 37n20
firmament, 180
first heaven, 104-5
form-fill pattern, 173, 175
forming, 180
formlessness, 176-77, 263-64, 270-71
Forms, the, 50, 52, 54-55, 56, 57, 58, 59-63, 75n26, 82
gematria, 224
gender, 47
genealogy, 48n55
generation, 89-90
Genesis
    accommodated, 265
    aporia, 4
    eternity, 265-66
    God, 183, 242
    love, 241
    metaphysics, 28, 66, 67, 157, 235-42
    and Plato, 63-64
    and simplicity, 117
    and *Timaeus*, 64, 66
    time, 268-77
    Trinity, 166-69, 203-4
    Word, 242-43
geometry, 65
gift, 155-56
glory, 22, 140n48, 295
God
    absoluteness, 266-67
    accommodation, 17-22, 290
    actuality/actualized, 120-21, 126, 133, 149, 158, 160, 207-8, 241-42, 287
    actus purus, 208, 242n63, 287
    analogy, 95-96
    ancient Near Eastern grammar, 185-87

'ani hu, 234
Aristotle, 72-73
attributes, 71-72, 204, 239
begetting, 125n20
and being, 90-91, 128, 210-14, 217, 220-22, 235-36, 241
between God and God, 281-99
Bulgakov, 134-35
cause, 96, 97-98, 101, 104, 106, 124n19, 126
command, 244
and composition, 93-95
and cosmos, 15
and covenant, 20
and creation, 21-22, 116-17, 120-21, 124-25, 133-39, 149-51, 154, 155, 163, 258-59, 266-68, 281, 288, 292-95, 300-301, 303
and creatures, 66, 126, 131, 137, 150, 153, 157, 168, 179, 182, 236-37, 245
demonstrations (Thomas), 97-98, 100
dependence, 154
derivation, 108
difference, 288-89
ecstasy, 245
effects, 97-98
'ehyeh, 215-16, 218, 219-20
'el, 185-86
'elohim, 185-89, 222, 227, 239-40, 245
energies, 145n66
erōs, 194
esse, 90-91, 96n80, 117, 208-9
essence, 113, 208-9, 287
eternity, 258-66, 297-98
existence, 107, 113
Father, 3, 10, 20, 25, 91-92, 110, 125n20, 167-70, 232, 237-38, 249, 286-89
first mover, 100-101, 115
Forms, 82-83
freedom, 132-33, 135, 149, 159
generation, 89-92, 232, 238
Genesis, 183
goodness, 84n55, 124, 129-32, 184, 194-95
hayah, 245
and history, 266, 296-97
Holy Spirit, 3, 20, 169, 189-95, 197, 284-85, 286-89

and humanity, 21, 239-40
"I am," 210-13, 215-22
idipsum, 210-11, 212n5
image of, 24, 200-202
immanence, 8-9
immobility, 108-9, 111-12
immutability, 95, 108-9, 116-17, 120-21, 159, 212n5, 261, 298-99
impassibility, 298
independence, 152-53, 155
intellect, 126
kenosis, 138-39
knowledge, 132
knowledge of, 3, 11, 97, 151, 156-57
and language, 264-65
language about, 4-7, 10-11, 12-13, 15, 17-19, 22, 93-95
light, 247-49, 270
love, 135-36, 139, 141-42, 146, 155, 183-84, 245, 249
motion/movement, 87-88, 92, 98-109, 111, 114-15
and mystery, 8
names, 6, 12, 13-14, 17n36, 211-13, 217-20, 227-30, 231, 235
nature, 127, 132
needs the world, 134-35
omnipotence, 84, 179
ousia, 139-40, 141
passivity, 108, 110-11, 114
perfection, 82-83, 239
personal, 140, 41-42
plurality, 92-93, 187-88, 199, 200-205, 207-8, 284
potency, 107, 120-21, 126, 144, 159-60, 241-42
power, 183
processions, 86-89, 109, 242n63
promise, 244-45
qui est, 212-13
real relation, 258-59
receptivity, 90-92, 114, 246, 250
relational, 136, 154, 207, 266-68, 299
relations, 70n10, 92-93, 114, 117n1, 125, 158n83, 163
resemblance of creatures, 14, 96n80, 245-46
ruakh, 189-95
sacrifice, 183

God (*continued*)
  say-see sequence, 281-85, 291-92,
    294, 296, 298, 300, 303
  and Scripture, 11-13, 15, 20, 23, 150
  self-diffusive, 124, 131-32, 184
  self-giving, 240-41, 249
  self-revelation, 13, 21
  Shema, 188-89
  simplicity, 78, 83-95, 98, 99, 111-12,
    116-17, 120-21, 127, 129n26,
    131-32, 158, 204, 208
  Son, 3, 20, 91-92, 110, 125n20,
    167-69, 232, 237-38, 240, 249,
    286-89
  and Sophia, 140-47
  source of being, 9
  speaking of, 10
  speaks, 23, 157, 175, 176, 195-99,
    203-5, 231, 237-40, 244-45, 248,
    260-62, 264-65, 295, 296-97
  speaks to God, 20
  spoken God, 231-35, 237-38, 282,
    295, 297
  static, 95, 99
  Thomas, 82-89
  and time, 217, 257-66, 271, 276-78,
    288-90, 292, 297-300
  transcendent, 8-11, 152, 228, 259
  unity, 165, 205-6, 236
  unrelated, 158
  voice, 262
  will, 124n19, 126, 127, 128, 129-33,
    134n31
  and Wisdom, 142-43, 144, 170
  without creation, 150-53
  Word, 9, 10, 21, 23, 25, 88, 89,
    167-68, 184n52, 193, 195-97,
    231-32, 236-38, 242n64, 243-44,
    262-63, 297
  works, 145n66
  and world, 134-35, 137-38, 142-43,
    146, 151-52, 160, 300
  yearning, 193-95
  YHWH, 222-24, 227, 228-35
  YHWH 'elohim, 228-29
  See also Trinity
gods, 47-48, 52, 61-62
goodness, 63-64, 75-76, 84n55, 124,
  129-32, 171-73, 184, 194-95, 270-71,
  284-85

gospel, 29-30
happenings, 251
hayah, 222-24, 229, 245.
    See also being
heaven, 174-75
Hellenization thesis, 28
history, 182n46, 230, 266, 272, 281,
  294, 296-97
how God creates, 148, 207
humanity
    creative activity, 182
    and God, 21, 239-40
    image of God, 24, 200-202
    listeners, 247
    naming, 181-82
    and world, 182
hypostasis, 74, 83, 113, 142, 144-45
hypothetical necessity, 131, 133, 155,
  160
idealism, 140
images, 55-56
incarnation.
    See also Jesus Christ
infinite regress, 101, 119
intellect, 80, 126
interiority, 247, 250, 253
Israel, 230
Jeremiah, 7
Jesus Christ
    archē, 198
    bere'shit, 198
    egō eimi, 232-33, 235
    incarnation, 24-25, 194, 211n4, 239
    light, 197
    and Scripture, 25
    Word of God, 24-25, 197
    YHWH, 235
Johannine Prologue, 197-98
kingdom-king pattern, 173, 176
knowledge
    of God, 3, 11, 97, 151, 156-57
    God's, 132
    knower, 150
    the One, 76
    and reason, 97
    scientific, 11
    Thomas, 97
    and world, 8
koinonia. See communion
kyrios, 234-35

language
  abstract, 17-19
  accommodation, 17-18
  analogy, 95-96
  apophatic, 6-7, 10, 94n75
  and God, 4-7, 10-11, 12-13, 15, 17-19,
    22, 93-96, 264-65
  linguistic analogy, 88
  Scripture, 17-18
  simplicity, 93-95
  theological, 15n30, 17-18
  triple, 249n85
liberalism, 17n35
life, 250-51
light, 180-81, 247-49, 261-63, 270
logos, 31-32, 36, 238n57
logos asarkos, 161
love, 106, 135-36, 141-42, 146, 155,
  183-84, 206-7, 241, 245, 249, 254
mediation, 51n63, 59, 60, 63, 80, 123,
  143-44, 146-47
metaphor, 18
metaphysics
  archē, 32n9, 40, 157
  Arian, 108
  Aristotle, 103
  and Christianity, 29, 66, 67-70, 214
  and creation, 66
  Creator, 242
  and eternity, 256
  of Exodus, 214, 242-43
  eye, 243
  of Genesis, 25-26, 222, 235-42
  Greek, 28, 66, 67, 157
  idipsum, 212n5
  incarnation, 239
  and intelligibility, 255-56
  and method, 2-3
  and physical sciences, 2-3
  and physics, 103
  Plato, 52-53, 59
  Plotinus, 75n22
  revisionary, 222
  and science, 2-3
  and Scripture, 66, 70-71
  and theology, 29-30, 69
  Thomas, 70n10, 111-12
  and time, 255-56, 269n40
  and Trinity, 111-13
  unbaptized, 111-12

  unbiblical, 29-30
  the word, 243-44
methexis, 58n82, 59
method, 1-3, 26-27
mind, 39-40, 74, 253
Moses, 20, 219-20
motion/movement, 53, 58, 71-73, 87-88,
  92, 98-111, 114-15
multiplicity, 34, 75, 129n26
music, 192-93, 205
mystery, 8
mysticism, 157n82
mythology
  Aristotle, 42n38
  elements, 50-51
  Greek, 30-32, 42-43
  Plato, 41-43, 44, 50-51, 52, 63-64
  poetic, 42-43
  Republic, 43-44
  Socrates, 42
  world, 51-52
mythos, 31-32
naming, 6, 12, 13-14, 17n36, 181-82,
  217-20, 227-30, 231
necessity of creation, 122, 130-36,
  147-48
  See also hypothetical necessity
nihilation, 169n22
nous, 39-40, 74-76, 80
numerology, 224, 229, 231
Odysseus, 43, 44, 45, 230
One, the, 34, 73-83
opera ad extra, 80
opera ad intra, 79
origin
  archē, 32, 34-35, 37
  necessity, 65
  and the One, 78
  Plato, 46, 51
  Thomas, 84
  Timaeus, 65
  world, 19
Other, the, 53-54, 55, 56, 57
panels of Genesis, 173, 175, 176, 177,
  178
panentheism, 137-38
pantheism, 81n48
participation, 56-57, 58n82, 59, 96, 107,
  147n67, 156n80, 184n51, 237, 242n64,
  247

parts. *See* composition
perfection, 81
person, 70n10
philosophy
   archē, 35n15, 38
   eternal creation, 123
   Hellenistic/Greek, 28-29, 33, 38
   and metaphysics of Genesis, 253
   and myth, 31-32
   odyssey, 44-45
   origin, 32n9
   and poetry, 49n60
   and politics, 45
   Presocratics, 31
   Republic, 45
   sensible world, 33-34
   temporal creation, 123-24
   and theology, 23n44, 33n11, 35n15,
     52n66, 67-69
plants, 175-76, 279-80, 292-94
poetry, 41-43, 246
potency/potentiality, 99, 100, 107,
  118-21, 126, 144, 146, 159-60, 241-42
prayer, 266, 268, 299
preexistence of Forms, 82-83
   See also Forms
principle of noncontradiction, 36
process theology, 150n71, 162-63
prodigality, 184
promise, 172
reason, 37, 46n46, 97, 112-13
receptacle, 46-47
receptivity, 90-92, 114, 245-46, 250
relation, 70n10, 92-93, 114, 117n1, 125,
  136, 154, 158n83, 163, 207, 221,
  258-59, 266-68, 299
relativists, 266-67
Republic (Plato), 42, 43-45
revelation, 112-13, 240n59
Sabbath, 171, 172, 271
Same, the, 53-54, 56
science, 2-3, 15n31
Scripture
   accommodation, 16-18, 20, 21-22
   anthropomorphic, 13, 15-16
   and apophaticism, 7, 10
   and Christ, 25
   counterfactuals, 160n86
   and creation, 4, 21-22, 150
   and God, 11-13, 15, 20, 23, 150

   and Hellenization, 29
   language, 17-18
   and metaphysics, 66
   monotheism, 171
   and simplicity, 117-18
   and theology, 68-69
   and time, 260
   and Trinity, 25
   Word of God, 23
self-transcendence, 251
sensus plenior, 24, 25
separation, 180, 181
Shema, 188-89
sight, 283-84
simplicity
   and apophaticism, 94n75
   and attributes of God, 71
   Cappadocians, 85n56
   Christian transformation, 71-72
   and creation, 117-19
   and demonstrations, 98
   and eternal creation, 126, 128
   and generation, 90-91
   and immutability, 116-17, 121
   linguistic, 93-95
   and motion, 111-12
   and necessity, 131-32
   the One, 75
   Plotinus, 78
   and potency, 120-21
   and Scripture, 117-18
   speaker and hearer, 204
   Thomas, 83-95, 98, 99, 111-12,
     116-17, 127-28
   and Trinity, 78, 86-88, 92-93,
     111-12, 208
   and will, 129n26
   and world, 79
sin, 170n22, 253-54
Sophia, 139-48
Sophist, The, 55-56
sound, 192-93
space, 266n30, 269n39, 273
sphere, 64-65
Stranger (*Sophist*), 38, 55-56
substance, 79-80, 246-47
successiveness, 252
temple, 277, 282n68
temporal creation, 117-18, 122-25, 128
theogony, 296

Theogony (Hesiod), 42, 46, 48n53, 49, 50, 51
theology
    apophatic (negative), 5-10, 94n75, 95-97, 157n81
    and *archē*, 157
    Aristotle, 52n66
    and being, 36n18
    cataphatic (positive), 5-6
    and creation, 156
    Creator, 157, 159-60, 161-62
    Dionysian, 6-7
    God beyond God, 163-64
    Greek, 28, 29-30, 157
    and language, 15n30, 17-18
    and metaphysics, 29-30, 69
    and philosophy, 23n44, 33n11, 35n15, 52n66, 67-69
    Plato, 52n66
    reorientation, 25
    revisionary, 68-70
    and Scripture, 68-69
    time and eternity, 256-57
Timaeus (Plato), 40-41, 43n40, 45-46, 50, 51, 57, 60, 64, 66
time
    Augustine, 261-64, 268-69
    and being/nonbeing, 53, 217, 269, 287-88
    body-time, 274
    and creation, 271, 273-76
    creatures, 289, 290, 292
    days of creation, 270-74, 277-81, 292
    day three, 292-93
    and death, 255
    distention, 269, 290-91
    and eternity, 41, 57, 256-57, 259, 270, 290, 297-98
    future, 260, 268-69, 286, 288, 289, 291n83
    Genesis, 268-77
    and God, 217, 257-66, 271, 276-78, 288-90, 292, 297-300
    metaphysics, 255-56, 269n40
    and nothingness, 268-69
    past, 260, 268-69, 286, 288, 289, 291n83
    personal, 276
    present, 268-69, 274, 286, 288, 291n83

rhythm, 274-76, 294-95
    and space, 273
    succession, 257-58
    Timaeus, 53
    and Trinity, 286, 289-92, 298
    utterances, 260-65
translation of Gen 1:1, 153n78
treatises on God, 112
triangles, 65
Trinity
    actuality, 241-42
    analogies, 250n87
    Augustine, 166-70
    Barth, 237n53
    and being, 221
    and creation, 3, 91-93, 185, 288-89, 303
    development, 241-42
    'elohim, 187-88
    and eternity, 298
    Father, 10, 20, 25, 91-92, 110, 125n20, 167-70, 286-89
    and Genesis, 166-69, 203-4
    Holy Spirit, 20, 169, 189-95, 286-89
    "let us," 199-207
    life, 289
    love, 206-7
    and metaphysics, 111-13
    and motion, 109-10, 114-15
    name, 221
    negation, 221
    nonbeing, 58n84, 221
    and Old Testament, 166
    one and many, 206
    passivity, 114
    potentiality, 241-42
    principle, 286
    relations, 221
    rhythm, 294-95
    say-see sequence, 285-86
    and Scripture, 25
    and simplicity, 78, 86-89, 92-93, 111-12, 208
    Son, 20, 91-92, 110, 125n20, 167-69, 286-89
    speaker and hearer, 203-5
    taxis, 134, 167, 264n26, 289
    termini, 286
    and time, 286, 289-92, 298

Trinity (*continued*)
  trinitarian ontology, 58n84, 89n66,
    110, 112, 113, 206, 254
  unity, 260
  and Word, 167-68, 170, 231-32
  YHWH, 231-32
truth, 4
twenty-sixfold patterns, 224-26
union, 76
unity, 51n64, 56-57
unmoved mover, 72-74, 101-6, 109-11
utterance, intelligible vs. audible, 196
via eminentiae, 83, 89, 109
via negativa, 89
voluntarism, 128-29, 132
water, 33n12

wind (*ruakh*), 191
Wisdom, 142-43, 144
world
  and *archē*, 35-36
  and God, 134-35, 137-38, 142-43,
    146, 151-52, 160, 300
  human creative activity, 182
  myth, 51-52
  needed by God, 134-35
  origins, 19
  and simplicity, 79
  Theogony, 46
  Timaeus, 46
  and Wisdom, 142-43, 144
  See also divine world
Zeus, 49

SCRIPTURE INDEX

OLD TESTAMENT

Genesis
1, 4, 19, 23, 24, 25, 26, 64,
   82, 84, 117, 127, 128, 147,
   153, 159, 164, 166, 167,
   168, 169, 171, 172, 174,
   175, 176, 177, 178, 180, 181,
   182, 183, 184, 185, 189,
   190, 191, 192, 195, 196,
   197, 199, 200, 202, 203,
   205, 207, 215, 222, 224,
   226, 227, 228, 229, 230,
   231, 234, 237, 244, 245,
   260, 261, 262, 263, 264,
   266, 267, 268, 269, 271,
   273, 274, 275, 277, 278,
   279, 280, 281, 283, 284,
   291, 297, 298, 300
1–2, 226, 228, 231, 245
1–3, 19, 174, 198, 273
1–4, 175, 278, 280
1–11, 189, 195, 225
1–15, 153, 189
1–17, 190, 191
1:1, 25, 32, 106, 148, 149,
   153, 156, 157, 161, 162, 174,
   175, 202, 231, 261, 303
1:1-2, 174, 175, 234
1:1-5, 171
1:1–2:3, 1, 171, 173, 178,
   222, 223, 278
1:2, 64, 153, 170, 174, 176,
   180, 189, 191, 192, 202,
   223, 224, 231, 234, 263,
   264, 269, 285
1:3, 153, 173, 175, 195, 196,
   223, 231, 244, 260, 262,
   263, 281
1:3-5, 180, 270

1:3–2:3, 279
1:4, 173, 281
1:5, 173, 223, 246, 278, 279
1:6, 173, 175, 223, 231, 270
1:6-7, 282
1:6-8, 180
1:6-13, 172
1:7, 173, 223
1:8, 173, 223
1:9, 173, 175, 177, 180, 223,
   294
1:9-10, 176, 279, 282
1:10, 173, 177, 180, 271, 281
1:11, 173, 175, 177, 179, 223,
   248, 271
1:11-12, 125, 176, 177, 292
1:11-13, 282
1:12, 173, 179, 281
1:13, 223
1:14, 173, 175, 180, 231, 271
1:14-15, 223, 249
1:14-16, 274
1:14-17, 282
1:15, 173, 223, 231
1:16, 180
1:18, 173, 281
1:19, 223
1:20, 170, 173, 175, 177, 285
1:20-21, 282
1:20-22, 125
1:21, 173, 177, 179, 281
1:22, 175, 177
1:23, 223
1:24, 173, 175, 176, 223,
   292
1:24-25, 125
1:25, 173, 281
1:26, 154, 176, 180, 199,
   200, 201, 202, 225, 231
1:26-27, 24, 200, 203, 205

1:27, 179, 200
1:28, 176
1:29, 176, 203, 223, 231,
   248
1:29-30, 176
1:30, 173, 223
1:31, 173, 223, 281, 282
2, 178, 181, 191, 227, 228,
   239, 240, 265, 279, 280,
   292
2–3, 171, 227, 265
2:1, 126, 174, 199, 282
2:1-3, 172, 293
2:2-3, 172, 293
2:4, 174, 222, 226, 229, 231,
   234, 279
2:4-7, 280
2:5, 279, 280
2:7, 176, 227
2:8, 235, 280
2:8-9, 227
2:9, 181
2:11, 181
2:15, 227
2:16, 227
2:18, 225
2:18-22, 227
2:19, 181, 281
2:19-20, 181
2:21-22, 227
2:23-24, 227
3, 199, 226, 285
3–4, 226
3:8, 192, 227, 285
3:8-9, 228
3:14, 228
3:21, 227
3:22, 202, 225
3:23, 228
4, 167

Genesis (*continued*)
4:1, *151*
5:29, *218*
6:3, *193, 225*
6:6, *193*
6:7, *225*
8, *199*
8:21-22, *225*
11:4, *202*
11:6-7, *225*
11:7, *202*
14:18, *185*
15:1, *181*
16:7-16, *232*
16:13, *185*
17:5, *181*
18:17-19, *225*
18:20, *181*
21:17, *181*
22:9-22, *232*
23:6, *191*
24:9, *186*
30:8, *191*
30:13, *186*
31:3, *216*
31:30, *186*
32:28, *181*
38:28-29, *219*
46, *25*

Exodus
2:10, *219*
3, *212, 213, 215, 216, 219,*
   220, 222
3–15, *225*
3:6, *232*
3:12, *216, 219*
3:13, *211*
3:13-15, *210*
3:14, *210, 211, 215, 218, 222,*
   233, 234
3:14-15, *210*
3:15, *211, 235*
3:17, *225*
4:3, *215*
4:9, *215*
4:12, *216, 219*
4:15, *216, 219*
4:24, *215*
5:2, *220*

6, *226*
6:7, *216*
7:5, *220*
12:23, *187*
13:17, *225*
13:22, *187*
14:19, *187*
15:6-7, *187*
15:10, *187, 191*
19:16, *196*
19:19, *196*
20:1, *186*
20:2, *187*
20:3, *186*
20:11, *175*
20:18, *196*
25–31, *190*
25:1, *282*
25:9, *282*
30:11, *282*
30:17, *282*
30:17-21, *282*
30:22, *282*
30:34, *282*
31:1, *282*
31:1-5, *283*
31:3, *190*
31:12, *282*
31:12-17, *190, 282*
31:18, *282*
33, *224*
33–34, *220*
34:6-7, *220*
35:31, *190*
36:1-2, *283*
38:8, *282*
40:6, *283*
40:7, *283*
40:8, *283*
40:18, *283*
40:20, *283*
40:22, *283*
40:30, *283*
40:33, *283*

Leviticus
1–16, *68*
11:1-23, *181*
21:13, *186*

Numbers
24:2, *190*
33:52, *201*

Deuteronomy
1:22-23, *200*
6:4-5, *187*
9:20, *278*
13:2, *186*
21:10-13, *68*
22:14, *186*
22:15, *186*
22:17, *186*
32:10-11, *191, 193*
32:11, *190*
32:20-27, *225*
32:39, *233, 234*

Joshua
3:11, *186*
3:13, *186*
24:19, *186*

1 Samuel
10:1-13, *192*
10:10, *190*
16:13-23, *192*
16:15, *190*
27:5-6, *200*

2 Samuel
11:16, *200*
15:14-17, *200*
21:6, *200*

2 Kings
8:22, *278*
11:18, *201*
19:16, *283*

2 Chronicles
4:3, *201*
6:40, *283*

Job
33:4, *191*
38:7, *199*

Psalms
1, *224*

1:3, *224*
2:7, *86*
8, *246*
11:4, *283*
19, *246*
23, *225*
23:4, *225*
29:3-9, *196*
32, *225*
32:6, *225*
33:6, *191, 195*
35:1, *11*
50:12, *152*
72, *225*
78:41, *187*
78:48-50, *187*
78:56, *187*
90:1-2, *151*
94:9, *14*
104:5-6, *191*
104:7-9, *192*
104:10-13, *192*
104:14-17, *192*
104:18-23, *192*
104:27-30, *191, 192*
104:28, *294*
104:29, *192*
104:30, *192*
115:1-8, *14*
122:3, *210*
123:2, *186*
134, *220*
145:8-9, *220*
148:5, *195*

Isaiah
6, *217*
11:15, *191*
40:7, *191*
40:22, *152*
41:4, *153, 217, 234*
41:10, *234*
42:17, *186*
43:10, *233, 234*
43:11, *233*
44:6, *233*
44:8, *233*
45:5, *233*
45:6, *233*
45:18, *174, 233, 234*

45:21, *152*
46:9, *233*
46:9-10, *152, 153*
46:10, *153*
47:8, *233*
47:10, *233*
48:12, *234*
48:12-16, *234*
52:6, *234*
59:1-8, *225*
59:1-14, *225*
59:9-14, *225*

Jeremiah
26:1, *153, 198*
27:1, *153, 198*
28:1, *153, 198*
31:20, *193*
32:41, *193*
49:34, *153*

Ezekiel
1:5, *201*
1:10, *201*
16:6, *193*

Daniel
4:34-35, *152*
9:18, *283*

Joel
1:16, *283*

Amos
9:8, *283*

Jonah
3:3, *191*

Zechariah
1:12-21, *232*

NEW TESTAMENT

Matthew
12:30, *3*
22:32, *232*
28:20, *233*

Mark
14:61-62, *233*

Luke
11:23, *3*
24, *11, 25*
24:25-26, *166*

John
1, *24, 25, 153, 231, 232,*
  262
1:1, *25, 151, 198, 231*
1:1-2, *197*
1:1-3, *196*
1:1-5, *195*
1:3, *231*
1:4, *197*
1:4-5, *196*
1:9, *196, 197*
1:12, *197*
1:19, *197*
1:29, *12, 197*
1:35, *197*
1:43, *197*
2:1, *197*
2:1-11, *197*
3:22-29, *11*
3:35, *249*
4:25-26, *233, 234*
6:20, *232, 234*
8, *232*
8:12, *232*
8:24, *232*
8:28, *232*
8:42, *86*
8:58, *232*
11:25, *234*
13, *12*
13:19, *232*
16:15, *249*
17, *20*
17:5, *151*
17:11, *202*
17:21, *202*
17:22, *202*
17:24, *151*
18:5-6, *232*
18:8, *232*

Acts
17:25, *152*
17:26, *181*
17:28, *152, 291*

Romans
1:18-20, *21*
1:20-21, *157*
4:13, *153*
4:17, *230, 235*
11:36, *291*

1 Corinthians
3:21-23, *67*
8, *188, 217*
8:4, *188*
8:5, *188*
8:6, *188, 235*

2 Corinthians
4:6, *195*

Ephesians
1:4, *151*
3:14-15, *14*
5:13, *248*
5:18-19, *192*

Philippians
2, *183*

Colossians
1, *198*
1:16, *198*
1:16-17, *238*
1:18, *32, 153, 166, 198*
1:19-20, *198*

1 Timothy
6:4, *248*

Hebrews
1:1-3, *23*

1:3, *248*
11:3, *195*

1 Peter
1:20, *151*

Revelation
1–11, *216, 230, 285*
1:4, *216*
1:4-5, *216*
1:8, *216*
1:14, *283*
2:18, *283*
3:14, *153*
4:8, *217*
5:6, *285*
19:12, *283*
21:6, *153*
21:23, *273*
22:5, *273*
22:13, *153*

ALSO BY PETER J. LEITHART

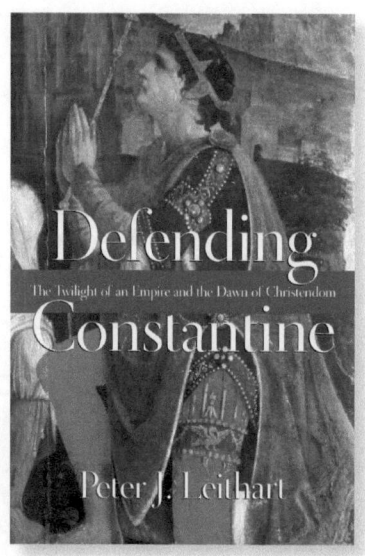

Defending Constantine
978-0-8308-2722-0

**Delivered from the Elements
of the World**
978-0-8308-5126-3